THE POWER OF
THE ACTOR

THE POWER OF
THE ACTOR

The Chubbuck Technique

IVANA CHUBBUCK

GOTHAM BOOKS

GOTHAM BOOKS
Published by Penguin Group (USA) Inc.
375 Hudson Street, New York, New York 10014, U.S.A.
Pegnuin Group (Canada), 10 Alcorn Avenue, Toronto, Ontario, Canada
M4V 3B2 (a division of Pearson Penguin Canada Inc.);
Penguin Books Ltd, 80 Strand, London WC2R 0RL, England;
Penguin Ireland, 25 St Stephen's Green, Dublin, Ireland
(a division of Penguin Books Ltd); Penguin Group (Australia), 250
Camberwell Road, Camberwell, Victoria 3124, Australia (a division of
Pearson Australia Group Pty Ltd); Penguin Books India Pvt Ltd,
11 Community Centre, Panchsheel Park, New Delhi – 110 017, India;
Penguin Group (NZ), Cnr Airborne and Rosedale Roads, Albany, Auckland,
New Zealand (a division of Pearson New Zealand Ltd); Penguin Books
(South Africa) (Pty) Ltd, 24 Sturdee Avenue, Rosebank,
Johannesburg 2196, South Africa

Penguin Books Ltd, Registered Offices: 80 Strand,
London WC2R 0RL, England

Published by Gotham Books, a division of Penguin Group (USA) Inc.

First American printing, August 2004
10 8 6 4 2 1 3 5 7 9

Gotham Books and the skyscraper logo are
trademarks of Penguin Group (USA) Inc.

LIBRARY OF CONGRESS CATALOGING-IN-PUBLICATION DATA
Chubbuck, Ivana.
The power of the actor / by Ivana Chubbuck.
p. cm.
ISBN 1-592-40070-1 (hardcover : alk. paper)
1. Acting. I. Title.
PN2061.C573 2004
792.02'8—dc22
2004007033

Printed in the United States of America
Set in New Caledonia
Designed by Mia Risberg

Contents

Introduction   vii

PART I:
The 12-Step Chubbuck Acting Technique   1

CHAPTER 1   Tool #1: Overall Objective   7
CHAPTER 2   Tool #2: Scene Objective   21
CHAPTER 3   Tool #3: Obstacles   41
CHAPTER 4   Tool #4: Substitution   53
CHAPTER 5   Tool #5: Inner Objects   77
CHAPTER 6   Tool #6: Beats and Actions   91
CHAPTER 7   Tool #7: Moment Before   107
CHAPTER 8   Tool #8: Place and Fourth Wall   124
CHAPTER 9   Tool #9: Doings   142
CHAPTER 10   Tool #10: Inner Monologue   172
CHAPTER 11   Tool #11: Previous Circumstances   195
CHAPTER 12   Tool #12: Let It Go   204

PART II:
Other Acting Tools and Exercises 211

CHAPTER 13   **Substance Abuse**   213

CHAPTER 14   **Creating Sexual Chemistry**   228

CHAPTER 15   **Playing a Serial Killer**   233

CHAPTER 16   **Creating Organic Fear**   237

CHAPTER 17   **Creating Organic Feelings of Death and Dying**   243

CHAPTER 18   **Experiencing Feeling Pregnant**   250

CHAPTER 19   **Experiencing Parenthood**   253

CHAPTER 20   **Playing a Paraplegic or Quadraplegic**   255

CHAPTER 21   **Creating Emotional Realities for Scars and Bruises**   257

CHAPTER 22   **Organically Realizing the Character's Occupation, Profession or Career**   259

PART III:
The Practical Application of the 12 Tools 267

Script Analysis for *Uncle Vanya* Using the 12 Tools   269

Practical Application: Three-or-More-Person Scenes   379

Epilogue   385

Acknowledgments   389

Introduction

....

Acting is a complex and elusive art to define. Yet almost everyone can tell good acting from bad acting—or good acting from brilliant acting. Why can one actor be riveting in a play and another actor be dull and boring in the very same play, doing the same character, the same lines? If it were just the script, the beauty of its language, the artful turn of a phrase, we would only need readings. But the words are not just read with sterility from the page. They are performed and brought to life by actors.

Every actor knows that discovering and understanding your personal pain is an inherent part of the acting process. This has been true since Stanislavski. The difference between the Chubbuck Technique and those developed in the past is that I teach actors how to use their emotions not as an end result, but as a way to empower a goal. My technique teaches actors how to win.

If you look closely at virtually all drama and comedy—in fact, all literature—you will find that the will to win is the one constant element. In every story, a character wants or needs something (their goal)—love, power, validation, honor—and the story documents the way in which they try to win that particular desire or need. While *what* and *how* the characters try to win is defined in many ways and takes many forms and shapes, when you distill these goals down, you find that every character's conflict and struggle is about fighting to win whatever their goal is.

I teach actors how to win because this is what people do in real life! They go after what they want. Interesting and dynamic people go after what they want in interesting and dynamic ways, creating greater emotion and intensity in realizing these goals. They do this subconsciously, whereas the actor must understand himself thoroughly and have the tools to break down a script in order to make this interesting and dynamic behavior appear and feel like a subconscious process. The Chubbuck Technique stimulates this behavior, allowing for this natural and powerful human drive to be realized.

The Chubbuck Technique grew out of my search to understand and overcome my own personal traumas—particularly, how they impacted my acting and my life. I had no idea how powerful and profound this concept would become.

I grew up with a distant/dysfunctional/workaholic father and a physically and emotionally abusive mother. I developed deep-seated abandonment issues and felt unworthy of being loved. In essence, I rose to the occasion of being diminished. As an adult and an actress, I took all my childhood and adolescent horrors and wallowed in them. I was looking for sympathy and understanding, which I thought would help relieve the suffering of my past. As any actor would strive to be, I was truly in touch with my emotional pain.

But I began to wonder, "To what end am I feeling all of this? How do the feelings and emotions from my past shape my work as an actor? How do they shape who I am as a person? How can these fractured, scattered and sometimes divergent emotions be focused to serve a character in a script?"

As a working actress, I would see so many actors who were truly dredging up deep, painful emotions, but whose work seemed self-indulgent. I realized that having deep and profound feelings didn't necessarily make me a deep and profound person. I saw that coddling one's pain—in life and onstage—creates almost the opposite effect. It seems self-involved, self-pitying and weak, the key characteristics of a victim. Not the most compelling choice for an actor to make.

I began investigating how to put the legacy of emotions I had inherited to better, more effective use in my work. When I examined the lives of successful people, I noticed that they seemed to use their physical and emotional traumas as a stimulus, not to self-indulgently suffer, but to *inspire* and *drive* their great achievements.

I suspected that very same formula could be applied to actors and their approach to their work. I watched the great actors of our time and I saw in their performances the same emotional drive to overcome adversity, and, in fact, to use those very obstacles to necessitate achievement of a goal and win. In their performances, great actors were instinctively mirroring the behavior and nature of great people.

I needed to create a system that would reflect and guide this process. A system to replicate real, dynamic human behavior. A system that, once the actor committed to making fearless choices, would guide and empower the actor to use their own pain to win their character's goal. A system that would also provide a way to craft risky choices that would allow an actor to *break the rules* and *make new rules,* inspiring exceptional work and characters. A system that would create an emotionally heroic character rather than a victim.

I realized that an actor must identify their character's primal need, goal or OBJECTIVE. With this OBJECTIVE in mind, the actor must then find the appropriate personal pain that can effectively drive this OBJECTIVE. After working with this idea for a while, I understood that the pain must be powerful enough to inspire an actor to fearlessly commit to doing *whatever it takes* to WIN their OBJECTIVE. If the emotions were not strong enough, then there wasn't enough there to help the actor sustain their fight to win. But when the appropriate personal pain is paired with an OBJECTIVE, it connects the actor to their character's predicament, making winning the OBJECTIVE real and necessary for them as a person, not just as an actor playing a part. With this new approach, my cutting-edge technique was born.

I began working to refine this theory of overcoming personal pain to empower a performance into a technique. I had to figure out how to help actors find a way to psychologically personalize and feel their character's drive to win as their own.

Once I began applying these concepts I found the process so personally enriching that it literally took over my life. I began teaching seven days a week, many hours a day. Because I primarily taught and coached working actors, word spread through the professional acting community quickly. I opened an acting studio. Shortly thereafter, the studio had a rather lengthy waiting list. I never advertised and refused to do any promotion or have my school listed in any of the trade publications for actors. I didn't even have a website. In fact, for a number of years, my studio's telephone number was unlisted. I wasn't being snobby or arrogant, I just figured that if an actor really wanted to find me, they would. Some people went to great lengths to get into my class, sometimes taking months just to get the school's phone number. As a result, I attracted those who were truly dedicated to the craft—whether they were a writer, director or actor. I truly believe that the quality of my students, the majority of whom are committed, working actors, has been a part of elevating and advancing my technique.

Over the past twenty years, I have coached thousands of actors on thousands of parts in literally thousands of movies, television shows and plays. These actors are a living (and acting) research lab for my acting technique. Often, I have coached several actors auditioning for the same part in the same movie. I have seen, firsthand, what works and what doesn't. Over time, I have identified the common denominators of what is most effective. When I would see certain approaches succeed again and again, I would develop, explore and refine them until they were easily reproducible. When my actors would get parts or win great reviews and awards, I found that it frequently came from using similar fundamental tools, all rooted in basic human psychology and behavioral science.

Another pattern I've observed over time is that my acting technique has a tendency to bleed into an actor's personal life. To actually *use* adversity as a way to overcome it and win is so inspiring and effective that many of my actors unconsciously incorporate this way of being into their lives, becoming more personally realized and empowered. They take the victimization out of their lives, as they do for a scripted character.

What's important for you as an actor or a director, screenwriter, or even a non-actor who wants to learn how to use your pain and win your goals, is that I have a technique that profoundly deepens actors' performances and changes their lives.

This book will give you the precise methodology for the Chubbuck Technique, which is ultimately a rigorous, step-by-step, nuts-and-bolts script analysis system. A script analysis system that will help you to access your emotions and give you a way to not just feel them, but *use* them with dimension and power. *The Power of the Actor* will show you how to take your conflicts, challenges and pain and turn them into something positive, both from the standpoint of the character you are portraying and the human being behind the character.

Throughout my career as a teacher I have received many personal cards, notes and letters from my students expressing their gratitude for the technique, which seems to always change an actor's, writer's and director's life and career. Let this book be my way of saying "Thank you" right back. For I've learned just as much, if not more, from my students—through who they are as people and their diverse life experiences—as they have from me.

PART I

The 12-Step Chubbuck Acting Technique

An actor who merely feels tends to turn his performance inward and does not energize or inspire himself or an audience, whereas watching someone do *anything and everything* to override pain in an attempt to accomplish a goal or an OBJECTIVE puts an audience on the edge of their seats, because the outcome becomes alive and unpredictable. Taking action results in risk and, therefore, an unexpected journey. It's not enough for an actor to be honest. It's the actor's job to make the kind of choices that motivate exciting results. You can paint a canvas using real oil paint, but if the final painting isn't a compelling image, no one will want to look at it.

This technique will teach you how to use your traumas, emotional pains, obsessions, travesties, needs, desires and dreams to fuel and drive your character's achievement of a goal. You'll learn that the obstacles of your character's life are not meant to be accepted but to be overcome, in heroic proportions. In other words, my technique teaches actors how *to win*.

More than two thousand years ago, Aristotle defined the struggle of the individual to win as the essence of all drama. Overcoming and winning against all the hurdles and conflicts of life is what makes dynamic people. Martin Luther King, Jr., Stephen Hawking, Susan B. Anthony, Virginia Woolf, Albert Einstein, Beethoven, Mother Teresa and Nelson Mandela all had to overcome almost insurmountable struggles in their lives to achieve their goals. Indeed, the greater the obstacles and the more passion these people brought to overcoming their obstacles, the more profound the achievement or contribution they made. They didn't become amazing, accomplished people despite their challenges, but because of them. These are qualities we want to duplicate in characterizations. It's much more captivating to watch someone who's trying to win against the odds than someone who's content to put up with life's travails. A winner doesn't have to actually win to be a winner—a winner tries to win, a loser accepts defeat.

The better you know yourself, the better an actor you'll be. You need to understand what makes you tick, profoundly and deeply. The following twelve acting tools will help you to dig into your psyche, allowing for discovery and a way to expose and channel all those wonderful demons that we all have. Your dark side, your traumas, your beliefs, your priorities, your fears, what drives your ego, what makes you feel shame and what initiates your pride are your colors, your paints to draw with as an actor.

The twelve tools:

1. **OVERALL OBJECTIVE**: What does your character want from life more than anything? Finding what your character wants throughout the script.
2. **SCENE OBJECTIVE**: What your character wants over the course of an entire scene, which supports the character's OVERALL OBJECTIVE.
3. **OBSTACLES**: Determining the physical, emotional and mental hurdles that make it difficult for your character to achieve his or her OVERALL and SCENE OBJECTIVE.
4. **SUBSTITUTION**: Endowing the other actor in the scene with a person from your real life that makes sense to your OVERALL OBJECTIVE and your SCENE OBJECTIVE. For instance, if your character's SCENE OBJECTIVE is *"to get you to love me,"* then you find someone from your present life that really makes you need that love—urgently, desperately and completely. This way you have all the diverse layers that a real need from a real person will give you.
5. **INNER OBJECTS**: The pictures you see in your mind when speaking or hearing about a person, place, thing or event.
6. **BEATS and ACTIONS**: A BEAT is a thought. Every time there's a change in thought, there's a BEAT change. ACTIONS are the mini-OBJECTIVES that are attached to each BEAT

that support the SCENE'S OBJECTIVE and, therefore, the OVERALL OBJECTIVE.

7. **MOMENT BEFORE:** The event that happens before you begin the scene (or before the director yells, "Action!"), which gives you a place to move from, both physically and emotionally.

8. **PLACE and FOURTH WALL:** Using PLACE and FOURTH WALL means that you endow your character's physical reality—which, in most cases, is realized on a stage, soundstage, set, classroom or on location—with attributes from a PLACE from your real life. Using PLACE and the FOURTH WALL creates privacy, intimacy, history, meaning, safety and reality. The PLACE/FOURTH WALL must support and make sense with the choices you've made for the other tools.

9. **DOINGS:** The handling of props, which produces behavior. Brushing your hair while speaking, tying your shoes, drinking, eating, using a knife to chop, etc., are examples of DOINGS.

10. **INNER MONOLOGUE:** The dialogue that's going on inside your head that you don't speak out loud.

11. **PREVIOUS CIRCUMSTANCES:** Your character's history. The accumulation of life experiences that determines *why* and *how* they operate in the world. And then personalizing the character's PREVIOUS CIRCUMSTANCES to that of your own so you can truly and soulfully understand the character's behavior and become and live the role.

12. **LET IT GO:** While the Chubbuck Technique does use an actor's intellect, it is not a set of intellectual exercises. This technique is the way to create human behavior so real that it produces the grittiness and rawness of really *living* a role. In order for you to duplicate the natural flow of life and be spontaneous, you have to get out of your head. To achieve this you have to trust the work you've done with the previous eleven tools and LET IT GO.

These twelve acting tools create a solid foundation that will keep you present and inspire a raw, profound, dynamic and powerful performance.

My work with Halle Berry in *Monster's Ball* is a good example of how this technique works. Using one pivotal scene, I'll give you a glimpse of how we used some of the elements of my technique. In this scene, I'll show how we used just a few of the acting tools from my script analysis system. Keep in mind, we used all twelve steps in the final performance, but to break down each scene using all twelve tools would be a book in itself. So here's a taste, using a few of the tools to illustrate how effective the technique can be.

Monster's Ball is an extremely heartrending story, and Halle's character, Leticia, is a tragic woman. We had to find a way to prevent Halle, as Leticia, from being a victim of her circumstances and thereby becoming resigned to the multitude of tragedies that her character has suffered. In the film, the heartbreak begins with Leticia taking her obese son to his last visit with his father (her husband), who is on death row and about to be executed. Shortly after her husband's death, her son is killed in a car accident, and then Leticia is fired from her job and evicted from her home. As the story evolves, Leticia discovers that her new boyfriend—her one hope—has a horribly racist father. And, as if all this wasn't enough, at the end of the film, she learns that her boyfriend was a part of her husband's death and never told her. Leticia is incensed and overwhelmed.

How was Halle going to take these events and not give up? What personal experiences did she have that would relate to her character? How could we possibly make this oppressive story hopeful, thereby allowing her character to win in the end? Once someone gives up the struggle to win, the story is over, leaving an audience unfulfilled. We applied the twelve tools, starting with determining her character's OVERALL OBJECTIVE. Then we found Halle's personal pain that emotionally duplicated Leticia's and set out to overcome these issues within her performance.

Betrayal Scene

Illustrating the use of OVERALL OBJECTIVE (tool #1), SCENE OBJECTIVE (tool #2) and INNER MONOLOGUE (tool #10).

- The Scene: The betrayal is established when Leticia discovers that Hank played a role in her husband's execution and never told her.
- Leticia's OVERALL OBJECTIVE: *"to be loved and taken care of."*

With all that Leticia has experienced in her past and present life, what she needs more than anything is the feeling of safety and support that comes from being loved and taken care of. The SCENE OBJECTIVE has to support the OVERALL OBJECTIVE in order to complete an arc to the entire script and a focused journey for the actor, the character and the audience. This is the last scene in the movie, so she must resolve her journey by defeating her OBSTACLES and achieving and *winning* her OVERALL OBJECTIVE. To make this happen, her SCENE OBJECTIVE can't be about the betrayal but how she gets what she wants, which is love. This makes . . .

• Leticia's SCENE OBJECTIVE: *"to get you to love me."*

The last scene of *Monster's Ball* opens with Leticia discovering her dead husband's drawing of her boyfriend, Hank, in Hank's belongings. The drawing indicates that Hank knew her husband, probably while her husband was on death row, and has never told her. The intention of Marc Forster, the director, was to have an unresolved ending, nothing that was too pat. Something that would leave the audience wondering if Leticia was going to kill him, herself or both of them. Although independent and art movies often have dark endings, it is my belief that everyone, even someone who's a part of the art-house crowd, wants to feel hope (*the win*) at the end of a movie. In other words, provide moviegoers with an experience that will allow them to anticipate a joyful resolution in their life dramas the same way Leticia has found one in hers. We couldn't change the script, which didn't support a happy ending, so it was up to Halle's performance to infuse a sense of hope and possibilities.

Hank's omission is a huge betrayal, yet another heartbreak to add to Leticia's long list. For Leticia, this deceit is the straw that breaks the camel's back. She explodes with fury. We wonder if she's going to kill him or herself or both (keeping in line with the director's ideas). By using IN-NER MONOLOGUE that supported the SCENE OBJECTIVE of *"to get you to love me"* (not "I need to feel angry and desperate"—what person in their right mind wants that?) we changed the ending without chang-ing the director's vision.

To find the INNER MONOLOGUE, we had to personalize Leticia's painful discovery, which helped Halle create her intense rage. In the film, the rage in her face says, "How can he do this to me?!" To make her INNER MONOLOGUE produce a transition from rage to a place of hope, Halle and I talked about Leticia's survival instinct. In this scene, she must fight for Hank's love to be real, or she'll die. Leticia could view the discovery as an evil betrayal, which would mean that she would suffer an emotional death, possibly even a physical death. Because of her need to be loved by Hank, she is forced to find a way to perceive his lie differently. It's possible that Hank's motivation for lying wasn't an act of deception, but rather an action taken that expressed an ultimate sacrifice of love. Leticia could rationalize Hank's behavior by thinking, "He could've loved me so much, he was afraid to tell me for fear of losing me once I found out. He was willing to live and be oppressed by his guilty secret because he loved me so deeply. He didn't think he could live without me, so he didn't act out of deceit, but out of a great love for me. . . ."

Thus, without words said out loud, strictly by using INNER MONO-LOGUE, the audience was able to see exactly what she was thinking and feeling. The arc that was created by her INNER MONOLOGUE began with:

- The surprise of the discovery . . .
- Which turned into a murderous rage . . .
- Which turned into hurt and confusion . . .
- Which turned into a survival need to find a way to change the horror of what she's discovered . . .
- To actually finding the solution by viewing the betrayal as something positive . . . which allowed her to feel unconditionally loved (a feeling she's never had before).

All of this is played out in Halle's facial expressions and behavior. In the film, she processes all this before Hank returns. So when Hank comes home and feeds her a spoonful of ice cream on the front porch, she is able to look at him with love in her eyes and to say in her INNER MONOLOGUE, "After all that I have suffered in my life, your love is going to make it all better. I'm going to be all right."

I hope that relating this specific story of the work Halle and I did together in *Monster's Ball* has given you a clearer understanding of the technique. In the same way, I have found in my years of teaching that using case histories from my work with various actors has helped to create a visual that exponentially aided in the comprehension of a particular tool or aspect of the technique. In the following explanations of the 12 tools I will do the same, utilizing a broad range of stories—from actors with Academy Award status, to television, theater and soap opera actors, to up-and-coming actors from my class.

CHAPTER I

Tool #1:

OVERALL OBJECTIVE

> What your character wants
> over the course of the entire script.

The OVERALL OBJECTIVE is the tool that gives a script a beginning, middle and end. It defines the journey for the actor as well as for the audience. All the other acting tools must serve and support the OVERALL OBJECTIVE.

If you want to be a poignant and powerful actor, you must duplicate the true behavior of dynamic, powerful people. And these compelling people are always, in one form or another, goal-oriented. Many actors fall into the trap of believing that just being real or having real, deep emotional feelings is acting—it is not. Too many actors feel that if they have reached real tears in their work that they have successfully fulfilled the role. It's how you use those emotions to fuel your goal that makes the art of acting exciting to play as well as to watch. Without the purpose of a goal, without the struggle to win, the purely emotional actor will be a victim to the circumstances of the script, and no one likes to watch a victim be a victim. We want to watch a person change their life, not accept abuse.

An actor must learn to use emotions, not as an end result,
but as a tool to provide the passion to overcome
the conflict of the script.

Beyond providing the actor and the audience with something to root for and a journey to travel on, the OVERALL OBJECTIVE also infuses the action with a sense of urgency. As you know, time flies when you're busy trying to get something done. Because the actor is going for his or her goal in the moment and with great passion, it compresses the actor's as well as the audience's sense of time, causing the minutes to tick away faster, making everything a more exciting, anything-can-happen experience. The better the actor is at accessing his life experiences as a way of creating urgency and passion for the goals in the script, the higher the art.

> *Ask yourself, "What does my character want from life?"*
> *"What is the primal goal?"*
> *This is the OVERALL OBJECTIVE.*

Whether it takes place in real time or over the course of twenty years, the OVERALL OBJECTIVE is the main *need* that drives your character. Your OVERALL OBJECTIVE should always be a basic human need, a primal goal such as *"I want to find true love," "I want power,"* or *"I need validation."*

All the subsequent tools are there to support the journey (your OVERALL OBJECTIVE) as well as to make it more crucial, detailed, deeper, significant and truthful. Man's survival instinct makes us goal-oriented. Our emotional lives come *only* as a result of getting or not getting our goals. Say the OVERALL OBJECTIVE is *"to be loved."* If you win your goal (OVERALL OBJECTIVE) then you'll be happy; if you lose your goal (OVERALL OBJECTIVE) then you'll be sad and angry.

Emotions are a reaction to an action, not the other way around.

Finding your OVERALL OBJECTIVE first keeps you from having to pump up emotions before you begin acting, and it allows the emotions to emerge in a more natural, human way. It's a lot easier than spending an hour before performing remembering some awful past memory and trying to keep it alive. If you're attempting to pump up emotions from some disconnected place, the result is emotional vomit. And, as in life, throwing up is pleasant neither for the participant nor the viewer. It becomes an emotional explosion, accomplishing nothing.

More importantly, working scene to scene to win your OVERALL OBJECTIVE creates real behavior in every scene. As you fight for your character to overcome every obstacle, to achieve the OVERALL OBJECTIVE, real and unique behavior will instinctively emerge in your journey to achieve your goal. Your pure concentration on accomplishing a goal makes you unaware of what you look like, and allows your naturally dis-

tinctive mannerisms and quirks to come forward. It's this kind of real behavior that generates in-the-moment tension that makes an audience
breathlessly watch and cheer for your character. The audience gets to
watch the unresolved emotional and physical OVERALL OBJECTIVE
become resolved before their eyes and to relate to it as if it is their own
resolution. People will be more likely to support another person if they
feel their struggle is the same as their own.

Several years ago, Catherine Keener was studying with me. She has
an amazingly rich emotional life to draw from, but at the time, she was
using it without the benefit and motivation of an OVERALL OBJECTIVE.
In class, week after week, scene after scene, she would put up emotionally wrought performances. But while her classmates and I could see her
pain, we couldn't relate to it. We, as her audience, couldn't find a way to
understand her feelings, because all of those wonderfully profound and
accessible emotions were not attached to a reason—a need to win a goal.
Catherine felt that to go after a goal without reservation would result in
making her characters manipulative and unlikable. But I see manipulation as a strong and conscious effort to get what one wants. Using manipulation as a way to win an important OVERALL OBJECTIVE actually
makes the character effective, and effective people are always very appealing. Just think of Elizabeth Taylor in *Who's Afraid of Virginia
Woolf?* or Kevin Spacey in *The Usual Suspects.* I told her, "Once you
know that it's okay to manipulate in your work, *this* is when you'll be
truly recognized for your work." At this point, Catherine had a solid acting career, but without public recognition.

As it turned out, it was playing the role of the enthusiastically *manipulative* sexpot Maxine in *Being John Malkovich* that made audiences
and critics notice her. Catherine's character was imbued with such a calculated sense of winning and desire that she had to embrace her character's OVERALL OBJECTIVE and I-don't-care-about-anything-else-but-
winning attitude. And Catherine's worry that going after an OBJECTIVE
without mercy would make audiences hate her was completely un-
founded. In fact, it had quite the opposite effect. The audience didn't care
that Maxine was a bitch, because Maxine had a justifiable reason to ruthlessly go after her goal, something they could relate to: *getting my power
back in my life.* Audiences identified with her longing, and cheered for
her for her willingness to do anything, to completely debase herself, to
claw her way to getting that power back—because clearly her need
for present power was a reaction to being made to feel powerless in her
past. Because Catherine made the decision to win Maxine's OVERALL

OBJECTIVE, she was able to embody and behave the character of Maxine. As a result, for the first time in her career, Catherine was nominated for an Academy Award, a Golden Globe, and won the Independent Spirit Award for Best Actress. But beyond the awards, she learned how crucial it was to pursue an OVERALL OBJECTIVE, and it changed her career.

For an actor, the OVERALL OBJECTIVE fills in aspects of plot and gives them a high-stakes, viable way to personalize the role. The OVERALL OBJECTIVE essentially constructs a journey for the actor and the audience. At the beginning of a play or a film, the character (and actor) starts at A, at ground zero. This is where they need to establish the goal they need to accomplish. The rest of the play or film is how that particular character goes about accomplishing the goal to ultimately earn the right to get to Z.

The script informs the raw material to be analyzed, providing the specific information that makes a character do what they have to do. This includes the character's socioeconomic background; history of traumatic events; geographical location in which the character was born and raised; the time period; the character's history of personal and professional success and failure; the character's dreams; the character's modus operandi; how the character sees himself; and how the other characters view him. Then the actor personalizes, duplicating these elements from his or her own life. This will organically generate idiosyncratic speech patterns and behavior.

> *Your character's OVERALL OBJECTIVE*
> *must be worded in a way that establishes a change in*
> *their life that is necessary for physical*
> *and/or emotional survival.*

These are big-picture, universally human issues that can drive a character's journey of an entire script, whether it takes place over the course of one day or spans a lifetime. Good OVERALL OBJECTIVES that include basic human needs are:

- To find love
- To get power
- To be unconditionally loved
- To have children
- To get married
- To be loved by my mother or father
- To get my ex back in my life
- To have a great career
- To be validated
- To stay alive (to survive)
- To protect and keep a loved one alive

OVERALL OBJECTIVE is not about plot. George Bernard Shaw said that there are no new plots, only new ways for people to negotiate and create relationships. And since every person is unique, *how* they negotiate and create relationships will be special and one of a kind. *How* your character attempts to win their OVERALL OBJECTIVE, which is based in an essential human need, is the journey.

> ***We don't need an actor's interpretation to provide plot.***
> ***The script gives us that.***

You have to always keep in mind that an audience goes to the theater, the movies, or watches television to see human relationships take place. It doesn't matter if the plot takes us to the nonexistent planet of Nebulosa, or to a battle in World War II, or tells the story of giant roaches wreaking dirty havoc—an audience can always relate to the human element of people attempting to establish, build or negotiate a relationship. This is true no matter what locale or venue it happens to take place in.

In the movie *Out of Time*, Eva Mendes played a cop named Alex Whitlock, who works side by side with her ex-husband and fellow cop, Matt Whitlock, played by Denzel Washington, to solve a murder. As she works to solve the murder, it looks more and more like Denzel's character has committed the crime. The story ends with the revelation that he was framed, and they reconcile.

Eva could have worked with the plot's OVERALL OBJECTIVE: *"to solve the crime."* This would be dry, cold and passionless and lacking what an audience really cares about—a human connection. The human equation would be missing. Instead, Eva and I tackled her character using the OVERALL OBJECTIVE *"to get Matt* (Denzel's character) *back and loving me again."* This made it imperative that she solve the case for two reasons. One, she needed to impress him with her prowess as a cop. And two, disregarding her feelings that he might be guilty, she needed to help to clear his name. This OVERALL OBJECTIVE makes Eva's character indispensable in his life—both career-wise and love-wise. In this way, it *earns* her the way to get him back in her life, not just *wanting* him back, but taking viable actions to *get* him back. This also inspired more emotional reactions for her, because every little turn that takes place in the plot becomes more conflict for her to overcome in reaching her OVERALL OBJECTIVE of getting him back. This is how the complexities and texturing are infused in a performance. She must confront all of the plot's twists and turns and still be able to accomplish her OVERALL

OBJECTIVE. These complexities can only emerge if the OVERALL OB-
JECTIVE is driven by a simple and basic human need. This enables the
actor to keep the experience from being a cerebral, intellectual process
and instead turns it into a body experience.

The OVERALL OBJECTIVE Should Be Simple, Basic and Active

Keeping the OVERALL OBJECTIVE simple and human also creates an
arena in which the actor can stop acting and really be in the scene. The
most common mistake people make is to make the OVERALL OBJEC-
TIVE too complicated and, therefore, too complicated to play.

When I was coaching Jessica Biel for her starring role in the remake
of *The Texas Chainsaw Massacre*, we faced this very problem. It could
have been easy to state her OVERALL OBJECTIVE as *"to want to get
away from the crazy guy and keep my friends and myself alive because
the murderer is out of control and bloodthirsty and we're just a bunch of
young people, and I'm also pregnant and my boyfriend doesn't know. . . ."*
It's hard to act out such a complicated, plot-driven goal. Keeping it simple, we came up with the OVERALL OBJECTIVE *"to protect my unborn
child."* This allowed her to have an urgent need to survive, because if she
died, so would her baby. She could also act from a place that was desperate, hyperaware and primal (it doesn't get any more primal than protecting your unborn child). This OVERALL OBJECTIVE also created
more tension and reality in her relationship to the others, especially her
boyfriend, because she felt she couldn't reveal her pregnancy until she
felt the future infant would be emotionally safe in the hands of her
friends and the father of the child. A simple OVERALL OBJECTIVE allowed her more dimensions in what would otherwise be a hokey horror
story.

In the final editing of the remake of *The Texas Chainsaw Massacre*,
they cut all references to Jessica's character being pregnant. But although she wasn't pregnant in the version that audiences saw, Jessica, using the OVERALL OBJECTIVE of protecting her unborn child, gave the
performance a primal urgency to survive and to save those around her. It
didn't matter that we the audience were not privy to her pregnancy, because we interpreted her moves as a dire need to protect her friends and
to stay alive. As a result, her acting in what could have been viewed as a
generic horror-film performance was instead heralded, and Jessica re-

ceived the kind of movie offers (and salary) that she had never received before.

Don't intellectually decide your OVERALL OBJECTIVE.

Instead, decide on three or four—determined from the circumstances of the script—and try them all in rehearsal. By the end of the second page of dialogue, the simplest and most effective choice for OVERALL OBJECTIVE will become obvious.

Hedda Gabler is one of theater's most complex characters. She is often played as an evil, calculating, unsympathetic woman. Judith Light came to me looking for a way to avoid this frequent interpretation. She was preparing for a run at the Kennedy Center in Washington, D.C. Judith and I stepped back and looked at the circumstances of Hedda's life. Hedda's father is a major-general who wanted a son to continue the family's military legacy. Of course, at that time, it was impossible for a woman to have anything to do with the military. Having his daughter Hedda meant less than nothing to him.

It made sense then to assume that throughout Hedda's childhood, she had overheard her father ardently discuss war strategy and tactics and play war games, all the while ignoring young Hedda. Any child who is shunned by a parent is going to become obsessed with changing that relationship to one of pride, acceptance and most important, to one of love. Her OVERALL OBJECTIVE was *"to get my father's love."* This OVERALL OBJECTIVE gives a sympathetic rationale for Hedda's harsh and calculating behavior. She is trying to become, even after her father dies, the kind of person Hedda's father *could* love: a major-general.

To accomplish this, I had Judith behave like a major-general of the house. With every interaction, conversation and gesture she was at war, moving troops, engaging in subterfuge, spying, convincing Mrs. Elstead to destroy evidence, etc. The behavior may have been evil, but because Judith worked with a righteous, primal reason—to get a father's love— the audience and critics saw Hedda as a real and vulnerable woman doing what was necessary to win, rather than a calculating woman incapable of love. As a critic described her performance, "Although Ibsen's Hedda is written as a newlywed bride of twenty-nine years, the fifty-one-year-old Light makes her realistic and sympathetic." We found the driving OVERALL OBJECTIVE that would make the most sense for the given circumstances, one that would give her a primal reason to behave so badly. Even the most vicious criminals have a sympathetic reason for their behavior. It's up to the actor to find it.

The OVERALL OBJECTIVE has to be a simple, bottom-line, primal need that will make sense throughout the script.

Whether the script is two pages or two hundred, or spans five minutes or a lifetime, your OVERALL OBJECTIVE must provide a coherent and focused "throughline." Where your character begins and where your character ends up provides clues as to what your OVERALL OBJECTIVE might be. A few years ago, Rob Schneider came to me with the script for the comedy *Deuce Bigelow,* which tells the story of a male gigolo. After talking about the pitfalls of playing this role, I told him we had to come up with an OVERALL OBJECTIVE that not only made sense for the overall story, but that would also make the audience see Deuce as a hero rather than a sleazy guy looking for an easy way to have sex with women. After exploring several ideas, we agreed that the OVERALL OBJECTIVE should be: *"to be loved."* So badly, in fact, that he must be willing to do anything to get that love.

We also talked about what would motivate this OVERALL OBJEC-TIVE. What would make a man so love-starved that he would become a gigolo? The answer came: his character had been rejected by girls, constantly and continuously, ever since it mattered to young Deuce. This need to be accepted by females had never been resolved, even in the present action of the script. Because the social skills of Deuce have never matured, for all intents and purposes, Deuce behaves from a child-like base.

To go after his OVERALL OBJECTIVE from a childlike place gave Rob the innocence needed to make Deuce a sympathetic character. After all, a child will do anything to win. For instance, if a child really wants a Frisbee, that child will seduce, have a tantrum, negotiate, complain, accuse, become the victim and be a brat, and we forgive this behavior because it stems from innocence, a purity of spirit. If an adult maintains a childlike need and behavior, we will forgive as well. Look at Jack Nicholson in *As Good As It Gets.* He, too, created a character from a childlike place, a character that would have been viewed as abusive and cruel if he had played it as a mature adult.

This OVERALL OBJECTIVE, fueled by Rob Schneider's own personal childhood issues, did two things for the film. First, the OVERALL OB-

JECTIVE changed the film's form. Because he was behaving like a child, the issue of his being a gigolo wasn't about having actual sex. Although women would come to him for their initial objective—sex—Deuce would overpower this desire with his desire to get them to love him. Deuce earned the love by making the women feel empowered enough to overcome some pretty severe problems—narcolepsy, obesity and Tourette's syndrome. Audiences loved him for rescuing these women. Rob made Deuce a hero, which leads us to the second thing that the OVERALL OBJECTIVE did for the film: It made a potentially seedy topic high comedy, and a huge hit.

Read the Entire Script More Than Once

To find the OVERALL OBJECTIVE for your character in a script, it's important to read the entire script more than once. By doing so, you can determine more specific elements about your character and begin to think about how the other characters relate to you and talk about you, even when you're not there.

Without having read and reread the script for *The Silence of the Lambs,* Anthony Hopkins would never have understood that his OVERALL OBJECTIVE as Hannibal Lecter wasn't about becoming an even more dangerous serial killer, but was to gain the friendship of Agent Clarisse Starling (Jodie Foster). The script opens with Lecter testing Clarisse to determine if she is worthy of his advice and camaraderie. Hopkins used his character's bizarre and scary behavior as a very effective way to test her—intellectually, emotionally and physically. Hannibal Lecter is a very damaged man, damage that almost always comes from severe childhood abuse. His testing of Clarisse becomes necessary as a way to ensure that she won't become an abuser, too. His strange testing tactics are truly the only way to emotionally protect himself. She passes his stringent test. How? Not only does she prove her intellectual and emotional strength, but more importantly, they come to realize that they have similar emotional demons in their lives to overcome. Both of them have the same "screaming lambs" in their heads, but have found opposing solutions to overcome them—her by saving others, him by killing. The commonality of pain bonds them, and a friendship is formed. A friendship so strong that the audience came to trust that no matter what, Hannibal Lecter would never hurt or harm her. In fact, the bond created by the actors was so effective that at the end of the movie, when his character quips to Clarisse, "I'm having an old friend for dinner" the audience laughs rather than being appalled, even though we know he is going to literally eat his guest. Why? Because the OVERALL OBJECTIVE—*"to get a friend who truly understands me"*—made this final comment acceptable and even funny, because it was a friend talking to a friend rather than an accomplished and flesh-starved cannibal talking to a rookie FBI agent. Anthony Hopkins' relationship-based OVERALL OBJECTIVE made *The Silence of the Lambs* a movie about friendship between two unlikely people rather than being yet another typical thriller film. His OVERALL OBJECTIVE effectively raised the commerciality, the relevance and the integrity of the film.

It's important to note that Anthony Hopkins also didn't see his character of Hannibal Lecter as a bad man. Hopkins didn't judge his character. He saw his character as someone injured by the previous circumstances of his life, and his serial killing as a retributional reaction to a horrible and painful past. Because Hopkins wasn't burdened by moral judgments, he was allowed the freedom to explore all the facets of a very complex man, therefore creating a very complex performance.

Never Judge Your Character or His or Her OBJECTIVES

Noel Coward said, "You can't judge art." Likewise, you can't judge your character or his or her OBJECTIVES. A stupid person never thinks they're stupid. An evil person doesn't think they're evil—they always have a righteous reason for doing what they do. A pimp/prostitute/stripper doesn't necessarily hate what they do for a living, or think it's sleazy or wrong. You can't contaminate your canvas with moral doctrines and societal values. Nurturing your values takes energy and focus away from your character and their goals. Art needs room to breath, with the freedom to discover without restraint. The colors you use in your work have to include a buffet of attributes. This consists of the good, likable parts of who you are, but it also includes the parts that make you bad, the darker elements that reside in all of us. It may make you feel smarmy, but really, it's the darker parts of being human that usually drive us to seek a goal with vengeance, passion and urgency—making the journey taken by the OVERALL OBJECTIVE a more exciting one.

When determining your OVERALL OBJECTIVE, don't be afraid to investigate and use the ugly, darker parts of who you are. You may be playing someone who might, by society's standards, be considered a bad person, but that person feels that what he or she is doing is right. This needs to be reflected in your OVERALL OBJECTIVE. For instance, if the character is a rapist, the OVERALL OBJECTIVE isn't *"to rape people"* but rather *"to get my power back"* from the primal person who, through abuse, took it away. As we'll explore later on in this book, abusers, rapists and killers usually see their victims as symbols or representations of the original person who raped or abused them. So when they act—abuse, rape and kill—they feel they are getting revenge and hurting the person who cruelly took their power away. Striking back at a symbolic tormentor is often the only way the rapist/abuser/killer can cope with their horrible childhood abuse. It's a means for the rapist/abuser/killer to stop feeling like a victim to the childhood abuse and instead feel empowered. This makes the act of raping/killing in a performance justified.

This is true even with the issue of suicide—you can't judge it. To some it is a viable solution to overwhelming and untenable pain. *Leaving Las Vegas* is a story about Ben (played by Nicolas Cage) a man who wants to commit suicide by drinking himself to death and then comes across the path of Sera, a prostitute (played by Elisabeth Shue). I worked with Elisabeth on both her audition as well as the actual movie.

First, we had to get past the audition, which was difficult because the director, Mike Figgis, didn't think Elisabeth was right for the role. His reasoning wasn't groundless. Before this movie, Elisabeth had always played good girls, the girl-next-door type. But Elisabeth really wanted the part and Figgis finally agreed to meet with her. We knew that, at best, it was a charity meeting. It was up to us to change his mind and see Elisabeth as the perfect Sera.

Based on the script, it seemed like Sera's OVERALL OBJECTIVE was *"to keep Ben from committing suicide and make him want to live."* However, this OVERALL OBJECTIVE judged the act of suicide as something amoral and wrong, which, as you may have guessed, went against my belief about not judging characters and their actions. We played around with a few ideas and then I asked Elisabeth, "What if your Sera saw suicide as a solution for herself, as well, and instead of trying to get Ben to stay alive, she connects with him because they have both found the exact same solution to their pain?" Her OVERALL OBJECTIVE then became *"to get Ben to love me,"* a love that emanates from two people sharing the same answer to their unbearable emotional agony. This would change *Leaving Las Vegas* from a depressing, maudlin story about suicide to a great love story. It would be a love story about two people who are going to die soon, and who have the urgency to fit what might normally be fifty years of a loving relationship into a few weeks. This made the question that Sera asks Ben in the scripted dialogue—"Why do you want to commit suicide?"—an entirely different issue. Instead of meaning, "Why would you want to do something like that?" which implies judgment, her question means, "Do you have the same reason for committing suicide that I do?" which makes it more about how similar they are and provides for further bonding. Staying in the nonjudgmental mind-set, we also made the choice that she really liked being a prostitute—this occupation, after all, would be the only way a person like Sera could experience power in her life, and that's always a good thing.

Elisabeth auditioned and presented our vision of the script to Mike Figgis. This interpretation surprised and intrigued him. He had seen several other actresses and they all had presented the OVERALL OB-JECTIVE of Sera as someone trying to save Ben, essentially a hooker with a heart of gold. The result of such an OBJECTIVE is patronizing and demeaning to Ben's course of action. Figgis couldn't get this new vision of Sera out of his head. He not only hired Elisabeth to play Sera against type, but also rewrote the script with her OVERALL OBJECTIVE in mind—two people who find great love fueled by a mutual need to commit suicide. Elisabeth was also able to bring true love and hope to a potentially relentless story of addiction, prostitution and rape. In fact, in his review of the film, Peter Travers of *Rolling Stone* magazine wrote, "The film, directed by Mike Figgis from an autobiographical 1991 novel by John O'Brien, is a tragedy that unspools with astonishing buoyancy and sneaky wit, as if no one told the lovers their story should be depressing." In fact, most of the reviewers echoed one critic's opinion that the film "is a strangely uplifting story about suicide." Elisabeth Shue was nominated for an Oscar, Nicolas Cage won the Oscar, and Mike Figgis was nominated for Best Director and Best Screenplay.

You must analyze the psyche of the character and find a way of making your character feel righteous in his behavior by investigating the probable primal issue(s) that makes your character behave the way he or she does today. You look at the character's psyche and then find out how that duplicates itself emotionally in your life, thereby making the character's amoral, outrageous behavior actually make good sense.

The character of Blanche Dubois in *A Streetcar Named Desire* is one of the most celebrated antiheroes of American theater. Her OVER-ALL OBJECTIVE is *"to get Stella* (her sister) *away from Stanley* (Stella's husband) *and back to me."* In her attempt to win her sister back, she's willing to lie and steal, but worst of all, she has sex with Stanley, her brother-in-law, by seductively driving him to rape her. Why push your brother-in-law to go this far? Blanche does *anything* and *everything* to win her OVERALL OBJECTIVE, because if she doesn't, she will die. And not just in the spiritual sense—if she can't get Stella to leave Stanley and be with her, she will be penniless, homeless and utterly alone.

Personalize Your Character's OVERALL OBJECTIVE

Barry Pepper came to me to prepare for his role as Daniel Jackson in Steven Spielberg's *Saving Private Ryan*. It would seem that Daniel's OVERALL OBJECTIVE was *"to win the war."* The OVERALL OBJECTIVE had some of the right elements: it was simple and active; it wasn't overin-tellectualized; it fulfilled the overall needs of the script; and it wasn't judgmental of his character. However, the basic human need element was missing. Winning a war didn't mean anything to Barry, and since all act-ing is relationship driven in one way or another, we had to find the way that this was true in his performance as well.

Barry is a small-town boy from Canada whose life experience has never given him anything even close to a warfare experience. How does he go after an OVERALL OBJECTIVE that he knows nothing about? He could've made believe he was in World War II and brought historical de-tails to his performance. But, like telling a complex lie, it's hard to re-member all the faces of the lie, and in time you will get caught with your pants down. The same thing happens with acting. If there's too much in-formation that relies on pure imagination, it will be forgotten.

Instead, I suggested that war can take on many forms. There are emotional struggles that feel like a battlefield and are warlike that exist in everyone's life. And this was just as true for Barry, who at the time was engaged to be married. An impending wedding day is always terrifying, intimidating, and for many of us (including myself) bloodcurdling. The fact is that most couples, just before they get married, have the worst and scariest battles that they have ever experienced. The day before I got married, my fight with my then future husband was so bad that I threatened to jump from a moving vehicle on the expressway. I even had my door open, with one foot dangling precariously in the wind in my neurotic attempt to win whatever petty thing we were struggling over. Facing down your future sickness-and-health, death-do-us-part life part-ner can be intimidating, scary, terrifying and in many cases (like mine) life-threatening. This can be compared to facing down the enemy in an actual warlike situation. And if getting married can be considered a proverbial war, it would make sense that you would probably want to be victorious in that war. You'd like to triumph over any problems that you might be having with your future mate. I knew that fighting with his fiancée was going to be one of Barry's natural responses to his imminent wedding day, so I had him use the battles, fears, concerns and emotionally driven life-threats that emanated from his war. Therefore, Barry's OVERALL OBJECTIVE for the war picture *Saving Private Ryan* became *"to make my marriage work."*

As a result, Barry wasn't playing a fantasy war figure. Indeed, he went after his personal OVERALL OBJECTIVE in *Saving Private Ryan* with the ferocity of someone who had something very personal at stake: to win the war over his and his fiancée's fears so that he could have a peaceful and healthy marriage. He only had a few lines in the movie, but the audience never thought of Barry as anything but one of the leads, alongside heavyweights like Tom Hanks and Matt Dillon. This was because his OVERALL OBJECTIVE was so strong, was based in something so necessary to his present personal life, that the audience, critics and future employers (directors and producers) couldn't help but notice him, and it changed his career.

The OVERALL OBJECTIVE and SCENE OBJECTIVE are the driving forces of my script analysis technique. Without OVERALL or SCENE OBJECTIVE, there's no need, no point, no consequence, no path and most important . . . no journey.

CHAPTER 2

Tool #2:
SCENE OBJECTIVE

> What your character wants over
> the course of the entire scene.

The SCENE OBJECTIVE has to support the OVERALL OBJECTIVE. Each SCENE OBJECTIVE cannot negate the OVERALL OBJECTIVE of the entire script. This is because each scene is a consecutive link, collectively building into one chain that completes the arc of the entire story. If the OVERALL OBJECTIVE for your character is *"to be loved,"* each successive scene is going to shape your character's path to getting that love. This means that even if your character asks another character to marry your character in one scene, but in a later scene asks that same character for a divorce, the OVERALL OBJECTIVE is still being served. How? Because the second SCENE OBJECTIVE is motivated by your character's OVERALL OBJECTIVE. Your character is not getting love in his current marriage, so his circumstances have led him to seek love elsewhere. So the divorce doesn't negate the OVERALL OBJECTIVE of *"to be loved."* It fulfills it.

A SCENE OBJECTIVE is the specific drive of intercommunication between you and the other character within a scene, whereas the OVERALL OBJECTIVE is the broad strokes of what your character seeks throughout the whole script. The SCENE OBJECTIVE is the precise way that you're going to achieve the OVERALL OBJECTIVE, informed by the dialogue and activity of the particular scene that you're breaking down. In *Patton*, the OVERALL OBJECTIVE of George C. Scott—who played the title character of General Patton, a major player in World War II— was *"to get power"* over anyone, be it his enemy or his troops. In the monologue he made famous, Scott stands in front of an American flag and uses a SCENE OBJECTIVE of *"to empower and inspire you* (the troops).” This motivates Patton's troops to do whatever he asks of them, including die for him. Inspiring this kind of loyalty can't help but make Scott as Patton a more powerful man, thereby making the act of empowering his men to come back at him twofold. By using SCENE OBJECTIVE, a symbiotic relationship is formed in which everyone benefits. Scott could have easily talked *at* his troops, but instead he made this monologue about intercommunication and forging human relationships. This is why it remains one of the most memorable scenes in any war film.

Your SCENE OBJECTIVE Should Be Worded in a Way That Requires a Response

For instance, *“to get you to be my friend.”* In other words, something you can *get* from the other person in the scene. Going after your SCENE OBJECTIVE should *include* the other person, which prevents you from talking *at* the other actor—instead, it makes you talk *to* him. In this way you are looking for a reaction, not a sounding board. You must answer the question, “Have I worded my SCENE OBJECTIVE in a way that generates a response?” You have to bottom-line your needs, taking out the intellect and wording the SCENE OBJECTIVE so that it is basic, needy and primal. This will allow you to act from your body, not your brain. When you are being rational, you are in control. But when the stakes are high—whether you're incredibly angry or sexually charged—your rational brain goes out the window, your body and emotions take over, and you end up behaving in a way that often surprises you. “Where did that come from? I'm usually never like that,” is the thought that should arise as a result of a good bottom-line, high-stakes, basic-needy-and-primal SCENE OBJECTIVE. Two examples of a cerebral and rational thought process for SCENE OBJECTIVE are:

- “I want to figure out how your mind works so that I can see if we have enough in common to fall in love.”
    or
- “I need you to understand why I do the things I do because I was abused as a child and I wonder if you can relate to that.”

As you can see, this kind of phrasing for a SCENE OBJECTIVE becomes too heady and confusing to create a straightforward journey. Stay away from esoteric or overintellectualized concepts. No matter how smart or stupid your character is, primal needs are always the same—they're primal. Albert Einstein or the retarded character of Lenny in *Of Mice and Men* have the same primordial human drives, such as a need to be loved. They just manifest them differently.

You can avoid overintellectualizing your SCENE OBJECTIVE by trying three or four SCENE OBJECTIVES with the dialogue. The one that seems to make the most sense, the one that includes your body and emotions as you're saying the words out loud, is the right one. It will be obvious because the most effective SCENE OBJECTIVE will fit like a glove.

The SCENE OBJECTIVE never changes midway through the scene.

If the SCENE OBJECTIVE changes or feels like it changes somewhere in the scene, you have picked the wrong SCENE OBJECTIVE. A SCENE OBJECTIVE has to make just as much sense at the beginning of the scene as it does at the end in order to have a beginning, middle and end.

The SCENE OBJECTIVE should be a simple thought process—one that doesn't take a right turn with a new direction and new thoughts by using more than one SCENE OBJECTIVE. The complexities of your acting come from how that particular character manifests his needs. In other words, *how* the part is played will change radically depending upon the unique background, experiences, personality and priorities emanating from the character *and* the actor who is playing the part. It's the who-am-I of the character as well as who you are as a person that brings in the nuances of individual behavior for that character.

The SCENE OBJECTIVE has to be something you can process from your mind, heart, gut and sexuality—simple human needs like:

- *"To get you to love me"*
- *"To get you to give me a job"*
- *"To make you validate me"*
- *"To make you my ally"*
- *"To get you to give me my power back"*
- *"To get you to have sex with me"*
- *"To make you wrong so I can be right"*
- *"To get you to give me hope"*
- *"To get you to worship me"*
- *"To get you to help me feel better"*

The wrong approach for the SCENE OBJECTIVE would be phrased as:

- "I need love"
- "I need a job"
- "I want validation"
- "I need an ally"
- "I want power"

- "I'd like sex"
- "I want to be right"
- "I want hope"
- "I want to feel better"
- "I want to be worshipped"

The second set of examples is wrong because the structure and conceptualization of the wording does not demand a response. You're not affecting the other actor.

Acting is the interplay between people.

There is a powerful difference between someone saying, "I want love," and someone saying to you, "I'm going to get *you* to love *me*." With the first statement, you can shrug your shoulders and say, "Fine, great, good luck, don't we all?" Whereas the second statement *changes* the other person. They are forced to react. They may be ecstatic, destroyed, afraid, but the response will be real. It helps to think about SCENE OBJECTIVE as an affective action you need to take in order to establish a human relationship of some kind.

You have to change the other person to ultimately get what you want.

Your SCENE OBJECTIVE *must* be phrased to require a response. It must affect the other actor in a manner that generates a need within him to give a response. The back-and-forth interplay of two actors trying to win what they need from each other is as exciting as watching a good boxing match. The more powerful the SCENE OBJECTIVE you choose, the more powerful the response, and thus, the more powerful the scene. Going after a SCENE OBJECTIVE that requires a reaction will always keep you present, because you have no idea how the other actor is going to react. And based on that unknown reaction, you don't know how you're going to respond. It keeps the acting work you're doing truly a moment-to-moment experience.

In fact, it might help to actually think about acting as a kind of boxing match. If you're in the ring, you don't know what moves the other boxer is going to use to try to win the match. You only know what the other boxer is going to do when he actually does it. You start the bout with your best punch. The other boxer will respond with, say, an uppercut. You then respond to his uppercut by first taking it in and then countering it with the best counterpunch you've got, trying for the winning edge. The other boxer takes in your response to his uppercut and responds with his own countermove that will hopefully enable him to win, and so on. All of the action is present and in the moment.

OBJECTIVE (Whether It's OVERALL or SCENE) Is Your Most Important Acting Tool

Yes, your emotional life is important. But without the sense of movement, which an OBJECTIVE gives you, and without using the emotions to fuel a goal (OBJECTIVE), your emotions just lay there, a quivering mass of useless feelings. When an actor just emotes, the audience experiences it as a self-indulgent performance. Inner work by itself, without an OBJECTIVE, creates a static emotional arena and scene, because emotions by themselves have no forward motion. Emotions are the *reaction* to an event or stimulus. What you do with those emotions to achieve your SCENE OBJECTIVE is what creates a powerful performance. Let the emotions be the impetus, or motivation, to achieve your SCENE OBJECTIVE, not the end itself.

When Eriq LaSalle first came to study with me he was an introspective actor—deep and substantial, but with the tendency to keep all that substance to himself. It only took him a few short months to learn to incorporate the drive to win into his performances. The will to win is so ingrained in our human makeup that once you connect with it, it's hard to go back. He began to see his work and his scripts not as the opportunity to reveal his rich emotional life, but as the opportunity to gain and accomplish something. This allowed him to incorporate the innate human survival instinct—whether that survival is emotional or physical—into his work. Soon after he had this revelation, he auditioned for the part of Dr. Peter Benton for the hit television series *ER*. On the page, Dr. Benton read as an introspective, temperamental doctor. Eriq's competitors made the mistake of auditioning for the role by portraying a moody guy because the character was written this way. Most actors try to please the writing rather than thinking about and looking for what the character's human need and goal is. Eriq knew better. In the audition scene—where every other actor played Dr. Benton having a pensive, life-and-death, typical "doctor" moment, Eriq played it differently. He worked with the SCENE OBJECTIVE—a human need stemming from his own unique personal life—which became: *"To get you to stay alive."* Eriq also endowed the dying person with someone important from his own life—which magnified the SCENE OBJECTIVE's emotional need. This brought direction, movement, an extreme desire to win the goal and a possibility of failure to his work, which made Eriq, as well as his audience of network executives, anticipate that anything could happen—because anything could. Working with a SCENE OBJECTIVE created dramatic moment after dramatic moment. When I spoke to one of the executives after the audition, he confided in me that Eriq had no competition. He was the one that NBC wanted because he was the only actor who was going after something.

Always Make the SCENE OBJECTIVE About Relationship—Don't Play the Plot

If all an audience wanted to see is plot, then we wouldn't need actors. We'd just put the script on the screen and let people read. Actors exist to interpret the script by bringing in the humanity. This boils down to creating a relationship of one kind or another. Even when someone has a gun to your head, you need to create a relationship with the gun-bearer or that person will shoot you as soon as you try to run away. The movie *Misery* exemplifies this. James Caan has been drugged and tied up by a crazy, obsessed, homicidal fan played by Kathy Bates. When he tries to fight her or berate her it only makes her angrier and causes him further physical damage. His character realizes that the only way he is going to survive is by making her believe that he likes her, relates to her and trusts her. By creating a relationship with her, he saved his life.

In the series *The West Wing*, actress Janel Moloney was originally hired as a one-time, possibly recurring, guest star to play the character Donnatella Moss, assistant to Josh Lyman. The dialogue on the page was nonrelationship workplace chatter and plot driven. Janel, however, did not see her scenes with her "boss" as a way to be good at her job at the White House (plot) but created the relationship-driven SCENE OBJECTIVE of *"to get you to fall in love with and be sexually attracted to me,"* instead. She brought in sexuality because it's a primal need that *everyone* relates to. This is something Janel learned over and over again while doing scene work in my class. Making the SCENE OBJECTIVE involve sex and love opened up a whole can of worms to play with—there's the employee/boss relationship dynamic, which is always risky and dangerous for both because you risk losing your job and having a hard time getting another; then there's the risk that he's married and she's not, which brings the wife in as a potent enemy; and of course, there's the getting your job done properly, which becomes more of a challenge when your mind keeps wandering to thoughts of the flesh. This SCENE OBJECTIVE enabled Janel to take a simple, uneventful character and turn her role into one that was complex, layered and multifaceted, and her character into someone who we all could relate to. As a result, she turned that one-time guest-star role into a regular role on a hit series, and an Emmy nomination.

SCENE OBJECTIVE gives the scene a beginning, a middle and an end.

SCENE OBJECTIVE gives the scene a focused through-line and journey: a beginning, a middle and an end. It also gives a scene a reason for being—it answers the question, "Why does this scene exist?" SCENE OBJECTIVE makes the material make more sense by giving each character movement and direction for the emotions and ideas in the scene. Pure emotions, by themselves, are not part of the human spirit; they evolve from our need to gain or accomplish something. When Djimon Hounsou, who starred in *Amistad* and *Gladiator* and was an Oscar nominee for his role in *In America,* came to me soon after he had just arrived in the United States from Africa (he's originally from Benin, in West Africa), he could speak English, but it was not his native language. In class, his scene work was incomprehensible due to his heavy African accent. I knew he was talented and his emotional life was full, but who cares when the audience—the class and I—doesn't understand what the heck he is saying? The breakthrough came when he did a scene from the play *Women of Manhattan.* The scene was about a blind date where Djimon's character, Duke—an African American man—meets his date, a white woman who was never told that Duke was black. The first run of the scene was confusing because what he was saying was once again incomprehensible due to his exceptionally heavy dialect. He might as well have been speaking Chinese. Apparently, Djimon was solely playing his inner work of being uncomfortable with his date's seemingly racist attitude without the aid of a SCENE OBJECTIVE. I told him he needed to have a SCENE OBJECTIVE to make the story make sense. The SCENE OBJECTIVE was basic and simple—*"to make you like me"*—which would be an effective way to overcome his date's bigotry and earn the right to the sex they have at the end of the evening. He did the scene again, but this time with the tack someone takes when trying to make someone *like me*. He used charm, humor, sexuality, availability and challenge. Somehow the accent didn't seem to be a hindrance anymore, the class and I knew precisely what was going on and he got numerous laughs (the play is a comedy) where he had previously gotten nothing but baffled gawking. The point is you can even be speaking a foreign language, but if you have a strong SCENE OBJECTIVE, the other actor(s) and the audience will get it.

Figure Out Where and How the Particular Scene Fits into the Entire Script

A SCENE OBJECTIVE must support the OVERALL OBJECTIVE in order to enable your character to take a journey that begins at A and logically ends at Z. The path must be straightforward and easy to follow for both the actor playing the character and the audience that is viewing it. This requires you to consider exactly where that particular scene fits into the whole script. Does it take place in the beginning, middle or end? As time progresses in the script, the drama and the stakes rise exponentially. The best way to understand this scene-by-scene build is to think about the way a relationship evolves. Let's look at a first date that ultimately ends up in marriage. Say the first scene is the first date. There isn't as much heat in this scene because there is no history between the two characters. On the first date, the stakes come from previous hurtful relationships, not from events that have taken place between the two people on the date. On this first date, the characters are looking at each other, asking, "How are you like my ex who hurt me?" Another scene takes place six months later. The characters are moving in together. Now they have a shared history. There's fear of commitment, fear of getting hurt and tension created from the battles that have happened over those six months. The stakes are higher because each party is capable of hurting the other, potentially causing much more emotional pain than they could have in their first month together. The next scene takes place after they move in together. The woman finds out that the man has been cheating on her, yet she wants to continue their relationship. Now the stakes have become even higher because they both have a tremendous number of obstacles to overcome in order to keep their relationship going. Somehow, this happens. The next scene is the night before the wedding. The stakes are even higher. Marriage is a big commitment. It's forever. All the "what ifs" become cruelly apparent: What if he cheats again? What if we have no money? What if I find somebody better? What if he changes? What if she becomes her mother?! As you can see, knowing exactly where a scene takes place helps you more accurately analyze it with the proper minutiae of that moment in time.

Carrie-Anne Moss learned how to see a scene in relationship to an entire script while she was doing scene work in class and put it to great use in her audition scene for *The Matrix*. She had to read a scene that takes place at the beginning of the script, the scene in the film where her character recruits Keanu Reeves' character Neo at a nightclub. First she looked at the entire script and determined her OVERALL OBJECTIVE, which was *"to love and be loved"* (of which she had to make the world safe first in order to have a secure environment in which *to love and be loved* and have a family). Then she looked at the scene. Although the scene's dialogue was pure recruitment-speak and science fiction techno babble, she made the SCENE OBJECTIVE a basic need: *"To get you to like me."* This enabled Carrie-Ann to establish the beginning of her journey, which would eventually lead her to accomplish her OVERALL OBJECTIVE. Since it took place in the beginning of the script, where the characters of Trinity and Neo have yet to share a history together, her SCENE OBJECTIVE manifested itself in behavior that was flirty, sexy, enticing, smart (as the beginnings of relationships always are). She made her SCENE OBJECTIVE a human need that required a response, which generated a human interaction. She was one of a handful of actresses who auditioned who didn't play the science fiction plot but established the beginning of a powerful relationship instead. She got the job over hundreds of other hopefuls.

Earn the Right to Get to the End of the Script

An actor also has to keep in mind how the script ends, and earn the right—scene by scene—to get there. If the script ends with you being together with the other character, every scene has to be, in some form, about going after the love. If the end of the script finds you split up, then you must earn the right to break up. In the movie *The Way We Were*, the characters played by Barbra Streisand and Robert Redford end up estranged. Thus, even in the earliest scenes in which they are together, there must be apparent insurmountable differences. In the film, we watch them as they try to address these differences, which need to be dealt with and overcome in order for them to have a healthy relationship. He's a W.A.S.P., refined, gorgeous, and everything comes easily for him. She's Jewish, loud, opinionated, coarse and has had to work very hard to accomplish anything. In their attempt to come together, they find themselves having to give up too much, which contradicts both of their innate needs to grow and evolve as human beings. In other words, they're bad for each other. They both find themselves overcompensating in word and deed and trying to do the impossible: mix oil and water. In one scene, Redford's character goes to Streisand's character's house to break up with her. However, Streisand's character is doing everything she can to keep him in her life. She offers to change the way she looks; to learn "Gentile" cooking; to live in Los Angeles, which she vocally abhors; and to be a part of the film industry, which she feels is selling out. Looking at this scene as a separate entity, without seeing it in the context of the full script, it looks as though Barbra's character's SCENE OBJECTIVE would be *"to get you to love me."* But because they don't end up together and she must earn the right to be separated at the end of the film, the SCENE OBJECTIVE instead becomes *"to make you stay with me at any cost."* This SCENE OBJECTIVE earns the right because it implies that, in time, she's going to grow dissatisfied and resentful of him (and he of her), because they have to change and give up so much of who they are as people to be together. By including the "at any cost" idea in the SCENE OBJECTIVE, it is inevitable that, eventually, the cost will be too high and the only way either of them will emotionally survive will be to separate.

Even if your character dies, you must earn the right to die.

You have to use the knowledge of your character's looming death when making choices for the SCENE OBJECTIVE. When I worked with Elisabeth Shue on *The Saint,* it was written that she was to die two-thirds of the way through the movie from a terminal heart condition. In each scene we made the choice that the SCENE OBJECTIVE had to include her living life to the fullest in order to complete her life before she dies. SCENE OBJECTIVES like *"to make you love me before I die"* gave each scene the additional urgency of time. As a result, her choices and performance were so powerful that nobody wanted her to die. When they showed the first version of *The Saint* to preview audiences, they said that the movie ended when she did. The studio responded by spending millions more to rewrite and reshoot the last third of the movie to keep Elisabeth's character alive. Salon.com film critic Charles Taylor said, *"The Saint* was rewritten and reshot after preview audiences objected to Shue's character being killed off. As much as I loathe prerelease testing, I can't blame those audiences. Without Shue's warm, pliable presence, there's nothing to hang onto in *The Saint."* *New York Times* critic Janet Maslin added, "Ms. Shue manages to be better than the movie." High praise that came from making high-stakes SCENE OBJECTIVES.

You're probably wondering, "Well, what if my character is not terminally ill and the death is unanticipated? How can my character know about the impending death?" While it's obvious that actors must use their five senses to re-create human behavior, they must also rely on their sixth sense, which is an honest and viable tool. Somehow we always know when danger or tragedy is about to befall. An actor has to develop and use their sixth sense alongside the other senses to create the fullest performance. If some huge tragedy befalls your character, have some sense that it's going to happen and make adjustments to your SCENE OBJECTIVE. In *The Godfather II,* Fredo, Michael Corleone's brother, is murdered at Michael's request. While alive, Fredo has to be constantly aware that Michael is capable of killing even his own brother. He thinks about this every time he screws up, which in Fredo's case happens a lot. A SCENE OBJECTIVE like *"to make you forgive me"* might just help to keep his brother from fitting him with cement shoes. An actor playing the part of Fredo has to maintain conscious contact with the idea that he might be murdered at any and every turn. This SCENE OBJECTIVE will cause intensified feelings of fear and panic, which would, in turn, create more dramatic results.

If you kill someone, you must earn that, too.

The play *Edmund* is material I frequently use in class because it is a good illustration of how to play a serial killer (the kind of character that seems to be in so many movies and television shows). In one scene, the character of Edmund has sex with a girl he's just picked up. After the sex, Edmund tries to provoke her, to push her buttons so that she'll become enraged, say horrible things, act out terribly and therefore deserve to be killed. The SCENE OBJECTIVE is *"to get you to deserve to die."* He tries bigotry, violence, sex, making her feel stupid. None of it works. Finally, he puts her down for never having worked as an actress even though she calls herself one. Under the guise of helping his victim face her reality, Edmund says, "Just say it with me, 'you're a waitress, you're a waitress.' . . ." But Edmund's true intention is to goad her to explode with rage. And lo and behold, it works—she becomes a human cherry bomb. She furiously and viciously acts out (just as he had intended), thereby justifying Edmund's SCENE OBJECTIVE. From his point of view, she now deserves to be killed, and he's just the guy to do it.

Don't Judge Your SCENE OBJECTIVE

Don't contaminate your choices with societal views, morality or personal issues. That judgment becomes a form of censorship. And censorship contradicts art. Sometimes what looks like a horrible situation can be viewed as something positive. If your character gets beaten up at the end of a scene, there's a really good chance that he or she wanted it that way. In *Raging Bull* there's a scene where Jake LaMotta questions his wife Vickie about where she's been all afternoon. She lies. They're obvious lies that intimate she's cheating on him. Vickie doesn't have to lie. She wasn't cheating and has witnesses to prove it. Yet she tells the kind of insinuating lies that she knows will make Jake's blood boil. Why? She wants him to hit her because after the beating, they'll have sex, violent sex— just the way they like it. It's the game they play, their special game that makes their relationship thrive . . . for them. And because the abuse will help her get what she wants, it becomes a positive act. Her SCENE OBJECTIVE is *"to make you beat me up so we can have great sex."*

In addition to not judging your SCENE OBJECTIVE, you must find the human reasons that compel the SCENE OBJECTIVE, even when your character seems to be engaging in heinous acts. This was how I worked with James Marsden and Kate Hudson on the movie *Gossip*. Derrick (Marsden) and Naomi (Hudson) are high school sweethearts. The night of the prom comes and there's an unspoken agreement that they will have sex on prom night. Indeed, sex is pursued by both of them until the moment of truth: the time for actual penetration. Naomi gets scared and changes her mind. She tells him she doesn't want to do it anymore. Derrick does it anyway. Naomi publicly announces that he's a rapist. The whole town shuns Derrick. Even his own parents want nothing to do with him. Derrick moves to New York and tries to get his destroyed life back together by going to NYU. In his second semester, Naomi coincidentally enrolls at NYU. Via gossip, Derrick sets Naomi up to believe that another student has raped her when she was passed out drunk at a party. In the script, James's character looks like the perpetrator, the rapist, and Kate's character the innocent victim. But life isn't always that simple—rarely is it a case of someone wearing the vicious black hat and the other the pure white hat. I suggested that instead of playing this story as a black-and-white scenario in which Kate's character would be good and James's would be bad, we play with the gray area. We consider the human element, that these two characters were human beings who were reacting to an untenable situation. Playing the roles this way would make the audience ask, "Was it rape? They were going together, in love, and the foreplay was consenting. Why did Naomi ruin the life of someone she supposedly loved without talking to Derrick first? And out of the thousands of schools in this country, why did she find herself at the one university that Derrick had enrolled in? It's likely that she was following him. Considering all of this, what is the real truth?"

In one scene, Derrick confronts Naomi about why she's ruined his life and why she's decided to attend the same school as him if he had really raped her. Naomi loses it, saying horrible things that she knows will hurt and probably enrage him. Kate and I talked about the possibility that her character was wrong. What if it wasn't rape? If it wasn't, then she must feel some guilt for ruining his life. And if it was rape, then her character, like most rape victims, probably feels at fault and somehow responsible. So Naomi's confrontation SCENE OBJECTIVE isn't *"to make you go away and not hurt me,"* but *"to make you wrong* (a violent rapist) *so I can be right* (not feel responsible for ruining your life)." The more she triggers his anger, making him commit violence, the more she can prove that he has a violent temperament and is capable of being a rapist. This enables her to assuage her guilt. Indeed, she pushes him so hard that he does attack her at the end of the scene, making her trip to NYU worthwhile. He, on the other hand, confronts her with lines like, "I loved you and I thought you loved me!" which would question the validity of an actual rape having taken place, at least in his mind. His SCENE OBJECTIVE then becomes the same as hers: *"to make you wrong so I can be right."*

Watching these two characters struggle with their guilt, their need to free themselves of it by making it the other person's fault, becomes very human. That's what we do. Nobody likes to take responsibility for being a bad person. Blame, making it the other person's fault, is a great way of alleviating responsibility. The human choice was made with all the facets and contradictions that go with it. At the end of *Gossip*, the audience is left to make the decision about who's right and who's wrong. Introducing this kind of human equation to SCENE OBJECTIVE makes a potentially black-and-white story gray, and thus artful, because it makes the viewer question, it disturbs convention and it affects the viewer's awareness. Like Kate and James, you must read between the lines to make the most compelling choice.

Even when you're playing someone who appears to be a shy, unassuming character whose behavior seems inactive, you must use SCENE OBJECTIVE.

The character of Laura in the classic play *The Glass Menagerie* illustrates this. At first glance, Laura looks like a shy, put-upon woman who doesn't want anything. But if you read deeper, you'll see that Laura has great desires and actually uses her shyness to get what she wants. Throughout the play she accomplishes a great deal by utilizing her timidity: she gets out of going to her typing class; she keeps her brother living at home and with her; she makes her mother continue to financially support her; and she gets a date with a guy she's always had a crush on. She gets all this done by using her incapacity, her fear and the victimization of her crippled leg to make people take care of her and love her. In the gentleman-caller scene she is victorious in her SCENE OBJECTIVE of *"to get you to like me."* He talks to her, he gives her advice, he opens up to her, he tells her he likes her, he dances with her, he kisses her. She gets what most women would consider to be a successful date. Laura's success is driven by her ability to use her supposed weaknesses to get what she wants.

There's always a goal, or a SCENE OBJECTIVE, when you are communicating and conversing with someone else. Always.

Your SCENE OBJECTIVE will never be *"to get you to leave me alone"* or *"to make the other person leave."* If a conversation is more than two sentences, then you must have a reason to want to engage in dialogue with that person. Think about how you behave in your own life. If you really want to leave, you leave. If you want to split up with someone and your mind is made up, the easiest way out is to send a letter, e-mail or fax, something that doesn't require being there emotionally or physically. That's how I extricated myself from my first husband (I've only had two marriages; the second one is a keeper): I left a letter on his bureau while he was away having one of his multitudinous affairs. If you bother to have a long, involved conversation, then it's clear that there's something more that needs to be resolved. Perhaps you don't want to split up after all (S.O.: *"to make you want me back"*), perhaps you want closure or piece of mind (S.O.: *"to make you take the blame"* or *"to get you to give me my power back"*), or perhaps you want that person to suffer—a payback, of sorts (S.O.: *" to make you feel my pain"*), so that person can feel as bad as you feel. In any of these cases, there's a reason to stay in the room or need the other person to stay.

Always Make Selfish Choices

We always do more to get something when it involves something for ourselves rather than for someone else. To help another selflessly can make you feel good, but it doesn't have heat to it because there's nothing personally at risk for you. You can be helping a friend with a problem, with the SCENE OBJECTIVE of *"to make you feel better."* But what do *you* get out of it? However, the SCENE OBJECTIVE *"to get you to feel better so you'll like me"* gives you something in return for all your hard work. It also gives you the possibility of failure. If you can't make the other person feel better, then there's a good chance that person won't like you. The apprehension that your attempt at gaining your SCENE OBJECTIVE may or may not succeed keeps you anticipating the worst, and therefore you keep trying harder and harder. This takes the ordinary and turns it into something extraordinary. Joan of Arc is a historical figure who has been realized again and again in art, theater and film. The essence of this woman's story is that she hears voices from God and believes that she's been put on this earth to connect God to the masses. Imagine watching two hours of a performance that reveals Joan of Arc as a woman who is fully confident in her voices and her belief that she's there to help people by bringing them religion. It makes Joan of Arc seem patronizing and superior. That's because, in this light, there's no vulnerability, no human side to seeing her story. Conversely, imagine that same woman who, through painful life experiences, has become so desperate to make people love her that she *needs* to believe in those voices, *needs* people to follow and worship her—in fact, her *needs* are so dire that she's even willing to die the horrible death of burning at the stake to realize her SCENE OBJECTIVE of *"to make you* (everyone she comes across) *love me."* This brings in the possibility that she might personally question her voices, but won't allow herself to disbelieve, because not being connected to God would eliminate any reason for people to love her. And that simply cannot happen. Now that's dramatic!

SCENE OBJECTIVE works for commercials, sketch comedy and cartoon voices.

If you are acting using a SCENE OBJECTIVE, you are creating relationship. It doesn't matter what the medium is—from high drama to sketch comedy, a commercial or even a cartoon. SCENE OBJECTIVE will make the sketch funnier, the commercial more saleable and the cartoon voice more real, because it brings in the human equation, thereby making it universally appealing.

When Rob Schneider was on *Saturday Night Live* he had a very popular recurring character: Rich the Copy Boy. Basically, Rich would sit by the copy machine waiting for a coworker to enter his enclave, and then chat away. If, for example, the coworker was named Sandy, Rich would welcome her with, "Sandy! The Sandster . . . making copies . . . Sandarama . . . Sandana . . . needing a Xerox . . ." and on and on until Sandy would get annoyed and walk away. When I discussed this character with Rob, we didn't address his behavior as a bigger-than-life comedic character, but as a frightened and very lonely man. We decided that the character of Rich is a guy who goes home alone, lives alone and dines nightly on home delivery—not for the food but for the company. One can imagine Rich answering the door and exclaiming, "Pizza Man, delivering a pizza! The Pizza Manster! The Pizza Pie-arama! . . ." until the pizza man flees, eardrums aflame from Rich's constant babble. Now this is a lonely guy. I told Rob that Rich was acting out because of his terrifying loneliness. Rich's only human contact was when someone would come to him to make a copy, so he had to make the most of each short visit. The humor of these sketches emanated from his desperation and his willingness to do *anything* (no matter how silly or strange) to get his SCENE OBJECTIVE of *"to get you to be my friend."*

There is a SCENE OBJECTIVE in every scene—
NO EXCEPTIONS!

Sometimes a director will give you direction such as, "Your character is just thinking out loud, he doesn't need anything from the other character," or "Your character is a force unto himself, he doesn't need anything from anyone." It's up to you as the actor to privately translate notes such as these into a SCENE OBJECTIVE. Otherwise your performance will have no forward motion, no journey, making it flat and uneventful.

Even when the director is a major force, don't be intimidated. You don't have to challenge the director, just privately use your SCENE OBJECTIVE—it will benefit your performance, and by doing so, make the director look good, too. In the movie *Space Cowboys*, Clint Eastwood was the star *and* the director. I worked with Loren Dean, who played the young astronaut in the film, and his OVERALL OBJECTIVE was to prove he was better equipped for the space mission than the older astronauts (Eastwood being one of them). In one scene, Dean was to operate the flight simulator alongside Eastwood. With the SCENE OBJECTIVE of *"to make you the loser and me the winner!"* in mind, I told Dean to play with the prop-simulator until he felt like an expert before they began filming the shot, so that he could actually *be* better than Eastwood. As he was becoming familiar with the knobs, dials and switches of the simulator, Eastwood came up to him and told him he didn't need to prepare. That he should just go for it. Eastwood added, "You don't have to learn the details to make it look real." In the meantime, unbeknownst to Loren, Eastwood had the technical expert on the set teach him how to expertly and accurately manipulate the simulator. Of course, once the scene was shot, Eastwood looked like he was the better astronaut as he went after his own personal SCENE OBJECTIVE of *"to make you the loser and me the winner!"* and successfully won the scene, both on and off-camera. No wonder Clint Eastwood has longevity both as an actor and as a director. He understands the importance of winning in his work.

Working with SCENE OBJECTIVE in Three-or-More-Person Scenes

If a scene is comprised of more than two people, you can't want something from everyone, never mind try to get a response from everyone.

It would be too confusing to play and for the audience to understand. Generally, there's one hot person in a scene, someone you do everything for. All the other characters then serve to be a witting or unwitting ally in your attempt to accomplish your SCENE OBJECTIVE. This is true in life as well—in a group, there's always that hot person that you want something from (SCENE OBJECTIVE), and everyone else is there to wittingly or unwittingly help you get what you want from that hot person.

Life examples:

- **Unwitting ally:** When you are at a party, there's always that cute guy or gal, or that important producer or director, in the crowd. Now, you may never actually talk to this hot person, but everything you do is for that person, in order to get the hot person to notice you and like you (SCENE OBJECTIVE). The unwitting ally is that party guest who you are conversing with as you are being extra sexy, witty, intelligent and generally impressive—not for the benefit of the person you're actually talking to, but for your hot person to become aware of you from across the room.

- **Unwitting ally:** Think about the times you've been on a double date (four-person scene). Who's the hot person? Your friend's date, of course. The SCENE OBJECTIVE is *"to get you to want me."* It won't work to use your own date as the hot person, because you've already proven you can get that person, so your date wouldn't be hot enough. Getting your friend's date to want you is complex. First, you can prove to yourself and to your friend that not only can you get your own date to want you, but are attractive to your friend's date, as well. Second, there's a danger element in going after your friend's date. You can lose your friendship and your date with your flirtation. It's not that you ever have to take it any further than flirtation. It just raises the stakes, makes the evening more interesting for you (particularly if your date is a bore) and boosts your ego. Your date and your friend become your unwitting allies in accomplishing your goal. Think about past double dates that you've been on. You'll see how this is generally true.

- **Witting ally:** Say the scene consists of you playing a con in the midst of a game of three-card monte. The hot person would be the "mark," a.k.a. the person you're trying to fool. Your SCENE OBJECTIVE would be *"to get you* (the mark) *to trust me,"* so they'll spend lots of money on the game. The "shill" is your witting ally, who will help gain the mark's trust by appearing to be a stranger who's easily winning money in your game.

In the movie *The Day After Tomorrow,* there was a difficult four-person scene that Jake Gyllenhaal and I had to tackle. The scene takes place in New York's Museum of Natural History. In the scene, Jake's character, Sam, is talking to his friend and ally at one exhibit, but directly across the hall is the girl he's interested in, Laura, otherwise known as his hot person. Laura, on the other hand, is engaged in a flirtatious conversation with his nemesis and competition—a smart, good-looking preppy guy. Laura seems to be enjoying the preppy guy's advances a little too much, and Sam doesn't like it one bit. Although Sam never talks directly to Laura in the scene, his SCENE OBJECTIVE is *"to make you* (Laura) *pick me over the other guy."* We accomplished this by making his intellectual observations about the stuffed bear exhibit thinly veiled jokes at the expense of the preppy guy. Jake made sure his character was loud enough so that the girl could hear it. Sam's friend was the witting ally, and although Sam's friend didn't know that Sam was mocking "preppy boy," he was (unsuspectingly) complicit in helping Sam decimate his rival by being a willing participant in the mocking dialogue. The preppy guy was an unwitting ally because he was clearly affected by Sam's jabs—they made Sam appear as the more powerful guy to Laura, and he wouldn't wittingly do that on purpose. All of these machinations work—at the end of the movie, Sam gets the girl and ultimately befriends the preppy guy, turning an unwitting ally into a witting one.

I can't stress enough . . .

OBJECTIVES are the most important tools!

All the following tools that you're about to read and learn are there solely to make your OBJECTIVES more real and more urgent. You must figure out your OVERALL OBJECTIVE and then the SCENE OBJECTIVE before filling in any of your other choices. In this way, you are driving a scene by a goal, making it active and interactive. Basically, you're creating communication.

> ***Do NOT** do your inner work first and then*
> *try to layer **OBJECTIVES** on top of it—*
> *cart before the horse, as they say.*
> *If you do this, the **SCENE OBJECTIVE***
> *ceases to drive the scene.*

Once you've figured out the best, most effective SCENE OBJECTIVE, the rest of the choices you make regarding the other acting tools will be easy—they'll fall into place in a logical manner.

CHAPTER 3

Tool #3:
OBSTACLES

> OBSTACLES are the physical, emotional and mental hurdles that make it difficult for your character to achieve his or her OBJECTIVES.

OBSTACLES give power and intensity to your OBJECTIVES by making your goal harder to accomplish. If your OBJECTIVES have a risk to them, then it brings physical and emotional jeopardy and danger to the goal. Climbing Mount Everest is a much more exciting story to play (and to watch) than walking over a molehill. Mount Everest has the danger of avalanches, thin air, and a misplaced foot that could bring death to the player. The molehill has virtually no risk. While they are both goals, one has much bigger and more compelling OBSTACLES.

Winning is only satisfying when there is a possibility of failure. The possibility of failure emanates from OBSTACLES.

First you must figure out the OBSTACLES that make sense to the character in the script and your OVERALL and SCENE OBJECTIVES. Then you can go back through the scene and personalize them, making the OBSTACLES make sense to *your* life. For example, if you're working with a seduction scene, the character's OBSTACLES might be rejection, specific sexual inadequacies, self-worth issues, body insecurities or a history of past hurts from other mates or lovers. Once you've identified your character's OBSTACLES, then you must find personal OBSTACLES that correlate to your personal and unique history, which might include rejection, sexual fears, body image. (The part of your body that you hate the most—breasts, chest, legs, arms, whatever. Pick one. The worst one.) Are you shy, overbearing or submissive? How does it get in your way?

Do you have a small penis, a chronic bladder infection or smelly feet? OBSTACLES are both internal and external. They are *anything* and *everything* that get in the way of your OBJECTIVES.

Attempting to overcome OBSTACLES, large and small, to finally achieve your OVERALL and SCENE OBJECTIVES is what generates heat and the stakes in your acting and the script.

Using OBSTACLES Creates the Challenge

The more difficult and risky it is for you to realize your OVERALL and SCENE OBJECTIVES, the greater the journey for you as an actor as well as for your audience. The more OBSTACLES you put in a scene, the harder you work to get your SCENE OBJECTIVE. A scene begins. Your character begins to confront and try to overcome the innate OBSTA-CLES in their SCENE OBJECTIVE's path. The scene progresses. Your character continues to attempt to overcome the many OBSTACLES that come up along the way. The more your character tries to overcome the OBSTACLES as the scene progresses, and the more they can't, the harder they're going to try. This effort creates the "arc" of a scene. Work-ing with OBSTACLES keeps the intensity growing, driving the need and meaning of the scene, which eventually brings it to the crescendo that all scenes must have. It's also true that the more difficult it is to achieve a goal, the more satisfying it is to accomplish it and to watch it.

> *OBSTACLES generate the difficulty that make*
> *for a more dramatic result.*

Think of the snake scene in *Indiana Jones: Raiders of the Lost Ark*. The character of Indiana Jones was deathly afraid of snakes, yet he had to cross mounds of large, scaly, writhing serpents to escape. Without the audience's knowledge that Jones had a horrifying phobia of snakes (phys-ical and emotional OBSTACLE), his crossing of them would be unevent-ful. Yet bringing in the fear of these gruesome and often misunderstood creatures made the scene terrifying and Indiana Jones heroic.

It would be fruitless (and endless) to list every possible OBSTACLE you may encounter in script analysis. Anything and everything that is a hurdle or creates conflict is an OBSTACLE. Nonetheless, most OBSTA-CLES fit into one of three categories: physical, mental and emotional.

Physical OBSTACLES

- **Physical handicaps:** Include broken limbs, limps (*Midnight Cowboy*), paralysis (*Born on the Fourth of July*), palsy (*My Left Foot*), tics (*The Tic Code*), blindness (*The Miracle Worker*) or visual impairment, deafness (*Children of a Lesser God*), impotence (*Sex, Lies, and Videotape*).
- **Race and religion:** Racism (*Amistad*), religious issues (*Agnes of God*), religious rivalry (*Mary, Queen of Scots*).
- **Physical size extremes:** Short (any Woody Allen movie), too tall, fat (*Shallow Hal*), skinny, penis too large (*Boogie Nights*) or too small, breasts too large (anything with Pamela Anderson in it) or too small, nose too large (*Cyrano de Bergerac*).
- **Appearance:** A burn victim (*The Phantom of the Opera*), ugly (*Beauty and the Beast*) or too beautiful and therefore unapproachable, too old (*All About Eve*), too young (*Paper Moon*), you're dressed in drag and that's not your thing (*Some Like It Hot*), age differences (*The Graduate* and any Woody Allen movie).
- **Financial:** Too rich (*Ruthless People*), too poor (*Titanic*).
- **Mind altered:** Are you stoned, drunk or high? Do you have an addiction that needs to be overcome, such as heroin (*Drugstore Cowboy*), cocaine (*Hurlyburly*) or alcohol (*Days of Wine and Roses*)?
- **Medical:** Dying (*Terms of Endearment*) or someone you love dying (*Love Story*). Is suicide your only option (*Death of a Salesman*)? Do you have to overcome the death of a loved one (*Lethal Weapon*)? Abortion (*Loose Ends*), pregnancy (*The Turning Point*)?
- **Professional:** Dangerous professions such as being a cop (*Die Hard*), prostitute (*Klute*), secret agent (James Bond movies), military (*Platoon*), drug dealer (*Scarface*), gangster (*The Sopranos*), bank robber (*Bonnie and Clyde*). Or high-stress occupations such as high finance (*Wall Street*), politics (*Angels in America*), big business (*The Apartment*), actor (*Bullets Over Broadway*), lawyer (*To Kill a Mockingbird*), sports player (*Bull Durham*), student (*Ferris Bueller's Day Off*), salesman (*Glengarry Glen Ross*), doctor (*The Doctor*), teacher (*Oleana*), journalist (*All the President's Men*), psychiatrist (*Antwone Fisher*).

- **Social status:** Being an immigrant (*Enemies, A Love Story*), class differences (*Pygmalion*), homosexuality (*Far from Heaven*), sexual deviancy (*9 1/2 Weeks*), victim of gossip (*The Women*).
- **Place:** Haunted house (*The Shining*), a dark imposing alley, concentration camp (*Schindler's List*), a place that contains a killer (*Halloween,* et al), a place riddled with physical hurdles (*Home Alone*), a place that reminds you of a traumatic event (*Sophie's Choice*), an unfamiliar and faraway locale (*The African Queen*).
- **Event:** War (*Apocalypse Now*), giving birth (*Same Time, Next Year*), graduation (*Dead Poets Society*), high school reunion (*Romy and Michele's High School Reunion*), deadline for owing money to a loan shark or drug dealer (*A Hatful of Rain*), gang war (*Romeo and Juliet*), a wake (*About Schmidt*), kidnapping (*Ransom*), unintentional homicide (*Thelma and Louise*), rape (*The Accused*), vengeance (*Cape Fear*), birthday (*Cat on a Hot Tin Roof*), a contest (*The Competition*), unwanted pregnancy (*The Pope of Greenwich Village*), getting married (*Honeymoon in Vegas*), divorce (*Kramer vs. Kramer*), an affair (*Unfaithful*), the Depression (*Waiting for Lefty*), dying on death row (*Dead Man Walking*), getting caught for a crime (*Fargo*).

Mental OBSTACLES

- **Brain capacity:** Too smart, too analytical (*Geniuses*), too stupid (*Dumb and Dumber*), retarded (*What's Eating Gilbert Grape*), overthinking everything (*The Real Thing*), simpleminded (*Forrest Gump*).
- **Political beliefs and principles:** Fighting the system (*Erin Brockovich*), being true to your ideals, pushing the envelope (*Norma Rae*), risking your job and stability in standing by your character's beliefs (*The Insider*), risking your life in standing by your beliefs (*Silkwood*).
- **Mental illness:** Phobias (*Arachnophobia*), split personality (*Sybil*), schizophrenia (*A Beautiful Mind*), depression (*Girl, Interrupted*), sane but locked up (*One Flew Over the Cuckoo's Nest*).
- **Secrets and lies:** Having a secret (*No Way Out*), keeping the lies straight (*A Streetcar Named Desire*).

- **Formal education or lack thereof:** Educational disparity—one character's educated, the other is not (*After the Fall*).

Emotional OBSTACLES

- **Relationship issues:** Intimacy issues (*About Last Night*), history of love gone wrong (*The Age of Innocence*), history of family problems (*Hamlet*), history of problems with a friend (*Beaches*), history of problems in the marriage (*Who's Afraid of Virginia Woolf?*), pent-up rage (*The War of the Roses*), sibling rivalry (*True West*), history of problems with the ex-mate (*Blithe Spirit*), obsession (*Fatal Attraction*), racial issues where there is love involved (*A Patch of Blue*), jealousy (*The Misanthrope*), history of parental problems (*Mourning Becomes Electra*), incongruent personalities (*The Odd Couple*), history of cheating or being cheated on (*Shampoo*), unrequited love (*Summer and Smoke*), ruthless rivalry with someone of the same gender (*Heathers*).
- **Personal problems:** Greed and extreme ambition (*Macbeth*), shyness (*The Glass Menagerie*), self-loathing (*Frankie and Johnny*), overbearing and controlling (*Ivan the Terrible*), feeling like a loser (*The Hustler*), abandonment issues (*An Unmarried Woman*), history of promiscuity (*Carnal Knowledge*), guilt (*Othello*), overwhelming anger (*Last Tango in Paris*), being a virgin at an older age (*Savage in Limbo*), being antisocial (*Kalifornia*), loneliness (*Marty*), history of self-sabotaging behavior (*American Pie*), paranoia (*The Collector*), fear of being judged.
- **Deviancy:** Homicidal tendencies (*American Psycho*); incest (*Fool for Love*); violent tendencies (*Raging Bull*); incestuous obsessions (*Oedipus Rex*); issues stemming from past abuse, rape or molestation (*Danny and the Deep Blue Sea*); other people's perceptions of a sexually deviant predilection (*Secretary*).

Anything that creates a hurdle, conflict, barrier or a stumbling block to accomplishing your OVERALL and SCENE OBJECTIVE is fodder for being an OBSTACLE.

The Graduate is riddled with OBSTACLES in all the categories for both Mrs. Robinson and Benjamin. My longtime student, Linda Gray, did the theatrical version in London's West End (England's Broadway) and received great reviews thanks to her thorough investigation of the

OBSTACLES that her character Mrs. Robinson had to overcome. She made Mrs. Robinson a living, breathing, multifaceted, vulnerable and fascinating human being.

Mrs. Robinson's OBSTACLES

- Benjamin might reject her. (The possibility of failure, the possibility that you might not get what you want, will always be an OBSTACLE in every script you analyze.)
- She's much older than Benjamin, which means that she's going to feel uncomfortable about her body. She'll compare herself to someone his age who would have an unlined, firm, lean body with perky breasts, versus her wrinkles, sagging skin and cellulite.
- Her husband hasn't touched her in a long time, making her needy for some male attention. This combined with her age issues makes for a very real fear of becoming that genderless age when women go from beautiful to "handsome."
- Benjamin is her neighbor and best friend's son. If this doesn't work out perfectly, Benjamin could tell others. As a result, she would lose her husband and social standing and generally become ridiculed.
- Benjamin falls in love with her daughter, Elaine. This heightens the risk of Elaine finding out about the affair. It would destroy Mrs. Robinson's relationship with her daughter.
- She may be discovered by friends, neighbors or a nosy acquaintance at the hotel where the sexual rendezvous takes place.
- She becomes attached to him. Maybe even falls in love with him, making it extremely difficult to give him up or to endure his love for her daughter.
- Her love for Benjamin also makes her jealous of his love for her daughter. It is not uncommon for jealousy to be an integral part of a mother/daughter relationship.

Mrs. Robinson's attempt to overcome all these OBSTACLES substantiates her OVERALL and SCENE OBJECTIVES.

Benjamin's OBSTACLES
(with Regard to Mrs. Robinson)

- Possible rejection.
- He's much younger than Mrs. Robinson. He is intimidated by her sexual experience and knowledge and his comparative lack of it. Will he ejaculate too quickly? Will he be able to get an erection? Will he touch her in a way that doesn't seem immature and stupid?
- His lack of knowledge. What will they talk about? Will he seem idiotic and naive?
- She's his mother's best friend, which makes having sex with Mrs. Robinson almost incestuous.
- She's watched him grow up. She knows way too much about him. She knows every embarrassing moment and event that happened in his life—if he was a bed wetter or was considered a nerd by his peers or spent his childhood eating boogers, she'd know.
- His fear of their affair being discovered by Mrs. Robinson's husband, Benjamin's parents and Mrs. Robinson's daughter, Elaine.
- When he falls in love with her daughter, Mrs. Robinson wages an all-out war against him.

As you can see, Benjamin's OBSTACLES coincide with Mrs. Robinson's, but come from a different point of view. When you are breaking down a script and looking for OBSTACLES, find as many of them as you can—physical, emotional and mental—because the more OBSTACLES a character has to overcome, the more intricate the performance.

The OBSTACLES you infuse in your work should always be the hardest, most demanding, problematic and challenging.

The more difficult it is to win, the more satisfaction you feel when you have achieved the goal. The OBSTACLES give you the difficulty factor. A challenging OBSTACLE makes you fight more passionately. You'll do more if you have a mountain of OBSTACLES to overcome, making your journey to reach your OVERALL OBJECTIVE, through your arc of SCENE OBJECTIVES, that much more moving.

OBSTACLES produce desperation, and desperation creates comedy.

OBSTACLES are there to heighten and intensify the drama, and the more OBSTACLES you have to overcome in realizing your SCENE OBJECTIVE, the more desperate you'll be in going after that SCENE OBJECTIVE. In the name of wanting something really badly, we often find ourselves behaving in a silly, crazy and outlandish manner. Think about that date you had when you really, really liked a person and wanted to impress them. Of course, the slicker and cooler you tried to be, the more awkward and stupid you became: tripping, bumping into walls, using the wrong doors, blurting out inane comments, spilling on yourself and/or the other person, breaking something and on and on.

Even something as seemingly trivial as passing gas can, in the wrong circumstances, be devastating—a potent OBSTACLE, if you will. Michael Richards' character of Kramer on *Seinfeld* had all kinds of comic behavior. But his motivation wasn't to be funny. His behavior came from his urgent and desperate desire to accomplish his character's frequently used SCENE OBJECTIVE of *"to make you* (Jerry) *like me."* While they were taping one episode, Richards passed gas while in character as Kramer. Jerry was across the room when it happened, so Richards felt it was safe to stop clenching and let 'er rip. Unfortunately, Jerry decided to come over to Kramer's side of the room at the exact time of the gaseous detonation. Knowing that his "silent but deadly" gas bomb would turn Jerry off, Richards, staying in character as Kramer, frantically and frenetically began to fan the air behind his rear end. Each time Jerry tried to get near Kramer, Kramer scooted away and fanned his behind. Humorous behavior was created by Kramer's desperate need to overcome a reeking OBSTACLE in order to attain his SCENE OBJECTIVE.

When I was working with the rapper/actor Redman on *How High,* he had to play a Harvard student who was from the ghetto and constantly stoned. For the purposes of the movie's storyline, Redman's character wasn't just smoking marijuana, he was also smoking the ashes of a dead body. The ashes made him smarter, which he needed to take tests and pass his courses. His character couldn't emotionally or mentally survive the social and academic rigors of an educational institution like Harvard without smoking. He wasn't just a pothead for fun. He needed to imbibe to subsist. Need equals addiction, and this need made it a viable OBSTACLE. So when his character was confronted with doing the most unghetto-like activity of rowing for the crew team with a bunch of preppy unhip white boys, he felt he *had* to smoke some weed. But how does one row and get stoned at the same time? In our struggle to find a way to overcome these OBSTACLES we found the solution. He would stroke (the oars) and then toke (the blunt). This phrase became a chant that he said out loud ("Stroke, toke, stroke, toke, stroke, toke . . .") as he attempted to do exactly that. In our effort to overcome his character's OBSTACLES, a comic bit was formed.

Just think about Jim Carrey's high comedy role as Lloyd in *Dumb and Dumber.* Everything was an OBSTACLE, because everything was hard for Lloyd to do, because he had to overcome the OBSTACLE of being dumb(er).

OBSTACLES help you better understand the motivations of your character.

When I was working with Joy Bryant on the movie *Three Way,* her character, Rita, was in love with a man who was older, a screw-up, secretive to the point of being untrustworthy, possibly responsible for killing two people, had no money, lived in a hovel, was still in love with his ex-wife, and wanted to involve her in the very illegal, lots-of-jail-time-if-you-get-caught activity of kidnapping. He sounds like every woman's dreamboat, right? Joy and I had to figure out why anyone, particularly someone as attractive as Joy, would want to be with a guy like this. The script provided no rationale. So it was up to us to dig deeper than the words themselves.

In the script there was no mention of Rita's friends or relatives. We presumed that, for all intents and purposes, her family was dead. Joy's character was literally alone in the world. "Loneliness" is an OBSTACLE that can drive us to be in a relationship that doesn't always make sense. And because most people duplicate a parent in their love relationships, we made the leap that Rita picked this man because he possessed the attributes of her character's father, a man who, we've already surmised, is either dead or MIA. Because Rita doesn't have the original, primal person to resolve her issues with, she finds someone who's just like him. This would enable Rita to resolve her childhood traumas with her father via a father surrogate. When we looked at some of the OBSTACLES that we surmised existed in Rita's relationship with this man, Joy and I were able to make sense of and fill out the character of Rita with tangible and significant reasons for what would appear to the outside world as a bad choice in a mate. This process of understanding the OBSTACLES gave Joy the ability to play the role in a believable way. Because her character needed to find some sort of resolution with her father issues, the OBSTACLES helped the OVERALL OBJECTIVE of *"to get you to love me and stay with me"* make sense, and they actually changed what would seem to be a negative goal of achieving a relationship with the wrong guy and justified his becoming Mr. Right.

All of Your Character's OBSTACLES Are Not Necessarily Written in the Script

When determining your character's OBSTACLES, some will be obvious— they'll be written in black and white on the pages of the script. Others you'll find by conjecture and supposition based on the facts of the script. But even when it seems that your character has no OBSTACLES, it's up to you find them. Without OBSTACLES and conflict, your character's journey to accomplish the OVERALL OBJECTIVE and SCENE OBJECTIVE will be too easy and therefore unsatisfying. It's stimulating to watch a storm and very dull to watch the calm.

When I was working with Peggy Lipton on her role for David Lynch's *Twin Peaks*, her character was written as the rock in the storm. All the other characters were outrageous and quirky to the max, yet her character was normal. Now a rock might be pretty, but after a while—a short while—watching that rock is going to get pretty tedious. Taking the facts of the script and the character, we found reasonable OBSTACLES, something for Peggy's character to overcome to create a viable dramatic struggle.

- **Fact:** Her character, Norma Jennings, was a waitress.
  Assumed OBSTACLE: Financial problems. Most waitresses don't earn a lot of money. Moreover, most people don't dream of becoming a waitress. We assumed that she was disappointed and dissatisfied with her lot in life.
- **Fact:** Norma Jennings was single.
  Assumed OBSTACLE: She's lonely.
- **Fact:** She lived in a small town.
  Assumed OBSTACLE: Her options for change socially, workwise and love-wise were slim.

- **Fact:** There was a murderer lurking about.
  Assumed OBSTACLE: Fear that she might be the next one to die.
- **Fact:** In this town of Twin Peaks strange happenings *and* strange people abounded.
  Assumed OBSTACLE: As the normal person, *she's* the fish out of water. She just doesn't fit in.

These OBSTACLES spawned nuances she otherwise wouldn't have had, and also made her character more relatable to the audience.

> *Once you've identified the most challenging OBSTACLES,*
> *never give up on your SCENE OBJECTIVE, even if*
> *the OBSTACLES seem impossible to overcome.*

Don't ever admit defeat. There's always a possibility that you will be able to overcome an OBSTACLE. Even if the chances are small, know that there's always hope. The person who gives up too easily is often perceived by the audience as a loser. You always want to act from a winning, anything's-possible point of view. The scene ends when your fight to overcome OBSTACLES to accomplish your SCENE OBJEC-TIVE ceases. This means if the scene isn't over, and your fight to over-come conflict stops, the forward motion is arrested and the audience will cease to care anymore. So always keep in mind that *it's not over 'til it's over.* Continue the struggle to overcome your OBSTACLES even a few beats after you exit, the director says "Cut" or the curtain comes down.

OBSTACLES: The Practical Application

It may sound obvious, but the first step when identifying OBSTACLES for a scene is to read the scene with a pencil in hand and note them as you go along. Then you can go back through and add another layer, and another. OBSTACLES should be written in pencil (this gives you a chance to erase if you change your mind) directly onto the script.

Do not solely consider your scenes or your lines when reading for OBSTACLES, because many of your OBSTACLES will be a result of the actions and words of other characters.

In this chapter, we've explored how to identify your character's OB-STACLES, which you must find in the script or presume would make sense to your character. The next step is to make it personal to you and your life. Personalization of your OBSTACLES can only be specifically determined by the choice you make for your SUBSTITUTION (the next chapter—tool #4). And your choice of SUBSTITUTION will change the choices you make to personalize the OBSTACLES.

The initial order for script analysis goes as follows:

1. Find your OVERALL OBJECTIVE.
2. Find your SCENE OBJECTIVE.
3. Find the OBSTACLES that make sense to the script and the character on the page.

Next you have to look at how this relates to *your* life, which makes it personal. This brings us to tool #4, SUBSTITUTION.

CHAPTER 4

Tool #4:

SUBSTITUTION

Endowing the other actor in the scene with characteristics of a person from your real life who best represents the need expressed in your SCENE OBJECTIVE.

We will explore how to apply and identify the best SUBSTITUTION choice. Once you have found your SUBSTITUTION, I will show you how to take your character's OBSTACLES and, considering your SUBSTITUTION choice, make them personal and relevant to your life. In other words, first you will find the most compelling and appropriate SUBSTITUTION. Then you will learn how to personalize those OBSTACLES you've already identified in the script (tool #3) to make sense to your SUBSTITUTION choice.

Applying and Identifying SUBSTITUTION

SUBSTITUTION gives you an immediate history with another character or problem and all the layered emotional responses that come with it. Using SUBSTITUTION enables you to attach emotions—emotions that have the depth and complexity that usually take years to develop—to another actor. You may have only known an actor you are working with for a few days, yet your character has had an intricate, lengthy relationship with the other actor's character in the script. With SUBSTITUTION you can endow the actor playing, for instance, your mother, with the involved history you have with your real mother—her love; the certainty or uncertainty of her love for you; and the memories, both joyful and painful. Working with your real mother as the SUBSTITUTION will make your interplay with the other actor as nuanced and complex as your relationship with your real mother—in every line, glance and gesture. In other words, SUBSTITUTION creates a truly human relationship, not an acted out interpretation that is merely motivated by a cerebral source.

We have all noticed that we act differently around different people. Likewise, a performance can change radically depending upon whom you are thinking about and responding to (your SUBSTITUTION). Think about it. You are different around your child, your mother, your lover, a crush, your husband or wife, your nemesis, your friend and your boss. We have a multitude of emotional responses to each person we come in contact with. Most actors, left to their imaginations, will take something like a love scene and just attempt to produce the feelings of love. This results in a one-note performance. Nobody *just* loves someone. Real-world love has moments of anger, pain, competition, jealousy, hate and sadness attached to it. Few of the complexities and minutiae of a real loving relationship—the layers of history and emotions—can emerge by acting a loving relationship from our imaginations. SUBSTITUTION is effective because we have such unique responses to each individual we come into contact with. Different aspects of our personalities are drawn out when we encounter different people. Each SUBSTITUTION choice will provide different reactions and stimuli.

> ***It's important to use real people in your acting work because you don't know how you'll really behave in front of a person when there's a lot at risk. You think you do, but you don't.***

After the first reading of a script, it's common for an actor to have a picture of precisely how a scene should look and operate. Then, the actor tries to create this picture as precisely as he sees it in his imagination. However, life rarely goes as we see it. Think about the disgruntled wife or husband who's been cheated on or lied to and wants their mate to change their ways. They imagine how they are going to confront their dishonest mate. They think to themselves, "I'm going to march right up and this time, I'm going to be strong. And I'm going to say, 'I'm great, I'm special, without me in your life you'd be screwed. So stop lying to me or I'm leaving. Really! This time I'm really outta here!'" In the disgruntled wife or husband's fantasy, the mate is hugely intimidated by this hard-line approach, realizes the depth of their wrongdoing, gets on his or her hands and knees, and with tears in their eyes, begs for forgiveness. Now, this is the picture in their mind of exactly how it's all going to occur in their "I refuse to be a victim to you anymore" scene. But as you know, it never goes this way. Ever. The disgruntled husband or wife may begin the confrontation with this picture in their mind, but when faced with the *actual person* who holds their future in their hands, the *actual person* who has the power to exile the husband or wife to a potential life of loneliness, all that strength goes out the window. The disgruntled husband or wife's imagination may have pumped them up, but ultimately, their fear wins. They'll often accept their mate's hateful behavior because it's still better than being alone. An actor's fantasy of what a scene should look like functions the same way. Rather than acting from these pictures, which are rarely accurate, SUBSTITUTION personalizes your work so that your actions and reactions are from your heart and body. In other words, SUBSTITUTION makes your behavior real.

SUBSTITUTION grounds an actor's work, providing them with real people to react and interact with. This leads to appropriate, real and original behavior, which even to you, the actor, will often be a surprise. Why? We think we know how we will act around specific people, but how we really behave around them is always quite different than what we imagine. We're weak when we think we'll be strong, we're seductive when we think we'll be standoffish, we're playful when we think we'll be boring. Using a SUBSTITUTION from your real life creates an arena for you to be whoever it is that you are around that person—with all the layers that naturally emerge.

Before we explore how to find and make your SUBSTITUTION choices, you need to understand how SUBSTITUTION works on a practical and physical level.

SUBSTITUTION: The Practical Application

In creating this SUBSTITUTION you would begin by finding one thing about the other actor's face that reminds you of the person you're using as the SUBSTITUTION. It can be anything—the eyes, eyebrows, skin color, nose, lips, cheekbones, forehead, etc. It's very important to use one specific feature, because our minds have a hard time latching on to vague ideas. Once you decide what it is, then concentrate on that one feature until the feeling of the person comes to you in your gut. No, you don't want to look cross-eyed until you see your SUBSTITUTION. You should simply wait to feel that person's essence in front of you. As you do this, remember key events (both traumatic and joyful) with the person you are using as your SUBSTITUTION while looking at that one facial feature. This entire exercise should only take five to ten seconds.

Working this way may seem awkward at first, but after trying it a few times, you'll find that this process will become as easy and natural as breathing.

Identifying Who to Use as a SUBSTITUTION

You must find the person (SUBSTITUTION) who provides the appropriate emotional and physical reactions. How do you find that person? Your SCENE OBJECTIVE answers this question. If the SCENE OBJECTIVE is *"to get you to love me,"* who is it that you need love from the most? Your mother, brother, ex-wife, ex-boyfriend or estranged friend? Don't worry about the appropriateness of the script's character to your SUBSTITUTION choice. Work from your SCENE OBJECTIVE. Because our psyche is strange, complicated and frequently incomprehensible, we aren't always aware of what we truly feel and need from the people in our lives. So it's important to try every person that feels even slightly right in answering the question of who best represents the need expressed in your SCENE OBJECTIVE. In rehearsal, try each possibility, going as far as the first half-page of the dialogue. The SUBSTITUTION choice that generates the most powerful and fitting emotions for the scene, and therefore the SUBSTITUTION that you will most likely want to use, will quickly become clear.

Or maybe your SCENE OBJECTIVE is *"to get you to give me my power back."* Here an appropriate SUBSTITUTION might be your demanding boss, a director that gave you trouble on your last film, your unforgiving mother, a wretched in-law, the person who abused you in some way, an ex, a mean sorority sister, that guy who beat you in a fight, an unreasonable teacher or a team member who ruthlessly competes with you. The issue of power comes in many shapes. Don't get stuck in the physical world—make choices that make emotional sense. The results are much more effective.

*Don't be literal about your SUBSTITUTION choice—
look at it from an emotional point of view.*

Just because the scene is about your lover doesn't mean that you have to use a person from your life who is, or has been, your lover. You want to find a SUBSTITUTION that you have similar emotional issues with.

Say you have a scene where your character's SCENE OBJECTIVE is *"to make you love me,"* and in the script, this SCENE OBJECTIVE is directed toward a lover. Your first instinct may be to use a past or present lover as your SUBSTITUTION. But what if your life circumstances include a father who abandoned you and your mother when you were eight? For most people, an event like this has a higher emotional charge than anything that ever happens with their lovers. By using your father as a SUBSTITUTION for your mate character in the *"to make you love me"* scene, you are more capable of finding a richer, more empowered and more profound emotional base to your SCENE OBJECTIVE. Besides, more often than not, we get involved with a mate who is, in psychological terms, a parental substitute. It's a simple psychological concept that most of us are more likely to be attracted to and attached to a mate that embodies the same unresolved issues that we have with one or both of our parents than with someone else who does not push these emotional buttons. It's just as legitimate to use your parent in a scene about a girlfriend/boyfriend situation as it is to use an actual lover.

I once assigned a scene from *The Hustler* for a pair to perform in class. The film tells the story of Fast Eddie, a brash pool shark who challenges the best pool player in town, loses and falls into a sea of self-pity and the arms of a woman named Sarah. In the scene I selected, Fast Eddie is telling Sarah that he's leaving, that he doesn't know for how long, but he's definitely coming back to her. Sarah gets angry, doesn't believe that he'll come back and uses every tactic she can think of to accomplish her SCENE OBJECTIVE: *"to prove that you love me by staying."* Shawna, the student playing Sarah, was doing a good job of going after her SCENE OBJECTIVE, but her performance was missing something. I didn't feel that her emotional life was in enough jeopardy if Fast Eddie did go and stayed away. Shawna was using her boyfriend as a SUBSTITUTION. I didn't think he provided Shawna with high enough stakes. If she lost her boyfriend, she, a gorgeous and smart woman, could easily find another guy. I also knew that when Shawna was young, her parents divorced and her father abandoned her. Now, this was a much more dramatic and traumatic event, filled with high stakes and pain. I thought it was safe to assume that she still possessed a fear of abandonment because of this event. I told her to go to the primal source of her fears and use her real father as her SUBSTITUTION. Let's just say the tears flowed freely, as did her passion to win. The second time through the scene, the class and I *felt* Sarah's need to get Fast Eddie to stay. She was wildly, desperately, vulnerably, violently, powerfully trying to get him *"to prove that you love me by staying."* It made the class and I want her to win her goal.

We rooted for her to win because we truly felt her goal *needed* to be accomplished for survival.

Your family members will often be your SUBSTITUTION choice.

When Jake Gyllenhaal starred as the awkward adolescent character of Warren in Kenneth Lonergan's *This Is Our Youth* at the Garrick Theatre in London, he initially had a hard time personalizing his character's circumstances in the script. The play chronicles what happens when Warren steals $15,000 from his self-made father, is thrown out of the house and spends a few days blowing the money with his friend Dennis, a guy he is envious of but looks up to. As the character of Warren, Jake's OVERALL OBJECTIVE was *"to be validated,"* with many of the SCENE OBJECTIVES being more specifically, *"to get you* (Dennis) *to validate me,"* because, by comparison, he felt small and inconsequential. The character of Dennis has a famous painter father, he's good with the girls and he's altogether wilier than Warren. Dennis has so much business savvy that he decides to invest the large amount of money in cocaine—which, to Warren, who's stoned all the time, seems like a damned ingenious idea. Jake's real life includes a father who is a very successful film director, a mother who is a thriving film writer and a sister who is a lauded film actress. He is very close to his family. We didn't know who to use. I suggested that he try his father, mother *and* sister because it's not a good idea to rely on intellectual decisions. The only way to really know if something works is to physically do it. So we tried everyone in his family as a SUBSTITUTION. As we played with the dialogue, we found that each choice—his father, mother and sister—drew out different behaviors. In the end, we decided that his father was the most powerful SUBSTITUTION choice for the character of Dennis, because Jake really looked up to his father and strove to always make him proud. It's hard not to be self-deprecating when you feel you have so much to live up to. This SUBSTITUTION choice made Jake take on Warren's needs and impulses—making the character live inside him. Jake won several awards for this performance, which is particularly amazing because it was Jake's virgin theater experience.

You don't know if it will work until you try it.

The best SUBSTITUTION choices are people that are currently important to your life and are emotionally charged. This keeps you in the present and from trying to regurgitate something that has already been resolved and that you have few feelings for or about. This doesn't mean you can only use a person as a SUBSTITUTION if they're presently in your life. Sometimes we have strong feelings for someone in our past, but these feelings remain current because they're unresolved. Now here's the tricky part: We don't always know which relationships are resolved and unresolved. Often, we feel we're done with a relationship when, in fact, we're not. The feelings reside hidden in our subconscious mind. Because our subconscious doesn't play fair, it rarely truthfully communicates with our conscious mind. Because only our subconscious knows, the only way we can know if a SUBSTITUTION will work or not is to try it.

Several years ago, when I was working as an actress, I needed a SUBSTITUTION for a character that I was supposed to passionately love. I wasn't dating anyone special at the time, so this was a daunting task. I tried a multitude of guys I had crushes on. None of them worked. Ex-boyfriends were next. Nothing. My father. Uh-uh. I was at my wit's end and decided, out of desperation, to try my ex-husband. He was someone I hadn't thought about for years (I swear!), and when I thought about him all that ever consciously emerged were thoughts of how good he'd look boiling in oil, skin peeling off, and yet apologetic for all the nasty, abusive things that good-for-nothing bastard had done to me (okay . . . take a breath). It was a long shot. I needed a SUBSTITUTION that would work for love, and I was trying a guy that I had nothing but hate and remorse for? But to my great surprise, it worked. Through using my ex-husband as my SUBSTITUTION, I realized that I still had a lot of unresolved feelings for him. I also discovered that you can't hate that much unless you love that much. To go along with this fortune-cookie wisdom, I discovered a SUBSTITUTION that worked for me in this material and again and again in other projects. So, you just don't know what will work until you try it. Art is rarely rational. Don't intellectually make your choices. Like me, most people are unaware of what is resolved and what is not. Are your issues with that SUBSTITUTION resolved and therefore unusable? The only way you'll know is if you try it. If you feel connected, it is the right choice; if you don't feel connected, it is the wrong choice. It's as simple as that.

The experience that taught me the true strength of our subconscious and made the argument for why we must always try our SUBSTITUTIONS happened when I was working with Jayne Brooke, star of shows like *The District* and *Chicago Hope*. Jayne was playing a character that felt threatened in her mate relationship by another woman who was having an affair with her man. At the time, Jayne was happily married. She couldn't think of anyone who threatened her relationship in any way. She completely trusted her husband, who apparently never even flirted with other women or gave a sideways glance to that buxom blonde walking in the opposite direction. There wasn't even an ex-girlfriend in his life who maintained any emotional hold on him. I finally said, "If I were to put a gun to your head and you *had* to come up with someone that your husband was having an affair with, who would it be?" There was no evidence of any hanky-panky in any shape or form, but she named a woman who was a neighbor. The SUBSTITUTION worked. But here's the astounding part of the story: A few months later, Jayne and her husband decided to split up. The first person her husband started seriously dating? That's right. The very neighbor Jayne had pictured him having an affair with. This story goes to show us that our subconscious always knows.

Your SUBSTITUTION is not always going to be a linear or literal path from the character in the script.

For instance, if your character has a fight with their mother, your SUBSTITUTION may not be your actual mother. You're going to have to look at your character's SCENE OBJECTIVE and then at the fight in the scene. What is it that your character needs from their mother? Approval? Maybe in life the person you seek approval from more than your mother is your teacher or best friend. Then you'd use that.

When working with Mary Stein, one of the stars in the movie sequel *Babe: Pig in the City,* her character was someone whose familial relationships were with a vast array of animals that she kept in her home. Instead of finding the best pet relationship she'd ever had, which wasn't very powerful, we made it more potent. We chose SUBSTITUTIONS that inspired her to behave and relate to the animals as though they were her human family. Each animal, then, was attributed with a human counterpart from Mary's life that made sense to how she felt about each animal.

Not all scenes require a SUBSTITUTION.

SUBSTITUTION is a tool that's there if you need it. Sometimes the person you're acting with (including a casting director in a casting setting) already provides you with the motivation to accomplish your SCENE OBJECTIVE, and you can use the person who's right in front of you.

When I first started helping Jessica Capshaw prepare for her role on the television show *The Practice,* we found that she didn't need a SUBSTITUTION in her scenes with Camryn Manheim. Her character, Jaime Stringer, a relatively new lawyer on the block, is supposed to be intimidated and feel naive around Camryn Manheim's character, Ellenor Frutt, a lawyer who has many cases under her belt. Because Jessica held Camryn's acting abilities and experience in high esteem, her need to please Camryn paralleled her character Jaime's need to please Ellenor. She didn't need a SUBSTITUTION to feel deferential.

**SUBSTITUTION is a tool that you use
if you need emotional history.**

For instance, for sexual connection you wouldn't use a SUBSTITUTION, you would use the actor who's right in front of you. Why? Because using a SUBSTITUTION takes away the intimacy. A SUBSTITUTION is there to provide a strong emotional connection, not a physical one. Sexual connections are what help create chemistry between two actors—which is essential in making a movie, television show or play a hit. I don't care how well written the script is, if the chemistry isn't there, the relationship is not worth rooting for by your audience. (Refer to the "Creating Sexual Chemistry" discussion in Chapter 14 for a full how-to exercise.)

**An emotional connection is different than a sexual one.
If the character who your character is
sexually interested in also includes an
emotional need, then use a SUBSTITUTION as well.**

What if the actor whose character you are supposed to be in love with is someone you cannot generate feelings for? Or worse, what if they're someone you don't like, which happens all too often? In that case, using a SUBSTITUTION for the other actor with someone you have a major crush on, or who you're in love with, is an option. But remember: this should always be *in addition* to the "Creating Sexual Chemistry" exercise (Chapter 14). When I was coaching a gay actress who needed to be boy crazy for her starring role on a hit television sitcom, she did the exercise with the actor who was playing her boyfriend du jour, as well as using her gay lover as a SUBSTITUTION so that she could add a dimension of love to the chemistry. She won an Emmy for her role, and no one was the wiser.

You'll find that there are only a handful of people in your life who are powerful enough to use as SUBSTITUTIONS.

Only a few people really shape and affect our emotional lives. For most of us, these people are our families—mother, father and siblings. And as life progresses, this core group may expand to include a partner, children and an employer. Because there are so many layers to these relationships that need to be resolved and understood, these people can and should be used again and again as SUBSTITUTIONS. Jack Nicholson frequently uses his mother as a SUBSTITUTION. Why? Because Jack's relationship with his mother is so complex.

As Jack was growing up he was led to believe that a woman named June was his sister and a woman named Ethel was his mother. When his "sister" June was dying, Jack was offered a part in Mike Nichols' *The Fortune.* He told June that he wouldn't leave her, that being with her as she was dying was much more important than any acting job. June assured him she was okay. She said she'd be alive when he came back and that he should just go and do the part. He left. A few days later June died. Devastated, Jack returned home. And to further his shock, he later discovered that June wasn't his sister. She was his mother. And Ethel, the woman he thought was his mother, was his grandmother. Ethel had died a few years earlier and now June was dead. There was no one for Jack to talk to or ask, "Why?" Jack was left to unravel this mystery himself—both emotionally and mentally. He had to investigate what had happened and why. And one of the ways he does this is by using his mother/sister as a SUBSTITUTION in his work. His unresolved feelings of anger, love, power and sexuality make for a powerful SUBSTITUTION. Instead of feeling sorry for himself, which is a common response to trauma like this, Jack used his pain to fuel his work. The result: full, ever-present and terrifically oddball characters. Jack's personal stamp makes his roles so Nicholson that they are impossible to duplicate.

SUBSTITUTION provides catharsis.

Acting allows us to do things we can't normally do because real events or convention keep us from experiencing them. Death takes away a relationship, but in our acting fantasy we can keep that person alive. That fantasy can extend to many issues. Whatever we dream of or truly want to be or do is doable in our acting. Because it's not truly real, in our acting fantasy we can kill people (who we think deserve to die), get married (even though you're not dating anyone), have children (even if you can't conceive), hate (those who are not politically correct to disparage), be divorced (from that person you can't leave) and be gay or straight. Acting allows our fantasies to take form. For Natasha Gregson Wagner, the daughter of the late (and great) Natalie Wood, the fantasy of having a mother was huge for her and the SUBSTITUTION work she did had a very positive affect on her life.

Natasha was very close to her mother. So when Natalie died when Natasha was only eleven, she was overwhelmed and in excruciating pain. In the years I've worked with her, we've discovered that her mother is a powerful SUBSTITUTION for Natasha. Clearly, her thoughts about her mother are infused with the kind of powerful issues that a SUBSTITUTION needs to have: abandonment, loss, and great love. Because Natasha is an actress, she can do what a lot of people can't. Using her work, Natasha can live out the fantasy of what her life would be like if her mother were still alive. For instance, if she's playing a role where love and loss is the issue, she will often use her mother as a SUBSTITUTION. And, in a way, this SUBSTITUTION work allows her to connect with her mother in a way that she never had the opportunity to do because her mother died when Natasha was so young. Some may view this as unhealthy, but keeping her mother alive in her work, as corny as it may sound, keeps her alive in her heart.

Every time you use a SUBSTITUTION that is infused with a loaded subject, the unresolved relationship gets worked out a little more in both your conscious and subconscious mind. Things you'd like to say or do to a high-stakes person in your past and/or present life—but *can't* do in real life—you can do in your acting.

Be Open to Change

When a new crisis enters our life, our minds cannot veer from thinking about the trauma at hand. Yesterday's dramas take the backseat to today's dramas. If, as you are doing a play, movie or a television show, something more distressing, crucial or more relevant happens in your life that introduces a better SUBSTITUTION choice, by all means change your SUBSTITUTION. This was the case when I was working with Charlize Theron on the film *Mighty Joe Young*. This movie tells the story of Jill Young (Charlize's character), who is left to care for a baby gorilla when her father, an American researcher, is killed by poachers in Africa. Charlize's character must raise this ape and make sure that he thrives, even when he is taken from his native Africa to a sanctuary in California. Jill feels she must protect the two-ton ape, Joe, from the perils of modern civilization. We had decided on a SUBSTITUTION for Joe, and had done extensive work on her role when, just a few days into filming, Charlize's brother died in an automobile accident. Naturally, this new and very traumatic event overshadowed everything else in her life. Like many people who lose family members, particularly siblings, Charlize's brother's death made her feel helpless. She wondered what she could have done to keep him alive. What should she have told him before his death that now she'd never get a chance to say? What never got resolved or accomplished? When she went back to work, she switched her SUBSTITUTION for Joe to her brother. By using her brother as a SUBSTITUTION, Charlize used her work as a second chance to take care of the unfinished feelings she had about her brother. Not only did it make her acting present and eventful, but it was also cathartic. In every scene, she got to bring her brother back and fight for him to stay alive, alleviating the helplessness that she was experiencing in her real life.

Of course, death isn't the only high-stakes event that can change your choices. Others include divorce, getting sued, getting caught doing something illegal or immoral, a big fight with a loved one, being sexually harassed, being lied to, or pregnancy, just to name a few. I was once hired by the producers of a high-profile television series to work with the leading actress. The director was verbally abusive to her. He would berate her with thinly disguised references to her being stupid and untalented while they were on the set and everyone could hear. This director served as a great SUBSTITUTION for the bad guy that appeared in the early episodes. Then life happened. She got pregnant. The father, who spoke words of love and attachment before the blessed conception, was suddenly nowhere to be found. The director was no longer the significant villain in her life. A more present and effective SUBSTITUTION took his place.

Take Risks with Your Choices

As you've probably noticed, I really believe in taking risks. If I got a nickel for every time I've said to an actor, "Always, always, take risks!" I'd have to buy a very large piggy bank. To create risk there must be huge, risky OBSTACLES to overcome. If you make a SUBSTITUTION choice that allows you to easily gain your SCENE OBJECTIVE, there's no real need to do anything exciting to get what you want. Let's look at how we behave with our friends. We often have two kinds of friends. There's the one who you know will do anything on your behalf—take a bullet if necessary—and then there's the friend that you try too hard for—try to be extra smart, helpful or funny, because you're still trying to win their approval and love. So you can see how, in a friendship scene, the friend you try too hard for is going to be the more compelling SUBSTITUTION choice. As with all the tools:

There must always be inherent OBSTACLES attached to your SUBSTITUTIONS.

When making a SUBSTITUTION choice, always ask yourself:

- Who do I most need to get my SCENE OBJECTIVE from? And from that list . . .
- Who is most *un*likely to give it to me?

This brings the possibility of failure into the equation, which will create unpredictability for you, the other actor and the audience. The possibility of failure also allows your personal flaws to emerge, which will create affectations and mannerisms that are unique to you.

Finding Your SUBSTITUTIONS

Beginning with the SCENE OBJECTIVE to help you figure out who the best and most effective SUBSTITUTION is to add reality and depth to your performance. Let's look at how this works for the character of Bonasera in the opening scene of *The Godfather*. The film opens, and it's Don Corleone's daughter's wedding. According to the story's tradition, on the day of a daughter's wedding, the Don of a family must receive and be open to requests. Bonasera, the undertaker, has a request for the Godfather. He is seated in front of the Don's desk.

THE GODFATHER
by Mario Puzo and Francis Ford Coppola
© 1972 Paramount Pictures

BONASERA
I believe in America. America has made my
fortune. And I raised my daughter in the American
fashion. I gave her freedom, but—I taught
her never to dishonor her family. She found a
boyfriend; not an Italian. She went to the movies
with him; she stayed out late. I didn't protest.
Two months ago, he took her for a drive, with
another boyfriend. They made her drink whiskey.
And then they tried to take advantage of her. She
resisted. She kept her honor. So they beat her,
like an animal. When I went to the hospital, her
nose was a'broken. Her jaw was a'shattered, held
together by wire. She couldn't even weep because
of the pain. But I wept. Why did I weep? She was
the light of my life—beautiful girl. Now she will
never be beautiful again.
             [*He breaks down*]
Sorry . . .
I—I went to the police, like a good American. These
two boys were brought to trial. The judge sentenced
them to three years in prison—suspended sentence.
Suspended sentence! They went free that very day!
I stood in the courtroom like a fool. And those two
bastards, they smiled at me. Then I said to my wife,
"For justice, we must go to Don Corleone."

Bonasera hoped to get justice on behalf of his daughter, who, in his
mind, was raped three times. Twice by men and then again by the American
legal system, a system he once dearly believed in. Feeling powerless
to do anything about the men that hurt someone he loved so dearly, he
went to the Godfather to seek vengeance.

- Bonasera's SCENE OBJECTIVE: *"to get you* (Don Corleone) *to
  murder for me."*

When picking your SUBSTITUTIONS, always consider the script's
OBSTACLES, which in this case are:

1. Possible rejection.
2. Fear of the Godfather. As the undertaker, Bonasera knows
   firsthand what Don Corleone is capable of.

3. Fear of being beholden to the Godfather.
4. If the Godfather doesn't grant the request, Bonasera will be left with horrible guilt and feelings of massive inadequacy.
5. In the story, Bonasera has gone out of his way to not socially connect to Don Corleone, which infuriates Don Corleone. Don Corleone feels particularly disrespected in this case because Corleone's wife is Bonasera's daughter's godmother. Therefore, Don Corleone is less inclined to grant Bonasera his request.
6. Corleone's going to do whatever he wants. Bonasera must be submissive to him. Bonasera has a feeling of utter weakness.
7. His desperate desire for justice through retribution.
8. If Corleone doesn't grant his request, Bonasera has no other options.

After thinking about your SCENE OBJECTIVE, *"to get you to murder for me,"* and the OBSTACLES attached to it, you then find out how this is true in your life by asking yourself, "Whom in my personal life do I currently need a huge favor from that I'm intimidated by because the power base is so uneven?" Or, "Who would it be emotionally painful to need anything from?"

As you look at the people that have come up as answers to the above questions, you have to decide who in your life would affect you the *most* as a SUBSTITUTION. Frequently, three or more names of people might come up as conceivably suitable SUBSTITUTIONS for the other character in the script. Because acting is a physical art form, you should never intellectually decide who the best SUBSTITUTION choice is. I repeat: The choices have to be actually tried out—on your feet, speaking the dialogue. It becomes clear upon trying each of your possible SUBSTITUTION choices which one affects you the most. Look for these reactions:

- Touching you emotionally.
- Giving you passion to succeed in achieving your SCENE OBJECTIVE.
- Having inherent OBSTACLES.
- Making sense to the script itself.

Someone may come to mind immediately and you might feel you have the perfect choice. Even so, you still must come up with at least two more alternative SUBSTITUTION choices, because we are not always aware, until we try it, who in your life affects us the most. Don't assume the most obvious SUBSTITUTION choice will work—sometimes it's someone you least suspect who will motivate the most passion to win your SCENE OBJECTIVE.

Here are possible SUBSTITUTION choices for Don Corleone:

- **Your father:** One common son/father dynamic is for a son to feel intimidation and fear toward his father. A son will put his father on a pedestal and feel that, no matter what he's accomplished, he has, in some way, disappointed his father. This makes the son constantly attempt to make his father proud and, at the same time, feel that whatever he does, it's never enough. Or if the father exhibits abusive tendencies, the son's need to overcome the abuse to get his father's love is limitless. A primal choice like a parent sets up an uneven power struggle, which is inherent in a parent/child relationship.

- **Your mother:** Perhaps in your family dynamic, your mother is the powerhouse. As with the father SUBSTITUTION, a son will put his mother on a pedestal and feel that, no matter what he's accomplished, he has, in some way, disappointed his mother. This makes the son constantly attempt to make his mother proud and feel like it's never enough. And if the mother is overdemanding or verbally or physically abusive, the son's need to overcome the abuse to get his mother's love is limitless. Again, a primal choice like using a parent sets up an uneven power struggle, which is inherent in a parent/child relationship.

- **Stepmother or stepfather:** Children often have problems with the person who steps in as an authority but hasn't earned it through blood ties. And they often blame this person for tearing the original family unit apart. A stepmother or stepfather relationship is wrought with issues, whether real or imagined (to a child, there's no difference). A common problem is the power struggle to capture the real parent's attention and focus. The child often loses this battle because the blood parent will often side with the person who shares their bed. As a result, having to ask this person for anything can be painful.

- **A teacher:** It's common for a person who's thrust into a position of power and authority to abuse that power. Some teachers thrive on making the student feel stupid, untalented, unliked, sexually harassed or ridiculed. If you have had a teacher like this, they can be a viable SUBSTITUTION.

- **Your boss:** It is rare that we have a healthy, fulfilling relationship with our employers. Your boss holds your present and future in their hands and is seldom responsible or held accountable for their actions. The appropriate power struggle is inherent in the employee/employer relationship.

- **Casting director, director, producer, agent, et al:** These people can make an actor's dreams come true. When a person holds this much power over people's hopes and desires, it's difficult to not feel tempted to abuse the people they have power over. This dynamic makes for an optimal SUBSTITUTION. What will you have to give up to get your request? Your dignity, your morality, your ethics? Are you expected to give unjustifiable adulation or sexual favors to make this request happen? Note that for this SUBSTITUTION to work, you must have a *real* problematic personal history with a *specific* individual holding a high-powered position in the industry.

- **Your ex-wife or ex-girlfriend:** Exes are our exes for a reason: we have major issues with them—especially power struggles. Who made more money? Who was better in bed? Who gave more to the relationship? Were you emasculated by an affair? Was your ex-mate physically and/or verbally abusive? Was your ex-mate condescending? To request something—anything—from an ex is humbling.

- **An older brother:** Obviously, this choice is about sibling rivalry. Perhaps your brother was the chosen son until you came along. The pain of spending an entire childhood dealing with an older brother possibly beating you up, tattling on you and mocking you doesn't easily go away just because you're both grown up and currently the best of friends.

- **A family member like an uncle/aunt or grandfather/ grandmother:** In some families, an uncle or grandmother may take on a more active, involved and complicated role. In cases such as these, family members have the responsibility and authority of a parent. As a result, your issues with this relative will embody a parental dynamic. Your power struggles will then be the same as they might have been with your mother or father.

- **Your present mate:** This SUBSTITUTION can only be used if there are major problems in your relationship. If all is well, barring the occasional flare-ups that plague all couples, there will be no conflict and nothing to really overcome to get your SCENE OBJECTIVE. But if the relationship is on its way out or there are *huge* issues, like your mate is having an affair or has a tendency toward emotional castration, then you've got something to work with. Eating crow in order to ask your detestable mate to do anything for you would make eating a rat seem like a doable alternative.

- **An abusive friend:** No matter how emotionally healthy we claim our friend relationships to be (I've often heard from students, "Oh, I don't have any friends like that, I got rid of them long ago . . ."), most of us seem to retain at least one abusive friend. You know the one. The friend that your other friends ask you, "*Why* are you friends with that person, anyway?!" What makes the friendship even worse is that the power struggle with the abusive friend has a friendly veneer to it. And then there's the fact that the abusive friend wins the power struggles most of the time, which infuriates you. This can be a powerful SUBSTITUTION, because these relationships are so complex and usually tap into our parental issues as well.

- **A person who molested you (babysitter, uncle, neighbor, etc.):** This person took your power away in the most heinous way, especially if it happened when you were a child and you didn't have the tools to either understand it or fight it. Asking a favor of someone like this might be devastating. Yet, if your daughter (or some loved one) had to be protected and the molester was the only one capable of doing this, you'd be forced to do so. This would create amazing drama, as the push-and-pull of the scene would be palpable.

Of course, there are many other possibilities for SUBSTITUTIONS, but these suggestions will give you an idea of how far you can go in making SUBSTITUTION choices that make sense emotionally and to the script, and that will further aid in making a character like Bonasera *live* inside of you.

Once you've determined your SUBSTITUTION, you can personalize the script's OBSTACLES. The personalization of OBSTACLES will be determined by whom you are using as a SUBSTITUTION. The conflicts or problems that exist are unique to each person in your life. Your needs, thoughts, and issues are different with your mother than they are with your father, and they're different with your friends, your teachers, your employees, and your children, etc. Thus, it's important to understand who your SUBSTITUTION is before you can analyze any of your inner work, because it will change radically depending upon who you're talking to. After you've determined your SUBSTITUTION, it's time to personalize the script's OBSTACLES.

Personalizing OBSTACLES: The Practical Application

The first thing you do to personalize the script's OBSTACLES is to review the OBSTACLES you've already listed and defined that are established from the script itself. Then, with your SUBSTITUTION in mind, determine what similar OBSTACLES exist within your relationship with your SUBSTITUTION.

For the purposes of explaining how to personalize your OBSTACLES, let's say that I've been cast to play the role of Bonasera in *The Godfather.* I'm using myself because this process is about making something personal, and I *know* my history, not yours. I've also found that telling an actor (or writer/director) I'm working with what personal choices I'd make if I were to play their role always seems to jog ideas for them. As you read my choices, let them inspire personal OBSTACLES that you would use from *your* life.

In the script, Bonasera's key OBSTACLES are:

1. Possibility of rejection.
2. Disparity of power.
3. Intimidation.
4. Fear of the person he's talking to.
5. A history of problems in the relationship.
6. The request is enormously important.

7. There are probably severe repercussions if the request is perceived as a sign of disrespect.

Considering these OBSTACLES, three possibilities for my SUBSTITUTION come to mind: my mother, a certain studio executive and my daughter's teacher. Now, let's take a closer look at how these SUBSTITUTIONS affect the OBSTACLES.

- **My mother:** She abused me as a child. So in our relationship, there's a history of abuse. And, although I'm an adult now, a kernel of the *fear and intimidation* of her still lives inside of me. Primal emotions like this die hard.

  My mother is also not particularly mentally stable. I fear that if I push her too hard (like asking a favor as big as Bonasera's), she might lose it. And then, as I'm already hardwired to feel guilty, I would have to live with the massive guilt for driving her over the edge. *Severe repercussions.*

  The *disparity of power* is intrinsic to our relationship, as she's the parent and I'm the child. This dynamic will never emotionally change, no matter what I've accomplished or how dependent on me she becomes in her old age.

  Based on this SUBSTITUTION, my request would be that I would ask my mother to become more financially dedicated to the needs of my mentally handicapped brother. She is my brother's caretaker. My father failed to set up any kind of trust for him before he died. My mother spends money extravagantly, rewarding any wayward salesman that rings her doorbell with unnecessary purchases. However, when it comes to my retarded brother's expenses, she makes Scrooge look like Imelda Marcos. If my brother doesn't get her financial support, he'll physically lose the roof over his head, the food to feed himself and the mental health care he so desperately needs. *An important request.*

- **A certain studio executive:** I've been in the entertainment business for a long time and know the power that a studio executive can exert. Hollywood is a small world and these folks can make or break a project, fire you, blacklist you with the other studios and generally wreak havoc in your life on a whim. With this executive, I have a combo platter of personalized OBSTACLES— *disparity of power, intimidation, fear of the person* and *severe repercussions.*

Based on this SUBSTITUTION, my request would be on behalf of a student who's starring in a television series. I want this executive to change some of my student's sentimental, hackneyed, on-the-nose dialogue that he's forced to recite episode after episode. Of course, this executive feels the dialogue has "award written all over it." By making the request, I'm taking the chance of destroying my student's career by angering this V.I.P. I also have to consider that, since this exec is paying me to work with this student and I don't live on hallowed ground, my ass might be grass as well. *Important request.*

- **My daughter's teacher:** My daughter is fifteen, that pivotal age when grades start to count for your future—college acceptance, summer internships, jobs. If she goes to a good university, it will increase her chances for a great future. Conversely, if she goes to a less prestigious university, her potential may not be fully realized and her life could go down the toilet. (Yes, this is a bit melodramatic, but I'm her mother and that's what mothers do.) *Disparity of power.*

A certain English teacher seems to have it in for my daughter, who is exceptionally gifted. And I'm not just saying this because I'm her mother. My kid is on the dean's list. But I digress. Anyway, I assume this teacher has a history of persecuting students (why else would he pick on my angelic and perfect kid?!). Recently, this teacher gave her an unwarranted lower grade.

My personalization for Bonasera's request will be to go to this teacher and ask him to change her grade. I have to be aware that if he perceives me as an enemy, that might make him give her future lower grades as a way to be vindictive. This would lower her overall GPA and negatively affect her getting into a good school. As much as I might hate this teacher for what I consider to be his irrational and evil behavior, I will have to find a way to ask and continue to empower the unjustifiably cruel teacher so that the letter grade is brought to the level where it should be in the first place. *Intimidation. Fear of the person I'm talking to. The request is important. Probable severe repercussions.*

Notice how each SUBSTITUTION changed my personal OBSTACLES. But more importantly, notice that the personal OBSTACLES still echo the character in the script's OBSTACLES. In all three of my SUBSTITUTION examples, the OBSTACLES talk about an imbalance of power, fear of the other person, a history of problems and a request that has a lot at stake. Personalizing OBSTACLES creates a more powerful and intimate investment in the material and adds need, heat and substance to your performance.

As with SUBSTITUTION, personalizing the script's OBSTACLES isn't always a linear thought process.

I helped the singer Macy Gray prepare for her guest-star role on the television series *M.D.s.* She played a singer who had life-threatening cancer that was attacking her vocal cords. In the story, the character had a choice. If she had her throat operated on, she would probably lose her voice, but the procedure would save her life. If the character didn't have the operation, she would die. The episode was about Macy's character grappling with this life-versus-death decision. In the end, the character realizes that her voice *is* her life and that she's going to take her chances, praying that there'll be some kind of divine intervention that will save her. In the story, Macy's character is single, childless and just on the verge of becoming successful. Macy, on the other hand, is an extremely successful singer and the mother of three children. We had to find a way to make the damaged world of her character parallel her own. As we worked together on the episode, we talked about how important her children were to her. Without her money and protection, her children would be left alone to fend for themselves. I asked Macy what she would do if she were to face this OBSTACLE-riddled choice: life without a voice or the possibility of an early death. Macy said she'd choose life without her voice. Although her career would be over, she'd at least be alive and able to take care of her babies. So when we personalized the OBSTA-

CLES for the episode, Macy's personal OBSTACLE was her children losing her as a mother, whereas her character's OBSTACLE was losing her
voice. Macy's personal life-and-death conflict is based on her maternal
needs and desires to be there and take care of her children, whereas her
character's conflict is based on her need and desire to finally succeed at
her dream before she dies. But their emotional desires parallel and reflect each other.

The OBSTACLES that need to be personalized are not always obvious or written in the script.

For many years, I worked with Adrian Paul on his role as Duncan
MacLeod in the television series *The Highlander*. Although he was playing a superhero, we had to create OBSTACLES to humanize his character so that the audience could relate to him. In one episode, Duncan
MacLeod was trying to help a friend who was a raging alcoholic. I told
Adrian that people with addictions rarely can or will listen to someone
who hasn't had similar problems. If his character hadn't experienced any
kind of addictive behavior, then his alcoholic friend would feel that Duncan's attempt to help him was judgmental and patronizing. And as you
know, no one likes to be patronized. Even though the idea of Duncan
being an addict of some kind wasn't in the script, we had to create this
OBSTACLE for his character and then personalize it for Adrian so that
he and his character could truly commiserate with this alcoholic character. We invented a back-story for Duncan: Somewhere in his 400-year
life, he too had suffered from alcoholism. But when we began to personalize the OBSTACLE, we had a new problem: Adrian Paul had never
had a problem with alcohol. We had to find a different vice. You may
be in denial, but everyone has at least one vice—sex, drugs, sleeping,
overeating, computing, etc. People who have chosen show business as a
career often have an array of vices to choose from. It's nothing to be
ashamed of. It's what makes you an artist. With Adrian's personal vice infused in his characterization of Duncan MacLeod, he could now truly
relate to his character's friend's obsessive and addictive behavior. This allowed Adrian, as Duncan, to profoundly understand his alcoholic friend,
which made this performance particularly affecting.

Dig deep. Look below the surface to those dark, tortured and hidden places that reside inside of you.

When you personalize a script's OBSTACLES, it requires you to look at your demons—especially those places we're often in denial about. Finding the appropriate SUBSTITUTION and personalizing a script's OBSTACLES asks you to dig deep within yourself and be rigorously honest about who you are and who and what pushes your buttons. There'll also be personal discovery. When you try different choices, it's sometimes really surprising what works and what doesn't. Issues you think you've resolved are not. People you think no longer hold any power over you still prevail in your heart. What is effective in your work is the *real truth* of what you feel. That's why it's important to try many choices, even the ones that seem wrong. Because underneath, in your heart and gut, there may be residual unresolved feelings—no matter how much your conscious mind may fight it. Working this way not only gives you a better performance, it gives you a better understanding of yourself.

The SUBSTITUTION you choose colors and changes what choices you make for *all* the inner work, including the mental images that are created by *what* it is you are talking about and *what* it is you are hearing. These are your INNER OBJECTS, and the next acting tool.

CHAPTER 5

Tool #5:

INNER OBJECTS

The images and pictures you see in your mind when
speaking or hearing about a person, place, thing or event.

In life, there's a natural movie that passes behind our eyes when we talk
and listen. These rolling images are associations we make based on our
past and present experiences. Likewise, any character you play must also
have a movie behind their eyes. But because your character's words and
life are not yours but that of the writer's, you need to make your own personal and appropriate associations to find the right pictures. This is so
that when you say or hear dialogue, the visuals and pictures that come up
should feel like they are emanating from your own personal life. If you
don't have clear associations to the words, they will seem and feel meaningless. It's your job as the actor to personalize the words that come from
the author's mind and make it appear and feel as though they come from
your mind. Using INNER OBJECTS makes this happen.

Our INNER OBJECTS are never random. Think about how we learn
to speak. First, a baby sees a picture and then forms the words. Often,
our first words are, "Ma Ma" and "Da Da." We learn these words first because these pictures are key to our survival, as well as the first important
images that an infant perceives. Similarly, when we're learning a new
language, we need a picture attached to the foreign word to recall it.
That is why we often learn the words for things like "bathroom," "bed"
and various food items first.

Our INNER OBJECT movie plays constantly. Your mind never goes
blank. *Ever.* Every person, place, thing or event you talk about or hear
another person talk about must have an INNER OBJECT attached to it.
Why? Because we are always thinking. To evoke any sense of reality, you

have to have your mind continuously generating images that will inspire your character's reality and feelings. The best illustration of our mind's ticker tape of activity is when someone says to you, "I've got something to tell you. . . ." It's rare when this statement forecasts good news. If you have good news, you usually just blurt out the good news: "Hey! I've won the lottery!" You don't say, "I've got something to tell you . . . I've won the lottery!" Yet when hearing, "I've got something to tell you," most actors wait for the news with a blank expression and an empty head. The reality is that when someone says, "I've got something to tell you . . ." you suspect it's something bad and your thoughts race trying to figure out what the bad news could be. If these words are coming from a mate, you might think, "Oh, my God, he's cheating on me!" or "She's leaving me!" or "He's gay!" or "He's not gay!" or "She's pregnant!" or "He's dying!" and so on. The pictures and thoughts of the anticipated bad news you've come up with may be right or totally off base, but it doesn't matter as long as the thoughts and pictures are plentiful and profuse. Your job as an actor is to have pictures and thoughts going on in your head as you talk and as your co-star lays out whatever news they have to tell you. This means that there should be INNER OBJECTS for every person, place, thing or event in the script.

The SUBSTITUTION choice you've made will determine your choices for the INNER OBJECTS. This means that if you're using your mother, your INNER OBJECTS should relate to your experiences with her. This way your work will track, filling out the larger inner story you're creating. Do not use one SUBSTITUTION and then work with INNER OBJECTS that relate to another person. It's too confusing to keep track of and ultimately creates a befuddled and unfocused performance. If you find that you're saying to yourself, "What am I thinking about now?" then you've made the wrong INNER OBJECT choices. Your INNER OBJECTS should flow, fitting together with your SUBSTITUTION, OBSTACLES, SCENE OBJECTIVE and OVERALL OBJECTIVE like a good jigsaw puzzle.

In *Gone With the Wind*, Scarlett O'Hara often speaks of her home, Tara. Actors who don't work with INNER OBJECTS will try to picture some generic plantation mansion rather than a home that means something to them. The result of generic choices like this will be general, vague and, well, generic. A generic plantation mansion has no personal meaning, relevance or emotional connection. Even if you happen to be from the South and you've seen many plantation mansions, the picture in your head is not infused with all the joys, traumas and real-life events that are attached to the places that have a real emotional history for you. Instead, you can use INNER OBJECTS and make charged choices. For instance, say you're doing a scene opposite Scarlett's archrival, Melanie, and you've chosen your mother as the SUBSTITUTION for Melanie, the INNER OBJECT (picture) you might use for Tara is the home you grew up in with your mother. Or perhaps you're doing a scene opposite Rhett Butler and you've chosen your ex-mate as your SUBSTITUTION. The IN-NER OBJECT that you choose for Tara is going to change because your thoughts, needs and history are quite different than they would be with your mother. With your ex-mate in mind, Tara now is pictured in your head as the home you lived in with your ex.

Your INNER OBJECT Choices Should Be Made on an Emotional Level, Not a Physical Level

The character of Bubba in *Forrest Gump* constantly refers to a shrimp boat. If you were playing Bubba and needed an INNER OBJECT, the idea wouldn't be to come up with the best boat reference you could think of. Bubba saw the shrimp boat not as a boat, but as something that symbolized his dream career, a reason to survive the Vietnam hell he was living in and an inspiration for him to get through his tour of duty. So, if you were playing Bubba, you might use the idea of getting a starring movie role opposite your favorite actor as an INNER OBJECT for the shrimp boat. Or the shrimp boat could be getting that dream house for your mother before she dies. There are no right or wrong choices, just more effective or less effective ones. When breaking down a script for INNER OBJECTS, just make sure the INNER OBJECT visuals relate to the SUBSTITUTION you're using and that the choices you make are the ones that hold the greatest value to you emotionally.

INNER OBJECTS should have inherent OBSTACLES attached to them.

The more specific and angst-ridden your choices are for the INNER OB-JECTS in a scene, the more they will evoke an emotional response for you, the other actor and the audience. Generally, high stakes are created by conflict—if a choice is unproblematic it becomes too easy to assimi-late and therefore not particularly interesting. The point is to not only concern yourself with finding INNER OBJECTS that make your performance the most honest, but to find the pictures that are the most precarious and risky. If the dialogue is, "I feel sick," you should use your worst nightmarish fear. The picture in your head shouldn't be of you being laid up with the flu, but rather of you in bed, in the final throes of cancer, the cancer that your grandma died from, the cancer that your mother has been diagnosed with, the cancer you might get because cancer can be hereditary. Using something like cancer as your INNER OBJECT choice is based on a *real* fear. If the choices you make for your INNER OBJECTS aren't infused with history and high stakes, then it won't naturally emerge when it comes time for performance. The hotter the choice you make the more likely you'll organically remember your images without having to think about them.

It's not just your own dialogue that requires INNER OBJECTS— the other actor's words must be attached to pictures that mean something to you.

People *hear* in pictures. Using INNER OBJECTS when the other person is talking also enables you to react more honestly. One of the biggest complaints that directors and casting directors have is that actors don't listen. They just wait to speak their dialogue. That doesn't imply that you as the actor aren't hearing the words from the other character—you're probably hearing every single word. But if the words don't mean anything to you and aren't summoning pictures in your head, then you're not effectively listening.

When we listen, we don't try to imagine another person's life, we relate everything we hear to our own world.

When we hear other people speak, we don't try to imagine what their pictures look like, even if we casually know the person, place, thing or event they're talking about. We listen with our own personal pictures because they mean something to us. Say your friend is talking to you about the recent death of his mother. You don't picture his mother dying. Instead, you recall an important death you've experienced, or you imagine what it would feel like if your own mother were to die. To truly listen as we do in life, we naturally match the other person's thoughts to relatable ones of our own. It's how we try to understand and relate to other people's emotional reality.

The function of INNER OBJECTS is to use them not physically but rather *emotionally* to duplicate the pictures used in the dialogue.

In class, Michael Ralph, an actor from the movie *Rules of Attraction* and the hit series *The Bernie Mac Show,* did a scene from LeRoi Jones' *The Dutchman. The Dutchman* is a play about a racist woman and an African American man riding the subway. As the play opens, it seems as though the woman is seducing the man, but as the story progresses her passion evolves into a rage—first with extreme racial slurs, then escalating into a fury that drives her to kill him. Michael read the script, listened to the character's bigoted statements and decided to use racism as his INNER OBJECT. Every black person in America has experienced racism. It's a heated issue, a solid INNER OBJECT choice. Yet I knew that Michael had an issue that was even closer to his heart. Due to impossible legal issues, he could not see his son, who lived three thousand miles away. Using his fight to get his son back rather than racist issues gave Michael a higher intensity and a larger emotional reaction to the racial slurs. It also motivated a stronger will to win over the evil white woman, because defending his child (a huge primal need) was at stake. The work Michael did as a result of his new INNER OBJECT was volatile and impulsive, because a parent will do anything to protect his child.

Make Your INNER OBJECTS Personal

My brother-in-law is an internationally recognized trial lawyer who wins nearly every case he argues. His clients are usually big corporations. Fighting cases on behalf of big business can be challenging. It's an uphill battle because most people—especially a jury—are inclined to side with the individual rather than the big bad corporate machine. So how does he win? He makes each case about himself, his wife or his children. He finds a way to personalize it, making it about defending his family and values. By doing this, he's not fighting for the depersonalized corporation, but for what he cares about the most. He argues hard and works fanatically. He does this because he knows that no matter how altruistic you are, you'll always do more for you and the things that matter to you (i.e., your family) than you'll ever do for others or their ideals.

I worked with one particular actress on many episodes of a popular television show about lawyers. (No, I won't reveal who she is, because the story would reveal too much about her personal issues and that wouldn't be fair to her. I plead the Fifth on this one.) Her character had to fight a particular case for a client who had been raped. In the show's storyline, the rape was personal to her character because she had been raped, too, but had never filed a police report. The challenge for this actress was to find the INNER OBJECT for being raped. Fortunately, she had never experienced this form of violation. I explained to her that rape is not just a physical violation—it's an emotional violation, as well. I asked her if there was any event in her life where she felt emotionally raped. She revealed that she was overweight as a child and that her father constantly criticized and humiliated her because of her excess poundage. Even though she is quite svelte and has been so for a long time, her father's ridicule has stayed with her. She looks in the mirror and sees someone who's horribly disfigured and fat. She came to realize that she indeed felt raped by her father's words and behavior, and, like a sexual rape victim, had been changed forever by it. She decided to try to use it as her INNER OBJECT. In her performance, every time she spoke of the rape that happened to her client and to herself, she pictured the worst and most humiliating events that happened regarding her weight and her father. By using this as an INNER OBJECT event, her emotions surfaced uncontrollably, much like they would have had she been sexually raped.

INNER OBJECT choices are not always linear.

Adam Baldwin, who has starred in films such as *Full Metal Jacket* and *My Bodyguard,* was acting in a play where his character was a newly sober character who was "qualifying" (the point at which an alcoholic tells their story) at an Alcoholics Anonymous meeting. In Adam's character's story, he has to talk about the injustices in his life—particularly, the fact that he sobered up to stop the abuse he was heaping onto his loving and patient wife, who then died. Adam's character is devastated and confused. Adam and I searched for appropriate INNER OBJECTS, and it was challenging. Adam is not an alcoholic and his wife is very much alive. We needed to come up with something that, when he talked about this eventful death, would destroy him as much as the untimely death of a loved one.

Adam had been in a series called *Firefly* that Joss Whedon of *Buffy the Vampire Slayer* fame had created. There were high hopes for the series. It was incredibly well written and Adam had the best character of his career to play. There was also the fact that Whedon, who had a hit series under his belt, was involved, which made it seem that this would be the role that would allow Adam to keep his wife and three children fed, clothed and living with a roof over their heads for a long, long time. Adam also felt that he had finally landed a soul-food kind of role, which, as any actor will testify, is a rarity. He loved the other cast members like family, as well. The series was canceled after only one season. Adam was devastated. It was a huge loss, much like losing a family member. As an INNER OBJECT, *Firefly* provided similar elements that a good wife offers—security, love, inspiration, nurturing and protection. The death of the series and his resulting moody behavior was perfect to use as a nonlinear INNER OBJECT. It allowed him to stay in the moment and feel feelings that were poignant and pervasive.

INNER OBJECTS can take a negative experience from your life and make it positive.

When I was working with a renowned actress (for what will be obvious reasons, I will not mention her name) on a thriller, her character had to have her unborn baby brutally carved out of her body. She needed an INNER OBJECT that would duplicate the severe trauma of a mother violently losing her baby. We'd worked together for many years and I knew that she'd had an abortion. This experience caused her such acute distress that it produced out-of-control shaking and weeping whenever she talked about it. I suggested she use the abortion as the INNER OBJECT for the scene. She did and out poured all of her rage, sadness, terror and horrific guilt that most women feel when they have had to abort their unborn child. Although sometimes necessary, an abortion can be the cause of great strife. And, whether in your opinion this is politically true or not, it can also make most women and men feel like they have murdered their own child. If you've suffered from either having had an abortion, or as a male, having endured an abortion on your behalf, find a way to use it in your inner work. You'll find that by using it, it will give you some emotional resolution.

INNER OBJECTS are enormously effective when working with material that is rich in jargon, be it political-speak, financial lingo, psychobabble, science or techno-gibberish.

The producers of the show *Star Trek: Deep Space Nine* hired me to help establish and make Terry Farrell's character Dax seem real. The producers described what they wanted to see: "Dax is a three-hundred-year-old worm who used to be a man and is now a gorgeous woman. She is wise (because she's so old) and unaffected by sexuality (again, with the old)—too wise, in fact, to have a sense of humor."

I told them, "Okay, no problem . . . makes sense to me. . . ." I am not as intrigued by science fiction as so many of those who count themselves amongst the "Trekkie" population, but I do know that in order for anyone to like a character they must relate to that character in some fashion. What the producers wanted was for Dax to be a character that the public would love and, at the same time, would stay true to her science fiction persona. This combination could only be achieved by humanizing Dax, by providing earthly duplications to her alien attributes so that those of us who still reside on planet Earth (and the Nielsen families) could understand and connect to her. Using INNER OBJECTS, I was able to give Dax sexuality (a primal force everyone can relate to), a sense of humor (humor appeals to most people) and to personalize all the technobabble (making words like "wormholes" and "quarks" feel like commonly used words). The producers saw the dailies after the first few days of Terry's work and were thrilled. Apparently, by humanizing the alien they got "exactly what we wanted." It's not that we were intentionally defying the powers in charge. They, too, want the best performance that will also accurately portray their vision of the character and inspire a large audience to tune in. Not being trained actors themselves, producers often don't have the right language to describe what they want. It's up to you to translate their words into a great performance by introducing the human quotient (yourself), making it exciting and relatable to the producers, the director and your audience.

Make the Most Current and High-Stakes INNER OBJECT Choices

Using recent painful circumstances from your life keeps you present and raw because you are still unaware of the ramifications of how it will resolve itself. The point is to not only concern yourself with finding INNER OBJECTS that make your performance honest, but to find the pictures that are presently the most volatile and risky.

Try different INNER OBJECT choices.

As with all the other tools, don't intellectually decide what should work. By trying different INNER OBJECTS, you'll find the ones that are the most effective. How do you figure out the best INNER OBJECTS? When you are rehearsing and performing, the weaker INNER OBJECT choices will float away—that is, they won't stick in your mind. However, the good INNER OBJECT choices *will* stick. You won't have to think about it—the pictures will emerge, organically and naturally. You'll even find that a strong INNER OBJECT choice will magnify your feelings.

Everyone has a wealth of significant experiences to call upon, and each and every experience has loads of pictures to match up. Most of us have fears to fill several volumes. Just look into your personal Pandora's box and you'll find good, strong INNER OBJECT choices.

Writing INNER OBJECT Choices on the Page: The Practical Application

To establish your INNER OBJECT choices, write in pencil so that you can erase if you change your mind (and you frequently will). Handwrite each INNER OBJECT choice directly beneath the word(s) that it's attached to.

To demonstrate how one applies INNER OBJECTS, let's look at how one of my students, Michael, personally utilized them in playing the role of Jack in Oscar Wilde's *The Importance of Being Earnest.* Here we have a story about two young men, Jack Worthing and Algernon Moncrieff. Jack and Algernon feel that their lives are dull, so they invent an imaginary brother, Ernest, as a way to escape the mundane and pursue excitement and romance. Jack uses the phantom "Ernest" as an excuse to leave his boring home in the country, which allows him to cavort in the city and spend time with his ladylove, Gwendolen. Because all lies tend to backfire, Jack and Algernon's deceptions cross paths, threatening Jack's relationship with Gwendolen.

THE IMPORTANCE OF BEING EARNEST
Oscar Wilde
(Act I, Scene 1)

[*Morning-room in Algernon's flat in Half-Moon Street. The room is luxuriously and artistically furnished. The sound of a piano is heard in the adjoining room.*]

[*ALGERNON enters*]

ALGERNON
How are you, my dear Ernest? What brings you
up to town?

JACK
Oh, pleasure, pleasure! What else should bring one
anywhere? Eating as usual, I see, Algy!

ALGERNON
[*Stiffly*]
I believe it is customary in good society to
take some slight refreshment at five o'clock.
Where have you been since last Thursday?

JACK
In the country.

ALGERNON
What on earth do you do there?

JACK
When one is in town one amuses oneself.
When one is in the country one amuses other
people. It is excessively boring.

ALGERNON
And who are the people you amuse?

JACK
[*Airily*]
Oh, neighbors, neighbors.

ALGERNON
Got nice neighbors in your part of Shropshire?

JACK
Perfectly horrid! Never speak to one of them.

ALGERNON
How immensely you must amuse them!
By the way, Shropshire is your county, is it not?

[ALGERNON takes a sandwich]

JACK
Eh? Shropshire? Yes, of course. Hallo! Why
all these cups? Why cucumber sandwiches? Why
such reckless extravagance in one so young?
Who is coming to tea?

ALGERNON
Oh! merely Aunt Augusta and Gwendolen.

JACK
How perfectly delightful!

ALGERNON
Yes, that is all very well; but I am afraid
Aunt Augusta won't quite approve of your being here.

JACK
May I ask why?

ALGERNON
My dear fellow, the way you flirt with Gwendolen
is perfectly disgraceful. It is almost as bad as the
way Gwendolen flirts with you.

JACK
I am in love with Gwendolen. I have come up to town
expressly to propose to her.

ALGERNON
I thought you had come up for pleasure? . . . I call
that business.

JACK
How utterly unromantic you are!

(and the scene continues)

As Jack, Michael's OVERALL OBJECTIVE was *"to get Gwendolen to
love me."* The SCENE OBJECTIVE was *"to get you* (Algernon) *to help me
get Gwendolen to love me."* Michael used as his SUBSTITUTION for Algernon his friend Tom, who is the one who initially introduced him to his
INNER OBJECT for Gwendolen (Samantha, the girl that Michael has an
unrequited passion for). Now, let's take this scene and write in Michael's
personal INNER OBJECTS under the words that require INNER OB-
JECTS, which will be underlined. It will be handwritten exactly how and
where you would write in the specific and personal INNER OBJECT
choices. Remember: INNER OBJECTS include the mental images of a

person, place, thing or event that you talk about or that you hear the other person talk about.

THE IMPORTANCE OF BEING EARNEST
Oscar Wilde
(Act I, Scene 1)

[*Morning-room in Algernon's flat in Half-Moon Street. The room is luxuriously and artistically furnished. The sound of a piano is heard in the adjoining room.*]

[*ALGERNON enters*]

ALGERNON
How are you, my dear <u>Ernest</u>? What brings you
Microstick (Michael's nickname, one
up to <u>town</u>?
he wishes to remain private and
Hollywood
between friends)

JACK
Oh, <u>pleasure, pleasure</u>! What else should bring one
Sex, drugs and rock and roll
anywhere? <u>Eating</u> as usual, I see, Algy!
Drinking whiskey

ALGERNON
[*Stiffly*]
I believe it is customary in <u>good society</u> to
Good friends
take some <u>slight refreshment at five o'clock</u>.
drink alcohol at 5 p.m.
Where have you been since last Thursday?

JACK
In the <u>country</u>.
Van Nuys (the Valley)

ALGERNON
What on earth do you do there?

JACK
When one is in <u>town</u> one amuses oneself.
Hollywood
When one is in the country one amuses <u>other</u>
<u>people</u>. It is <u>excessively boring</u>.   *suburbanites*
bowling and eating at Denny's

ALGERNON
And who are the <u>people you amuse</u>?
suburbanites

JACK
[*Airily*]
Oh, neighbors, neighbors.
boring families, no single people

ALGERNON
Got nice neighbors in your part of Shropshire?
families   the Valley

JACK
Perfectly horrid! Never speak to one of them.

ALGERNON
How immensely you must amuse them!
By the way, Shropshire is your county, is it not?
the Valley

[*ALGERNON takes a sandwich*]

JACK
Eh? Shropshire? Yes, of course. Hallo! Why
the Valley
all these cups? Why cucumber sandwiches? Why
plastic glasses   expensive Chivas Regal
such reckless extravagance in one so young?
Who is coming to tea?
For drinks

ALGERNON
Oh! merely Aunt Augusta and Gwendolen.
Kim (Samantha's best friend)   Samantha

JACK
How perfectly delightful!

ALGERNON
Yes, that is all very well; but I am afraid
Aunt Augusta won't quite approve of your being here.
Kim (who hates Michael)

JACK
May I ask why?

ALGERNON
My dear fellow, the way you flirt with Gwendolen
Samantha
is perfectly disgraceful. It is almost as bad as the
way Gwendolen flirts with you.

JACK

I am in love with <u>Gwendolen</u>. I have come up to <u>town</u>
               Samantha   *Hollywood (where she lives)*
expressly <u>to propose to her</u>.
      Ask Samantha to be girlfriend

ALGERNON

I thought you had come up for <u>pleasure</u>? . . . I call
that <u>business</u>.   *random sex*
   stupid

JACK

How utterly unromantic you are!

(and the scene continues)

As Michael was working on the scene for class, he found that some
INNER OBJECTS were effective and some were less effective. After
each rehearsal with his scene partner, he changed the less effective ones
to try ones that he thought might work better. Your work isn't done until
you've either finished shooting or the theatrical run is over. There are always new places you can go that will change and improve your work.
Acting is an infinite experience, there's always something more to learn
and more to experiment with. It's not over 'til the fat lady sings, and in
art, the fat lady has laryngitis.

CHAPTER 6

Tool #6:

BEATS AND ACTIONS

A *BEAT* is a thought change. ACTIONS are mini-OBJECTIVES attached to each BEAT. BEATS and ACTIONS are the various approaches one takes to achieve the SCENE OBJECTIVE.

Whenever a thought changes in the script, a BEAT changes.

Put a bracket around each [BEAT] to indicate when one BEAT ends and the next BEAT begins. How many BEATS are there in this dialogue?

> "Why did you hurt me the way you did?
> No, don't answer that . . . I know. Because you
> don't care, ya never did. And you know what?
> I don't care either. I don't care twice as much
> as you! So there!"

There are three BEATS:

> ["Why did you hurt me the way you did?]
> [No, don't answer that . . . I know. Because you
> don't care, ya never did.] [And you know what?
> I don't care either. I don't care twice as much
> as you! So there!"]

A BEAT can be one word, one line, or even as much as a page of dialogue. The criterion for a BEAT change is when the dialogue indicates a new thought. As with all of these acting tools, there are no absolutes. What will seem like a BEAT (thought) change in your initial script analysis might change when you are saying the words out loud. And the BEAT change might differ depending upon how the other actor(s) are responding to you. Always be open to the possibility of changing up the

BEATS. Staying open and being available to other choices will keep you present and raw. Think of BEAT analysis as an outline for you to draw from, a foundation you can use as a solid base to make the natural, in-the-moment adjustments that will arise in the heat of the live action.

ACTIONS are mini-OBJECTIVES, the different* approaches *you take to most effectively achieve your SCENE OBJECTIVE. ACTIONS are accomplished both verbally and behaviorally.

BEATS and ACTIONS produce a distinction between the various tactics you take to accomplish your SCENE OBJECTIVE. In other words, BEATS and ACTIONS are mini-OBJECTIVES. They are more precisely worded than your SCENE OBJECTIVE and must support the forward motion necessary *to win* your SCENE OBJECTIVE.

If my SCENE OBJECTIVE is *"to get you to give me a job,"* there are many ways I can go about getting you to want to do that. With words and behavior, the ACTION for a first BEAT may be *"to make you laugh."* With words and behavior, the ACTION for a second BEAT could be *"to impress you with my resume."* With words and behavior, the ACTION for a third BEAT might be *"to amaze you with my intelligence."* With words and behavior, the ACTION for a fourth BEAT could be *"to get you to trust me."*

Working with BEATS and ACTIONS allows me to go after my SCENE OBJECTIVE with specificity and a range of behaviors. BEATS and ACTIONS give the scene variation and diversity, not only affecting how you say the words, but also your behavior. As you go after a BEAT and ACTION verbally, you'll find that your body feels compelled to join in the pursuit. Thus behavior is formed.

Like the SCENE OBJECTIVE, BEATS and ACTIONS have to be worded to elicit a reaction, to affect the other person, not just to talk *at* them.

Using BEATS and ACTIONS to affect the other person allows you to work moment-to-moment. Without the need to change or affect another person, it's easy to fall into the trap of memorizing a way of being. This is not particularly human. You want to duplicate the part of your life that is unconscious, unintentional and unplanned, because this will produce unpredictable, spontaneous results.

BEATS and ACTIONS allow you to be present and authentic.

When you are going after a BEAT and ACTION to get a reaction, it can't be planned. You not only have no way of knowing how you're going to say it (because you are focused on the other person rather than yourself), but you also have no idea how the other person is going to react or how *you* are going to react to that person's reaction, and then their reaction to your reaction. As a result, life—rather than a simulation of life—is allowed to take place.

> ### *Your need for a reaction from the other person*
> ### *(BEAT and ACTION)*
> ### *empowers that person, because it makes the*
> ### *other person feel necessary and important.*

If you don't require a reaction from the other actor(s), you diminish them and weaken your ability to win your SCENE OBJECTIVE. Almost everyone has had the experience of being at a party where someone comes up to you and says, "Hey, how ya doin'?" But they don't really look at you or wait for your answer. Instead, they continue on their way or glance around the room looking for other party guests who might be more important/sexy/interesting than you to talk to. How does this make you feel? Bad, inconsequential, almost like you're not really there, right? This is exactly how you cause another actor (or a casting director in an audition) to feel when you throw a line at them and don't really care how they respond.

Using the same speech we broke down into BEATS, let's play with a few associated ACTION possibilities:

> ["Why did you hurt me the way you did?]
>
> [No, don't answer that . . . I know. Because you don't care, ya never did.]
>
> [And you know what? I don't care either. I don't care twice as much as you! So there!"]

Here are some possible BEAT and ACTION choices, staying true to the needs of the SCENE OBJECTIVE, *"to get you to stay with me"*:

- FIRST BEAT: "Why did you hurt me the way you did?"
  Action: *to get you to help me understand*
  Or: *to get you to comfort me*
  Or: *to make you feel guilty*

- SECOND BEAT: "No, don't answer that . . . I know. Because you don't care, ya never did."
  Action: *to get you to calm me down*
  Or: *to get you to admit that I'm right*
  Or: *to tell me it's not true*
- THIRD BEAT: "And you know what? I don't care either. I don't care twice as much as you! So there!"
  Action: *to make you feel my pain*
  Or: *to challenge you to "one up" me*
  Or: *to scare you into thinking it's "over"*

These BEAT and ACTION choices are all worded to get a reaction, so that you can establish interaction with the other person and, thus, a relationship. The wording gives you a way to make the other person your focal point and keeps you from being self-conscious and self-indulgent.

Read the above lines again, but this time recite them out loud, trying each BEAT and ACTION choice for the dialogue.

See how much the way you say the line and your behavior changes upon each BEAT and ACTION choice? And the above choices are just a few possibilities. There are many different ways that you could specifically accomplish the SCENE OBJECTIVE of *"to get you to stay with me."*

The following examples express the same sentiments, but do not demand a response. These are far less effective.

- FIRST BEAT: "Why did you hurt me the way you did?"
  Action: *I want to understand*
  Or: *I feel sad*
  Or: *I think you're guilty*
- SECOND BEAT: "No, don't answer that . . . I know. Because you don't care, ya never did."
  Action: *to be calm*
  Or: *I believe I'm right*
  Or: *I don't want to believe this*
- THIRD BEAT: "And you know what? I don't care either. I don't care twice as much as you! So there!"
  Action: *to feel pain*
  Or: *I feel challenged*
  Or: *It's over!*

These are feelings, not BEATS and ACTIONS. Feelings do not provoke a reaction. With this phrasing, you don't need another person to interact with. You can have these feelings by yourself. Phrasing your ACTIONS as inactive feelings causes an introspective result as well as a reality that has no goal, need or desire for human interaction. Consequently, no movement and no relationship is being established.

ACTIONS Have the Power to Change Meaning and Intention

This gives you the freedom to discover more interesting and unique ways of being and speaking the dialogue. Without BEATS and ACTIONS, you are likely to make an obvious, literal reading. Take the sentence, "I hate you" and use it as dialogue. On its own, the intention seems clear enough. But let's look at what happens when we switch the BEAT and ACTION up. Try saying, "I hate you,"

"To make you laugh."

Different than you originally thought? Now say it:

"To get you to admit guilt."

It has an entirely alternate meaning now. Okay, now say it:

"To get you to comfort me."

You get the idea. The BEAT and ACTION you choose will determine what you're trying to communicate, regardless of the actual words. The BEAT and ACTION make the meaning of the words change drastically. Have you ever said "I love you" when what you really wanted to do (BEAT and ACTION) was to get that person to have sex with you? Compare that line-reading to the time you've said "I love you" and what you wanted to accomplish (BEAT and ACTION) was to get the other person to say "I love you" back. Or the time when "I love you" meant you wanted the other person "to laugh at the absurdity of it all" (BEAT and ACTION). So you can see why, if an actor plays "I hate you" or "I love you" using obvious, black-and-white ideas of "I hate you" or "I love you," they miss out on and lose all the other possibilities—the shades of gray—that exist between the black and white. The gray area is literally and figuratively blank and begs for interpretation that is inspired by specific BEAT and ACTION choices.

***Ask yourself, "What do I want to win (SCENE OBJECTIVE)?
And how is the best, most effective way (both verbally and
behaviorally) to achieve it (BEATS and ACTIONS)?"***

The ACTIONS must support the SCENE OBJECTIVE to create a focused thread that weaves throughout the entire scene. The more you go
after trying to win your SCENE OBJECTIVE, BEAT by BEAT, ACTION to
ACTION (using different approaches and tactics in both speech and
physicalization), and the more you find that you are *not* winning your
SCENE OBJECTIVE, the more you'll be driven to try harder. This causes
a crescendo to the arc you're creating in the scene. You also have to
make the other character *want* to give you your SCENE OBJECTIVE, by
making the most effective choices for BEATS and ACTIONS.

Jennifer Beals kept this in mind and got compelling results when we
worked on one particular scene in an episode of the Showtime series *The
L Word*. *The L Word* is a series about lesbian women and all the inevitable
trials and traumas they face in a world filled with homophobia and intol-
erance. In one scene, Jennifer's character, Bette, is a guest on a talk show,
and she's engaged in a heated debate with Faye Buckley, this episode's
nemesis. Faye abusively argues that Bette's art exhibition is pornographic.
At the end of the scene, the character of Faye takes it too far and hits below the belt by using personal information about Bette, exclaiming,

> "The Bible condemns homosexuality, Bette. That's why God took
> your lesbian lover's unborn child. The baby will be spared all the
> degradation he would have been subject to if he had been born
> into your deviant lifestyle. That baby is lucky he was never born."

Bette retaliates by calling Faye a "monster" and by exposing a video
of Faye's teenage daughter performing in an adult film, a film that Faye
has done everything to keep under wraps. The ACTION for the BEAT when
Bette says "monster" and reveals the video on camera could be vindictive. But Bette's SCENE OBJECTIVE is *"to make you* (the viewing audience) *take my side over Fae."* If Bette were to act maliciously and
spitefully, she would seem cruel. The most effective way for her to win
her SCENE OBJECTIVE was to rise above Faye's caustic words. We used
the ACTION for this BEAT, *"to help you* [Faye] *understand your cruelty,"*
as she gently said "monster" (instead of the obvious, on-the-nose, and
very ineffectual explosion of anger), and then compassionately slid the
video across the table for Faye to see. If Bette were to respond vindic-

tively, she would not be sympathetic to her audience. By using this BEAT and ACTION, Jennifer made her character of Bette empathetic, a person whose side we, as the television viewing audience, would gladly take.

Apply BEATS and ACTIONS to Nonverbal Moments

In an argument with your lover, you might stomp angrily out the door, slamming it behind you. Even though no words are spoken, you are still going after a BEAT and ACTION: *"to get you to stop me from leaving."* More often than not, the harder and more violently you slam the door, the more you want the other person to follow you out the door and stop you, which would prove that the other person loves you. This makes the BEAT and ACTION, *"to get you to stop me from leaving,"* support the bigger picture of the SCENE OBJECTIVE: *"to get you to prove you love me."*

Or the stage directions say that you are getting ready for bed with irritation and annoyance . . . within the framework of a SCENE OBJECTIVE of *"to make you take the blame."* The BEAT and ACTION could be *"to make you admit you feel guilty,"* or *"to make you feel my pain,"* or *"to get you to calm me down."*

There's a lot we can attempt to win through using BEATS and ACTIONS.

> *Even when the other actor is speaking,*
> *your BEATS and ACTIONS should never stop.*

When you are listening you still need to make sense of what you want from the other character—*with or without words.* When you stop talking and the other person is speaking, you must continue to attempt to get the desired reACTION with behavior. Your needs don't stop just because your words do!

> *There are no right or wrong choices, just more effective*
> *or less effective ones.*

You Must Consider Your Character's Modus Operandi, the "Who-Am-I"

Keep in mind the "who-am-I" of your character, the specific M.O. of how your character would be most effective in winning the SCENE OB-

JECTIVE. A seductress or player generally wins a goal (SCENE OBJEC-TIVE) by using his or her sexuality. An intellectual generally wins a goal (SCENE OBJECTIVE) by using mind games and his or her intelligence. A class-clown type is going to use humor as his M.O. to win. A mobster, fighter, or gang member type would use violence and aggression to get his way. In other words, always keep in mind *who* the character is and *how* they generally operate in life when making specific BEAT and AC-TION choices.

I worked with Jon Voight on the movie *A Dog of Flanders*, where he played a father figure to a boy who believed he was an orphan. Until the end of the film, Jon's character does not know that he is the boy's bio-logical father. The boy's mother died before she had a chance to tell him. To help the audience accept the story's ending, Jon used every opportu-nity to show the audience that he was and could be paternal with the boy. Within the spoken dialogue, he used BEATS and ACTIONS like *"to make you feel safe," "to get you to believe in yourself," "to make you feel protected," "to impress you with my loyalty"* and *"to make you feel loved."* These BEATS and ACTIONS helped serve as a kind of bookend for the movie. When he and the audience finally discover his character's paternity, they can accept it. Due to his BEATS and ACTIONS, his being the biological father made sense.

You Must Consider the Other Character's Modus Operandi, the "Who-Are-They"

You also have to consider the type of person the other character is, which will help you determine *how* to get what you want. The other character might be someone who uses their intellect to get what they want in life. You have to attempt to appeal to that person on their playing field, be-cause they're more likely to give you what you want if they're getting what *they* want.

Your BEAT and ACTION Choices Should Be Focused and Driven

All your ACTION choices should come from the feeling of having a proverbial gun to your head. Because you're taking risks with your

OVERALL OBJECTIVE, SCENE OBJECTIVE, OBSTACLES, SUBSTITU-TION and INNER OBJECTS, the stakes should be personally very high for you. And, when the stakes are high, as you know, every little thing that you do or say is important. Nothing is ever a throwaway. Every *how*, *why* or *what* means something. Imagine making a throwaway comment while someone is holding a gun to your head. It wouldn't happen. Every remark, every move counts when you're trying to save your life. Every scene should be about trying to resolve, overcome and accomplish something that is extremely valuable or meaningful to you, too. Your BEATS and ACTIONS must complement and further the realization of an extremely important goal (SCENE OBJECTIVE). This infuses your work with the power of a life-and-death struggle. That means you can't discount any moment or call anything irrelevant. Everything you say or do should advance the accomplishment of your goal, making the use of BEATS and ACTIONS imperative for the entire script.

> **Don't go after your BEATS and ACTIONS as though they
> are a list of things to be accomplished, performing one after
> the other like a runaway train.**

With words and behavior, consciously pursue the BEAT and ACTION. Determine whether or not you have provoked the desired reaction or not. Take in your emotional response to winning or losing that BEAT and ACTION to fuel your response, and then go after your next BEAT and ACTION. Repeat this process—BEAT and ACTION to BEAT and ACTION, response to response—until you walk off the stage or the director says, "Cut."

For instance, say you're telling a joke and, obviously, your ACTION for that BEAT would clearly be *"to make you laugh."* Think of all the possible reactions that can happen to the BEAT and ACTION of *"to make you laugh"*—a patronizing laugh, a forced laugh, a smirk, a voiced "ha-ha, that's so funny I forgot to laugh," etc. You will have a different emotional reaction depending upon *how the other person responds* to your BEAT and ACTION. If the other person laughs you'll feel great inside, if the other person doesn't, then you might feel terrible. It's important to go after your BEAT and ACTION and then see what kind of reaction you're getting, feel it (the good and the bad) and then respond accordingly.

Working to get a reACTION keeps you out of your head and in the moment.

When you are deeply focused on getting a reACTION from the other person, it's difficult to watch yourself and set or preplan a way of saying and performing the dialogue. This creates spontaneity. Just think about those really high-stakes moments in your life, a situation when you wanted something so badly that you could just taste it. Remember how concentrated you were on the other person's (the person who could give you what you wanted) response. Every blink, sideways glance, inflection, diction, body language was interpreted, reinterpreted and retold to be interpreted yet again by your friends. You were hyperaware of everything they said or did. You need to be in the same state when you are acting.

You can repeat a BEAT and ACTION in the scene.

For example, you're trying to get someone to have sexual relations with you. Your SCENE OBJECTIVE would be *"to get you to have sex with me."* Breaking down the dialogue of the scene into BEATS and ACTIONS, you could look at a typical first-date BEAT and ACTION as being *"to turn you on."* The second ACTION for the second BEAT might be *"to impress you with my sexual prowess."* The third ACTION for the third BEAT might be *"to get you to trust me"* and the fourth ACTION for the fourth BEAT could very well be *"to turn you on"* again.

Try different BEATS and ACTIONS in rehearsal to identify the best ones.

As with many of the tools, do not intellectually determine your BEATS and ACTIONS. Let me repeat: Acting is a physical art form that requires you to experiment out loud and on your feet. You will not know what the most effective BEATS and ACTIONS are until you test drive them and discover whether or not they effectively propel your SCENE OBJECTIVE forward.

BEATS and ACTIONS Realize the Words

When we first began working together on *The Larry Sanders Show,* one of my first notes to Garry Shandling was that he had to make his work more physical. Garry rose up the Hollywood ranks as a stand-up comedian. This means that, as a performer, he was used to relying on the words to be funny. But I pointed out to him, as I do to all of my clients, that what usually makes us laugh is not what someone says, but what someone *does.* BEATS and ACTIONS not only serve the dialogue, but also create behavior that goes along with it. When we walk out of the movies or the theater, we usually say, "I love the way so and so *did* something." It's rare when we comment, "I love the way so and so *said* a line."

One of the first exercises I did with him was to teach him how to physically realize a script's words. I did this by utilizing BEATS and AC-TIONS. We would pick a scene, and then we'd figure out what the AC-TION was to each BEAT. Next, I would read the cue line in the script and then he would behave the BEAT and ACTION, rather than saying the lines. Let's look at a scene from an episode of *Larry Sanders* called "Adolf Hankler." Larry (Garry Shandling) is talking to his producer, Arthur (Rip Torn), about his brother, Stan, who's coming to visit. Larry is leaving his network talk show, and Jon Stewart (ironically played by Jon Stewart) is supposed to take over. For a long time, Larry's show is his obsession—working sixteen-hour days, even his social life is geared around the show. Larry is panicked; he has no idea what he's going to do with his time after the show is over for him. He reaches out to family, to his brother, Stan, hoping he can get the love and support he so desperately needs now that he feels so displaced. Stan is an entrepreneur—well, he thinks he is. He's actually one of those pie-in-the-sky types whose moniker would be "The-One-Who-Always-Has-a-Stupid-Plan-That's-Supposed-to-Make-Me-Rich-But-Actually-Puts-Me-in-the-Poorhouse." Arthur is not only Larry's producer, but his best friend. He knows that Stan is up to no good, because he's always up to no good. In the following scene, Arthur tries to warn Larry to stay away from Stan, no matter how much he might need him emotionally.

Now let's take this scene and break it down into BEATS, indicated by brackets, and ACTIONS (mini-OBJECTIVES or tactics), which are always handwritten (in pencil) on the side to the right. This is so they will not be confused with the other tools that you'll also be writing on the page. These are possible ideas for BEATS and ACTIONS from Larry Sanders' point of view. These BEATS and ACTIONS are not etched in stone. Like all the tools, they can change upon your personal interpretation.

These particular BEATS and ACTIONS are geared toward driving the SCENE OBJECTIVE of *"to get you to help me feel better."*

Larry Sanders has just finished the show, and is walking offstage when his producer Arthur stops to compliment him . . .

THE LARRY SANDERS SHOW
EPISODE "Adolf Hankler"

ARTHUR
[Ahoy Captain Sanders! The U.S.S. Hilarity is now
safely in her berth.

make you laugh

LARRY
Has anyone ever told you you should wear a sailor's cap?

ARTHUR
Yeah, the late Rock Hudson.

LARRY
That's another conversation.]

ARTHUR
[So your brother Stan's coming to town?

get you to feel how desperate I am

LARRY
He's staying with me.]

ARTHUR
[Ah.

get you to stop judging me

LARRY
What's that supposed to mean?

ARTHUR
Oh nothing. Just practicing my Chinese.
(*beat*)
Just mail him a check?

LARRY
[Because I can use the company.

make you feel my pain

ARTHUR
My advice? If you want expensive companionship,
buy yourself a shar-pei.]

LARRY
[Then there'll be two of us drinking out of the toilet.]
make you laugh

When Garry and I rehearsed this scene, I cued him using Arthur's dialogue; then Garry would wordlessly, physically express the BEAT and ACTION, using the INNER OBJECTS we had previously selected. Notice that Larry Sanders' M.O. is to be a funny guy, so the ACTION of *"to make you laugh"* is repeated. Garry's physicalized version produced some very funny, comic behavior. Once he successfully realized the BEATS and ACTIONS through physicalization, we went back and ran the scene using BEATS and ACTIONS with the dialogue. This time, the behavior underlined the dialogue, making it twice as effective. BEATS and ACTIONS inspire an actor to physicalize the dialogue, making the experience more three-dimensional and relationship focused. The test for any good performance is to be able to cut the sound and still be able to laugh, cry and feel because the BEATS and ACTIONS reveal and drive the character's intentions.

Commit to Your BEATS and ACTIONS

Go after your ACTIONS boldly and without fear. Push the envelope. And don't be afraid to boldly realize your BEATS and ACTIONS. The more risks you take and the more fearless you are, the more exciting the end result will be.

I worked with Christian de la Fuente on his audition and then his role as Memo Moreno in the movie *Driven*. Christian is from Chile, and English is still very much a second language for him. Going after his BEATS and ACTIONS without reservation would make him more understandable, as well as more effective. When I coached him for his audition with Sly Stallone (Joe), I encouraged him to courageously commit to his BEATS and ACTIONS, no matter how foolish he felt he looked while doing it. Although the majority of the film focuses on a racing story, one of the film's subplots includes the fact that Memo is married to the character of Joe's ex-wife. In one particular scene, Memo has to deal with Joe, who is being adversarial. For Christian to play the scene by matching Joe's antagonism would be a weak choice. The saying "keep your friends close, your enemies closer" comes to mind. So, I gave him the SCENE OBJECTIVE of *"to get you to like me,"* because if Joe likes Memo, then he's less likely to sabotage his relationship with his wife. The scene included a lot of verbal sparring between Joe and Memo, including a moment where Memo says, "I want you to marry me." For this line, we used the BEAT and ACTION *"to make you laugh."* When Christian auditioned, he went up to Stallone, got down on one knee and said, "I want you to marry me." Then he took a ring off his finger and attempted to stuff it onto Stallone's ring finger, which was thicker than Christian's. Christian tried for a while, pushing and shoving his ring onto Sly's finger, but it just wasn't going to make it past the knuckle. Incredulously, Stallone looked down at the hapless Christian, who wasn't sure if what he was doing was annoying Stallone or, worse, making him angry. He persisted. Finally, after what felt like a million years, Stallone burst out laughing and exclaimed, "I like this guy!" Needless to say, he got the part. On set, Christian continued to make risky and fearless I-don't-care-if-I-look-stupid BEAT and ACTION choices. When the studio saw the dailies from the first few days, they offered him a two-picture deal.

Don't censor yourself.

Try anything that might seem even vaguely appropriate. You'll be surprised at the choices that work the best. Try different BEATS and ACTIONS in rehearsal to identify the best ones. As I've said many times thus far—you can't know unless you try it.

> *Consider what the character is **really** **trying to do**
> in accomplishing the SCENE OBJECTIVE.
> Read between the lines.*

You could be doing a scene where an angry couple is discussing a divorce. Just because your lines say you want to split up doesn't mean that's what your character really wants. As we saw earlier with the slamming door, more often than not, when we threaten to leave, we're really trying to get the other person to make us stay or prove in some way that they love us. Or you may be doing a scene in which your character is talking about how much they loved and respected some piece of literature. The truth is they may have never read the book or did read it and thought it was boring, but they're saying they liked it because they want to impress the other person with their brilliance, or simply to make the other person like them.

Elisabeth Shue's critically acclaimed work for an off-Broadway production of Lanford Wilson's *Burn This* is a great example of how to read between the lines. Supporting her character's SCENE OBJECTIVE of *"to make you prove that you love me (so I won't get hurt),"* here's a small excerpt of the script along with our notes, which will show you how we broke it down into BEATS and ACTIONS.

Remember: Bracket your BEATS and write your ACTIONS to the right side of the BEAT so you know exactly the words they connect to. There is not just one way of going after your SCENE OBJECTIVE. As long as you are being true to your SCENE OBJECTIVE, the who-am-I of your character, and the who-are-they of the other character, you can use any of the hundreds of possible BEAT and ACTION choices. The choices below are the ones we initially made. Depending upon how her co-star Peter Skarsgaard responded, she would change her BEATS and ACTIONS accordingly.

BURN THIS
by Lanford Wilson
(Excerpt from Act II)

(Anna's living room. It's late at night.)

ANNA
[Pale, I have never had a personal life. I wasn't scared of it, I just had no place for it, it wasn't important. And all that is different now and I'm very vulnerable,

impress you with my vulnerability

I'm not going to be prey to something I don't want. I'm too easy. Go someplace else.]

PALE
[I come to you.

make you beg to stay with me

ANNA
No, I said no. I don't want this. I'm not
strong enough to kick you out physically.]
[Why are you being so damned truculent? I said I don't
like you. I don't want to know you. I don't want
make you sexually "want" me
to see you again. There is no reason for you to
come here. I have nothing for you. I don't like
you and I'm frightened of you.]

Even though the words *say* that Anna wants him to leave, the truth is that she wants Pale to stay. Too fragile and damaged by a tragedy that takes place earlier in the script, Anna needs to test Pale by pushing him away. If he stays, no matter how abusive she is, then that is proof that he really loves her. If Elisabeth were to just play these lines using a literal, black-and-white interpretation of the script, then she actually would be trying to get rid of this man. But Elisabeth knew that her character needed love as well as a stepping-stone to get her character to the end of the script where Anna and Pale profess an intense love for each other.

Your BEAT and ACTION approaches must support the character's SCENE OBJECTIVE, which supports the OVERALL OBJECTIVE. In Elisabeth's case, the SCENE OBJECTIVE for this particular scene in *Burn This* was *"to make you prove that you love me,"* which supported her character's OVERALL OBJECTIVE of *"to find passion in my life again."*

Look at BEATS and ACTIONS as a subset of SCENE OBJECTIVE, and SCENE OBJECTIVE as the subset of your OVERALL OBJECTIVE.

Seeing them this way, you can see how they make sense and fit together. They must drive an overall journey for the entire story.

Now that you have found the best way to put forward motion to the story in the scene, you have to understand *how* and *why* you got there in the first place. This is taken care of by using the MOMENT BEFORE.

CHAPTER 7

Tool #7:

MOMENT BEFORE

The event that happens before you begin the scene gives you a place to come from, both physically and emotionally.

The right MOMENT BEFORE will drive your SCENE OBJECTIVE, inspiring great need and urgency. There are three questions you must ask yourself when looking for your MOMENT BEFORE:

1. **What do I want?:** SCENE OBJECTIVE.
2. **Why do I want it so badly?:** OBSTACLES, SUBSTITUTION, and INNER OBJECTS. Your OBSTACLES, SUBSTITUTION, and INNER OBJECTS provide you with a need to win your SCENE OBJECTIVE.
3. **Why do I want it so badly right now?:** MOMENT BEFORE. The MOMENT BEFORE increases your need to win your SCENE OBJECTIVE by giving it *urgency* and *immediacy.* In other words, the MOMENT BEFORE provides the scene with the idea and pressures of *time.*

The MOMENT BEFORE ramps up your need to win your SCENE OBJECTIVE immediately. Whether you are playing a heated sex scene or having a verbal or physical battle, the MOMENT BEFORE is the tool that moves you into the appropriate urgent mental, physical and emotional space for the scene. Additionally, the MOMENT BEFORE gives you a place to begin because, like life, a scene never starts from ground zero. The MOMENT BEFORE helps you know *why* and *where* you're coming from and *how* badly you presently need your SCENE OBJECTIVE.

It's important to know that a scene doesn't begin where it begins in a

script. There is an assumed or implied event that has occurred to motivate the text. The practice of using a MOMENT BEFORE makes the on-
the-page scene become a continuation of an ongoing interaction rather
than the beginning of one. The MOMENT BEFORE allows you to treat
every scene as if you are already in the thick of it.

In a play, an actor will use the MOMENT BEFORE directly before the
curtain goes up, an act changes, and at the points where he leaves the
stage for a time and then returns.

The MOMENT BEFORE is an even more crucial tool for actors working in film and television, because more often than not, scenes are shot
out of order and as separate entities. For instance, the last scene of the
movie—the one where the wife dies in her husband's arms—may be the
first scene you have to shoot. The MOMENT BEFORE, in conjunction
with the other work you've done—OVERALL OBJECTIVE, SCENE OB-
JECTIVE, OBSTACLES, SUBSTITUTION, INNER OBJECTS, BEATS and
ACTIONS—will make it possible for you to have the heightened emotions and behaviors required for the scene.

Using the MOMENT BEFORE is also essential for film and television
scenes because they're generally quite short. You simply don't have the
time to start from nothing and build to a crescendo with less than three
pages of dialogue. To keep the tension high with material connected by
many short scenes, you must start each scene from an emotionally
charged place.

Furthermore, due to the slow physical process of filmmaking, there
are frequent delays. The MOMENT BEFORE is an essential tool for film
work because it enables you to get back into character whenever you
need to. The MOMENT BEFORE is the key to effectively and efficiently
reestablish the needs of your character and their predicament.

APPLYING THE MOMENT BEFORE

1. Determine what personal event will produce a high-stakes need.
   (We'll discuss how to determine and choose the best event next.)
2. Just before the director says, "Action!" or right before you walk on
   stage, give yourself about a minute to relive the personal event
   you've chosen. Think about it as if the event has just happened.
3. To relive the event, remember every detail. Think about the
   space—visualize what it looked, felt and smelled like, and what the
   other person looked, felt and smelled like; hear the actual words

you and he/she used; and feel your actions and reactions viscerally. Essentially, refeel it with all your senses. Let this reliving put you in a heightened emotional and physical state.

Applying the MOMENT BEFORE should never take more than a minute.

If it does, then you've picked the wrong event as your MOMENT BE-FORE. Your personal event choice for a MOMENT BEFORE must affect you easily and immediately. Many actors will spend hours trying to pump up the appropriate emotions to keep themselves in the proper head-space for the scene. If it is a highly charged, emotional scene, the actor may spend those hours trying to work up the memories of "the day their dog died." This way of working is not only draining for an actor, but also generates a huge mushroom cloud of feelings when the director finally calls "Action!" or the curtain goes up. And just like an explosion, it erupts quickly and then dissipates just as quickly. The resulting performance is vague for two reasons. First, a performance fueled by unrelated emotions will not be script motivated. This is problematic because when the feelings are unrelated to the story and the needs of your character there's no through-line or direction for the emotions to go. Second, pumped-up emotions don't last very long—particularly if they are not grounded by what's happening in the script. Unless we human beings have the gravity of an event pressing on us, pinning us to our pain, our bodies instinctively move away or shut down when there is pain. A story-driven MOMENT BEFORE event will keep the appropriate feelings going throughout the scene because it's related to the material and makes logical sense to the story being told. Also, artificially inflated feelings don't allow for the emotions to naturally build and evolve the way they do in life. If you use the first six tools and choose an effective MOMENT BE-FORE, it allows for all the details, subtleties and layers of emotion that real people display.

Always use personal events for your MOMENT BEFORE that are recent or based on past events where the issues remain unresolved—the lack of resolution keeps your feelings percolating in your heart and your mind.

Don't use an event that has been resolved. Knowing the outcome to an event, being aware of exactly how it's all going to turn out, doesn't inspire movement. It only creates regurgitated feelings. When choosing your MOMENT BEFORE event, it's important to think about what's going to motivate you to win. Using an event that you have anything less than a burning need to resolve undermines your fight to win your OVERALL and SCENE OBJECTIVES. If you use issues that are current, you won't need to emotionally stew for long periods of time, because you'll be trying to overcome a problem that you are living with every day and is therefore emotionally available to you. Likewise, there may be an experience you had a long time ago but have not had closure or resolution on. This event, for all intents and purposes, can be considered a present event because it remains unresolved in your heart and mind. The repercussions of the event and your burning need for its resolution make the event a viable and powerful MOMENT BEFORE choice. Using something that deals with a current life issue as your MOMENT BEFORE wipes away the need to play mind games with yourself or to arbitrarily dig deep to get to that place that you ceased to care about long ago.

**The only way to know if the feelings for an event
are resolved is to try it using the MOMENT BEFORE.**

Sometimes we think we have resolved an issue when in fact, lurking around in the dark corners of our mind, it continues to reside in a land I like to call *denial*, which is essentially the subconscious working overtime so that we don't have to deal with something that our brains and hearts deem too painful. Sometimes we'd like to think we're over someone or something because we need to feel that we are. My experience has found that, more often than not, the emotional residue of painful events lingers in our subconscious for decades. You'll only know if a MOMENT BEFORE event is unresolved and usable by trying it.

Recently, I had to come up with a MOMENT BEFORE for a film audition for Beyoncé Knowles that would make her feel the emotions that erupt when a sister commits suicide. These feelings include guilt, helplessness, anger, sadness and a need to resolve an event that is rarely resolvable. Often, when I'm trying to come up with answers to any of the tools for a student, I try to figure out what I would use given *my* life's circumstances. It helps me make sense of the character and also helps to jog my student's mind, inspiring them to think of a parallel or similar event in their lives. Beyoncé's character's situation reminded me of my father's death. He died more than ten years ago, and with the help of therapy and some deep soul searching, I had moved on and was over it . . . or so I thought. As I was going over the dialogue with Beyoncé, images of my father on his deathbed kept emerging. I told her that if I were doing this part I would try to use my father's death, but it probably wouldn't work because I had closure on it. As I was telling her how successful I was in overcoming my trauma, tears began to fall. I was wrong— apparently, my solid emotional health was being overshadowed by the all-encompassing and painful thoughts surrounding the fact that my father had never told me that he loved me. Which made me question if he ever really did. His death made it impossible for me to ever know, because death, being what it is, tends to limit one's ability to speak. By trying this as a MOMENT BEFORE, I became aware that I actually haven't resolved my feelings surrounding this event, and that truthfully, I probably never will.

As with all the tools, don't be afraid to change your MOMENT BEFORE choices. In the arts, change is inherent because interpretation is infinite.

You'll often come up with a great and powerful MOMENT BEFORE, but then something extreme occurs—someone unexpectedly dies, you have a car accident, you get dumped by your mate of ten years, you find out that your girlfriend's pregnant, you get fired and so on. Extreme changes in your life will be what is on your mind. The poignancy of the MOMENT BEFORE choice you've already made is weakened by the present, more pressing event. If this happens, change your MOMENT BEFORE to the tumultuous event that's just occurred.

One of my students, Susan, was doing a scene in class from Woody Allen's *Hannah and Her Sisters*. The scene opens with Holly, Hannah's sister, running into Hannah's ex-husband, Mickey, at a record store. Holly, an ex-actress turned screenwriter, asks Mickey, a television writer, if he will help her with her script. After many jibes at her expense, he agrees.

Susan performed the scene for the class. Her first run was lifeless because her MOMENT BEFORE event wasn't motivating her needs and feelings for the scene. The other problem was that her version of the scene—a Woody Allen scene—wasn't funny. And that's not good. I asked Susan what she was using, and she related to me a light event, because she had assumed that one should use light choices in humorous material. That's when I knew she was really on the wrong track. The truth of comedy is that the inner choices an actor makes must be more desperate, painful, angry and darker than drama! So I asked Susan what was going on in her life that would drive her to be more desperate and angry. She tearfully confessed that she had been violently carjacked a few nights before. She was mildly bruised, but her husband was critically injured. This event was so traumatizing that they were considering moving away from Los Angeles to safer shores. But the decision to leave L.A. meant that she would have to give up her dreams of pursuing an acting career. Her pressing dilemma was that she needed help to make the decision whether she should stay in Los Angeles, continue to follow her dreams and live in a constant state of fear, or leave, give up and feel safe.

The carjacking as a MOMENT BEFORE was a great choice because it was unresolved and wrought with repercussions that could conceivably be life-changing. This MOMENT BEFORE also allowed Susan to use her need to get help about whether she should move or not as her INNER OBJECT for Holly's need to get help on her screenplay. We had to also change her SUBSTITUTION for the character of Mickey to a friend who was a V.I.P. in the film business. All of this work heightened the personal stakes for Susan and her character. She ran the scene again. This time, when Holly asked Mickey for help with her writing, Susan felt like she was asking for help with her decision to stay or go from someone who she trusted would know the best answer. Changing the MOMENT BEFORE event to one that was more currently significant— which changed her INNER OBJECTS and SUBSTITUTION—allowed Susan to tell a linear story for both her inner and outer work. Her new MOMENT BEFORE choice also provided an edge and urgency to the scene and drove Susan to go after her SCENE OBJECTIVE of *"to get you to love and help me"* as if her life depended on it, because it did. And the laughs that were so sorely missing in the first run of the scene were plentiful in the rework.

Using "WHAT IF" Circumstances

If your life is pretty steady—there's nothing particularly pressing happening—and you can't come up with an unresolved past event that appropriately affects you, don't try to make more out of a present event than there is or try to use some past event that you've ceased to care about. Instead, use a WHAT IF event based on a real fear. A WHAT IF event is what it sounds like: an imagined experience born out of a deep-seated, well-founded personal fear. To use a WHAT IF event as your

MOMENT BEFORE, you imagine all the details of an event that *could* happen as if it *has* happened. For instance, if a loved one is terminally ill, then you could use your feelings—the fear, anger, sadness—to imagine and picture what it will be like when they actually die. Or, if you feel your job is in jeopardy but you haven't yet been fired, you can still imagine the event—the boss calling you into her office, sitting you down, getting cold sweats, not having a way to pay your bills, becoming homeless, etc.

When using a WHAT IF circumstance as your MOMENT BEFORE, it must be based on a real, plausible fear that is personal to you.

If you don't fear your mother's death because she's in good health, then you can't use her death as a WHAT IF event because it's too implausible for you to suspend disbelief. This is not an effective WHAT IF fear. It's too far-fetched for your psyche and imagination to latch on to. Although, if a fear is well founded, the possibility of the event manifesting itself is often more intimidating and powerful than actual events, because we have no idea how they are going to turn out. And, as you know, we always imagine the worst. It's part of being human. People are paranoid creatures and we gravitate toward the negative. But ironically, our negative tendencies and fears often produce a positive result in acting by providing us with weightier and more powerful MOMENT BEFORE events. The MOMENT BEFORE event must have a germ of possibility, and even better, the odds of probability.

Amy Smart had a particularly difficult role in the movie *The Butterfly Effect*. The film tells the story of Evan Treborn (played by Ashton Kutcher), who tries to recover his memory by traveling to his past. But every time he changes something about his past, it changes his present reality. Amy plays the character of Kayleigh Miller, Evan's childhood friend and love interest. As a result, each time Evan changes something in his past, it affects Kayleigh's life, too—who she is as a person, her life events, her memories. As the result of one of his trips into his past—in which Evan abandons young Kayleigh after he discovers that she was being molested by her father—Kayleigh becomes a prostitute and a heroin addict. In one particular scene that explores this prostitute-addict scenario, an older Evan runs into the older Kayleigh and sees how destroyed her life is. Evan knows it's his fault and tries to fix it. Amy and I came up with the SCENE OBJECTIVE of *"to make you take the blame,"* not only so her character doesn't have to take responsibility for her predicament, but because it is, after all, his fault.

We needed a good MOMENT BEFORE for this scene. Something that would not only duplicate Kayleigh's damaged persona, but that would include the pain and abandonment caused by someone she once loved very much. We had to find something in Amy's life that would parallel this kind of pain, so she could become Kayleigh.

Needless to say, Amy is not a prostitute or a drug addict. Primal abandonment issues were not available to her because Amy has a terrific relationship with her happily married parents. The only painful thing we could identify was that Amy and her longtime boyfriend had split up right before the movie began to shoot. But it wasn't anything huge that had happened; in fact, they got back together soon after the film wrapped. So we needed to use a WHAT IF as her MOMENT BEFORE.

It's natural in any split-up to fear that you are dispensable and easily replaced. Most people fear that their estranged mate is bound to find someone else and that sex is likely to happen. Even though there was no real issue of Amy's boyfriend having sexual liaisons with anyone else, the fear that he might be was real. It *could* be happening. As a result of this organic fear that she was feeling, we came up with her MOMENT BEFORE: WHAT IF she found out that her boyfriend was with someone else? Amy then made the fear real to her by picturing it happening— actually visualizing her boyfriend in sexual congress with a girl. She became upset, angry, and felt betrayed and abandoned. Her MOMENT BEFORE made her feel inordinately ugly, replaceable, hurt beyond repair and needy of relief from the pain (giving her the reality of a heroin addict). With this WHAT IF MOMENT BEFORE, sweet, even-tempered Amy became a foulmouthed, in-your-face, drug-addled whore.

> *Or you can take a real event from the past—a rape, abuse,*
> *violence, or abandonment event—but instead of trying to*
> *re-create the past event, imagine the same event*
> *happening again, a second time, right now.*

In other words, WHAT IF it were to happen again? Imagining a traumatic event happening yet again is an effective choice to use for your MOMENT BEFORE. It works on two levels. First, as we saw with my student Susan, who was carjacked, traumatic events cause us to live with a profound fear of the event happening again. Traumatic events will always live in our minds in vivid detail, along with the constant apprehension that it could come to pass once again. Working with this ever-present fear makes this WHAT IF MOMENT BEFORE event accessible and intense. Second, imagining WHAT IF it happens again, *now*, makes the MOMENT BEFORE present. You know how it turned out last time, but a second time leaves you with other possible repercussions. Why? Essentially, the second time becomes an entirely new event, because you're a different person now, and the differences are informed by the original trauma—you may be more leery and less naive now. This gives you great OBSTACLES to overcome, because if it happens again, it might just be your fault for being a magnet to your personal trauma, a self-saboteur. This kind of MOMENT BEFORE drives you to especially need to accomplish your SCENE OBJECTIVE because there's so much at stake.

When he was thirteen, one of my well-known students was repeatedly molested by his babysitter. At one point in his career, he came to me to prepare to play the role of a serial rapist without a conscience. He needed a MOMENT BEFORE that would give him a sense that he wasn't actually doing anything wrong; that each girl he raped deserved it, thereby making it not a crime but a justified act. I had him use his babysitter as his SUBSTITUTION for all of his victims. And, as his MOMENT BEFORE for all of the scenes that required him to rape someone, I had him remember the worst events of the molestation, picturing the babysitter molesting him *again, today*, doing all the wretched things he did to him when he was thirteen. In each rape scene, the MOMENT BEFORE gave the actor the organic feelings of violation, anger and a desire for retribution that he needed to feel so that each act of rape became an act of righteousness, rather than a random act of violence. As I've said before, it's vital that you never judge your character, no matter how heinous your character behaves. People who do evil acts don't see them as such—they always have a justifiable reason.

Always Make a MOMENT BEFORE Event Choice Come from an Emotional, Relationship Point of View

Rather than an event that is exclusively script inspired. Your MOMENT BEFORE event should come from an emotional relationship point of view. Your interpretation should be motivated by your unique, individual life story. This creates a more compelling and one-of-a-kind performance because there's only one you. In one episode of the critically acclaimed series *Once and Again,* Susanna Thompson's character of Karen Sammler is having a nervous breakdown and then has a horrible accident—she's hit hard by a speeding car while out walking—that forces her to reassess her life. At the time, Susanna was going through a similarly disruptive time in her personal life. After living in the same house for eight years, she was told that she had to move within a month. It was Christmastime and the cast and crew were in the midst of a heavy shooting schedule (working days). For Susanna, this home was her base, her sanity. We talked about how displaced she felt. That her whole orientation—where she shopped, ate, did her dry cleaning, not to mention the ease of knowing where her personal effects were—was off. The situation caused her to feel discombobulated, alone and terribly insecure about her future. Therapists and studies alike say that moving is one of the most stress-inducing experiences there is. I'm sure if you've suddenly had to move from a safe haven to an unknown, future abode, you know what an anxiety-ridden experience it is. And to add to her stress, it was December, the holiday season, a very difficult time to find new digs in L.A., which gave rise to the not so unreasonable fear of being totally homeless. So duplicating a true nervous breakdown via thinking about a move isn't so far-fetched. I told Susanna to picture being homeless and horribly displaced in midwinter as her MOMENT BEFORE event for the car accident scene. An accident that the audience has to believe might have been no accident at all, but a suicide attempt. By imagining her own personal horrors of being homeless, she was allowed to feel the shock, upset and disorientation that one feels when having a nervous breakdown. This helped her create an eerily accurate representation of how a real nervous breakdown looks and feels. Why? Because she was really feeling it.

Sometimes using a straw-that-broke-the-camel's-back event from your life as your MOMENT BEFORE choice can be very effective.

Although a particular event might not be so terrible when viewed in and of itself, when it is compounded by previous other bad events, it can turn an otherwise unpleasant event into something excruciating. What if you were to just find out that you've lost your job, and soon after your mate told you that they were leaving you? The previous event makes the present event that much more bleak.

When David Spade was in my class (before *SNL* and fame), he had a straw-that-broke-the-camel's-back experience to work with when he did a scene from the movie *Broadcast News*. In the scene, his character of

Aaron Altman is home alone, lamenting how badly he's screwed up his first opportunity to be a news anchor. Aaron was so nervous and sweating so profusely on the air that audience members had called in because they were afraid he was having a heart attack. Needless to say, Aaron wasn't going to get another chance at his dream. But who should pop by unexpectedly but Jane Craig, the girl he's in love with. For a moment, it seems like things are looking up. But unfortunately, Jane has stopped by to tell Aaron she's in love with his archrival, Tom. Not Aaron's day. As Aaron, David needed a strong MOMENT BEFORE to make Jane's news feel lethal. As his MOMENT BEFORE, David chose to use a straw-that-broke-the-camel's-back event of his own—he had recently blown a showcase for *The Tonight Show*, which is considered a career maker for stand-up comics. When it happened, David was at his wit's end and feeling completely distraught about his career, which made for a potent MOMENT BEFORE.

Common MOMENT BEFORE Examples

Remember: The MOMENT BEFORE is an event that takes place before the scene begins and makes you not just want but *need* the SCENE OBJECTIVE, urgently and immediately. Your MOMENT BEFORE must make sense to your SCENE OBJECTIVE and your SUBSTITUTION choice. Working this way keeps your OVERALL OBJECTIVE and SCENE OBJECTIVE in sight, and your character's arc linear as well as logical throughout the script.

The following MOMENT BEFORE choices are just a few ideas to get you thinking about how to choose an appropriate and effective MOMENT BEFORE. Any of the following suggestions for these common MOMENT BEFORE examples may be actual events, or WHAT IF events that you may imagine. But if you choose a WHAT IF event, you must have a genuine, plausible fear about it.

If the SCENE OBJECTIVE is *"make you love me,"* then an appropriate MOMENT BEFORE is something that has happened to you recently or a worst fear event (a WHAT IF event) that makes you shamelessly and desperately need to be loved *right now*. Some possible events include:

- Your mate has broken up with you. The loss of one love makes you need the new person's love with much apprehension and immediacy. Right before you launch into the scene, imagine the breakup has just happened (or WHAT IF an impending breakup happened). Picture the place, smells, what he/she was wearing, what was said and your pained feelings.

- You fear your mate is fooling around on the side (WHAT IF). Even though there's no evidence and it's just a fear, imagine finding out. Picture it—*who* they're doing it with, *where* it would take place, *what* you would be doing, *how* they would tell you, *how* you caught them in the act. Viscerally see your mate making love in the same way your mate makes love to you, and then feel your hurt feelings that result because of it. Then begin the scene.

- If you presently don't have a mate, use a real or a feared WHAT IF split-up with a friend, agent, boss, business partner, family member or anyone that would cause your life to change if you were to lose them. It should be somebody that you'd work very hard to win back. Picture the breakup, re-creating or creating it in your mind—get as detailed as you can and then start the scene.

If the SCENE OBJECTIVE is *"to get you to give me my power back,"* then an appropriate MOMENT BEFORE is something that has happened to you recently or a worst-fear event (a WHAT IF event) that makes you urgently need to get your power back right now. Some possible events include:

- You've just been made to feel very stupid by your boss, your lover, a family member or a friend. Viscerally re-create and relive the event in your mind.

- You've just been unreasonably fired and you feel compelled to seek revenge. Viscerally re-create and relive the event in your mind.

- You've gotten into a violent fight with someone and lost the battle. Viscerally re-create and relive the event in your mind.

- You've been raped, molested, mugged, robbed, carjacked or have experienced some sort of physical violation that made you feel powerless. Viscerally re-create and relive the event in your mind.

- A person has emasculated or diminished you in a horrible, life-changing way. Viscerally re-create and relive the event in your mind.

- You've been lied about or to, and it has caused irreparable damage. Viscerally re-create and relive the event in your mind.

Rapper MC Lyte came to me when she working as a guest star on a series called *Platinum,* which was a show about the African American music industry. This particular episode chronicled the fall of Camille FaReal, a successful but swiftly-becoming-yesterday's-news rapper who is being usurped by the new "it" girl. In the story, the label's record producer ignores FaReal no matter how hard she tries to get his attention with diva-like tantrums, teary diatribes and fights that would make the WWF proud. In one scene FaReal won't come out of her trailer to perform in a music video because the new "it" girl rapper, who's also in the video, is getting far too much attention. The producer comes to get her, and a power struggle ensues. Triggered by her feelings of abandonment and betrayal, FaReal screams and cries.

Her SCENE OBJECTIVE is *"to get you to give me my power back."* As FaReal, MC's challenge was to figure out what the heck to use for her MOMENT BEFORE, because MC had recently started her own record label, SGI/CMM, to get away from situations exactly like the one her character was facing. We talked and both agreed that though she may have presently avoided some of the pitfalls of being a recording artist by creating her label, she still had to contend with the fact that most artists in the music industry have about as much longevity as a pet rock. MC and I decided to use this insecurity as an inspiration for her MOMENT BEFORE. Working with a recent event in which she found out that one of her archrivals (and someone who was far less talented) was doing far better than her—platinum CDs, movie deals—sent MC into a rage. So when the director called "Action," and she faced her SUBSTITUTION—a heavyweight in the music world and a friend who seemed to be taking the other rapper's side—the MOMENT BEFORE caused her to honestly and organically fight for her SCENE OBJECTIVE, *"to get you to give me my power back."*

If your SCENE OBJECTIVE is **"to get you to worship me"** or **"to get you to look up to me,"** then you must have a MOMENT BEFORE that makes you feel so small and diminished that it becomes essential that you achieve your SCENE OBJECTIVE, because it's the only way to feel confident again. Some possible events include:

- You've just been fired from your job.
- You've had some recent sexual dysfunction.
- Your mate just dumped you.
- You've blown yet another audition.
- A parent berates you for something you have no control over.
- You've asked someone for a date and that person says no and acts like you're a bad smell that won't go away.
- You've been cruelly blamed for something you didn't do.

In class, one of my students, Matt, was doing a scene from the play *Private Wars* and was a having a hard time with his MOMENT BEFORE. He was playing the character of Salvio, a man whose "package" was blown off in a war and who now lives in a mental hospital. Needless to say, it's a devastating event for a man to lose what defines his gender. In the particular scene Matt was playing, Salvio is teaching his buddy Woodruff how to pick up women. Salvio's theory? "Tell them that you're a priest, the horniest, loneliest men on the face of the planet." Matt's first run of the scene was not passionately driven to win his SCENE OBJEC-TIVE of "*to prove my manhood to you.*" Even though Salvio isn't much more experienced than Woodruff, it is imperative, due to his lack of male organs, to make Woodruff look up to him as a lady's man. To get into the appropriate physical, mental and emotional mind-set for the scene, Matt needed an emasculating event equal to his character's cir-cumstances to use as his MOMENT BEFORE. I asked Matt if he had any sexual dysfunction, issue with his size, or if a woman had ever ridiculed his performance in bed. I told him that he didn't need to tell me or the class (I mean, that would have been humiliating), but that he should think about his insecurity. Most men have *some* insecurity in this area because most men—actually, just about *every man*—has an irrational fear when it comes to issues of their own sexuality. I told him to use whatever emasculating event came to mind, to work with it as his MO-MENT BEFORE and then to try the scene again. The second time through, his character had a swaggering gait, a swiveling pelvis, and spoke with the exaggerated tones of an I-can-get-anyone-I want-so-listen-and-learn voice. These were the moves of a man who feels compelled to overcompensate as a way to overcome his true feelings of being physi-cally and emotionally impotent.

Speaking of sex, the theater, television and movies often have the before-sex and/or after-sex scene. Here are some ways to think about your MOMENT BEFORE for these circumstances.

MOMENT BEFORE for First-Time Sex Scenes

It's never easy the first time you're with someone, especially if you really like that person. Before anything happens (and you just *know* it's going to . . .), there are moments that tap into our deepest insecurities and desires. For these scenes, your MOMENT BEFORE should be driven by your real sexual neuroses and fantasies. For example:

- *Before* **first-time sex (for both men and women):**
  MOMENT BEFORE: First, think about your deepest insecurities in this area, what you fear *might* occur, or sexual issues that *might* emerge during the sex act. Imagine a time when the worst of your sexual issues/fears were realized or use WHAT IF it happens again. Then vividly fantasize sexually about the person/actor in front of you and hope (and pray) that your sexual issues won't be revealed.
    If you're a man, think about size issues, sexual dysfunction, performance anxiety, weird sexual predilections that could be misunderstood and rejected, talking too much during the sex act, etc.
    If you're a woman, think about breast-size issues, fat or cellulite in places that only the act of sex can reveal, a propensity for being too vocal or too quiet, weird sexual predilections that might make you look like a slut or a prude, etc.

- *After* **first-time sex (for both men and women):**
  MOMENT BEFORE: Think about your deepest insecurities in this area and deal with your worst sexual fears or issues having *just occurred* in their full glory during the sex act and now you have to suffer the torturous consequences of the aftermath. As a MOMENT BEFORE relive viscerally an event when the worst of your sexual issues were revealed. Imagine your sex partner thinking the worst thoughts about your issue.
    If you're a man, think about size issues, sexual dysfunction, performance anxiety, weird sexual predilections that are misunderstood and can be rejected, talking too much during the sex act, etc.
    If you're a woman, think about breast-size issues, fat or cellulite that can and has been discovered during the act, your

propensity to be too loud or too quiet, weird sexual predilections coming forward making you look like a slut or a prude, etc.

MOMENT BEFORE for Fight Scenes

There's always a reason for a fight, be it physical or verbal. Consider your SCENE OBJECTIVE, which in a fight scene is usually *"to make you wrong so I can be right"* or *"to get my power back from you."*

- MOMENT BEFORE: You must first look at your SUBSTITU-TION choice and inner story that reflects this SUBSTITUTION, because whom you picture will establish the subject of the fight and the event you'll use as your MOMENT BEFORE. The MO-MENT BEFORE event should be one that will trigger the fight. So when the scene begins with the verbal and/or physical dispute in its full glory, you have a heightened reason and purpose to fight.

In the film *In the Bedroom,* there's a verbal war between a husband (played by Tom Wilkinson) and wife (played by Sissy Spacek) over which of them is to blame for their son's death. The SCENE OBJECTIVE for each character is *"to get you to take the blame so I don't have to feel guilty anymore."* Both characters were simultaneously taking responsibility *and* blaming each other for his death, which is a very realistic depiction of this kind of trauma. To play either character in this scene, a MOMENT BEFORE could be to imagine a tragic event that's happened to you (or a WHAT IF a specific tragic event that you fear could happen were to take place) and that you feel very guilty about. Your SUBSTITU-TION choice would be the person who you want to believe caused the tragedy. By using a tragic event that you feel guilty about as your MO-MENT BEFORE, it propels you to try to assuage your guilt by winning the SCENE OBJECTIVE of *"to get you to take the blame."*

Another classic fight scene is in Noel Coward's play *Private Lives.* In the second act, ex-lovers Amanda and Elyot are holed up in Amanda's apartment, trying to piece their relationship back together. Both characters have the SCENE OBJECTIVE of *"to get you to admit that you abused me (so that I can be the injured party)."* It's late at night, they're drinking, and, of course, the subject of their breakup comes up. They each have their own perspective about what happened and who is responsible, each blaming the other. Both Amanda and Elyot feel like they're the victim of the other's abuse. They begin to verbally spar and end up in a physical brawl. For this scene, your MOMENT BEFORE would be to recall the most abusive event that was caused by your SUBSTITUTION.

MOMENT BEFORE for a Make-up Scene

The SCENE OBJECTIVE for a make-up scene is usually *"to get you to forgive me,"* or *"to get you to give me absolution."*

MOMENT BEFORE: Think of an event that makes you feel that you were wrong, something that instills great guilt in you. This makes you feel like you must fix the problem because it's your fault. Pick events that are applicable to your SUBSTITUTION and the inner story you've created. Some possible MOMENT BEFORE events include:

- A specific time when you cheated on your mate.
- A specific time when you've been caught doing something illegal.
- A specific time when you've lied about substance abuse problems.
- A specific time when you've been caught lying to or slandering your SUBSTITUTION.
- A specific time when you've been verbally/physically abusive to your SUBSTITUTION.
- A specific time when you've been caught stealing from your SUBSTITUTION.

Remember: The MOMENT BEFORE is a real or WHAT IF event that takes place before the scene begins and that makes you need your SCENE OBJECTIVE to happen ASAP. You take this event and you imagine it happening, in its vivid entirety, right before the scene begins. You recall or imagine the space, the smells, what was said or could be said, and the high-stakes emotions that accompanied or would accompany the event, and you feel it viscerally happening in the present.

You've got to rehearse with your MOMENT BEFORE to find out if the MOMENT BEFORE event you've chosen—real or WHAT IF—is going to affect you and best compel an urgent need to win your SCENE OBJEC-TIVE. A powerful MOMENT BEFORE choice will push your buttons im-mediately. So if it doesn't affect you within a minute, then continue to try other MOMENT BEFORE choices until you find one that really drives your SCENE OBJECTIVE.

CHAPTER 8

Tool #8:

PLACE AND FOURTH WALL

Endowing your character's physical reality with attributes
from a PLACE and FOURTH WALL from your real life.

Using PLACE and FOURTH WALL creates privacy, intimacy, history, meaning, safety and reality. The PLACE/FOURTH WALL must support and make sense to the choices you've made for the other tools. Applying information from the inner story you have created, ask yourself the question, "What PLACE from my life will inform and make the choices I've already made have even higher stakes?"

Say your SCENE OBJECTIVE is *to get you to admit you're wrong and apologize,*" and you're using your mother as your SUBSTITUTION. You need a PLACE that heightens your reality—something that really magnifies the feeling of betrayal—and propels your need to accomplish your goal (SCENE OBJECTIVE). To find your PLACE, you must first identify where the scene in the script takes place. Inside or outside? Is the inside or outside space private or public?

Once you have identified what kind of space the scene is in, you then correlate the script's space with a PLACE from your life. In this case—getting someone to admit they are wrong and apologize using your mother as your SUBSTITUTION—you would need to think of a PLACE where your mother deceived you or let you down. This PLACE from your life should be either the PLACE in your MOMENT BEFORE or a PLACE where a similar event of betrayal happened with your SUBSTITUTION (in this example, your mother) that makes sense to the scripted scene. If the scene is in a public inside space, like a restaurant, think of a PLACE where your family always dined, where your mother always belittled you—perhaps the place where she berated you for being too fat. If the scene is an inside private PLACE, an effective PLACE could be your childhood bedroom where your mother frequently physically or verbally abused you. If the scene is an outside public space, you could use the elementary school steps that you waited on for three hours when she forgot to pick you up from school when you were eight.

No matter what kind of space a scene is in—inside and public, inside and private, outside and public, outside and private—the process of identifying the type of space and then identifying your personalized PLACE will help round out the inner personal story you've built with the first seven tools, which all support and reflect your character's feelings and goals.

The best way to understand how using PLACE can support an actor's work is by looking at a specific scene and breaking it down. At one point in the film *Titanic*, the character of Jack Dawson sketches the character of Rose DeWitt in her stateroom. Except for a priceless necklace, Rose is completely nude. Rose, a society girl, is engaged to Cal, a manipulative and wealthy young man. Jack is young, without a family, and poor. He won his steerage seat on the ship in a card game. Rose's SCENE OBJECTIVE is *"to get you* (Jack) *to fall in love with me."* Obviously, the scene's space is inside and private, although there is the chance that Rose's mother or fiancé, Cal, could burst in and surprise them at any time. This is just one of the many OBSTACLES that you would need to keep in mind for this scene. You must always consider the scene's inherent OBSTACLES in making a choice for PLACE.

Rose's OBSTACLES are:

1. Possible rejection.
2. I'm nude and I'm not comfortable with my body (be specific—hips, stomach, breasts, cellulite, etc.).
3. WHAT IF he thinks I'm too easy?
4. My fiancé could bust in at any time and kill Jack or me or both of us.
5. My mother could bust in at any time and have a fit.
6. The disparity of social standing between us.

If you were playing the character of Rose, the PLACE you find from your life wouldn't be the one that most replicates a luxurious, walnut-paneled ship's stateroom. Instead, you would have to think of a PLACE from your life that invites these six OBSTACLES and works with your SUBSTITUTION for the character of Jack.

As with all the tools:
Always reproduce the physical aspects of the script
from an emotional point of view.

PLACES that might work for the *Titanic* stateroom scene include:

- If you're using your ex-mate as your SUBSTITUTION for Jack because you still have feelings for him, then:
    PLACE: **Your ex-mate's living room.**
    This choice naturally infuses the stakes of history with your ex-mate, as well as the danger of being hurt again. The risky person who can burst in on you could be your present mate, or the friend and/or relative that always disliked that person.
- If you're using a crush or someone you have a crush on who is in some way related to your present mate by friendship, family or work associate as your SUBSTITUTION for Jack, then:
    PLACE: **Your present bedroom where you live with your mate.**
    A PLACE dangerous by the very nature of the constant reminder that you are being unfaithful. Furthermore, your mate could show up at any moment.
- If you're using a platonic friend (yet you have feelings for him that go beyond friendship) as your SUBSTITUTION for Jack, then:
    PLACE: **Your friend's apartment.**
    This choice incorporates the danger of loss of friendship. If the affair doesn't work out, it's unlikely you'll ever be able to get back to the way it was. The person that could burst in on you could be another friend who is a part of your group who would be alarmed at your state of undress and bound to tell everyone else.
- If you're using your boss as your SUBSTITUTION for Jack, then:
    PLACE: **Your boss's office.**
    A place that reminds you of the impropriety of the situation, as well as including the danger that a coworker, secretary, his wife, etc., can abruptly and uninvitingly enter. Also, if an affair doesn't work out with someone you're employed by, you might lose your job.

Of course, these are just four suggestions drawn from the infinite list of possibilities. If you were really playing the character of Rose, then in your rehearsal time, you would try as many SUBSTITUTION-related options for PLACE that came to mind to see which one felt the most powerful and fueled your SCENE OBJECTIVE.

Once you've identified a few locations that you might use as your PLACE, based on your SCENE OBJECTIVE and SUBSTITUTION, you must create it. Creating PLACE means that you endow the location—set, stage, classroom—with attributes from your personal PLACE. Let's look at how you would create PLACE with the first example for the *Titanic* scenario, your ex-mate's living room.

APPLYING PLACE

Remember notable parts about your ex-mate's living room. This includes thinking about the furniture, the flooring, the color of the walls, the posters or art on the walls, the windows and doors, the smells, the sounds, the temperature. Once you have conjured up as accurate an image as possible, match the shapes of the set with similar shapes that exist in your ex-mate's living room. For instance, match the couch in the set with the couch from your ex-mate's living room—seeing the colors, the fabric. Endow the side table on the set with the stereo system from your ex's living room. The paintings on the wall of the set are windows. The wood floor becomes the blue carpeting. The smells are his personal brand of cologne. The sounds are of the traffic that was constantly flowing by. Feel a chill in the air because your ex always kept the thermostat on low because he hated to sweat. As you endow each significant part of the PLACE, think about events—both traumatic and wonderful—that have taken place in that space. Remember the first time you made love on the couch. And then recall that this was the same couch where you discovered the flowered thong underwear that didn't belong to you. See the poster that you bought for him. Hear the CD he used to play ad nauseam. Picture the door that you slammed as you exited for the last time. Do this until you feel like you have transported yourself from the soundstage, acting class or theater to the actual PLACE you've chosen.

> *Once you choose the best PLACE, spatially endow the existing set with the reality of what's in the room of the personal PLACE you've chosen.*

If you're doing stage work, endow PLACE before every rehearsal. If you're doing film or television work, spend at least ten or fifteen minutes on the set of the scene you're about to shoot. Create your PLACE, get comfortable in your PLACE, and make it real to you by remembering emotionally appropriate events and experiences that happened in that PLACE.

I produced a movie called *Kiss Toledo Goodbye* starring Christopher Walken. With each new set and on every new location, Walken would walk around on the dark set (before the set was lit) touching and generally using the furniture—sitting in a chair, touching items on the coffee table, perusing the books on the bookshelf—until the space was real to him and contained the appropriate history and feelings. He was invoking his PLACE. So when it was time to actually film the scene, there was no distinction—Walken's world and the set were one.

The choice you use for PLACE should have *inherent* obstacles.

If the PLACE you choose is too easy to be in, you won't be compelled to win your SCENE OBJECTIVE. Let's say you're doing a scene in which your character is on a job interview and the SCENE OBJECTIVE is *"to get you to give me this job."* If you use a PLACE where you were once easily hired, there are no stakes. This is because that PLACE doesn't give you the nervous feeling that you get when you are on an interview and really want the job. A more effective PLACE choice would be a PLACE where you once blew an incredibly important job interview. This PLACE feeds your SCENE OBJECTIVE, infusing your work with a desperate need and desire to make the interview go well because you don't want to screw up the way you did last time.

It's amazing how substantially PLACE affects us. Think about a restaurant that you used to frequent with a past mate. Now think about how it would feel to eat at this restaurant with a new person just weeks after you've broken up with your former partner. The feeling changes, right? What was once a cozy second home becomes a PLACE that produces anxiety and discomfort. You'd fear your ex showing up (after all, it was your special place), remember the horrible arguments that occurred there and that could happen again if your date turns out to be a long-term relationship, and think that you may never have a mate again because the PLACE is a constant reminder that you failed so miserably with your ex. Where we are affects our feelings and needs.

David Hare calls attention to the importance of PLACE in *The Blue*

Room, a play based on *La Ronde* by Arthur Schnitzler and freely adapted by Mr. Hare. Just by naming his play *The Blue Room,* Hare calls attention to the integral role that PLACE plays in every story. The play chronicles a series of sexual encounters. In one scene, a senator is having an affair with a very young intern. I asked Bill Moses, star of *Melrose Place, Falcon Crest* and numerous television movies, to do this scene for me in class. Bill knew that his character's central OBSTACLES were that he was married and a senator. The senator would worry that his wife, the press and his constituents would discover his indiscretion. As we've seen so many times in our illustrious political past, this kind of discovery is a shortcut to the unemployment line. Additionally, there was the age OBSTACLE—the intern's Lolita-like age would not be good for the ol' resume. Bill and I talked about what PLACE would summon this kind of sexual heat and the danger of discovery. Bill had already gone through one divorce with a child involved. If he were to get caught having an affair, he would have to go through the whole ugly mess again—a trauma he would gladly forgo. So, Bill used his bedroom with the WHAT IF he was having an affair and his wife and child were out of the house. Having sex on the bed (having endowed it with his own bed) he shared with his wife, where their child was conceived, took on a dangerous heat when he imagined sharing it (in the biblical sense) with his SUBSTITUTION. Bill endowed PLACE using shapes and memories: picturing the furniture he'd bought with his wife, sniffing smells of his wife's clothes and perfume, and being aware of the bed's idiosyncrasies. This magnified Bill's feelings of guilt and fear (his wife could show up at any time) and he became sexually charged (it's always more erotic when there's danger involved). It was a powerful performance that was fueled by a strong, effective PLACE.

PLACE is an essential tool, even if it's supposed to be a PLACE your character has never been in before.

A lot of actors will try to play a trick on themselves by not going on the set until it's time to shoot if it's supposed to be a new PLACE to the character, or a PLACE they're entering for the first time. This works well for the first take, but what about the second or fourteenth? How about all the setups for each scene? You'll be using the set again and again for the master shots, two-shots, close-ups, etc. What do they do then? This is why making a conscious choice to use a personal PLACE is always important. You need a PLACE that you can rely on that will supply the appropriate feelings over and over. And believe it or not, there are many PLACES in your life that can duplicate the anxiety of being in a space for the first time.

For instance, if you're doing a horror film and the direction in the script is for your character to walk into a haunted house for the first time, a very effective PLACE choice could be the home you grew up in but haven't been in for years. And to make this "first time" experience scary—it is a haunted house, after all—remember and picture unpleasant memories (INNER OBJECTS) from your childhood as you look around the PLACE. This will give you the same eerie feeling that one has when walking into a haunted house. Note that by working this way, the PLACE also informs your SCENE OBJECTIVE by giving you even more OBSTACLES (the bad memories) to overcome.

Or in cases like Natasha Gregson Wagner's role as a victim in *Urban Legends,* we used a safe PLACE to enhance the surprise of her character's brutal murder. In the opening scenes of this horror movie, Natasha's character is in her car, innocently singing with the radio, when a psychopath surprises her from the backseat and does what murderers do so well: kill and create bloody, deadly mayhem. Even though our cars are surrounded by glass, they feel like a private PLACE to us. All of us are guilty of behaving in our car in ways we wouldn't dare in public—picking our noses, crying and rocking out to our favorite songs. I told Natasha to use her own car as her PLACE and to imagine seeing the streets leading to her childhood home as she looks out the windshield and the side windows.

> ***Personalizing what you're seeing outside your car window
> in doing car scenes is part of creating PLACE.***

Not only was she feeling the safety of being in her car, but she was also feeling the old safety of her childhood neighborhood. This sense of security allowed Natasha to sing with abandon—and Natasha's ability to sing is more like a cat being mauled than Melissa Etheridge, which made the audience relax and laugh. This PLACE got both Natasha and the audience feeling so safe that when the homicidal maniac popped up from the backseat, they were shocked and truly horrified because they were not expecting it. Using this PLACE was so effective that test audiences said that Natasha was their favorite character and this scene was their favorite part of the movie. Since she was killed at the beginning of the movie, the producers went back and recut the film, using her scene in flashbacks throughout.

Use PLACE to Create a Feeling of Privacy

PLACE helps you feel like you are unwatched and alone. We as the audience should feel like flies on the wall, watching something so intimate and private that we feel like we're observing events that we shouldn't be privy to.

Using a PLACE that originates from your childhood can be extremely powerful because it's so primal.

The memories that emanate from our childhood are potent because so much of who we are today stems from those past experiences. No matter how old we get, we always seem to vividly remember important childhood events. This includes not only *what* happened, but *where* it happened. And the *where* seems to instill very strong pictures and feelings. If you've ever revisited your old elementary school, or driven through the old neighborhood, or even gone to that Burger King where you and your friends used to hang out—the memories of experiences, good and bad, come flooding into your head.

Tatiana Ali (of *The Fresh Prince of Bel Air* fame) and I worked together on the film *Alicia Packer,* which she starred in opposite Ja Rule and Ving Rhames. Tatiana played the title character, a young woman who loses her father, a preacher, to a senseless shooting at an ATM. In one of the scenes, Alicia Packer is alone in her father's study looking at her late father's Bible, an old photo album, and his journal. Through nostalgia and reflection, Alicia is trying to keep her father alive. We used Tatiana's childhood bedroom as her PLACE, because it evoked events and a time that can never take place again. Even though Tatiana's father is still alive, picturing the bedroom and remembering its smells and objects gave her a sense of loss and mourning because, as an adult, she'll never be a child again. This means that she'll never experience the feelings of being nurtured and protected in that special way that a father protects and loves a little girl. We took the set's pictures and endowed them (INNER OBJECTS) with important father/daughter events. Alicia's father's journal entries became the encouraging words that her own father used to say to her when she was growing up that would fix childhood emotional wounds (INNER OBJECTS). Picturing her childhood bedroom helped her duplicate the feelings of having experienced the loss that comes from death, because it was real—it was the death of her youth and her role as daddy's baby girl.

Use PLACE to enhance your feelings.

Every PLACE from your life has an emotional base. It doesn't matter how innocuous a PLACE seems to be, an event has occurred there that has some form of an emotional attachment. You must choose a PLACE that has the most powerful emotional connections to produce the highest dramatic intent.

For many years I've worked with Emmy Award–winning actress Michelle Stafford on her character of Phyllis, one of the mainstays on the daytime drama *The Young and the Restless*. In one of her storylines, Phyllis is framed for setting fire to her husband Jack's guesthouse, which, at the time, housed his ex-fiancé and mother of his child, Diane. Phyllis is thrown in jail. Diane uses Phyllis's time in the hoosegow as an opportunity to seduce Jack. Jack succumbs and then expects Phyllis to forgive his infidelity because he was just having sex (more than once, I might add) with Diane to finagle the truth that it was Diane herself who was the guilty arsonist. Phyllis isn't buying it (who would?), but can't do anything about it because she's behind bars. Oh, and there's more (it is daytime television after all). Phyllis, feeling alone, betrayed and defeated, goes crazy. She hears voices, talks to herself (literally, Michelle plays two people in these scenes) and tries to do bodily harm to herself. We talked about what we could use for PLACE that would be rich with the sense of being imprisoned. I told her that prison can be any PLACE that motivates a sense of being physically and/or emotionally caged. So Michelle used a PLACE where a traumatic childhood event occurred. Like all childhood traumas, they color and affect our feelings and behavior as an adult. They also cause the ever-vigilant need to protect ourselves from similar emotional injuries. Michelle's PLACE choice gave her the general sense that she had no way out and no one to turn to, the same feeling she had when she was a child experiencing her trauma for the first time. In other words, the feeling of being imprisoned. This particular PLACE was also a reminder of an event that made her feel powerless and out of control. And when you add it all up, feelings of fear, powerlessness, being out of control, having no way out and no one to turn to is a perfect recipe for insanity. Michelle's personal choice for PLACE gave her performance truth, accuracy and a more enhanced emotional life.

FOURTH WALL

The FOURTH WALL is the dimension of the PLACE that makes the space you're working in (stage, set, classroom, location, et al) private, separating the actors and the stage or set from the audience or camera crew.

The FOURTH WALL is the edge of the stage or set. The FOURTH WALL encloses your PLACE, establishing a sense of intimacy and privacy. When you are personalizing the floors, walls and furniture of the set from your PLACE choice, you have to personally endow what's on the FOURTH WALL, as well. In your personal PLACE choice, the real FOURTH WALL could consist of a chest of drawers, a sculpture and a window, even though on the set there is a camera and lights in the actual area where the FOURTH WALL would be.

APPLYING THE FOURTH WALL

When you are looking at the FOURTH WALL area of the soundstage, imagine seeing the camera as the chest of drawers or a key light as the sculpture and a light diffuser as the window. In other words, even though the set lacks a literal fourth wall, you must fill out your entire PLACE, spatially duplicating and completing what would be on that wall in your PLACE choice. Pick big items from your PLACE choice—a window, television, painting, art object, chest of drawers, armoire, etc.—things that are similar in shape to the actual items there so that it's easy to spatially endow your personal FOURTH WALL.

PLACE coupled with the FOURTH WALL also enables you to take away the intimidating force that the camera and the audience always has on an actor. PLACE and the FOURTH WALL establish a feeling of privacy—it takes away the feeling that we are watching actors acting and instead makes us feel that we are watching human beings truly interact. The best acting you can do should make your audience feel like they're

Peeping Toms, catching real live people going through truly intimate moments. It's always important to create privacy in your work, but particularly crucial when doing a highly charged emotional or sexual scene.

Accurately assimilate the FOURTH WALL of the PLACE you have chosen and endow it accordingly.

Take what's on your personal FOURTH WALL and endow it onto what's actually there—the actual wall dressings, furniture, camera or whatever. Endow the space with choices that make it easy to imagine, otherwise you'll have to play mind games that make it complicated and confusing. If there's clear space with an audience, as in a theater, just pick some of the more obtrusive items on your FOURTH WALL and imagine them there. Or, if it's a small theater space, see the wall that actually exists beyond the audience. Then take the actual shapes that exist there and endow the wall with the items that would generally exist there.

When endowing PLACE and the FOURTH WALL, you don't have to imagine each and every item in that PLACE and on that FOURTH WALL.

Just picture the key pieces that define your personal PLACE/ FOURTH WALL—particularly the items that hold some history or special meaning. Picturing these few specific and key pieces will transport you to the PLACE/FOURTH WALL, because the items are significant enough to conjure it up. And, if you've picked the correct emotionally charged objects to project, they will often inadvertently call up less-charged objects that will flesh out the space you're endowing.

APPLYING AN OUTSIDE FOURTH WALL

In an outdoor PLACE, the FOURTH WALL is what would be on the horizon. On a beach, you'd see the surroundings of that special beach that you've picked as your PLACE, and the FOURTH WALL would be the view of that specific body of water—the color, the sounds, the movement of the waves. If you were outside in the city, your FOURTH WALL would be the specific buildings that face you in that familiar and poignant street from your life.

When making PLACE/FOURTH WALL choices, you have to
keep in mind whether it's a PRIVATE/INSIDE PLACE, a
PUBLIC/INSIDE PLACE, a PRIVATE/OUTSIDE PLACE,
or a PUBLIC/OUTSIDE PLACE.

Different PLACE/FOURTH WALL(s) naturally create different feelings. When you're inside and alone, you don't feel you have to be secretive because you're not encumbered by peering eyes and ears. On the other hand, when you're outside in public, there's always the possibility that you can be overheard or seen by the wrong people.

Inside/private PLACE/FOURTH WALL.

- Your home (including bedroom, living room, study, kitchen, etc.)
- Your office
- Hospital room
- Hotel/motel room

In a private/inside PLACE/FOURTH WALL, you are alone with only one or two other people. In this kind of PLACE, anything can be said and done because there's no one else there to spy, reveal, judge or change the tone of your activity. You can still be aware of the possibility of interruption or being discovered, yet without the other invading person(s) actually being in the room, you are left to feel that anything privately can and will happen. This includes the privacy of sex, secrets told or experienced, violence or death.

Inside/public (or populated) PLACE/FOURTH WALL.

- A restaurant
- A hospital waiting room
- A doctor's waiting room
- A courtroom
- Your home with a party going on
- A movie or stage theater
- A bar
- A police interrogation room (there's the possibility that others may be spying through a two-way mirror)

- An airplane
- A train
- A store
- A mall

PLACES that are inside but public change the tone of the scene because you can possibly be overheard and/or seen. In public/inside PLACE/FOURTH WALL(s), you always have the OBSTACLE of other people in the scene discovering and then disclosing what they've seen or heard to that person or persons that your character wishes not to know—their mate, the police, their boss, their friend that they're disparaging, their parent, their child.

> *Personalizing a nonspeaking person around you in a*
> *PUBLIC/INSIDE PLACE will enhance your behavior—*
> *especially if the specific person threatens you either*
> *emotionally and/or physically—because it*
> *amplifies the scene's OBSTACLES.*

When thinking about an inside/public PLACE/FOURTH WALL, it's helpful to identify exactly who it is that is lurking around your public place, which ups the stakes. Imagine a first date scene that takes PLACE/ FOURTH WALL in a restaurant. Take one of the actors/extras at one of the other tables in the restaurant, and for your SUBSTITUTION for that actor/extra, use your ex-mate (who'll judge your present date as less good-looking, stupid, weird or perverted and make you feel that you have substantially lowered your standards); or use a parent who is obsessed with your single status being changed to a status of married with children (this choice makes you feel compelled to make this date work out, no matter how wrong this person is for you); or use a friend who always finds a way to ridicule you (making you overcritical in watching your date, which will taint your interaction); or use a friend of your ex who will be happy to gossip to your ex about how you've lowered your standards. Depending on who you use as a SUBSTITUTION choice, placing and then endowing someone who has meaning around you will absolutely vary and enhance your behavior.

Another instance of endowing an actor/extra in an inside/public PLACE/ FOURTH WALL is a scene in a bar where your character is regaling their life's troubles to a stranger. Using a SUBSTITUTION—someone who really matters to you—for the idle patron sitting nearby or the nonspeaking bartender can deepen the conflict and the drama of the scene. The inconsequential observer is now your mother who has issues with your drinking, or an enemy (or friend of your nemesis) who would gain pleasure in knowing your secrets and the retelling of your flaws and failures.

Or perhaps your character is the defendant in a court case. If you use SUBSTITUTION, imagining that one member of the jury is a person from your life who would love to see harm done to you (an ex, a longtime enemy, someone whom *you've* hurt in the past, etc.), you will deepen your desire to win your SCENE OBJECTIVE, *"to make you believe in my innocence."* Because there's someone in a position to control the decision-making process who has a vendetta against you, who's going to be negatively subjective when looking at the facts of the case, you will work harder to win. Again, this adds to the drama in your work and in the scene.

Outside/private PLACE/FOURTH WALL.

- A secluded beach or a beach at night
- A park at night
- A secluded parking lot
- A dark alley
- A pool
- A backyard
- A street or road in the middle of the night
- A car
- The woods

The difference between outside/private PLACE/FOURTH WALL(s) and an inside/private PLACE/FOURTH WALL is that when you are outdoors, there's an even greater possibility that you can be discovered or caught. There are no walls to keep a person out. In an outside/private PLACE, the FOURTH WALL is the horizon. Always use what would truly exist in your personal FOURTH WALL of the PLACE you've chosen.

Outside/private PLACE/FOURTH WALL suggestions:

- A beach: The FOURTH WALL would be the shore and the waves crashing against the shore.
- A park: The FOURTH WALL would be the specific trees, park benches and park signs that are in the PLACE you've chosen.

- A secluded parking lot: The FOURTH WALL would be the specific buildings that you know surround the parking lot. Or, in the case of an underground parking lot, the walls that line the structure.
- A dark alley: The FOURTH WALL would be the buildings that you know exist outside the mouth of the alley.
- In a backyard: The FOURTH WALL would be the specific house that the backyard is a part of.
- On a street or road in the middle of the night: The FOURTH WALL would be the buildings and/or homes or foliage (trees, etc.) that line the street or road.
- In a car: Cars are different because generally you're not stationary—cars move, and as a result, the FOURTH WALL is always changing. Also, you're in an *inside* place, but you're outside. You'll find a car scene in just about every movie or television show, so listen up.

APPLYING PLACE/FOURTH WALL IN AUTOMOBILE SCENES

First, endow the inside of the car with a car you're familiar with, one that brings up the appropriate history to the script. For instance, if the scene is a happy joyride, use the car your family had when you were five and your entire family drove cross-country; or, if the scene is a sex scene, use the car you had unbridled sex in for the first time; or, if the scene is about freedom and excitement, use the first brand-new car you ever bought; or, if the scene is traumatic, use the car that you drove your child around in before the child died or was taken away from you in a custody battle. You get the idea.

Once you've identified the car, then you must personalize the scenery, making sure that what you're passing makes logical sense with the script. For example, your character is driving through a dark, scary wooded area. You can picture an area where something frightening occurred, or imagine an area filled with creatures that terrify you—spiders, rats, snakes, roaches. This creates additional imagery from the thought: "What if my car breaks down and I have to actually face down those spiders, rats, snakes or roaches?" Or perhaps your character is driving home. Then you would endow the neighborhood they're driving through with your route home, including the neighborhoods you drive through, or a childhood neighborhood that brings up the proper emotions for the script. Or maybe your character is driving through a city they've never been in. Here you would endow the city with a specific town in which you've experienced awful events. This will give you a feeling of being displaced, uncomfortable and needing to assimilate and fit in.

Make a choice for your car and the contiguous area that you see outside the car, double-checking to see if these choices follow and make sense to the linear inner work you've already done.

Outside/public PLACE/FOURTH WALL.

- A crowded beach
- A populated park in the day
- In a parking lot, daytime, with lots of cars and people
- An alley in the middle of the day, close to a heavily trafficked street
- A pool with other people swimming and lounging about
- In a backyard with other people, or with people who can come out of the house at any time
- A crowded street
- A sidewalk on a street that has lots of cars buzzing by

Obviously, an outside/public PLACE/FOURTH WALL offers the greatest risk of being exposed. You must not only endow a familiar, emotionally duplicated PLACE/FOURTH WALL from your life with the PLACE/FOURTH WALL you're actually in, but, as with an inside/public space, you must also use SUBSTITUTION to endow one of the non-speaking people who are located around you with someone who would emotionally affect you in some way. Say you're doing a scene where your character is in a park buying heroin from a shady drug dealer. Choose a PLACE/FOURTH WALL where you did something illegal or immoral. Then choose one of the innocuous characters—perhaps the woman walking by with a poodle—and SUBSTITUTE a parent, a critical friend, a teacher, a policeman, your child, someone who will make "drug shopping" a truly nerve-racking experience.

PLACE/FOURTH WALL also infuses a history to your work, making not only the event of the script real but where it is happening real, too. It acclimates you.

The following are varied samples of how some of my students and I have beneficially used PLACE/FOURTH WALL in their work.

PLACE/FOURTH WALL student examples used in movies and television.

- Rick Gonzalez used a street in Brooklyn where he grew up to duplicate the (outside/public) PLACE/FOURTH WALL of the ghetto of Richmond, California, when playing the character of Cruz in the movie *Coach Carter* opposite Samuel L. Jackson.
- Travis Fimmel used his family's farm in Australia as his (outside/public) PLACE/FOURTH WALL for Central Park in New York City while playing Tarzan in the television series *Tarzan.*
- John Adams used the church where his father was a preacher when John was a teenager as his (inside/public) PLACE/FOURTH WALL for the funeral scene in the series *The Dead Zone,* in which John's character of Bruce has to say good-bye for the last time to his dead father. (John's real father is very much alive, so the use of his father's real church as PLACE and his father as a SUBSTITUTION for the dead father made this episode for John extremely profound.)
- Rene Russo used a bathroom from a childhood home for her (inside/private) PLACE/FOURTH WALL of the bathroom she was forced into in the movie *Get Shorty.*
- Melissa Joan Hart used the dock where her father used to fish when she was a child for her (outside/private) PLACE/FOURTH WALL, as a way to reproduce the field in which she and her character's father are alone in the movie *Drive Me Crazy.*
- Tasha Smith used the space where a childhood trauma happened for her (inside/private) PLACE/FOURTH WALL to replicate the space where her heroin-addicted character shoots up in the Emmy-winning HBO miniseries *The Corner.*
- Hoyt Richards used his current home bedroom as his (inside/private) PLACE/ FOURTH WALL to create privacy and intimacy for the sex scene that he had to perform with bare buttocks in the HBO series *Black Tie.*

PLACE/FOURTH WALL are necessary acting tools—
don't ignore or forget to use them.

In my many years as a teacher, getting actors to use PLACE/FOURTH WALL is like pulling teeth. The rationale for using the other tools is more obvious because they clearly allow the emotions to flow, and actors like emotion—a lot. Though the power of PLACE/FOURTH WALL is less obvious, it is essential for maintaining and intensifying the emotions that the other tools induce. But more important, PLACE and the FOURTH WALL lessen the feeling of being watched and judged, which is often what prevents actors from being able to stay present and in the scene. In many cases, the self-consciousness created by a live audience or a running camera actually nullifies an actor's feelings. PLACE/FOURTH WALL serves to strengthen your emotional reality and the sense of privacy, which helps foster even more feeling.

CHAPTER 9

Tool #9:

DOINGS

> The handling of props to produce behavior.

DOINGS are the physicalization of our intentions through the use of props. All the things that people do in life are DOINGS—brushing your hair while speaking, washing the dishes, getting ready for bed, setting the table for company, cooking, primping and cleaning.

DOINGS also tell us more about the who-am-I of a character. Imagine a kitchen argument scene in which your character uses food as a way to deal with the rising tension. The simple act of getting a gallon of ice cream out of the freezer, grabbing a spoon, slamming the silverware door shut, foregoing a bowl and ravenously shoveling spoonfuls of ice cream down your throat while the other person is yelling at you speaks volumes to the other actor(s), as well as to the audience. Or, envision a therapy scene where you, the patient, make intricate origami paper sculptures out of Kleenex. Without hearing the words of the script—simply through the behavior created by making origami sculptures out of the facial tissue (which, given the delicate nature of facial tissue, requires a lot of skill and extreme focus)—the audience understands that the character is anal-retentive, obsessive and incapable of exposing his feelings.

Words can lie. Behavior always tells the truth.

In conversation we often say what we think the other person wants to hear. We use words to conceal our true feelings. They enable us to lie, deceive and sometimes protect others from the truth. Even when you think you're telling the truth, whether you like it or not, your most honest reactions are going to emerge through your behavior. You may be saying one thing, but your behavior betrays your true feelings. This is because most of our behaviors are subconsciously motivated, which makes them impossible to consciously control. No matter how much personal inner work you've infused into your character, your feelings—expressed solely through dialogue—will produce minimal behavior. The handling of props allows you to naturally behave, and the inner work will inform *how* you handle them.

Only actors think standing around, staring intensely at another person and emoting is a powerful and true depiction of life. However, reality is that when human beings are faced with hyperdramatic situations, we do things. And more often than not, we do them fervently.

When the Stakes Are High, We *Do* a Lot

Think about the time you were in the apartment of someone you really liked, alone together for the first time. The sexual tension was high. What did you do to ease your nerves? You might have moseyed over to the person's bookshelf and attempted to casually peruse their collection. Or you might have anxiously eaten some jelly beans out of a bowl on the coffee table as a way to deal with the tension. In your discomfort, you might've even handled something fragile as you cruised the joint. Did you break something or see something you weren't supposed to see? Probably. Coping with your nerves produced spontaneous behavior. These unplanned moments cannot happen without DOINGS.

Or picture being in a scene where your character is in the middle of an argument with a loved one as they are preparing a salad for dinner. You could stop cooking and just stand there and yell at the other person, but it's much more effective and realistic to simply continue making the salad. It allows the other character, as well as the audience, to understand what you're really feeling when you forcefully and with vengeance cut that cucumber as if it is humanly attached to the subject of your wrath. You could viciously tear at a head of lettuce as a threat, showing the other person what's to come if they continue to be so damn critical and derogatory. In this context, making a salad, usually a fairly benign activity, becomes a menacing one. With these DOINGS, there would be no need to yell. The use of DOINGS is so powerful that they allow you to convey your rage even if you're speaking softly.

DOINGS also gives the actor an alternative place to go. When the stakes are high, it's simply impossible to look that person straight in the eye *all the time*. DOINGS gives you a legitimate reason not to have to face the other person. It's so much easier to "lie" while you are busy stirring a pot, rolling a cigarette, preparing a drink, dressing or fixing a pipe under the sink—legitimate activities that prevent you from ever having to look that person directly in the eyes, which, if you were forced to, would reveal that you were being dishonest or uncomfortable.

The next time you're in a highly charged situation of any kind, just watch how physical you become. It's surprising how much activity takes place when you're excited or upset about something. Jim, one of my students, challenged this idea. He insisted that any time he was involved in a heated argument, he stood there and yelled. Nothing more. He maintained this theory until he had a fight with his estranged father, whom he had not seen in years. They were standing on the lawn in front of Jim's house and the old look-what-*you*-did-to-*me*-blame-game evolved into a heated confrontation. As things grew more intense, Jim's father unconsciously began ripping dandelions out of the lawn and tearing them apart. Jim saw this DOING and smiled because he realized that I was right. Unfortunately, Jim's father thought the smile was for him, that his son was being condescending, which, of course, infuriated him even more. The lawn suffered, but Jim got the point: when we get scared, upset, angry or excited, we DO.

The choices you make for your DOINGS flesh out your character's neurosis, social background, educational background, financial status, and how they *really* feel about the other character. Your choice of props/ activities should be appropriate to the character's life (psyche, economic background, present job status, history, sexual predilection, geographical location, time period, etc.).

DOINGS for a low-rent character on a date at a fancy restaurant with someone who is making them feel hostile could be:

- You might find yourself playing with your food in an aggressive way—stabbing the lettuce with your fork, hacking your meat or stuffing food in your mouth to avoid blurting out, "You're such a boring moron," which is what you really want to say.
- You might clean the silverware with your cloth napkin by spitting on it and then wiping it down with ferocity.
- You might play with your food, perhaps rudely sucking the pimento out of an olive and then making hand puppets by slipping the empty olives onto your fingers.

- You might drink too much wine, swigging it down and filling and refilling your glass as the conversation gets more painful and uncomfortable.

Whatever you choose to do, hiding your animosity with DOINGS gives us more information about *what* you're really feeling and *how* you deal with those feelings.

DOINGS can create a sense of unpredictability.

Let's explore a character who would be considered a bad guy, someone who is attempting to scare their intended victim in a gangster scene. Some standard approaches might be to stand and yell and/or grab and/or physically pin the other actor. A DOINGS-driven approach might be to eat Girl Scout cookies (a seemingly innocent act) while you threaten the other character with heinous, unspeakable acts of torture. Munching on cookies that he's acquired from some innocent Girl Scout makes the fear inspired by the bad guy more palpable, because it makes him look like he hurts, mutilates and kills casually—as if it's something he does every day. He can kill you just as easily as he idly consumes a sugar wafer. When someone is violently yelling and pushing you up against the wall, it's pretty obvious that pain and death is bound to follow. DOINGS allows for other possibilities, which disarms and confuses the victim about what's going to happen next. Not knowing what your predator is going to do moment to moment is much more frightening.

DOINGS are essential because we see before we hear.

A picture is worth a thousand words. A cliché? Yes. But it's a cliché for a reason. We should be able to take the sound out of a scene and still know precisely what's going on from the behavior.

DOINGS Must Further Your SCENE OBJECTIVE

DOINGS are not a random handling of props. You must consider your SCENE OBJECTIVE. If your SCENE OBJECTIVE is *"to get you to love me,"* then throwing sharp items at the object of your affection is hardly going to help you accomplish this goal.

A great illustration of considering a character's life circumstances, the who-am-I of the character and the SCENE OBJECTIVE is Brad Pitt's very first scene for class. Brad had just arrived in Hollywood and hadn't taken any professional acting classes. (Yes, there was a time when Brad Pitt was a young man with dreams and no money. He started out like everyone else, taking three menial jobs as a way to support himself and pay for his acting classes.) I assigned him a scene from a play called *Tribute*. In the scene, Brad's character, Jed, is having an indoor picnic with a girl hired by his gregarious and charismatic father to seduce him. Jed is unaware that his father has arranged this. Jed's father feels justified—Jed is painfully shy, a presumed virgin and someone who's spent his childhood having to live in his father's shadow. Brad's SCENE OBJECTIVE was *"to get you to like me."* His OBSTACLES were sexual tension and a lack of knowledge of how one plays "the game." It's not written in the script that Jed serves the girl wine, but Brad brought two long-stemmed wineglasses along with a bottle of wine (a facsimile, not real alcohol—*never* use real alcohol when you are acting) to class for the scene. Brad began the scene by emerging from the kitchen with the bottle and the glasses. Although the dialogue consisted of I'm-just-getting-to-know-you babble, the scene implies se-duction and sex. Eating the food for the picnic—the DOINGS written in the script (the handling and eating of food can be very sexy)—along with using the wine and glasses created an unspoken sexual tension between Brad and his scene partner. Brad's apparent lascivious thoughts made him unconsciously place the glasses on his breasts and seductively twist the stems of the glasses. Although the dialogue was some nebulous discussion of the girl's high school days, it was clear by Brad's DOINGS and the re-sulting behavior that school was not on his mind. We saw what Brad (as Jed) was *really* thinking about through his behavior. This provided the scene with realistic and layered first-sex tension, because a player would have been more slick and self-assured. When you are going after your SCENE OBJECTIVE and really need reactions from the other person, it creates unconscious behavior. By going after his SCENE OBJECTIVE so strongly, Brad wasn't, as the actor, self-conscious or self-aware—his be-havior was allowed to happen the way it does in life, without premedita-tion. It allowed Brad to become, *as the character,* self-conscious and self-aware, because it became so real to him. When I asked Brad, "Did you know you had the wineglasses on your chest and were twisting the stems like one would do to nipples?" He looked at me truly surprised and blushed a deep purple. Apparently not.

In the same scene from *Tribute,* there is a scripted direction (DO-

ING) for the character of Jed to open a jar of pickles and eat one, and the girl is then supposed to ask him to share. It's imperative that he open the jar and begin nibbling on the pickle, or the girl will never be cued for her line, "Could I have a bite of your pickle?" Brad got to the pickle part of the scene and could not get the lid off. No matter how hard he tried, it just wouldn't budge. Instead of doing what most actors would do—stop the scene, get flustered and pull out of character, or change lines to accommodate the unexpected mishap—he silently gave up and handed the pickle jar to her so that she could try her hand at it. Of course, she slipped the lid off effortlessly, which made the audience laugh at his apparent wimpiness. He dared to be spontaneous and look foolish, and by doing so created a real moment and a real connection with the other actor.

Brad knows the benefits of using DOINGS, and he continues to explore them in his career. In the movie *Ocean's Eleven*, he plays Dusty Ryan, a con man in the midst of a complex Las Vegas casino heist. Las Vegas is infamous for its cheap food, which is designed to lure the unsuspecting bargain hunter into the casino to gamble. Brad's character Dusty is a con man, and all con games involve aspects of wanting and needing to feel powerful. Keeping in mind Dusty's OVERALL OBJECTIVE of *"to be empowered in my life,"* Brad figured that Dusty would beat the system and get the food without being tempted into the glitz of possible riches via slots and blackjack. He told the director, Steven Soderbergh, that he felt his character would always be indulging in Las Vegas food, like the 99-cent shrimp cocktail. Soderbergh was all for it, and with the use of DOINGS, Brad turned a typical and slick con-man role into a quirky, flawed and unique character.

DOINGS spark mannerisms, unique affectations and quirky behavior.

Directors often workshop their scripts in class before they go off to shoot or stage their productions. Screenwriter David Marconi, who has written blockbuster movies such as *Enemy of the State,* brought a scene from a feature that he was about to direct called *The Informer.* The scene he put up in class was a necessary expository scene to establish the backstory. The character of Iverson, a handsome and sexy FBI agent, tries to convince Tulsa, a young, gorgeous, drug-addled model, to go undercover to help him discover which wrongdoer killed her best friend. In order to do this, Iverson must explain the case's history, including who he is and

why she would be the right person for the job. The scene takes place after Iverson has spent the night at Tulsa's place—she was so drunk and
stoned and in trouble with the cops that he chivalrously brought her
home and tucked her in (it doesn't go *there* yet—he slept on the couch).
The first time the scene was performed in class, it was static. Basically,
we watched two people sitting on a couch talking. I told the actor playing Iverson, Rod Rowland, to take off his socks (his character had been
wearing them for a good twenty-four hours) to get more comfortable.
Rod did this as he relayed the details of the case. As soon as he had his
socks off, he noticed a smell, as did Sarah Brown, the actress playing
Tulsa. Rod's socks stank. Embarrassed, he teasingly put them in front of
her face. Sarah's face soured and then she giggled. Then, still talking
about the case, Rod put one foot to his nose and realized that his socks
weren't the only things that reeked. Sarah laughed. These simple DO-
INGS bonded Rod and Sarah, along with their characters. They now
shared a private joke, and the humanity and trueness of the moment
made a dry expository scene absorbing.

The characters of Tulsa and Iverson end up together at the end of the
movie, so these simple DOINGS served as an original way to establish
their intimate relationship. And the DOINGS were so effective that
David Marconi not only added them to his script, but also went back
through the story and added more DOINGS to the scene, including Iverson finding some moldy old cheese under the couch, which is also
smelling up the joint and that he has to throw out. David also had Tulsa
smoke a joint throughout the scene. As a result of including these DO-
INGS, David was able to communicate who his characters were through
their behavior.

Through DOINGS, the audience learns that Tulsa:

- Is a slob
- Prioritizes drugs over cleanliness
- Is bold, showing no fear of doing something illegal in front of a
  law enforcement agent.

Through DOINGS, the audience learns that Iverson:

- Has been doing this job for a long time (he's rather casual)
- Must like Tulsa, because he's feeling comfortable enough to play
  with her and not question her drug use
- Is in bad need of some Odor-Eaters.

DOINGS give your character a safe place to go.

Whether we're lying or sexually attracted or simply in danger, we have a tendency to need someplace to go and do something that's familiar. DO-INGS help provide a safe haven. Remember my student Jim's father pulling the lawn out? The DOING of pulling the grass out was a safe place for him as his son berated him for not being a good dad. And this wasn't acting—it was a scene that happened in real life.

Obviously, if DOINGS help provide us with a sense of safety in the real world, then they are just as valuable (if not more) in the world an actor creates. When Barry Pepper played the sharpshooter Private Daniel Jackson in *Saving Private Ryan,* his character in the midst of war (terrifying to even the strongest of veterans) needed something that would give him a sense of well-being. Because Barry is a religious man, we came up with the idea of using a cross that he would always wear around his neck and whenever the war got too scary, he would touch it and look at it, garnering strength and peace from it. This DOING was not written in the script, but ended up giving the audience a deep insight about this character—that God and religion are his resource when he is frightened.

DOINGS bring out a script's humor.

I often assign the same scene over and over again so that my students can see how using the tools and doing the inner work from their own personal events and feelings allows their unique mannerisms and quirks to emerge, thereby making the scene a different and distinct experience for the actor and the audience. For instance, I asked Matthew Perry to do the same scene from *Broadcast News* that I also gave to David Spade, which we discussed for MOMENT BEFORE (tool #7). To recap, this is the scene in which the character of Aaron Altman (played by Albert Brooks) is at home, ruing his poor performance as a news anchor. He knows that he's blown his shot at his dream. Aaron is momentarily elated because Jane Craig (played by Holly Hunter), the love of his life, has come by to see him. He thinks she's there to comfort him after his horrible day. But Jane has stopped by to tell Aaron she's in love with his rival, Tom, a successful news anchor.

The first time Matthew Perry did the scene, he had no props. Matthew, being an inherently funny guy, made the scene mildly amusing. I told him that the scene could be much funnier. We discussed the who-am-I of the character, which is essential in making DOINGS choices. The character of Aaron is a guy who uses humor as his defense and as his way to win. Through working with people like Garry Shandling, Rob Schneider and Jim Carrey, I have found that really funny people seem to collect and own a lot of toys. So I asked Matthew if his home resembled a mini–Toys "Я" Us. He gave me a surprised "yes." Then I asked him to bring a large sampling of his toy collection to use as DOINGS for the rework of the scene. He didn't think this was such a great idea. "What newscaster wannabe has toys?" he asked. He challenged me by saying, "I'm going to bring so much and do so much that you're going to hate it." I'm always up for a debate, so I told him to "bring it on." The following week, Matthew brought in a huge suitcase filled with the kind of toys only Matthew Perry would own. Throughout the scene, he played vigorously with his toys. Through the activity of his playing and his choices of specific toys, we as the audience were better able to understand Aaron's angst, his love for Jane, and who he was as a person. We saw Aaron's humanity—his frustration, insecurities and failed history with women. These DOINGS gave Aaron a three-dimensionality that made him more accessible and a person who we as an audience could relate to. An audience will feel much more compelled to laugh if they're relating to the way a character handles an extremely uncomfortable situation, saying to themselves, "Been there, done that." Matthew, fully expecting to prove me wrong, used the DOINGS with a vengeance. Yet the more DOINGS he did, the bigger the laughs he got. In fact, he had to stop speaking several times because the class's laughter was so strong. Matthew learned a valuable lesson, and this scene turned out to be his breakthrough scene. Soon after he began to book just about everything that came his way, including his heralded and Emmy-winning performance on the long-running series *Friends*.

You can change the DOINGS.

The writer may have put particular DOINGS in the script, but these are often just suggestions. If the DOING doesn't rely on the scripted dialogue, then it's up to you, the actor, to use your imagination—always considering the who-am-I of the character, the time period and the character's SCENE OBJECTIVE. Don't just use DOINGS where they're indicated in the script. The more DOINGS you have, the more behavior can emerge.

Personalize Your DOINGS by Infusing Information About Your SUBSTITUTION and INNER OBJECTS

You must personalize your DOINGS so they mean something special to you. If you are at a future lover's home and happen to pick up one of the photographs displayed on a counter, you need to use your SUBSTITU-TION and endow what's pictured in the photo with a person that makes emotional sense to the scene and you. Let's look at the first date scene in Neil Simon's *Chapter Two,* when the character of George picks up a photo of Jenny's ex-husband. George's wife of ten years has recently died, and this is his first time out. Because it's been so long since he's dated and he's still mourning the death of someone he loved, he's ex-tremely awkward. In the dialogue, George asks Jenny who the man is in the photo. Jenny tells him that it is her ex-husband. If you were playing the character of George, you might endow the picture with someone from your personal life who is a competitor, a nemesis or someone that could put a damper on having a future relationship with your SUBSTI-TUTION for Jenny.

You might be playing an alcoholic who's DOING is—surprise, surprise—drinking alcohol. If you actually have a propensity toward al-coholism, you would endow the liquid in front of you with your alcohol of choice. If not, then you'd endow the drink in front of you with the vice you do have (and most people have at least one): drugs, sex, sleep, food, shopping, a computer obsession—you name it. Anything done in pro-found excess can be considered a vice.

A scene might require your character to put a CD in the stereo and play some music, so you'd then endow the particular music playing with that special song that you shared with your SUBSTITUTION for the scene. Or you might endow the CD with the music that reminds you of emotionally charged past events that match up to the feelings you're supposed to have, as supplied by the script's text.

Charmed is a television series that brings the supernatural to three women's lives, which means the DOINGS often don't make sense for those of us who are not witches or warlocks. In a number of scenes in one episode, the character of Chris, played by Drew Fuller, has a ring that he holds, touches, muses over and gives to his one true love, who then returns it. It's not just a ring that signifies love—there's a mysticism attached to it. The ring originally came from the future and now resides in the past, which, by the way, equals today. Confusing, yes, but it doesn't have to be. By endowing this magical ring with something real from Drew's love life, Drew could make the ring into something that inspired great significance. As we were trying to figure out what he would use for this ring, I happened to notice a leather band on his wrist. I asked about it and he told me that his girlfriend and he wear matching leather bands to symbolize their love for each other. They never take them off. In fact, their agreement is that if either one of them does take the band off, it means the relationship is over. Eureka—the perfect solution! I told Drew to endow the ring (his DOING throughout a good part of this episode) with his leather band, infusing all of its personal implications. Endowing the ring in this way made it easy to elicit the proper emotions that he needed the ring to represent—love and the eventual loss of love that was supposed to come from the scripted DOING.

When Identifying Your Character's DOINGS, Consider Their Neurosis, Career Path and Modus Operandi

DOINGS visually expose a character's neurosis.

Most characters have a defining phobia or neurosis. If not, then it's up to the actor to come up with something that makes the character stand out. In *Scarface,* Al Pacino's character of Tony Montana wouldn't have been as rich without his extreme paranoia. *Othello* would not be *Othello* without Othello's obsessive jealousy. Lady Macbeth would be just another nagging wife if she didn't have her fanatical ambition. Joe Pesci needed his Napoleon complex to justify the character of Nicky Santoro in *Casino.* The character of Virginia Woolf would have been just any morose writer if she didn't have suicidal tendencies in *The Hours.* Brick in *Cat on a Hot Tin Roof* would be a bore without his alcoholism and his unresolved father issues. And Oedipus would merely be a mama's boy without his mother obsession. DOINGS help to create a deep, visual understanding of how and why a character's neurosis or psychosis exists.

In *Uptown Girls,* Marley Shelton played Ingrid, a character with profound anal-retentive tendencies. When I helped Marley prepare for the role, we decided that we didn't want to just rely on the dialogue or costuming to convey this. We decided that everything Ingrid did would have a system. She would apply Chap Stick right to left, sit the same way every time, and her tiny purse would be filled with items that would keep her prepared and protected from the world. Things like lavender-scented hand towels, nail scissors, gloves for reading the newspaper, hand-gel purifier, breath mints, facial tissues, a mini-fan (to blow away smoke in the nightclub scenes) and air fresheners. We also agreed that Ingrid would use these towels and tissues to constantly clean surfaces like seats, coffee tables and glasses. I told her to commit to becoming anal-retentive, to take any and every opportunity to arrange, organize and perfect her surroundings. In the film, the financially broke character of Molly Gunn, Ingrid's best friend, holds a garage sale to raise some money. Marley, as Ingrid, made sure in the scene that everything was stacked perfectly, excessively organized and priced accurately. She even ran around with a hand steamer for wrinkle emergencies. Every scene was so heavily laden with anal-retentive activities that Marley began to act like Ingrid in her own life. The DOINGS became so organic to her that much to her husband's dismay, she began to behave as an anal-retentive after hours. The act of her doing her DOINGS helped her to truly *become* the character.

Under the same category of neurosis are those characters that have serious substance-abuse problems. The following are examples of how some of my students and I realized their character's particular addiction by the use of DOINGS.

Overeating

In class, Robin McDonald put up a scene from the play *Pizza Man*. She played the character of Alice, an overeater who has lost weight for her married boyfriend. In the scene, Alice comes home after she discovers that her boyfriend has gone back to his wife. This is a great excuse for her to do some major consuming. She quickly notices that her alcoholic roommate and friend has spent all their money on liquor. Most people with a substance-abuse problem will have secret stashes hidden for binge crises. For this scene, Robin put a Kit Kat in a flower pot, Twinkies behind the curtains, potato chips under the couch and beef jerky underneath the couch's cushions. This setup gave Robin the motivation to move around the room, surreptitiously finding each item and trying to find a way to eat it without the roommate noticing. Most addicts don't display their addiction; they imbibe secretly. Alice's words were underlined by behavior that was created by her sneaky and on-the-sly munching.

Alcoholism

Leticia in *Monster's Ball* is a woman in denial. Who wouldn't be, after your husband is executed, your child dies in a car accident and you lose your job? Halle and I decided that Leticia would make her alcohol abuse seem like less of a problem by having her only drink out of little airplane bottles of whiskey. This way, Leticia could drink ten bottles in one sitting, but rationalize her behavior by thinking, "I don't have a drinking problem. I mean, how much could I *really* be drinking if the bottles are so small?" The small containers made her feel like she was drinking a whole lot less. When she daintily offered Hank a drink, Leticia could feel as though she was entertaining in style—daintily screwing off the tiny metal cap and handing him the mini-bottle—without revealing that she might have a drinking problem. In the film, the characters sit together, talking about her dead son and sipping from these doll-size whiskey bottles, which provides the film with a great visual that also indicates her social, financial and emotional status.

Drug Abuse

An integral part of drug use and abuse is the ritual of getting high or stoned. For instance, as part of their ceremony, potheads will pull the marijuana from the baggie, smell it, lick the papers together, flake the weed onto the papers, roll it and then lick the joint so as to make it firm and compact. Cokeheads will chop, cut and snort cocaine with their preferred devices on their preferred surfaces. These DOINGS create anticipation and are an integral part of the intoxicating experience.

Eriq LaSalle directed and starred in the HBO miniseries *Rebound,* which is about a diehard junkie and basketball player who pulls his life together to become a basketball coach and mentor to young people who've felt the magnetic yet destructive pull of heroin. Eriq played Diego, a diehard junkie, yet Eriq had never taken or done any drugs of any kind. He had no idea what it felt like to do heroin and was oblivious to the heroin-using rituals. We talked about how there's a sexual quality to "entering" a needle in a vein and releasing a "feel-good" substance into it. The cooking of the liquid in the spoon and the needle sucking the heated liquid into the needle's cylinder is like sexual foreplay. And that sex, when it gets to a certain point, becomes a must-have event, a necessity, the same way heroin is to an addict. When he fully understood this DOING, Eriq could feel the gritty reality of the why, the how and the desperation of his heroin-addicted character.

Sexaholism

Sexaholics use sex as their way to feel powerful. Sex, too, is such a strong, primal force that often it makes people do things they wouldn't ordinarily do. Using sexuality is a great way to win what you want. A sexaholic is aware of the power that sex has over people. Deborah Kara Unger understood the power of using sex when she put up a scene in class from Shakespeare's *The Taming of the Shrew.* As the character of Kate, Deborah needed to find a way to have power over her worthy adversary and future mate, Petruchio. Considering the day and age of the play, Deborah knew that Kate's sexuality was her most valuable commodity. She came up with the DOING of cutting an orange and then forcefully squeezing the pulpy juice so that it poured into her mouth and then dripped sensually down her lips, chin, neck and chest (she was wearing a low-cut top with plenty of cleavage). She then wiped her lips with the back of her hand and luxuriously rubbed the juice and pulp into her chest. The actor (I don't remember who he was—frankly, I was so entranced by her DOING that I can't remember much else) became putty in her hands, and Deborah won the scene.

No matter what your character is addicted to, addicts take huge risks—robbing banks, killing, having multiple affairs, and being willing to lose a friend, family or a job just to get their drug. If you're playing an addict, your DOINGS should consider and reflect these extreme behaviors.

DOINGS reveal your character's modus operandi.

Neuroses and psychoses are different than one's modus operandi. Mental and chemical imbalances are not in our control. They are usually OBSTACLES, additional hurdles to jump over in attaining and winning the SCENE OBJECTIVE. A modus operandi (how we operate) is a set of behaviors that we use to *help* us to achieve and win our goals.

All of us have an M.O. we use to get our way and win. When in doubt, we use what we know has successfully worked for us in the past. Some of us use sex; some use violence; some humor; some intellect; some use physical prowess and some use their authority or power position in life. The following are examples of possible DOINGS for these M.O.s. Don't be limited by these suggestions. Be creative.

M.O. for People Who Use Violence

Films and plays featuring this type of character: *In the Boom Boom Room, Goodfellas, American Psycho, Streamers, Reservoir Dogs, A Clock-*

work Orange, Danny and the Deep Blue Sea, Edmund, Secretary, Cape Fear

- Playing with a gun or knife or practicing moves with it; cleaning your gun or knife; whittling with a switchblade; hitting a punching bag or some facsimile; using hand-exercise equipment; throwing or breaking something; violently squeezing clay to mold an object; eating the kind of food that makes hard sounds; making a salad by wielding a large knife and viciously cutting into the carrot, cucumber, lettuce, etc.; building something that requires a hammer or a saw; doing drugs like smoking a joint, snorting coke; using sharp scissors to clean and cut your fingernails; etc.

M.O. for People Who Use Humor
Films and plays featuring this type of character: *Annie Hall, Gingerbread Lady, Lost in Translation, Animal House, Chapter Two, Bringing Up Baby, Life Is Beautiful, Frankie and Johnny, When Harry Met Sally, A Thousand Clowns*

- Playing with funny toys like windup dolls; mini-figurines; paddle sticks; toy army men; a doll that speaks, burps or passes gas, etc.; trying on weird hats or clothes; playing with food like sucking up spaghetti, or trying to eat peanuts by throwing them up in the air and catching them in your mouth, or making a puppet show out of carrot sticks; crumpling up paper and trying to make baskets into any circular object; picking up and playing with items that belong to the other person, maybe even intimate things; drinking wine by gargling with it first; drinking anything that allows for a spit-take; putting underwear on your head; etc.

M.O. for People Who Use Their Intellect
Films and plays featuring this type of character: *Geniuses, The Real Thing, Speed-the-Plow, Uncommon Women and Others, My Dinner with Andre, Brideshead Revisited, Reversal of Fortune, Dead Poets Society, True West, Equus*

- Using a computer; reading something scholarly, doing Sunday's *New York Times* crossword puzzle, writing, taking photographs; always pulling out a writing pad and jotting down your thoughts;

eating food that is exotic; drinking brandy or fine wine; fixing or installing something that is technically difficult; sketching or painting; cooking something that's complicated; playing with a pen or pencil; etc.

M.O. for People Who Use Sex
Films featuring this type of character: *The Misfits; The Last Seduction; Sexual Perversity in Chicago; American Gigolo; Body Heat; Last Tango in Paris; The Unbearable Lightness of Being; Summer and Smoke; Sex, Lies, and Videotape; Fool for Love; Desire Under the Elms*

- *Women:* Eating a juicy peach; shooting whipped cream directly into the mouth; drinking and letting some of the liquid drip down your chin and chest; bending over to choose a CD to put in the stereo; dancing and swaying to music as you play with the CD cover; eating something phallic; putting cream on chest and arms; sensuously lapping up sweat with a tissue above your breasts; fixing your nylons; drinking alcohol and playing with the ice in the glass or the stem of a wineglass; etc.

- *Men:* Chugging down a beer; breaking nuts with your bare hands; seductively fixing something mechanical with a screw-driver; lasciviously eating a mango or kiwi; using any excuse for legitimate contact with the person who is the object of your desire, like picking lint off her sweater, etc.; creating an excuse to take off your shirt and taking it off; wiping sweat off chest or brow; etc.

M.O. for People Who Use Power/Authority
Films and plays featuring this type of character: *Wall Street, Nixon, Angels in America, Working Girl, Hamlet, The Great Santini, A Few Good Men, Speed-the-Plow, Sweet Bird of Youth, Hedda Gabler, Mary of Scotland, Faustus*

- Balancing your checkbook or writing a check; using a tape recorder or videotape recorder; entering data into your cell phone or PalmPilot; cleaning off your utensils before you eat; writing on a pad in a way that says, "I'm writing something 'telling' or 'secretive' about you . . ."; dressing or undressing in an impeccable manner; going through your billfold and counting a large amount of money; smoking a cigar; shining your shoes fastidiously; drinking fine brandy; eating exotic and expensive foods like oysters, quail or paté; etc.

M.O. for People Who Use Athletic Prowess

Films and plays featuring this type of character: *The Wager, Raging Bull, Bull Durham, The Hustler, The Color of Money, Rocky, The Great White Hope*

- Playing basketball, golf, football, etc.; using mini-exercise equipment like barbells, travel-size foot bikes, a StairMaster, mini-trampoline, etc.; dressing or undressing in a manner that allows you to show off your physique; throwing a ball into the air and catching it constantly; waxing down a baseball glove; picking up anything heavy and using it as a barbell; drinking Gatorade; lifting and/or moving heavy objects; hitting a punching bag; making and drinking a protein shake; practicing your sport in some way; etc.

DOINGS define the career of the character.

Here are some examples of classic jobs that are represented again and again in movies, television and theater, and the DOINGS that can be used. These are just a few of the thousands that can be done. Use your imagination to come up with DOINGS choices that are career appropriate. Remember to also consider the neurosis and the M.O. of the character when making your decisions for DOINGS.

- **Police Officer**

  Cleaning or unholstering or holstering your gun; playing with your handcuffs; fiddling with the police radio; using a tape recorder; writing on a pad; smoking; drinking, spilling, cleaning up coffee; eating on-the-run junk food like doughnuts, Slim Jims or PowerBars; putting on makeup; using Handi Wipes (for those anal-retentive cops who have to touch filthy things in a crime investigation); etc.

• Doctor

Writing out a prescription; organizing or giving out pill samples; putting on or taking off surgical gloves; sterilizing medical instruments; washing hands; playing around with medical instruments; buttoning the white lab coat; perusing the medical records; looking at X-rays; looking something up in a medical manual or on a computer; etc.

• Psychiatrist

Writing on a pad; using the tissue dispenser; making coffee or tea; drinking coffee or tea; playing with worry beads; writing on or perusing the patient's records or previous notes made; knitting; doing a crossword puzzle; etc.

• Nurse

Writing into or examining a patient's records; preparing medical instruments; putting paper on the examining table; rearranging a patient's personal items; eating junk food; eating off the patient's food tray; sterilizing medical tools; preparing for a patient to come in or cleaning up after a patient; taking a patient's temperature or blood pressure; adjusting an IV; preparing a needle; emptying bed pans; making a bed; etc.

• Computer Expert

Using the computer; eating junk food; smoking cigarettes; fixing the computer with items such as a screwdriver; cleaning off eyeglasses; preparing or drinking coffee, tea or juice; downloading music into an iPod; messing around with a PalmPilot; playing music on a stereo; eating microwave popcorn; etc.

• Painter

Painting or sketching; cleaning paint brushes; arranging the model or things that are to be painted; drinking or doing drugs; preparing unique and colorful food; organizing studio space; taking pictures; munching on jelly beans; etc.

• Housekeeper

Sweeping; polishing tables, silverware, etc; mopping; dusting; plumping pillows; sponging off dirty areas; using cleaning products; washing or drying dishes; cooking; eating; doing laundry; going through the owner's personal effects; etc.

• Bartender/Waiter

Cleaning or polishing drinking glasses; cleaning the counter or table; organizing the bar; counting the tip money; arranging the cash register; drinking; preparing the bill; refilling peanut bowls, ketchup or mustard bottles; restocking the drink condiments or preparing drink condiments (like cutting orange or lime slices); etc.

• Prostitute/Stripper

Putting on or taking off sexy clothing; putting on makeup; preparing and/or drinking alcohol; smoking marijuana; preparing and snorting cocaine; taking pills; cleaning off body parts like neck, arms, upper chest or legs; putting on body cream; eating something phallic-shaped, like a lollipop, licorice stick or baguette; spooning out something like ice cream or oatmeal and licking the spoon; smoothing your nylons while wearing them; putting on or taking off nail polish; styling hair; etc.

• Politician

Going through your briefcase; reading your own press coverage in the paper; highlighting items in a newspaper or magazine; shaving; putting on cologne or aftershave; jotting down notes; checking yourself in the mirror; talking into a tape recorder; eating mints; using hand-exercise machines; putting product in hair; etc.

• Receptionist/Secretary/Assistant

Filing; organizing papers; eating a brown-bag lunch; preparing or drinking coffee; using the computer; taking notes; filing nails or putting on nail polish; putting on makeup; putting on hand cream; massaging one's hands or feet; sharpening pencils; using correction fluid; paper-clipping papers; brushing hair; filing; programming the phone; using a calculator or an adding machine; sharpening pencils; perusing files; using scissors or a paper-cutter; looking for appropriate items in desk drawer; etc.

• Housewife/Mother

Cutting out coupons; folding laundry; cleaning; picking up the kids' toys; making the bed; putting away groceries; making lists; styling your hair; putting on various anti-aging products; using a ThighMaster; cooking; flipping through magazines such as *Redbook* and *Family Circle;* dusting; taking pills; doing a crossword puzzle; etc.

• Construction Worker

Eating fast food or a sandwich; drinking beer, soda or water; going through or organizing your tools; chewing on breath mints or gum; adjusting safety goggles; sandpapering calluses off fingers; using a Walkman; cleaning tools; etc.

• Actor

Primping by using hair products like gels and hairspray; looking into a hand-mirror; eating lo-cal snacks; putting on showy accessories; putting on makeup; perusing a script; playing with toys, props or awards from previous acting jobs; drinking designer water; trying new facial expressions or moves; etc.

• Lab Technician

Using, fixing, cleaning or storing the appropriate scientific tools; making a sandwich with the tools; eating in a precise way; experimenting; etc.

Eric Szmanda plays Greg Sanders, a lab technician, on the hit television series *CSI.* The key to playing this role is to use as many DOINGS as possible. In fact, Eric got the role by miming the use of macabre DOINGS in his audition. A medical examiner's lab is filled with devices ranging from the norm—swabs, sutures, scalpels—to the gruesome— morbid tools that perform all sorts of ghastly tasks on the dead. Eric's audition scene was about Greg Sanders reporting to the ME what he's done to determine the cause of death of a body. The dialogue included a lot of medi-speak. I instructed Eric to physically illustrate everything his character discusses. For instance, in one of his monologues, Greg has to discuss his findings, which he gathered from "an anal swab." In the audition, Eric (playing Greg) mimed what his character had done with an anal swab and then unconsciously brought the swab to his nose and smelled it. As a result, Eric realized a character who was distinctive and unique from all the other actors who auditioned. He also made his character easy to write for. This is key, because more often than not, television writers are also the producers, the very ones making the casting decisions. Eric inspired the show's writers/producers so much that his role, which was originally supposed to occasionally recur, was expanded. Because of his DOINGS, which were so compelling and quirky, Eric's character eventually became a regular starring role.

Outside Place DOINGS

In addition to considering your character's neuroses, M.O. and career, you should always consider the space you are in. The possibilities for outside DOINGS can be slim, because there are often not as many legitimate props available. This does not mean that this is an excuse to not have DOINGS. Here are some suggestions for outside DOINGS.

- **Car**

    Going through your purse; playing with the radio; tapping the steering wheel; rolling a window up or down; eating candy or fast food; drinking coffee or soda; spilling coffee or soda or food; cleaning the mess up; putting on makeup; etc.

- **Park or Bus Stop**

    Drinking a soda; drinking coffee in a Styrofoam container; eating candy or fast food; playing with the leaves on the ground; playing with a tree twig; whittling; listening to a Walkman; watching a Watchman; people-watching; playing with the buttons or zipper on a sweater or jacket; using a toothpick; throwing bread crumbs to the birds; drinking out of a flask; reading; writing; going through a purse or wallet; taking photos; looking at photos; drawing; etc.

- **Beach**

    Putting on suntan lotion; making a sand castle; drinking beer; pulling food out of a cooler; eating; rocking out to rock and roll coming from a boom box; putting on colored sun blockers; flipping through a magazine; people-watching using binoculars; reading a beach book; taking photos; drawing; eating fast food; cleaning sand off your body; etc.

- **Walk and Talk**

   Using a toothpick; playing with change in your pockets; playing with a rubber band; putting on a scarf or gloves; sipping coffee; drinking designer water; playing with the buttons or zipper on your shirt or jacket; eating candy or fast food; applying Chap Stick; kicking a rock; tossing a rock; etc.

Inside Place DOINGS

Inside place DOINGS will be determined by the space itself and what props and furniture might naturally exist within that environment. Don't be afraid to use what already exists in the space. Suggestions for inside place DOINGS:

- **In an Office**

   Make a copy on the Xerox machine; get a cup of water from the water cooler; make yourself some coffee out of the office coffeepot; work on the computer; use a calculator; go to the file cabinet and rearrange the files; etc.

- **In a Restaurant**

   Occupy yourself with the utensils, napkins, bread and butter, crudités, water, wine and wineglasses, sugar packets, condiments like mustard or ketchup, salt and pepper shakers, etc.

- **In a Hotel/Motel Room**

   Peruse the inevitable Bible; fill or empty drawers from or to your suitcases; look through a local guidebook; raid the mini-bar; steal towels; play with the mini-shampoo, conditioner, body cream, sewing kit and shower cap; play with the black-out curtains; etc.

- **In a Garage**

   Fool around with the tools; play with the parked car; dust off the stored furniture; investigate what's in the stored boxes; use the out-of-commission exercise equipment; etc.

Sometimes a great prop-person will fill the space with the right props to help an actor with their DOINGS, but don't necessarily leave it up to someone else. It's up to you, the actor, to make sure that you're not left with nothing to do, becoming a boring, uninteresting "talking head." You can bring personal props or talk to the prop master and director about providing the props you need. Don't worry about offending the director or production designer. As long as everyone sees that it's in the best interest of telling the story, most directors and designers will welcome your input. If you have a good idea, it only makes the director and designer look better because it enhances the production, which is good for everyone.

By now, you should have a pretty good sense of how to think about a character's DOINGS—by considering your character's SCENE OBJECTIVE, neurosis, career, M.O. and locale. Finding the appropriate doings is a game of mix and match. There are no right or wrong DOINGS choices; let your personality and imagination be your guide.

DOINGS: The Practical Application

The following is a scene I have written to illustrate the application of DOINGS. My suggestions for DOINGS are handwritten on the left side of the dialogue (to avoid confusion with BEATS and ACTIONS, which are always written on the right). This is the way you should write DOINGS onto your script. Always handwrite your DOINGS choices in the general vicinity of where in the script you want to accomplish your DOINGS. The DOINGS choice you write on your script doesn't have to happen precisely where you put it. Your DOING choice should be a general indication of what you should be doing and when it should happen. Don't stick to your DOINGS choices like glue. Let them emerge organically. The DOINGS you write on your script are merely ideas—you can veer off to other DOINGS that are available on the set. Also, if you find that you're only accomplishing a few of your DOINGS ideas, that's all right. Better to have too much than be left with nothing to do. There will not be a DOINGS for every line or BEAT because DOINGS take time to accomplish. Actual dialogue follows.

THE CONFRONTATION

[*Int. one-room apartment—night. John is sitting alone on the couch looking alone, desperate and tipsy. We hear a key turn in the lock. Tina, his wife, opens the door and enters.*]

TINA
Aren't you supposed to be at work?

JOHN
I got laid off.

TINA
[*Suspiciously*]
I don't understand. Usually, when you get laid off,
they give you some notice.

JOHN
I guess my boss didn't read the *Laying Someone
Off* book of etiquette. Remind me to get him a copy.

TINA
You were fired, weren't you?

JOHN
Why do you think that?

TINA
Oh, gee. Maybe it's because you've lost six
jobs in three months.
JOHN
Give me some credit—it's not easy making
that many people hate you in such a short
period of time.

TINA
[*Fed up*]
Same reason?

JOHN
Yep.

TINA
Drinking on the job. When are you going to
realize you have a problem?

JOHN
[*Dripping with sarcasm*]
The only problem I have is that we've run out of
scotch. Do you mind running to the store, dear,
and getting me a fifth?

TINA
Sure, let me go right now . . . oh, but I forgot—I don't
have any money because someone I know can't
keep a job. Which, since last I heard, is a requirement
for a paycheck.

JOHN
That's a nasty rumor—don't believe it.

TINA
[Screaming with frustration]
I've had it. I can't do this anymore!

JOHN
Witty repartee isn't enough?

TINA
No.

JOHN
I didn't think so. What if I threw in a set of
dish towels?

[She exits, slamming the door behind her.]

JOHN
[Yelling after her]
What if I get you a turtle? They make nice pets . . .

[Nothing.]
I'll teach him how to roll over . . .
[One last try.]
Tell ya what, I'll let you name him!
[She doesn't return.]

Possible DOINGS from Tina's P.O.V.

Keeping in mind Tina's SCENE OBJECTIVE, *"to get you to change so we can stay together,"* here are some possible DOINGS:

THE CONFRONTATION

[Int. one-room apartment—night. John is sitting alone on the couch looking alone, desperate and tipsy. We hear a key turn in the lock. Tina, his wife, opens the door and enters.]

Carrying in a bag of groceries

TINA
Aren't you supposed to be at work?

unloading the
"generic" groceries   JOHN
into the   I got laid off.
cupboards

TINA
[*Suspiciously*]
I don't understand. Usually, when you get laid off,
they give you some notice.

JOHN
I guess my boss didn't read the *Laying Someone
Off* book of etiquette. Remind me to get him a copy.

*"accidentally" drop a glass
jar that you're pulling out of the*   **TINA**
grocery   **You were fired, weren't you?**
*bag, just to let him know
how frustrated you are*

JOHN
Why would you think that?

get a sponge, paper   **TINA**
towels and   **Oh, gee. Maybe it's because you've lost six**
dustpan to   **jobs in three months.**
clean it up

JOHN
Give me some credit—it's not easy making
that many people hate you in such a short
period of time.

*clean up the glass
fragments and the jar's*   **TINA**
contents and dump   [*Fed up*]
into garbage **Same reason?**
(this will take time)

JOHN
Yep.

TINA
Drinking on the job. When are you going to
realize you have a problem?

JOHN
[*Dripping with sarcasm*]
The only problem I have is that we've run out of
scotch. Do you mind running to the store, dear,
and getting me a fifth?

TINA
Sure, let me go right now . . . oh, but I forgot—I don't
have any money because someone I know can't
keep a job. Which, since last I heard, is a requirement
for a paycheck.

JOHN
That's a nasty rumor, don't believe it.

grab an overnight bag and
stuff it with clothes   TINA
and personal   [*Screaming with frustration*]
effects,   I've had it, I can't do this anymore!
hastily pulling drawers open,
roughly grabbing items from   JOHN
the closet   Witty repartee isn't enough?
(This lets him know
how serious you are.)   TINA
                No.

JOHN
I didn't think so. What if I threw in a set of
dish towels?

[*She exits, slamming the door behind her.*]

JOHN
[*Yelling after her*]
What if I get you a turtle? They make nice pets . . .
[*Nothing.*]
I'll teach him how to roll over . . .
[*One last try.*]
Tell ya what, I'll let you name him!
[*She doesn't return.*]

Possible DOINGS from John's P.O.V.

Consider John's SCENE OBJECTIVE of "*to get you to love me in spite of my problem*" in making your choices for DOINGS.

THE CONFRONTATION

[*Int. ONE-ROOM APARTMENT—NIGHT. John is sitting alone on the couch looking alone, desperate and tipsy. We hear a key turn in the lock. Tina, his wife, opens the door and enters.*]

Hide empty "no-label" liquor
bottles. Perhaps, throw away
a "box" of wine before   TINA
she enters   Aren't you supposed to be at work?

grab a banana and in an
attempt to hide   JOHN
your real   I got laid off.
activities, nonchalantly peel it.

TINA
[*Suspiciously*]
I don't understand. Usually, when you get laid off,
they give you some notice.

eat the banana   JOHN
I guess my boss didn't read the *Laying Someone
Off* book of etiquette. Remind me to get him a copy.

TINA
You were fired, weren't you?

JOHN
Why would you think that?

TINA
Oh, gee. Maybe it's because you've lost six
jobs in three months.
                                        JOHN
Give me some credit—it's not easy making
that many people hate you in such a short
period of time.

*get the newspaper and
pull out the classified   TINA
section*   [*Fed up*]
        Same reason?

JOHN
        Yep.

TINA
Drinking on the job. When are you going to
realize you have a problem?
*get a pen, read and
circle job opportunities*   JOHN
[*Dripping with sarcasm*]
The only problem I have is that we've run out of
scotch. Do you mind running to the store, dear,
and getting me a fifth?

TINA
Sure, let me go right now . . . oh, but I forgot—I don't
have any money because someone I know can't
keep a job. Which, since last I heard, is a requirement
for a paycheck.

JOHN
That's a nasty rumor, don't believe it.

                              TINA
                    [*Screaming with frustration*]
                  I've had it, I can't do this anymore!

                              JOHN
                  Witty repartee isn't enough?

                              TINA
            No.

                              JOHN
                  I didn't think so. What if I threw in a set of
                  dish towels?

            [*She exits, slamming the door behind her.*]

violently throw the pen at the door
open the door and   JOHN
call after her   [*Yelling after her*]
                  What if I get you a turtle? They make nice pets . . .
            [*Nothing.*]
                  I'll teach him how to roll over . . .
            [*One last try.*]
                  Tell ya what, I'll let you name him!
slam the door as hard as she did
            [*She doesn't return.*]

John's DOINGS communicate:

  • PLACE and poor financial status: the one-room apartment and
    his use of generic, no-label liquor, and/or the use of wine that
    comes in a box
  • His alcoholism, which includes an alcoholic's need to conceal
    the problem
  • That he covers using humor
  • Their long-term relationship problems
  • His long-term job problems

Tina's DOINGS communicate:

  • Their poverty status, indicated by her "generic," no-label gro-
    ceries
  • Her caretaking
  • Her long-term frustration (displayed by her breaking things and
    the violent way she packs up her belongings to leave)

- That she covers using humor (part of what bonds them, because they both use the same M.O.)
- Her sense of being a bit of a drama queen

It's important to note that even though this is, at the very most, a three-minute scene, so much can be DONE and conveyed within such a short period of time using DOINGS. DOINGS further intensify the scene's arc as well as supports and strengthens the character's (and actor's) journey, which is initiated by the SCENE OBJECTIVE. And DOINGS are important because behavior rarely happens by just standing there and saying the words.

CHAPTER 10

Tool #10:

INNER MONOLOGUE

> The dialogue inside your head
> that you don't speak out loud.

While INNER OBJECTS are the pictures and images in our minds that are attached to the words in the script, INNER MONOLOGUE is actual *dialogue*—words and sentences going on inside our head. Although IN-NER MONOLOGUE and INNER OBJECTS are separate tools, they are inextricably linked, because they must work together to create a linear and comprehensive inner story. For instance, in the movie *The Wizard of Oz,* Dorothy speaks often about wanting to go home. The INNER OB-JECT would be the visual of the home the actor would want to return to and the INNER MONOLOGUE would be the inner dialogue regarding going home that she can't speak aloud. So, as the actress playing Dorothy is visualizing the picture of the home she's using, she might be saying as her INNER MONOLOGUE, "I'm never gonna get home with you losers helping me out. I mean, you, Scarecrow, don't even have a brain, and you, Cowardly Lion, well, I think your name says it all. And your pal, the Tin Man, is a heartless shell of a man. I am so screwed." These would be her real thoughts, even though she's expressing in the scripted dialogue that these weird creatures are her friends. Just working with INNER OBJECTS is not enough. You need a dialogue around them. The tools complement each other, providing your brain with pictures (INNER OBJECTS) and words (INNER MONOLOGUE) that make your charac-ter's thinking truly human. Using INNER MONOLOGUE in conjunction with INNER OBJECTS serves to accurately duplicate the way a real per-son's thought process works.

The spoken words are available to the actor in the script, but it's up to the actor to fill in the inner conversation. Generally speaking, INNER MONOLOGUE is defined paranoia: all the things you can't say because it will make you seem wrong, vulgar, mean, insecure, crazy, stupid or prejudiced.

INNER MONOLOGUE includes:

- Thoughts and ideas of what you're going to say next.
- Second-guessing what you've already said or done as inane, inappropriate, too forward, not forward enough, stupid, trying too hard, scary, not scary enough, etc.
- Interpreting what the other person is really saying and doing— is he/she covering? Does he/she like me? Does he/she hate me? Is he/she trying to get away from me? Does he/she think I'm stupid? Does he/she think I'm ugly? Anything that makes you question the other person's feelings and perception of you.
- Remembering thoughts of past history with that person, or past history that occurred in a similar circumstance.
- Your slanted and paranoid interpretation of what the other person is trying to say to you (at the same time the other person is saying it.)
- Anything you would censor if you were to say it aloud. Dialogue that remains in your head can be smutty, not politically correct, inappropriate, evil, judgmental, paranoid and ignorant. After all, you're the only one who knows what you're *really* thinking.

Using the word "you" enables interactive behavior as a result of the INNER MONOLOGUE.

The INNER MONOLOGUE is always stated in a way that connects with the other person. INNER MONOLOGUE is not talking to yourself. INNER MONOLOGUE is the unspoken communication between people. It creates an unspoken interaction. Write your INNER MONOLOGUE in a way that establishes intercommunication with you and the other character(s). To do this, use the word "you" when addressing your thoughts to the other person, instead of expressing your thoughts to yourself by using "he" or "she."

For example, it is *not:*

- "Why is *she* looking at me so weirdly? *She* must think I'm crazy. . . ."

Using "she" creates introspection, which means the actor is acting in a vacuum.

Instead, it *is:*

- "Why are *you* looking at me so weirdly? *You* must think I'm crazy. . . ."

This interactive INNER MONOLOGUE will help to produce behavior, as well. Just think about the physical actions and facial expressions you might instinctively make if you're thinking, "I'm so not qualified for this job. In fact, *you'd* be making a mistake if *you* hired me . . ." while you are saying aloud, "I really think I'm the best person for the job, and I feel I will be an asset to your company."

In the same way we all use spoken dialogue to generate a response from another person, INNER MONOLOGUE is also used to create a reaction from your fellow actors.

INNER MONOLOGUE helps you work to create a relationship even when you are not speaking. We as an audience will pick up on an actor's INNER MONOLOGUE. The truth of what you're thinking versus what you're saying will make us relate and respond. We identify with it because we rarely say what's *really* going on in our minds. Saying what's really on our minds is often contrary to achieving our goal. We couch what we really want to say to elicit the response we desire. If you want someone to have sex with you, you can't very well say, "Hey you, I really want to have sex with you." Instead, you tell the person they're attractive; you wine and dine them; you're sympathetic, understanding and charming; you pretend that you're actually listening when that person is aimlessly babbling; and you generally spend too much time talking about a lot of things you don't care about. When Jack Nicholson's character of Melvin Udall in *As Good As It Gets* visits Carol Connelly (Helen Hunt) at the restaurant where she is a waitress, they discuss Carol's asthmatic son's health. While she talks about her son's critically bad health problems, Jack, as Melvin, clearly has an INNER MONOLOGUE that has nothing to do with her son's health. When you watch Jack listening to Carol, you see in his behavior that he's thinking about something a lot more risqué. Of course, Melvin can't say anything that would remotely touch the romantic arena—it would be insensitive and cavalier—but he *can* and *does* think it. This INNER MONOLOGUE not only establishes Melvin as a flawed and human man but also generates a chemistry between the two characters.

Another example of a common INNER MONOLOGUE that you may have experienced is when you ask someone, "Do I look like I've gained weight? I feel like I might have put on a few pounds." But your INNER MONOLOGUE is actually driven toward trying to provoke the other person to tell you that you look like you have *lost* weight. You're thinking, "Please, just say I look thinner. . . . I've spent so much time and money on frozen, minuscule, pre-prepared, cardboard-tasting meals. . . ."

Your INNER MONOLOGUE should be written out the way your mind really thinks.

This means that even if you are a Rhodes scholar, your thoughts are simple, unrefined, rudimentary, uncomplicated and just plain base. Sometimes our inner dialogue is so simplistic that it can seem akin to childlike, non-sequitur ramblings. Most of our intellectualizations and rationalizations take place when we're speaking out loud. What we say and what we think is dissimilar and often even contradictory. INNER MONOLOGUE is the script attached to the ever-present movie (INNER OBJECTS) that plays behind our eyes at all times. By having an INNER MONOLOGUE, an actor can realize their character's actual inner life and truths, which adds details that could not otherwise be achieved.

INNER MONOLOGUE is what you can't say out loud because it will be antithetical to winning your SCENE OBJECTIVE.

Imagine a scene where your character is on a date in a restaurant. Your character's date is extremely attractive, smart and worldly, and your character isn't. If you let your date know how insecure and stupid you are then there's a really good chance that this date will be the last date. Sample dialogue:

YOUR CHARACTER
This is a great restaurant. Even the music is great.

THE DATE
Yeah, it's Mozart, I find it stimulating and calming
at the same time.
    [*Knowingly hums a few bars*]
So, who's your favorite composer?

YOUR CHARACTER
I'm so hungry. I wish the waiter would come.

Let's look at the same scene with the INNER MONOLOGUE of what you're really thinking and feeling—riddled with your lack of savvy, fears and anxiety. Handwrite your INNER MONOLOGUE in quotes and in pencil underneath the dialogue it relates to in the script.

Remember: SCENE OBJECTIVE, OBSTACLES, SUBSTITUTION, MOMENT BE-FORE and PLACE/FOURTH WALL are written at the top of the scene; INNER OB-JECTS underneath their attached words; BEATS and ACTIONS to the right of the BEATed parenthesis; DOINGS to the left; and now, INNER MONOLOGUE in quotes, below and across the page exactly where you would think it in the script.

Date Scene with Sample INNER MONOLOGUE:

I.M.= "I've got to say something to you soon, I'm just sitting here looking like an idiot and I don't want to screw up. . . . You are soooo good-looking. What are you doing with me? Stop it, be positive, say something, and say something smart . . ."

YOUR CHARACTER
This is a great restaurant. Even the music is great.
I.M.= "Oh yeah, gee whiz, that was smart. I'm such a moron. If there was a jail for stupid people, I'd have a life sentence . . ."

THE DATE
Yeah, it's Mozart, I find it stimulating and calming
at the same time.
I.M.= "Oh no, all I know about Mozart is that he was German . . . or is it Austrian? Or Swiss? Why do _you_ have to be so sexy and _me_ so dumb? Please, oh, please, for the love of God do not ask me anything about classical music . . ."
    [*Knowingly hums a few bars*]
So, who's your favorite composer?
I.M.: "What?! I don't have a clue. Quick, change the subject . . ."

YOUR CHARACTER
I'm so hungry. I wish the waiter would come.
I.M.: "*Oh boy, that was smooth. You're probably thinking that I'm slick and on top of my game . . . oh yeah, right, creepy loser would be more accurate . . . Oh man, I'm gonna be alone forever . . .*"

. . . and so on.

As you can see, the INNER MONOLOGUE infuses your portrayal with human vulnerabilities. This makes your character more audience-friendly, because an audience can feel and relate to a person who is insecure and apprehensive more than they can relate to someone who is fearless and confident.

INNER MONOLOGUE makes you work harder to win your SCENE OBJECTIVE.

This is because your spoken words are frequently so different than what you're really thinking that it forces you to gush and overdo as a way to make the other person believe that what you're saying is true. You always know the two people at a party who hate each other the most. They are the two who, when they meet, squeal with mutual delight about their reunion. They say things like, "It's been too long! It's so good to see you! You look amazing! We really have to get together. Let's do lunch!" When what they are really thinking is, "It hasn't been long enough! Seeing you reminds me of all the wretched things you've done to me! You are repulsive! If we do have lunch, I'll probably vomit on your ugly face!" The equation goes something like this: the bigger the greeting glee, the bigger the hatred.

INNER MONOLOGUE is indicative of what you are really thinking, but can't say without repercussions.

Envision a scene where your character, a journalist, is being denigrated by their boss, the newspaper's editor.
Actual dialogue:

EDITOR
This piece you wrote is awful—a ten-year-old
could have done better.

YOUR CHARACTER
Thank you, sir. I'll work on it.

EDITOR
Great. If you need help, my assistant Edna will work
with you.

YOUR CHARACTER
Edna's good. That's an excellent suggestion.

EDITOR
Now, get out of here and get on it.

Your INNER MONOLOGUE might go something like this:

EDITOR
This piece you wrote is awful—a ten-year-old
could have done better.
*"You no-talent ass. What would you know about writing? You
spend more time with the bottle than the page . . ."*

YOUR CHARACTER
Thank you sir. I'll work on it.
*"Yeah, thank you for sleepless nights. Thank you for making me
loathe myself. And thank you for making me want to kill
myself . . ."*

EDITOR
Great. If you need help, my assistant Edna will work
with you.
"Edna the slut. Yeah, she's gonna be a lot of help . . ."

YOUR CHARACTER
Edna's good. That's an excellent suggestion.
*"Edna's good, all right. She's got the scuffed-up knees to prove
it . . ."*

EDITOR
Now, get out of here and get on it.
"You should die a slow and horrible death . . ."

Obviously, your character can't say what they really think or they'll
lose their job.

> ### Our INNER MONOLOGUE can spice things up when
> ### we're having banal, boring conversations.

Having inappropriate, vulgar, illicit thoughts makes these conversations a whole lot more exciting. Whenever you're spending time with a

member of the opposite sex (or the sex you're attracted to), there's always an opportunity and an inclination to think about them sexually. We wonder what it might be like to kiss them, what they are like in bed, etc. Even when there's no chemistry between you and the other actor, it's up to you to create it. Sexuality is a primal force that everyone can relate to, making boring dialogue and a boring scene hot.

When I was an actress, I had an actor friend who had a bit part on *Archie Bunker's Place,* the spin-off of *All in the Family.* Ordering from an attractive waitress, his dialogue was, "I'd like the steak, please." My friend, not being aware of the adage, "There are no small parts, just small actors," gave a reading of the line that he felt it deserved, about five words worth. Carroll O'Connor, the star of the show, walked up to my friend and whispered in his ear, "Hey, do you think the girl who plays the waitress is pretty?"

"Heck, yeah!" my friend responded.

"Would you like to sleep with her?" O'Connor asked.

"Oh, yeah!!" my friend said with all the testosterone he could muster.

"So, when you say your line, 'I'd like the steak, please' . . ."

"Yeah?"

My friend waited for O'Connor to continue.

"Use it!"

INNER MONOLOGUE *provides information that the actual dialogue does not—helping you earn the right of future events in the script, which is not often in the written word because it would reveal too much too soon.*

One of the early scenes of the Neil LaBute film *Your Friends and Neighbors* is a dinner party given by the characters of Mary and Barry, who have just moved to the country because they've had enough of city life. In the scene, Mary extols the virtues of country living—how glad she is that they've moved, how improved her life is, and how much better her relationship is with Barry. She says all of this despite the fact that she's completely miserable. She feels isolated from her friends and her former work life. Mary has also discovered that spending more time with Barry, one of the main reasons for moving out of the city, is *too much* time.

In the film, Mary's unrest ultimately leads her to have an affair with the handsome and slick Cary (Jason Patric). When looking for inspiration for the character of Mary's INNER MONOLOGUE in this scene, I told Amy Brenneman, who plays Mary, that she needed to feel an earlier pull and yearning for Cary, which would support her affair with him in later scenes. We decided that when Mary is talking about her terrific decision to move to the country, her INNER MONOLOGUE would be something like this: "I hate being here. No, 'hate' is too weak a word. I loathe and detest being here. Barry has become country boring." This line of thinking would be interrupted by Mary (Amy) looking over at Cary (Jason) and thinking, "You are so hot. I'd like to (fill in the blank with Amy's personal version of porn and lust). . . ." Even though the dialogue for Mary had nothing to do in any way with her relationship—past, present or future—with Cary, Amy's use of INNER MONOLOGUE made Mary's feelings and intentions loud and clear to Cary and the audience. Using INNER MONOLOGUE for this scene achieved two things. First, by using the INNER MONOLOGUE, Mary (Amy) is subconsciously and subliminally telling Cary (Jason) that she wants him. This gives him subconscious permission to pursue her, which he wouldn't have done otherwise because she's married and seemingly unavailable. People don't generally put the moves on someone unless they feel there's a good shot that they won't be rejected and that they are wanted. Second, by establishing that the heat is rising between these two characters, the INNER MONOLOGUE helps to foreshadow events to come, which creates audience anticipation. From this example you can see how:

INNER MONOLOGUE gives you something to say when there is no dialogue.

In theater and especially in film, there are scenes where there is no dialogue or the other character is reciting a long monologue and you're the listener. Instead of merely standing around feeling and looking like a sounding board, INNER MONOLOGUE keeps the listening active. For instance, in *Unfaithful,* Diane Lane had the challenge of portraying her character Connie Sumner's feelings about her first unfaithful tryst with Paul, her younger lover, on a silent train ride home. She had to convey the fact that this experience had left her character feeling elated, guilty, angry, sad, desiring more and alone. How did she relay all of this without any dialogue? With the help of INNER OBJECTS and INNER MONO-LOGUE, we, the audience, see these contrasting feelings play out on Diane's face and body. Diane makes us feel that we are in her skin, experiencing the event and all the consequential thoughts and emotions.

**INNER MONOLOGUE can give purpose and magnitude
to scripted moments that seem mundane or insignificant.**

When doing script analysis, there should be no moment in time or a piece
of dialogue that should be considered unimportant. When the stakes are
high, even a sigh has significance; a step away, a sense of emotional
urgency. Nothing should ever be thought of as throwaway, because when
you throw it away, so does your audience.

For example, in many scripts you'll find a character singing along with
a group. This might seem innocuous enough, a group of people singing,
say, "Happy Birthday" or drunkenly belting out show tunes around the
piano at a party scene. It is up to you to find more personal and note-
worthy meaning to the event itself and the words of the song. In *Their
Eyes Were Watching God,* an ABC movie, executive produced by Oprah
Winfrey and Quincy Jones, there is a scene where the townspeople sing
as a group. The movie tells the story of Janie (played by Halle Berry), a
young woman in the early 1900s who has spent most of her young life being subjugated, controlled and criticized. She meets Joe Starks, who offers her a new life, a great life, filled with the freedom to explore and
discover. Joe takes her to Eatonville, the first city in America run by, as
Joe tells her, "colored folks that's got together. They've made their very
own town." She leaves with him, and when they get to Eatonville, they
find it needs Joe's moxie and know-how to create a true and real city. Joe
becomes the official mayor and Janie, the first lady. The first street lamp
is delivered to Eatonville by a Sears and Roebuck truck. To mark the
auspiciousness of the occasion there is a lamp-lighting ceremony to mark
that Eatonville is now considered "the first incorporated colored town-
ship in all America!" as Joe expresses in his speech to the townfolk. When
Amos requests a few words from Mrs. Mayor Starks (Janie), Joe quickly
shuts him down, saying, "Mrs. Mayor Starks don't know nothing about
speech making. I didn't marry her for that." This devastates Janie. Joe
had promised her the world but instead does what everyone else has
done in her life: squelched her spirit by making her feel stupid, powerless, and inconsequential. She isn't allowed to speak. Joe finishes his rous-
ing speech to his constituents and gets them all singing. There's a look of
hope on the townspeople's faces in direct contrast to Janie's look. Joe was
her only hope for a different life and future and clearly that was a lie.

As Halle and I broke down this scene, we could've easily infused the
truth of a woman who feels the pain and disappointment of a life gone
terribly wrong. But solely providing the reality of hurt and betrayal would

imply that she has given up and has been defeated. There's no win in admitting and giving in to defeat. It creats hopelessness, not only for the character but also for the actor and the audience. You as an actor should never make the choice of becoming helpless and victimized by life's traumas. The journey stops when you cease to try and change even the most untenable of situations. To accomplish a winning scenario, as opposed to Halle becoming a victim to defeat, we first infused Halle's personal issues that require hope and change, issues that at the time of shooting this scene seemed to weigh in at the doomed-to-fail end of the scale. Then we provided INNER MONOLOGUE that would create a sense of hopeful expectation. As she closed her eyes she sang the words to the song . . .

> "This little light of mine, I'm gonna let it shine.
> This light of mine, I'm gonna let it shine. This little light
> of mine, I'm gonna let it shine. Let it shine, let it shine,
> let it shine . . ."

. . . And at the same time infused hopeful possibilities by thinking an IN-NER MONOLOGUE that went something like this:

> **I.M.:** *I hate him and he lied to me just like everyone else in my life, but I won't give in to hating myself. I won't be a victim! Not anymore. I'll find a way, there's gotta be a way, there's hope for me, there's light for me, I'm not giving up. I can't—if I do I'll die. This light is mine, I'm not gonna let anyone take that away from me again, I'm gonna let my hopes and dreams shine. I won't give up, I don't know how and when it's gonna change but I'm gonna expose the light of who I am, and I'm gonna let it shine, let it shine, let it shine!*

This INNER MONOLOGUE enabled Halle and her character to garner strength to carry on and fight the inevitable battles that she was going to face—as a woman, as well as a woman of color. In a scene that was written to express Janie's downfall, INNER MONOLOGUE gave the scene purpose, hope, and possibility.

INNER MONOLOGUE can be the obnoxious, brazen translation of the scripted dialogue.

This is especially true in duplicating hyper-real situations like soap opera catfights. These fights are hard to realistically feel or portray, because fortunately life rarely provides females with the excuse for a pull-your-hair-out, scratch-your-eyes-out, tug-of-war with another female unless you mysteriously find yourself on *The Jerry Springer Show*. Yet in drama (especially daytime drama), it comes up time and time again. Sharon Case, the Emmy Award–winning actress who plays the character of Sharon Newman on *The Young and the Restless,* has had to become a professional catfighter. Her character has had these fights with her mother-in-law, sister-in-law and her character's former best friend (who became a former best friend by having an affair with Sharon's television husband). The dialogue in these scenes is spicy, or at least as scandalous as one can get on daytime television. When Sharon came to me for help with these scenes, I suggested that she use INNER MONOLOGUE to help her find the need (SCENE OBJECTIVE) for a catfight. Sharon and I created a very brazen, brass and audacious INNER MONOLOGUE. We did this by using strong expletives and personal information that related to her SUBSTITUTION—the kind of material that would cause even the strongest adversary to weaken because it's so insinuating, revealing and vulgar. This INNER MONOLOGUE allowed Sharon to truly feel the need to have a catfight, which otherwise would have looked and felt theatrical and staged.

You might be wondering, "What did Sharon say in her INNER MONOLOGUE?" Unfortunately, I can't tell you. But this is the point of INNER MONOLOGUE: It should be so private, so personal and so humiliating that it creates a sense of secret, which adds to the audience's experience by making them feel somehow in on emotions and thoughts beyond the written word.

When you personalize your INNER MONOLOGUE, make sure it makes sense with your SCENE'S OBJECTIVE, SUBSTITUTION, personalized OBSTACLES and INNER OBJECTS.

Because of the nature of INNER MONOLOGUE and my work—an acting coach's ethics are similar to that of a psychiatrist's client/patient confidentiality—it's impossible for me to discuss someone else's personal INNER MONOLOGUE work. An actor must trust that I'll never reveal their secrets so that they'll feel comfortable telling me intimate information they often don't even share with their family or therapists. I use these secrets for the inspiration, dimension, shadings and hues for an actor's work. The use of secrets in an actor's work is essential for producing a dynamic performance. Because I cannot reveal anyone else's secrets, I will use a case from my own life using a miscreant cad of an ex-mate (if you're wondering if it's *you*, it probably is) to show you how to personalize your INNER MONOLOGUE. In the play *A Boy's Life,* there is a scene where the character of Lisa finds another girl's panties in her bed as she begins to make love with her boyfriend Don. Don has indeed been fooling around and feels he must cover his misdeed in order to keep Lisa around because, despite his indiscretion, he loves her. Lisa loves him, too, but letting him off the hook too easily would make Don feel he could do it again—so she must put him through his paces before she takes him back.

- **OVERALL OBJECTIVE:** *"To be loved"*
- **SCENE OBJECTIVE:** *"To make you say or do something that will fix it"* (so we can stay together)
- **The script's OBSTACLES:**

  1. Don is likely to do it again.
  2. Don's lack of remorse.
  3. Don's charm and humor mean that he's used to getting away with his bad behavior.
  4. Lisa's history with "bad boys."
  5. If Lisa becomes too aggressively antagonistic, she just might lose Don.

- **SUBSTITUTION:** My ex. A man who, by and by, cheated on me with not just one but several nubile beauties, as well as one gay man named Alan.
- **Personalized OBSTACLES:**

  1. My ex seemed to be a sex addict, which would make it that much harder to change or fix.
  2. My ex wasn't particularly remorseful when he was caught, unless I threatened to leave.
  3. My ex said he was sorry so many times, yet committed his unfaithful acts anyway, again and again.
  4. My belief quotient, because I've been lied to so many times in the past.
  5. My history with dishonest men.
  6. His history of cheating with prior girlfriends.
  7. And what the heck was his sexual preference, anyway?!

- **MOMENT BEFORE:** The event when we were hosting a party and I found him in our bedroom with Connie in the "middle" of breaking one of God's commandments. As I stood there in disbelief, wondering if my presence (or cold water) would stop them, he said, "Leave, can't you see I'm busy?!" (I'm not making this up, he really said this—a vivid memory, no doubt, that will stay with me forever.)
- **PLACE/FOURTH WALL:** Our bedroom we shared when we were going together, and the sight of the above crime.

Following is an excerpt from *A Boy's Life,* which considers my character's OVERALL OBJECTIVE, SCENE OBJECTIVE, my SUBSTITUTION for Don, my personal OBSTACLES, MOMENT BEFORE, PLACE/FOURTH WALL and INNER OBJECTS—which will become obvious from the following INNER MONOLOGUE.

In the scene, Lisa carefully lifts the offending underwear and begins to confront Don, who is silently staring at the incriminating panties.

A BOY'S LIFE

"So who's stinky, cheapo panties are these? Slutty Jillanne? Skanky Connie? Or how-did-he-get-in-the-mix Alan? Huh? Huh?!"

LISA
Is that all you have to say about it?
"You always put me down, calling me stupid all the time. Well, who looks like an idiot now, you jerk!"

DON
What else do you want me to say?
"You think you're such a big-time writer, yet you have nothing to say . . . all those big words that you use—incorrectly, I might add—can't help you now! . . ."

LISA
How about sorry?
"Hey, pea-brain. Has it ever occurred to you to say 'I'm sorry' and actually mean it?! Perhaps, mister writer-man, you don't know the meaning and derivation of the word. God, I'm such an idiot for always taking you back . . ."

Now, looking at it from the P.O.V. of being Don or Lisa, go through this scene and try using your own INNER MONOLOGUE (based on doing the prior tools). See what behavior comes of it. Notice how the IN-NER MONOLOGUE provides another dimension of behavior, allowing you to speak and think at the same time—just like real people do.

> **INNER MONOLOGUE is not to be memorized,**
> **but the thoughts and ideas behind the monologue are.**

An INNER MONOLOGUE will vary every time a scene is run, but the general concepts of what were written down will be retained. Think of the INNER MONOLOGUE you've written down on the page as an extensive outline, then let your imagination run from there.

INNER MONOLOGUE: THE PRACTICAL APPLICATION

Let's work with a scene from Shakespeare's *Macbeth*, Act II, Scene II, to explore how the practical application of INNER MONOLOGUE works. Previous to the action in this scene, Lady Macbeth's extreme ambition inspires her to manipulate her weak husband, Macbeth, convincing him to kill the king so that he will be king and, more importantly, she will be queen.

This scene is, at its core, a fight between a husband and wife. Actual dialogue:

MACBETH
(Act II, Scene 2)

MACBETH
[*Looking at his hands*]
This is a sorry sight.

LADY MACBETH
A foolish thought, to say a sorry sight.

MACBETH
There's one did laugh in's sleep, and one cried "Murder!"
That they did wake each other: I stood and heard them:
But they did say their prayers, and address'd them a gain to sleep.

LADY MACBETH
There are two lodged together.

MACBETH

One cried "God bless us!" and "Amen" the other,
As they had seen me with these hangman's hands
Listening their fear, I could not say "Amen,"
When they did say "God bless us!"

LADY MACBETH

Consider it not so deeply.

MACBETH

But wherefore could not I pronounce "Amen"?
I had most need of blessing, and "Amen"
Stuck in my throat.

LADY MACBETH

These deeds must not be thought
After these ways; so, it will make us mad.

MACBETH

Methought I heard a voice cry "Sleep no more!
Macbeth does murder sleep"—the innocent sleep,
Sleep that knits up the ravell'd sleave of care,
The death of each day's life, sore labour's bath,
Balm of hurt minds, great nature's second course,
Chief nourisher in life's feast,—

LADY MACBETH

What do you mean?

MACBETH

Still it cried "Sleep no more!" to all the house:
"Glamis hath murder'd sleep, and therefore Cawdor
Shall sleep no more: Macbeth shall sleep no more."

LADY MACBETH

Who was it that thus cried? Why, worthy thane,
You do unbend your noble strength, to think
So brainsickly of things. Go get some water,
And wash this filthy witness from your hand,
Why did you bring these daggers from the place?
They must lie there; go carry them, and smear
The sleepy grooms with blood.

MACBETH

I'll go no more:
I am afraid to think what I have done;
Look on't again I dare not.

LADY MACBETH
Infirm of purpose!
Give me the daggers: 'tis the eye of childhood
That fears a painted devil. If he do bleed,
I'll gild the faces of the grooms withal,
For it must seem their guilt.
[*She exits*]

The following INNER MONOLOGUE choices are only suggestions based on the script. When actually creating an INNER MONOLOGUE, you must make it personal, incorporating the information and choices you have made with the other tools. When reading my INNER MONOLOGUE suggestions for *Macbeth,* try to imagine what you might write for your personal INNER MONOLOGUE.

Remember: The INNER MONOLOGUE should be handwritten, in quotes, between the dialogue. The thoughts should lie exactly where you would think the INNER MONOLOGUE when you are speaking your lines or listening. And INNER MONOLOGUE always starts before the actual dialogue.

INNER MONOLOGUE from Macbeth's P.O.V.

• Macbeth's SCENE OBJECTIVE: *"To get you to absolve me of my guilt."*

MACBETH
(Act II, Scene 2)
". . . Was it worth it? There's blood all over my hands. I've killed a human being and I'll never be the same . . . I'm an evil, horrible man and I'm going to hell!"

MACBETH
[*Looking at his hands*]
This is a sorry sight.
". . . There was blood everywhere. I didn't want to do it and you made me . . . Why did I ever listen to you?"

LADY MACBETH
A foolish thought, to say a sorry sight.
". . . How could you say that?! It was horrible! But you can say anything you want because you weren't there! What am I going to do?! I think someone might have seen me. I think I heard voices or am I just going stark raving mad? . . ."

MACBETH

There's one did laugh in's sleep, and one cried "Murder!"
That they did wake each other: I stood and heard them:
But they did say their prayers, and address'd them a
gain to sleep.

"... See how bad it is?! You think you're right all the time.
Maybe this time you were wrong ..."

LADY MACBETH

There are two lodged together.

"... Hey Lady, didn't you hear me? I said that I think I might
have been caught! But no, you never listen to me. You don't care.
You don't love me. You think I'm so weak and stupid, but I'm
telling you, there may have been a witness. Wait a minute,
maybe you wanted me to get caught, you conniving ..."

MACBETH

One cried "God bless us!" and "Amen" the other,
As they had seen me with these hangman's hands
Listening their fear, I could not say "Amen,"
When they did say "God bless us!"

"... I'm feeling so guilty and God-awful and you just stand
there, patronizing and above it all? What's wrong with you,
woman?! Who are you? Why did I marry you? ..."

LADY MACBETH

Consider it not so deeply.

"Oh yeah, if you're so smart, answer me this ..."

MACBETH

But wherefore could not I pronounce "Amen"?
I had most need of blessing, and "Amen"
Stuck in my throat.

"... Then why did that happen, huh?! Are you going to give one
of your heartless answers? When did you get so cold? Huh?! ..."

LADY MACBETH

These deeds must not be thought
After these ways; so, it will make us mad.

"... There you go. Putting me down again. I might be losing my
mind, but ohhhhhh you don't care. Listen, you shrew, I REALLY
THINK I'M GOING CRAZY!"

MACBETH

Methought I heard a voice cry "Sleep no more!
Macbeth does murder sleep"—the innocent sleep,
Sleep that knits up the ravell'd sleave of care,
The death of each day's life, sore labour's bath,
Balm of hurt minds, great nature's second course,
Chief nourisher in life's feast,—

"... Yep, a lot of crazy talk from a crazy person, like me. Do you
need any more proof that I'm really losing it!!! ... jeez ..."

LADY MACBETH
What do you mean?

". . . 'What do you mean?' What do I mean?! I think I've made it really simple to understand. I'm GOING INSANE!!! You never listen to me, do you? Never think I have anything important to say. OK. Let's try this again. But listen to me this time! I'll make it really, really clear!!! . . ."

MACBETH
Still it cried "Sleep no more!" to all the house:
"Glamis hath murder'd sleep, and therefore Cawdor
Shall sleep no more: Macbeth shall sleep no more."

". . . Do you understand now?! I mean, even an idiot could get it, but you don't want to get it. It's always about you . . . you, you, you, you. You're so self-centered . . ."

LADY MACBETH
Who was it that thus cried? Why, worthy thane,
You do unbend your noble strength, to think
So brainsickly of things.

". . . There you go. Putting me down again. Is it possible for you to breathe without making me feel stupid?"

Go get some water,
And wash this filthy witness from your hand,
Why did you bring these daggers from the place?
They must lie there; go carry them, and smear
The sleepy grooms with blood.

"No damn way am I'm going to do one more thing. I've risked my life for you and this is what I get? I thought killing the king was crazy, but if you think I'm doing anything more, then you're even crazier than me! . . . Oh God, just thinking about all that blood makes me want to spew . . ."

MACBETH
I'll go no more:
I am afraid to think what I have done;
Look on't again I dare not.

"You think you control me, but I'm not going to do it. No way in hell!!!"

LADY MACBETH
Infirm of purpose!

"There you go, calling me dumb again!"

Give me the daggers: 'tis the eye of childhood
That fears a painted devil. If he do bleed,
I'll gild the faces of the grooms withal,
For it must seem their guilt.

"Yeah, <u>you</u> do it. You think you do everything better than me, anyway. Well, let's see how well <u>YOU</u> deal with all that BLOOD! . . ."

INNER MONOLOGUE from Lady Macbeth's P.O.V.

• Lady Macbeth's SCENE OBJECTIVE: *"To make you give me the power."*

MACBETH
(Act II, Scene 2)

". . . Finally, you killed him. Last time you chickened out. Why? Because you're a loooooser! I can't believe I married you . . ."

MACBETH
[Looking at his hands]
This is a sorry sight.
"No it's not. Don't you get it?! Now you'll be king. And, more important, I'll be queen . . ."

LADY MACBETH
A foolish thought, to say a sorry sight.
"Now let's be done with all of your ridiculous paranoia and make plans to abuse our newfound power . . ."

MACBETH
There's one did laugh in's sleep, and one cried "Murder!"
That they did wake each other: I stood and heard them:
But they did say their prayers, and address'd them a gain to sleep.
". . . So what?! What difference does it make? You're the king now. You can do whatever you want . . ."

LADY MACBETH
There are two lodged together.
". . . There you go. Easy answer, but you're too much of a moron to figure it out . . . Boy it's going to be fun being queen . . ."

MACBETH
One cried "God bless us!" and "Amen" the other,
As they had seen me with these hangman's hands
Listening their fear, I could not say "Amen,"
When they did say "God bless us!"
". . . Don't think about it . . . Thinking has never been your strong suit, anyway . . ."

LADY MACBETH
Consider it not so deeply.
". . . Do what I do: think about the money, the power . . . Don't you get how great it's going to be running a whole country?! You're such a weakling. What did I ever see in you in the first place?!"

MACBETH

But wherefore could not I pronounce "Amen"?
I had most need of blessing, and "Amen"
Stuck in my throat.

". . . Guilt is a pain in the ass. . . . God, you're just like your sorry mother . . ."

LADY MACBETH

These deeds must not be thought
After these ways; so, it will make us mad.

". . . See how easy it is? Just listen to me and you'll be fine . . ."

MACBETH

Methought I heard a voice cry "Sleep no more!
Macbeth does murder sleep"—the innocent sleep,

"Whine, whine . . . whine, God, you're a sorry excuse for a man. It's no wonder nothing's been happening in the bed department for I don't even want to think about how long . . ."

Sleep that knits up the ravell'd sleave of care,
The death of each day's life, sore labour's bath,
Balm of hurt minds, great nature's second course,
Chief nourisher in life's feast,—

"Yeah, yeah . . . get over it . . ."

LADY MACBETH

What do you mean?

". . . You did it. You killed the man and you can't take it back. You might as well take advantage of it . . . But you always look at how bad everything is, you're such a downer . . ."

MACBETH

Still it cried "Sleep no more!" to all the house:

"Here we go again . . . try a new thought on for size . . ."

**"Glamis hath murder'd sleep, and therefore Cawdor
Shall sleep no more: Macbeth shall sleep no more."**

". . . All this ranting and raving is scaring the crap out of me. You're not going crazy, you're going to be fine. Calm down, if you can't sleep you can take some of my sleeping pills . . ."

LADY MACBETH

Who was it that thus cried? Why, worthy thane,
You do unbend your noble strength, to think
So brainsickly of things.

". . . Do I have to think of everything?! . . ."

Go get some water,
And wash this filthy witness from your hand,
Why did you bring these daggers from the place?

". . . Why in heaven's name would you bring the murder weapon back here?! How can you be so, excuse the expression, bloody stupid?!!! . . ."

They must lie there; go carry them, and smear
The sleepy grooms with blood.

". . . Why is it that I have to be the brains in this marriage? I thought the man was supposed to take care of the woman . . . When I first met you, you were strong and handsome and brave. What happened? Now you're a brainless wuss . . . It's a good thing you're king or I would be so out of here . . ."

MACBETH

I'll go no more:
I am afraid to think what I have done;
Look on't again I dare not.

". . . Ooooo, now you're going to stand up to me. I'm soooooo scared . . . ."

LADY MACBETH

Infirm of purpose!

". . . Okay, that didn't work. All right, as usual, if I want something done right, I've got to do it myself . . . God, you're worthless . . ."

Give me the daggers: 'tis the eye of childhood
That fears a painted devil. If he do bleed,
I'll gild the faces of the grooms withal,
For it must seem their guilt.

"You're such a crybaby. Just throw some of the king's blood on the others and voilà, they look guilty and we're in the clear. Ya know, you could have easily done this yourself, but you're such a spineless dumbass . . ."

As demonstrated in the above INNER MONOLOGUE, the scene could be any long-term married couple having a power struggle. Even with Shakespeare's poetry and language, the INNER MONOLOGUE provides us with a basic human reality. It doesn't matter what time period or arena a script takes place in, the bottom line is that people are people and our truest, most fundamental inner thoughts and feelings, like those that occur between a married couple, are going to remain the same and span the decades. INNER MONOLOGUE makes any dialogue from any time period relevant and relatable to the actor as well as to a modern audience.

**Continue the INNER MONOLOGUE until you've made a
clean exit or the director has said, "Cut."**

Just because you are heading off stage, or walking out the door, or the
spoken dialogue is finished, it doesn't mean the scene is over. INNER
MONOLOGUE is an essential tool.

Your mind continues to think even when you're not speaking.

Great actors always have a strong INNER MONOLOGUE playing behind their eyes at all times. Watch a scene with one of the legendary actors and notice how much time the camera stays on him or her. Why did
the film editors cut back to him or her even when they were not speaking and the other actor was delivering an impassioned speech? More often than not, it's because the nonspeaking actor or actress is using
INNER MONOLOGUE. Their INNER MONOLOGUE plays out on their
face, in their eyes, in the way they hold their bodies, their hands. Frequently, the actor who is using INNER MONOLOGUE displays more
need and passion than the actor who is speaking. INNER MONOLOGUE
is one of the most powerful tools an actor can use.

CHAPTER 11

Tool #11:
PREVIOUS CIRCUMSTANCES

> The character's history that makes them
> who they are today.

Who we are today is an accumulation of past events, our reactions to these events and other people's reactions to us. This is also true for any character you are playing. When you are playing a thirty-year-old character, you must give your character the details of thirty years of existence. In every script the character has PREVIOUS CIRCUMSTANCES that define *who* they are; *how* they move in the world; and *what* they feel they must do to survive, both emotionally and physically. You have to look at the character's who-am-I today by investigating the information provided in the script and making assumptions based on the dialogue and your character's past and present activities. This will tell you *why* your character embodies a specific nature. The next step is to consider your character's history and the kind of psyche and behavior that results from that particular history. In other words, *how* the PREVIOUS CIRCUMSTANCES have manifested themselves in present word and deed. Finally, you must personalize by identifying how your character's history relates to yours. So, to recap, the formula for:

APPLYING PREVIOUS CIRCUMSTANCES

1. You look at the PREVIOUS CIRCUMSTANCES of the character by reading and investigating the character's dialogue, as well as how your character is discussed in other dialogue (whether or not your character is in the scene).

2. You consider how your character deals with life physically by examining the activities, past and present, that your character chooses and relies on to exist and survive in their world.

3. You look at why the character makes the choices they do—both socially and career-wise. This information is derived from your exploration of the character's PREVIOUS CIRCUMSTANCES, considering the actual information written into the script, as well as anything you might be able to assume based on the written information.

4. Personalization. You look at how this information relates to you and your own personal PREVIOUS CIRCUMSTANCES.

Let's look at how this works with a character who is a killer. First, you would look at the character's dialogue and what others say about the killer for the first layer of understanding of why your character kills, considering how they speak, what language they use, how they relate to others, behavioral traits and how others see them. Next you would look at why, how and who your character chooses to kill. Then you would examine the PREVIOUS CIRCUMSTANCES that are described in the script, as well as speculating and exploring what kind of temperament their particular history would establish. Generally speaking, a murderer kills because of some need to assert the ultimate power. After all, there is nothing more power-inducing than taking someone's life. More often than not, a person who feels the need to go to this extreme has had, in some way, their power cruelly and heinously taken away (and it's usually by a primal somebody)—either through physical and mental abuse. The act of killing allows the killer to feel like they are getting their power back. Usually, killers subconsciously make their victims a symbolic version of the abuser. When they are killing, they feel that they are asserting their dominance over the original offender. The killer is acting out as a way to *heal* their past. As you can see, thinking about a killer in this light takes the act of murder out of the one-dimensional evil realm and humanizes the behavior.

If you were playing the role of a killer, you must relate this desire to assert the ultimate power over someone to your own life. You might be asking, "What does this have to do with me? I have no massive trauma like this in my history nor do I have a desire to assert this kind of power." But the fact is that everyone has, at some point in their life, thought about killing someone. For most of us it's a brief and momentary fantasy to murder as a way to resolve a relationship that has been ruthlessly intolerable, but nevertheless, the killing instinct is there. It's up to you to figure out when and what triggered these feelings so that you can use them to fuel your character's words, feelings and actions. This is a way to look at the PREVIOUS CIRCUMSTANCES of the character and then identify how they are duplicated in your own personal PREVIOUS CIR-CUMSTANCES.

Tatum O'Neal and I were working on an obscure piece of material as an exercise for class. The script was about a character who maliciously and without remorse runs over and kills a man with her car. The charac-ter feels justified because the man she's murdered has callously left her. Tatum, despite her very public life and even more public tumultuous up-bringing and personal history, was adamant that she wasn't capable of doing such a thing—even in her darkest fantasies. Even though she claimed she had forgiven and forgotten the many offences and abuse, I persisted, making her acknowledge that she still had a lot of unresolved feelings—particularly anger—with the various and sundry characters from her past. I helped her recall the experiences and then feel the rage and deep hurt. As she went through her history, one particular scoundrel rose to the surface. Through listening to her speak about him, it was clear by her voice and behavior that this experience could provoke Tatum's killer instinct. When she described the horrific details of her ex-perience, for the first time, she understood how her character, a killer, might derive pleasure by running someone over. Her anger and instinc-tive desire to hit back could lure her into feeling that killing this guy would empower her and be cathartic. This changed her original feeling of love and forgiveness toward the guy to a need for violent payback and retribution as a way to give her emotional closure. Remembering events that included this guy's most offensive behavior as her PREVIOUS CIR-CUMSTANCES helped Tatum realistically and righteously discover and relate to her character's very real need to kill.

Let's look at the movie *The Silence of the Lambs* again. But this time, from the point of how one might personalize the character of Clarisse Starling's (played by Jodie Foster) PREVIOUS CIRCUMSTANCES. Based on the script, we know that Clarisse Starling is an FBI agent who has grown up on a "backward" sheep farm. Through her dialogue with the character of Hannibal Lecter, we learn that Clarisse's family never paid much attention to her and was emotionally abusive. We can also assume from their conversations and her behavior that she became an FBI agent in order to find a way to "silence the screaming lambs" in her head and her heart. We can also presuppose that Clarisse is using saving the life of a senator's kidnapped daughter as a salve for her own emotional disquiet and pain. To play this role you would have to find corresponding history (PREVIOUS CIRCUMSTANCES) of your own to make Clarisse's needs and issues yours. It's not very likely that you have ever been an FBI agent or the daughter of a lamb farmer, or, as a child, have run off with a screaming lamb coddled in your arms. However, you probably do have "emotional disquiet and pain" that emanates from another source. For example:

- You may have become an actor (likened to becoming an FBI agent) as a way to deal with an abusive stepmother ("screaming lambs in your head") and grown up wanting to run away (running off with the lamb in your arms). Or . . .
- You seek great success as a way to overcome that bully you grew up with who always made you feel diminished, small and inconsequential, and seek comeuppance with the same type of people that are currently in your life. Or . . .
- You have (had) an abusive boyfriend or girlfriend whose demoralizing, terrorizing remarks and attitude plague you with self-loathing, and you seek to estrange yourself from this person but don't have the courage.

Creating these kinds of parallel similarities between the written character's history and your own will help you become the character.

What if you have to play someone whose PREVIOUS CIRCUMSTANCES are all about growing up as an orphan, and you are not? Here you would find something in your history that would duplicate the feelings of growing up as an orphan. For instance, maybe at a critical moment in your life, one or both of your parents was not emotionally there for you, which left you feeling lost and alone, like an orphan.

All of this is to show you that you don't have to experience the hard realities of the character you're playing to bring realism to the role. While being homicidal or orphaned are singular experiences, the feelings of being powerless or abandoned are things that we can all relate to, at least at some point in our lives. You have a lifetime of experiences and a myriad of feelings attached to them that you can call upon to give you a history that corresponds to the character on the page, which will enable you to embody that character heart and soul.

Michael T. Weiss, star of the series *The Pretender,* played the character of Larry in the feature film *Iowa.* Larry is a parole officer and a rapist in a small town in Iowa. In the film, Larry beats up on women, rapes them and then tells them that they loved it and "don't be bothering me for more, cuz I'm busy." In fact, one of the women does love it so much that even after he breaks her nose, cracks some of her front teeth and beats her up, she begs for more, pleading with him to stay with her. To win Larry's love, this woman even goes so far as to try to set up her own son's murder so that Larry can get the insurance money. We can assume that Larry sees himself not as a destructive force, but as a hard-edged Romeo. Otherwise, he would have to admit that his behavior is wrong, and nobody, no matter how heinous their behavior, wants to believe that their most fundamental characteristics and behaviors are flawed. Michael and I deduced that Larry probably came from an abusive father who beat up on his mother, and that his father, being a role model, made Larry's behavior toward women a part of his legacy and therefore justifiable. Or perhaps Larry came from a childhood riddled with physical abuse from his mother (with no father around to protect him), and his present need to assault women as a way to make love to them would make psychological sense.

Michael and I talked about what personal PREVIOUS CIRCUM-STANCES might relate to his character of Larry. We found a past relationship with a woman who was sadistically vicious to Michael, a woman whom he felt deserved a little bit of what she dished out. Using this as a trigger to justify his character's behavior as his PREVIOUS CIRCUM-STANCES, Michael recalled events in which she was particularly savage. Michael originally thought it would be an ugly experience to play someone like Larry. But by thinking about his character as a man who views his violence as a really macho way to make love to a woman (rather than an evil person inflicting pain), the role became, in Michael's words, "a whole lot of fun!"

Using PREVIOUS CIRCUMSTANCES gives you substantial reasons from past events to have to win your OVERALL OBJECTIVE.

It becomes a way to heal the past, creating an opportunity for catharsis. Everyone has had painful events in their past (PREVIOUS CIRCUM-STANCES), but how someone deals with these experiences is the difference between everyone and an artist. Simply put, there's a fork in the road of life—to the left are those who take past traumas and *destruct* with them. It's a road well-traveled, because it's the path of least resistance. Then there are the few who choose to take those same past traumas and *construct* with the information. A road less-traveled that is more like a dirt path riddled with all sorts of hazardous obstacles and gruesome creatures—it makes the journey difficult, but ultimately it's a far more satisfying journey. "Constructors," in other words, take adversarial situations rather than making the safe choice, accepting life's horrors and becoming self-pitying, and they use the conflict and pain to fuel their passion to win. These are the true winners and artists.

By using your painful PREVIOUS CIRCUMSTANCES as a way to fortify your need to win your OVERALL OBJECTIVE in the script, you are establishing a dynamic journey that will be cathartic to play and will create hope in your audience, because if you can win despite all your past conflicts, perhaps so can they.

The problem is that a lot of us bury those painful events because it hurts too much to remember them. It's part of our human survival instinct. People don't want to feel bad. They want to feel good. Denial is a great and powerful balm. Many of our most horrible memories are hidden away in our subconscious. And it's those very same hidden terrible memories that supply the most potent need to win a goal. How do you get to them if they're buried? I have created an acting tool I call the "Emotional Diary" that seems to be able to bring the traumas to the surface.

In class, I was critiquing a scene from the film *The Banger Sisters*. My student Ben was playing the role of Harry Plummer (played in the movie by Geoffrey Rush), a suicidal, frightened, anal-retentive, celibate (for the last ten years) male. In the first run of the scene, it was clear that Ben hadn't done his PREVIOUS CIRCUMSTANCES work. He wasn't in touch with his character's need to commit suicide, nor had he investigated the character of Harry's father issues or why Harry was so frightened of women and life. I asked Ben if he had any traumatic back-story that could substantiate Harry's behavior. He said he didn't. I sent him to another room to do an Emotional Diary.

How to Do an "Emotional Diary"

1. Identify your SCENE OBJECTIVE.

2. Determine your SUBSTITUTION.

3. Using a pen (always use a pen, because it glides easier on the paper) and writing on lined paper, begin the diary with your SCENE OBJECTIVE. Address your SUBSTITUTION within your SCENE OBJECTIVE statement, then continue the SCENE OBJECTIVE need with the word "because." Example:

SCENE OBJECTIVE: "*To get you to love me.*"
SUBSTITUTION: Your father

Begin your Emotional Diary with "I want you to love me, Daddy, because . . ."

4. Once you start writing, don't stop to think. Let it flow organically. Write with abandon. When you stop and think you'll end up in your conscious/cerebral mind. Continuing to write without thought of spelling, grammar or text allows you to access your subconscious—this is where all your true traumatic events and feelings lie. Continue to write nonstop without premeditation. (The Emotional Diary is not a list—it's diary-like ramblings.)

5. Write for at least two to three pages. The most revealing information often comes later as you warm up and can dig deeper into your subconscious. As you write, you'll find that telling events will come up that you've forgotten about, feelings and forbidden thoughts you didn't know you had.

6. The end of your diary should have a death resolution. "If I don't get my (SCENE OBJECTIVE) then I'll kill myself" or ". . . I'll kill my (SUBSTITUTION)" or ". . . I'll be alone forever" or ". . . I'll lose my family forever" or ". . . I'll never achieve my dreams," etc.—anything that has a deathlike finality to it. This ending gives you even more passion to win your SCENE OBJECTIVE because a life (yours or your loved one's) is riding on it.

What you write should be so private and so intimate and so revealing that you'd be mortified if anyone else were to see it. As you write the Emotional Diary, it should motivate tears and the need to destroy the pages that are filled with all your personally incriminating thoughts. If you haven't achieved this, then start again. It will happen.

It is vital to let the writing in your Emotional Diary flow. It is writing without thinking. The Emotional Diary is a form of automatic writing that helps give you strengthened purpose and passion to accomplish your SCENE OBJECTIVE. Each time you do an Emotional Diary something different will come up—you'll never have the same one twice.

Ben's Emotional Diary for Harry Plummer in *The Banger Sisters* began with "*I need you* (Ben's personal SUBSTITUTION) *to give me a reason to live because* . . ." The fact that the SCENE OBJECTIVE was about wanting to live implied that he wanted to die. Ben's Emotional Diary brought up events that made him feel hopeless and insignificant, which in turn brought up feelings that death might be his only solution for dealing with his utter despair, thus requiring an important someone (Ben's SUBSTITUTION) to give him hope and life. When Ben came back after writing his Emotional Diary (they generally only take five to ten minutes to write, which makes it an especially valuable tool for film work) he re-did the scene, but this time Harry's desperation and history were tangible.

Try doing an Emotional Diary by starting with the SCENE OBJEC-TIVE *"to get you to love me* (fill in a primal SUBSTITUTION—mother, father, mate, sibling, child—anyone that you need love from) *because . . ."* and continue to write for two or three pages until you get to some form of a death resolution.

What are you waiting for? Do it now.

Didn't know you had those feelings, did you? It's been my experience that Emotional Diaries really work. They have been an instrumental tool for helping my students achieve great and profound acting moments—on stage and in film. An Emotional Diary is useful for all media—comedy and drama—and can be done directly before a performance to provide immediate and enhanced need and emotion. And they provide the detailed personal information that is required to apply PREVIOUS CIR-CUMSTANCES most effectively.

Never Ignore Who *You* Are
When You're Getting into Character

The actors that are the most celebrated for their talent are those who never lose sight of who they are as people when they perform. Robert DeNiro, Jack Nicholson, Meryl Streep, Cate Blanchett and Al Pacino have each played a variety of characters, but you can always see traces of their true selves in their work. This comes from infusing their personal PREVIOUS CIRCUMSTANCES in their work. They know that who we are today is shaped by our histories. Besides, all you've got is *you.* You aren't DeNiro, Nicholson, Streep, Blanchett or Pacino, which is good because that makes you distinctive and unique and, therefore, special.

When Jim Carrey first came to me, it was at a time in his life when he couldn't get arrested. He had done three movies that had failed miserably, along with a series called *The Duck Factory* that was also considered a colossal bomb. Jim was blamed for the failures and was having trouble even getting in the door for auditions. He realized that if something's broken, you've got to at least make some effort to fix it, especially if it's your livelihood. So he came to me to see if he could change what looked, at this point in his life, like a bleak future.

In true Jim Carrey fashion, he would arrive at my door fully animated, saying and doing things that invariably caused a nonstop laugh-fest. But as soon as we began working with a script, he would become soft-spoken, still and, well, boring. I asked him why he wasn't bringing himself to the work. He said he was afraid it would be considered over-acting. Over the years, I've found that most actors' biggest fear is that they'll be told they are overacting. This causes them to censor their nat-ural impulses and prevents them from taking risks—and, as you should know by now, risk-taking is essential to being a great actor. I told Jim what I tell all my students: "What's the worst that can happen if you overact? The overacting police will come and arrest you and put you in overacting jail? The overacting police don't exist, so you're pretty safe to go balls to the wall." I assured him that as long as his work was honest, and he had strong OBJECTIVES and a heightened need to win them, he couldn't ever go too far. That in fact he should risk going too far. When we humans are faced with urgent needs and the necessity for survival, we have a tendency to do strange and outrageous acts. Think about that date with that special person where you blurted out inanities and be-haved absurdly. Or that important job interview where you expressed yourself too boldly, perhaps even fudging the truth in insane propor-tions. In his acting, Jim needed to communicate and relate the way he did in his day-to-day life. I told him not to pull back. I explained that when the stakes are high, we're always a hyper-version of ourselves, and that to truly reflect real behavior, he must be himself.

We found that by using his daughter Jane as a frequent SUBSTITU-TION in his SCENE OBJECTIVE statements, he was motivated to win. His love for her connected him to the work and inspired him to work hard to overcome the script conflicts, because he was doing it for her. By relating himself and his life to his work, it gave all the crazy Jim Carrey behavior a context and made his acting work make sense, because he was doing it for his little girl. Once we figured this out, any time Jim would perform a scene, I'd say, "You can do more!" He'd say, "Really?" And I'd respond by saying, "Yes, *you* can do more, because who you really are as a person *is more*." And, well, we all know how this story ends.

Your past constructs your present and future, thereby making you a three-dimensional human being.

PREVIOUS CIRCUMSTANCES will stop the playacting and help you *become* the character from within by supplying you with the *why* your character is who they are and behaves the way they do.

CHAPTER 12

Tool #12:

LET IT GO

> Trust all the work you've done with
> the previous eleven tools and let it go.

Once you've analyzed the script using the eleven tools, you will have comprehensively established a strong and detailed foundation for living the role. Now you must take all of the work you've done and trust that it will be there and LET IT GO. The focus as you LET IT GO should only be on your SCENE OBJECTIVE, which will propel you and the action of the story forward. Trusting all of the other work you've done, letting it go and concentrating only on accomplishing your goal (SCENE OBJEC-TIVE) helps re-create the way we act in life.

For spontaneous and original behaviors to emerge, you need to be and feel free. You must LET IT GO and try not to retain all the detailed thoughts that your script analysis inspired. You don't want to be stuck in your head. You must *trust* that all the preparation you've done with the first eleven tools will come up naturally. This will happen because, by the time you've applied the first eleven tools to a script, you've built a pow-erful muscle structure and foundation that will activate and respond to true human impulses. The trigger to activate these tools is to LET IT GO. This is crucial, because without letting it go, you can't help but be in con-trol, trying to duplicate something you did in rehearsal and overintellec-tualizing.

To reproduce real life you have to feel like anything can happen and anything's possible.

You can't successfully LET IT GO unless you trust that all the work you've done won't disappear *when* you LET IT GO. Yes, I know you feel it's difficult to trust that if you don't constantly concentrate on the choices you've made it will all just float away. But if the choices are weighty and have high stakes, it will not only stay, but the act of letting it go will *magnify* your feelings and needs. This is because your rational, thinking head isn't involved and therefore is unable to stop the flow with cerebral rationalizations. If you haven't made strong enough choices, it will be apparent very quickly, because those will be the choices that will not emerge when you LET GO. This is good, not bad, because it tells you what you need to revisit and work on, providing you with the opportunity to go back and find a more effective choice. Even in performance, you can change the less effective choices to better ones in your next take or setup, or the next night on stage.

How Do You LET IT GO?

Don't think about the work (except SCENE OBJECTIVE). Don't try to remember the choices you've made. Trust and allow the information you derived from your script analysis and rehearsals to permeate and inspire your feelings and needs to organically surface. This will also provide space for you to truly listen to the other person (people) in the scene, because you won't be in your head thinking about all the work that you've done. Watching an actor's wheels turning makes the work visible and less compelling to an audience. In life, who we are—how we speak and behave—is seamless. Letting it go allows the actor to organically move from each action and reaction, creating a natural flow of life. New responses will come up spontaneously because of the detailed and layered foundation you've established. This means that if you don't do all of your work, not much will happen when you LET IT GO. So . . .

Don't be lazy!

You can't LET IT GO unless you've created a strong enough base via the previous eleven tools. You must do the work. The formula goes like this:

If there's* nothing *to LET GO of,* nothing *is what you'll get.

Exactly how much work you accomplish will be exactly the amount of work that will remain when you LET IT GO. That is to say: Do a little work, and a little is what you'll get. Do deep work and deep is what you'll get. The more work you've put in, the more substantial the results you'll get when you LET IT GO. Which brings us to . . .

Work Ethic and Rehearsal Time

Every time you rehearse, you'll find more nuance and detail about the human being you're trying to become. Every rehearsal gives you more information about the choices you've made—what's effective and what isn't as effective. Remember: there are no right or wrong choices, just more effective and less effective ones. Any choice is a good choice, because no matter what, it always provides you with more information about your character. Making no choice makes the moment empty. So take a stab at coming up with something. It just may work! And if it isn't very effective, it will still inspire more thoughts that will eventually lead you to that ideal choice. Extensive rehearsal time, where you can continue to try new ideas and choices for each tool, is what leads you to the most powerful choices, because it provides the space for you to find the subtleties, textures and layers of a scene. The more you work out, the more your skills as an actor will grow.

The more time you put in, the better you'll be.

The Rehearsal Process

1. Read the script at least once.
2. Do some of the rudimentary, broad-stroke script analysis as homework before you meet with your scene partner. (Write in pencil so you can erase, because you will be constantly experimenting with alternative choices.)
3. Get together with your scene partner and, by running the scene several times, figure out which choices work for you and which choices need to be changed.

4. At home, based on your experience in rehearsal, reconfigure the choices you've made. Identify new possibilities for your next rehearsal.

5. Rehearse again with your scene partner. Stop when you feel the choices you've made aren't working and redo that section of the script over and over until you find a choice that does work.

6. After rehearsal, go home and find alternative choices for the ones that didn't work in the last rehearsal . . . and bring the new choices to the next rehearsal.

7. Repeat until you feel you've gone as far as you can or until it's time for the performance.

And to answer a question my students ask *all* the time:

No, you cannot rehearse too much!

All actors of note know this. When I was working with Charlize Theron on the film *The Devil's Advocate*, I discovered that Al Pacino is an actor who is enormously committed to the rehearsal process. In one scene that was only three pages long, Pacino stopped and started for each beat of the scene, altering choices that didn't work, refining the ones that did. He moved on to the next beat only when it felt right. This rehearsal process, for a tiny three-page scene, lasted for a few days!

Your rehearsals should include lots of starts and stops so that you can make sure:

- You're being true to your OVERALL OBJECTIVE.
- You're going after your SCENE OBJECTIVE.
- There are OBSTACLES getting in your way.
- The SUBSTITUTION is the most compelling choice.
- The INNER OBJECTS are emotionally loaded.
- The BEATS and ACTIONS are the most effective.
- You're using a MOMENT BEFORE that creates a pinnacle of urgency.
- You're using a PLACE/FOURTH WALL that is full and informed.
- You're utilizing DOINGS that are appropriate and helpful to promoting the reality and SCENE OBJECTIVE.
- You're employing INNER MONOLOGUE that is free-flowing.
- You're being substantiated by PREVIOUS CIRCUMSTANCES.
- And each rehearsal provides you with enough of a foundation so that you can LET IT GO in performance.

The more you study and work out, the more likely you are to succeed. In the many years that I've been teaching, I've found that among the many prominent and successful actors that I've been instrumental in establishing, there's one common dominator for success as an actor. No, it's not being pretty or handsome, or even talented. Especially in Hollywood, pretty and handsome actors are a dime a dozen. Unnurtured talent is around every corner. What's the secret?

Be open to learning.

Know that there's always more. Jon Voight once told me that a great actor never stops training and learning.

Take risks.

Fear stops the creative process. Never be satisfied; don't rely on safe choices. In doing your script analysis, always make the deepest, darkest, boldest, don't-be-afraid-to-look-foolish choices. And most important . . .

Work hard.

The more ardently an actor (writer, director, et al) works, the higher the success rate. Charlize Theron was open to learning, a risk-taker in her choices and one of the hardest workers I've ever seen. The years when she was in class she rehearsed all the time, often asking for double the work and to do two scenes at a time. She also always asked for challenging scenes, and would show up doing her scene work by making the boldest and riskiest choices. Her fellow students watched her with great anticipation, waiting for another unpredictable original move. When she was working on one of her movies that happened to be shooting at a studio half a mile away, she would come to my class during her lunch hour. When she was on the final days of a movie shoot, she'd call me to ask for a scene partner so she could start working on a scene for class. And to back up her bets, she would call one of her friends from class and ask if they wanted to do a scene during her two- or three-week downtime— just in case I didn't come through with someone. That was how dedicated she was to learning her craft. It wasn't a surprise to me or to her fellow students that she reached the spectacular heights of respectability and award-worthy performances. She worked hard and prospered. Sure, she's gorgeous. But the fact that her role as the unseemly and very unattractive Aileen Wuornos in *Monster* won her an Academy Award is a testament to her dedication to her craft and the work, not her beauty. You can do the same, so let this story inspire you. Charlize is just one actor's success story. I could go on and on about actors who walked through my door, never having acted a day in their lives, but through openness to learning, making fearless, risky choices and doing dedicated hard work on the craft—became renowned, award-winning actors.

Now you have the tools. It's up to you. The more time and effort you put toward exercising them, the better you'll become. You can't be expected to win an Olympic gold medal if you don't practice, practice, practice. Reward will follow if you . . .

Stay open, take risks and work hard.

PART II

Other Acting Tools
and Exercises

The following acting tools are not to be confused with the twelve-step system. It's important to do the work using the twelve tools first and consider any of the other acting tools as icing on the cake—to be utilized *only* after you've accomplished the twelve steps using the twelve tools.

Certain scenes require very specific states of being, such as being high (from alcohol or drugs), being afraid, dying, feeling the death of a loved one, being pregnant, being a parent, being physically impaired or injured, experiencing sexual chemistry and having the psyche of a serial killer.

These particular states of being affect us physiologically as well as emotionally.

These states of being affect our body chemistry. For instance, if we're afraid, our fight-or-flight instinct kicks in and our bodies react. Our pupils contract, our heart beats faster and adrenaline surges through our system. These are involuntary muscle reactions. While you cannot make your pupils contract, you can provoke these states of being, which will compel your involuntary eye muscles to respond.

I have developed a system of formulas to help the actors I coach access and organically feel these primal states, even if they have never felt them before. Because these reactions are so scientifically predictable, they can be assessed, calculated and broken down into a kind of mathematical equation.

I've found that the best way to truly feel one of these states is to first understand *why* a particular state of being works for our human condition. Therefore, the following will first explain *why* our bodies respond to these states of being, from a psychological base. And second, I will explain how to provoke the biological and physiological response. In short, I'll show you why the formula works, and then how to do it so you can truly and organically feel it.

CHAPTER 13

Substance Abuse

Creating organic feelings
of being on drugs or alcohol.

When playing a substance abuser, the first thing you must consider is *what* the character uses and *why* they use that particular drug. This will help you understand the actual feeling that takes place when under the influence, as well as the psychological reason why that exact drug is necessary in the character's emotional survival. Each substance supplies a different cure for a variety of emotional aches. Here's how they are broken down:

- **Alcohol** literally drowns misery, sorrow, suffering, regret and guilt, providing alcoholics with what they perceive as liquid strength. Alcohol gives an alcoholic the permission and the power to do and say what's on their minds and in their hearts without the consideration of consequences. For those who have been subjugated and beaten down in their lives, alcohol is a way to feel powerful, to be "right" and capable of taking on any adversary that comes their way. And in the alcoholic's mind, there are many.

- **Opiates** (heroin, opium, morphine, codeine, Vicodin, Percocet, etc.) numb the pain, making the user feel that all is right with the world and providing a sense of euphoria, allowing the user to more easily cope with new and old traumas. Users are drawn to opiates because they numb the deepest emotional and physical pain while allowing them to feel elated at the same time.

- **Cocaine and crystal methedrine** give you a sense of power and strength. They are often used by those who have been made to feel powerless in life. The user either has a powerful family or parent and continuously feels as though they can never reach their potential, or they have a career in which power is an issue (show business, law, medicine, politics, etc.) and the power in that field isn't easily attained. Thus, cocaine or crystal meth offers a way to feel powerful effortlessly. Users think of it as powdered strength.

- **Cocaine and heroin combined** ("speedball") offers the user both the feeling of power and the numbing of pain. This combination takes care of the person who feels powerless in their life and is also overwhelmed by emotional pain.

- **Marijuana** gives you a sense of freedom and lightness. Users generally feel they don't have permission to let go, be silly and have fun, and they are often generally inhibited when not under the influence. Reasons for marijuana abuse range from militant parents, highly critical parents, peer-group humiliations or growing up with religious constraints. Marijuana provides a way to rise above the repression and control that creates habitual inhibitions.

- **LSD, peyote, mescaline and other psychedelics** give the user a sense of intellectual strength (revelations abound) coupled with a sense of great creative capacity. Those who frequently ingest psychedelics are those who feel in some way creatively and intellectually repressed, perhaps by parents who were excessively controlling, hypercritical, or creatively and/or intellectually repressed themselves by the choices they made in life.

Now that you understand why your character takes that particular drug, find a way to use your own circumstances in life to personalize why you would use this substance. Determine the catalyst that might cause you to need to take your character's substance of choice. In other words, find your trigger. For instance:

- If you're playing a cokehead and something tumultuous is happening in the scene, or someone just said something emasculating to you, you would go to the cocaine and snort some up as a way to deal with it and feel powerful again.
- Or, if the other character reminds you of a time when you experienced someone's death or a calamity in your family that might have been your fault, then your character might shoot heroin or take a few opiate pills to eradicate the rush of emotions that overtake you.

The occasions when addicts drink, snort or smoke are always times when they *need* to do it. This means that they use when they need to feel—or not feel—something emotionally.

Even if you are playing a recovered substance abuser, if your substance of choice is presented to you, you must respond to it as if it still has a hold on you. As any recovering addict knows, you may be presently sober, but that doesn't remove the extreme desire and pull that your drug of choice has on you, which lasts for a lifetime. But no matter what you're playing—a recovering addict or an active one—if you are in a scene where your character's drug of choice is readily available, use the pull of the drug. Talk to it in your INNER MONOLOGUE.

Behavioral Formulas

Once you have a deeper comprehension of *what* and *why* your character uses (alongside your personal reasons), then you can use the following behavioral formulas to generate the organic feelings associated with the drug.

- **Note #1:** With these formulas, you never have to have actually used a particular substance to truly feel the affects of it. *And* more important, you NEVER have to use or experiment with the substance to create a more realistic performance. The following formulas will take you there: it's cheaper and there's no hangover or health risks.

- **Note #2:** Before you do any exercise to feel inebriated or stoned, it's key that you do your script analysis first. Otherwise the scene will only be about intoxication and will lack your character's OBJECTIVES and the intricacies of your inner work. So remember, first complete emotional and active script analysis and then do the substance exercise.
- **Note #3:** DO NOT DRIVE OR OPERATE MACHINERY AFTER DOING THESE EXERCISES. I'm not kidding. These exercises really do alter the way you think and behave and can seriously impair your ability to react and act. The effects last for about ten to fifteen minutes.

Feeling Drunk

When drunk, one loses control of one's faculties, which prompts our survival instinct to try to appear sober to other people as well as to ourselves. Our mind attempts to compensate for our faulty vision, slurred speech and poor coordination and overreacts so that it can feel sober and in control again. In essence, *it's our need to overcome our loss of faculties in order to feel and appear sober that creates drunken behavior.*

The specific body part—eyes, tongue or legs—that is affected most by alcohol, depends upon the individual. If you are visually inclined, and if your eyes are not working properly, you would naturally focus on overcoming your off-kilter vision. If you are verbally inclined, and if your speech is slurred, you would be driven to overcome your lack of cohesive speech. If you are physically inclined, then not being in total control of your legs would cause you to attempt to override and overcompensate your sloppy movement.

Often my students don't know what kind of person they are, so I have them try all three of the following exercises. Even though you're only using one element of your body, if it's the right choice it will make your whole body feel inebriated. You'll know which one works for you after you try all three. One will make you feel drunk, while the others will not. I have found that most people are visually inclined, so I ask my students to try the *eye* formula first. After that, the *tongue* seems to be the second most effective exercise. Those that rely on their physical ability number much fewer, and they should therefore try *legs* last.

Formula for Feeling Drunk

Eyes

1. Without focusing on anything in particular, fog up your vision. Don't cross your eyes; just randomly cloud your vision.

2. Think of the verb "focusing" as a noun and put "The Focus" at the back of your eyeballs, then move it around the actual ball of your eyes (not through the eyeball, because you will actually focus). Think: "The Focus" *around* the ball of the eye until it gets to the front. *Around* the fog, *around* the actual ball of the eye, around the *ball* of the eye itself until "The Focus" lands at the pupil. Put "The Focus" *around* the ball of the eye at least three times.

3. Now walk around for a few moments and let it go. If the eye element works for you, it should stick and you'll feel drunk without thinking about it.

Tongue

1. Take your tongue and let it rest in your mouth and feel like all the muscles of your tongue are useless and gelatin-like. Don't stick your tongue out, just let it idly rest in your mouth without being able to use it; let it become just a mush of tissue.

2. Then, take your lips and overpronounce your speech so as to overcompensate around your useless, mushy tongue. In other words, isolate the lip muscles around the unusable tongue and try to speak.

3. Do it for a few moments and then let it go.

Legs

1. Standing, feel like all the muscles in *one* knee become entirely useless, formless, gelatin-like. Barely be able to stand because the muscles have melted away in the one knee.

2. Next, use the muscles around the knee to walk in a way that overcompensates for the liquidity of your knee muscles. Keep walking, the knee muscles feeling like oozy pulp, and the other muscles in your legs working overtime, overcompensating around the mushy knee muscles.

3. Walk around for a few moments, then let it go.

No matter which exercise works for you, the goal is to effectively affect one body part so that it does not function properly and you must overcompensate for its failure. Once you pinpoint which exercise affects you the most when it's not functioning, you will have found your impetus for feeling drunk in the rest of your body. You should feel really drunk, act drunk, because for all intents and purposes—you *are* drunk. You are overcompensating for the impaired body part; you're working within the psychology of drunken behavior.

Once you set these feelings of being drunk in motion, which should take a few moments, always let it go. This enables you to color the scene with the drunken behavior, as opposed to making the scene *all about* being drunk.

- **Note #4:** Don't do all three drunk exercises at the same time. The specificity of using one physical trait will be more powerful in producing a true feeling of being drunk.
- **Note #5:** Redundant, yes, but worth repeating: Do your script analysis first and add the drunk element last. The state of being drunk should be an additional layer, not what the scene is about.

Formula for Creating a Marijuana High

1. To feel a marijuana high, begin by thinking that your brain has been replaced by a large gob of pink cotton candy. Think of the fluff, think of the pinkness of it, the sweetness of it and see how the air hits the cotton candy and how it becomes tiny sugar icicles . . .
2. Now, attempt to *think* and *see through* the fluff, the pink and the drippy warmed sugar . . . your brain no longer exists—*think* and *see through* those pink, pink, fluffy, sugary hairy filaments, a whipped up, sugary cottony mass . . . your brain no longer exists, it is now a large gob of pink cotton candy. *Think* and see *through* the fluff, the pink and the drippy warmed sugar . . . your brain is gone and that feels so good . . . continue to *think* and find a way to *see through* all that pink, pink, fluffy, whipped up, sugary-sweet cottony mass . . .
3. Now let it go, and begin the scene.

Feeling High on Heroin

A heroin high makes you feel euphoric to the extent that when you're faced with a problem or obstacle, the problem or obstacle ceases to exist—a heroin high seems to make life's encumbrances and difficulties disappear. Life feels good when you're at the peak part of the high, and you feel you can overcome anything. This is probably one of the reasons that heroin addiction is one of the hardest addictions to overcome.

Formula for Feeling High on Heroin

1. Begin by thinking that your brain has been replaced by a large gob of pink cotton candy. Think of the fluff, think of the pinkness of it, the sweetness of it and see how the air hits the cotton candy and how it becomes tiny sugar icicles . . .

Now, attempt to *think* and *see through* the fluff, the pink and the drippy warmed sugar . . . your brain no longer exists—*think* and *see through* those pink, pink, fluffy, sugary hairy filaments, a whipped up, sugary cottony mass . . . your brain no longer exists, it is now a large gob of pink cotton candy. *Think* and *see through* the fluff, the pink and the drippy warmed sugar . . . your brain is gone and that feels so good . . . continue to *think* and find a way to *see through* all that pink, pink, fluffy, whipped up, sugary-sweet cottony mass . . .

2. Then, give yourself a feeling of nausea in your stomach—think about whatever you most recently ate and feel it churning around and around in your stomach.

3. Then, pick a point of entry (where the hypodermic needle would go to inject the heroin)—a good place is in the crook of your arm where you're used to getting blood tests taken and begin there.

4. Then, think *"liquid warmth, peace, love, power"* and imagine it going into your veins starting from your point of entry. Feel the *"liquid warmth, peace, love, power"* slowly course through your veins up your arms . . . across your shoulders . . . feel the comforting, exquisite *"liquid warmth, peace, love, power"* travel your veins up your neck . . . to your chin . . . to your lips and then let *"liquid warmth, peace, love, power"* settle and engorge the fullness of your lips—feel that for a moment . . . feel the sensuality, the tingle as it fills your lips with *"liquid warmth, peace, love, power"* . . . Then feel the *"liquid warmth, peace, love, power"* go up your face, nose and to your eyes, and feel the *"liquid warmth,* *peace, love, power"* engorge your eyes and lids—feel that for a moment, let it linger in its heated pleasure as it fills your eyeballs and lids. Then take the *"liquid warmth, peace, love, power"* down your face, neck, chest, until you get to your nipples and let the *"liquid warmth, peace, love, power"* engorge your nipples, feel them swell with the sensual heat of the *"liquid warmth, peace, love, power."* Feel that for a moment, then take the *"liquid warmth, peace, love, power"* and bring it down your torso, then to your stomach, until it gets to your sexual zone, and then let the *"liquid warmth, peace, love, power"* engorge that area . . . feel the tingly warmth swelling that area with sensuality. Feel that for a moment, then take the *"liquid warmth, peace, love, power"* and travel it through your veins down your legs, your knees, your feet and out your toes.

5. Then, attempt to open your eyes by slowly lifting your eyelids (this will organically create the junkie nod).

6. Let it go.

Experiencing Organic Heroin Withdrawals

Before you can "jones" (have withdrawal symptoms) on heroin, you must first experience the high of heroin. This is so when the high starts to dissipate and the sickness begins to permeate your system, you'll truly need a fix to feel good again. Begin with the heroin exercise and continue from there.

Formula for Organic Withdrawal Symptoms for Heroin:

1. Do the high on heroin exercise. (Refer to above heroin formula.)

2. Now take tiny, icy-cold cockroaches . . . swarms of tiny, icy cockroaches jumping around on the back of your neck and the back of your hands going up the back of your arms. Thousands of sharp, icy, creeping antennae and legs stomping all over your neck and the backs of your hands and arms.

3. Add to the nausea you've already created and make yourself really feel like you're going to vomit. Feel the semidigested pieces of your last meal surging and swirling, attacking the lining of your stomach. Feel a sour taste coming up your throat and laying putridly on your tongue.

4. Let it go.

Feeling High on Cocaine or Crystal Methedrine

Cocaine gives the user a feeling that every thought is a revelation, one that is effusive, unrestrained and irrepressible. A thought, furthermore, that must be spoken aloud. The revelations can be extraordinary in the positive and extremely intense in the negative, causing profound paranoia. There is no subtlety to a cocaine user—the discovery is monumental, the rage like a volcano, the self-loathing enormous, the feeling of power Herculean. There's a lot of INNER MONOLOGUE when you're on cocaine. Every move, every word the other person is saying is worthy of several interpretations—after all, that's the basis of paranoia, and paranoia is an integral part of the cocaine/crystal meth experience.

Formula for Organic Cocaine/Crystal Methedrine High

1. Begin by thinking that your brain has been replaced by a large gob of pink cotton candy. Think of the fluff, think of the pinkness of it, the sweetness of it, and see how the air hits the cotton candy and how it becomes tiny sugar icicles. . . . Now, attempt to *think* and *see through* the fluff, the pink and the drippy warmed sugar . . . your brain no longer exists—*think* and see *through* those pink, pink, fluffy, sugary hairy filaments, a whipped up, sugary cottony mass . . . your brain no longer exists, it is now a large gob of pink cotton candy. . . . *think* and see *through* the fluff, the pink, and the drippy warmed sugar . . . your brain is gone and that feels so good . . . continue to *think* and find a way to see *through* all that pink, pink, fluffy, whipped up, sugary-sweet cottony mass . . .
2. Then, put thousands of tiny spiders on the back of your neck and hands, feeling the little spider legs piercing like little needles, dancing, frolicking on the back of your neck and the back of your hands.
3. Acknowledge everything you say aloud as a revelation.
4. Let it go.

Heroin and Cocaine Combination (AKA: "Speedball")

A person that uses both heroin and cocaine at the same time is someone who requires both an emotional pain reliever and a feeling of power. In replicating this behavior, you must first follow the formula for a heroin high, then do the formula for a cocaine buzz. This will reflect the way both highs physiologically affect your body.

Formula for an Organic Heroin/Cocaine High (a.k.a.: "Speedball")

1. Do the high on heroin exercise. (Begin by thinking that your brain has been replaced by a large gob of pink cotton candy. Think of the fluff, think of the pinkness of it, the sweetness of it, and see how the air hits the cotton candy and how it becomes tiny sugar icicles . . .

Now, attempt to *think* and *see through* the fluff, the pink and the drippy warmed sugar . . . your brain no longer exists, *think* and *see through* that pink, pink, fluffy, sugary hairy filaments, whipped up, sugary cottony mass . . . your brain no longer exists, it is now a large gob of pink cotton candy. . . . *think* and *see through* the fluff, the pink, and the drippy warmed sugar . . . your brain is gone and that feels so good . . . continue to *think* and find a way to *see through* all that pink, pink, fluffy, whipped up, sugary-sweet cottony mass . . .

Then, give yourself a feeling of nausea in your stomach—think about whatever you most recently ate and feel it churning around and around your stomach.

Then, pick a point of entry (where the hypodermic needle would go to inject the heroin)—a good place is in the crook of your arm where you're used to getting blood tests taken—and begin there.

Then, think *"liquid warmth, peace, love, power"* and imagine it going into your veins starting from your point of entry. Feel the *"liquid warmth, peace, love, power"* slowly course through your veins up your arms . . . across your shoulders . . . feel the comforting, exquisite *"liquid warmth, peace, love, power"* travel your veins up your neck . . . to your chin . . . to your lips and then let *"liquid warmth, peace, love, power"* settle and engorge the fullness of your lips—feel that for a moment . . . feel the sensuality, the tingle as it fills your lips with *"liquid warmth, peace, love, power"* . . . Then feel the *"liquid warmth, peace, love, power"* go up your face, nose, and to your eyes and feel the *"liquid warmth, peace, love, power"* engorge your eyes and lids—feel that for a moment, let it linger in its heated pleasure as it fills your eyeballs and lids. Then take the *"liquid warmth, peace, love, power"* down your face, neck, chest, until your get to your nipples and let the *"liquid warmth, peace, love, power"* engorge your nipples, feel your nipples swell with sensual heat of the *"liquid warmth, peace, love, power."* Feel that for a moment, then take the *"liquid warmth, peace, love, power"* and bring it down your torso, then stomach, until it gets to your sexual zone and let the *"liquid warmth, peace, love, power"* engorge that area . . . feel the tingly warmth swelling that area with sensuality. Feel that for a moment, then take the *"liquid warmth, peace, love, power"* and travel it through your veins down your legs, your knees, your feet and out your toes.

Then, attempt to open your eyes by slowly lifting your eyelids.

2. Then bring in the cocaine by putting thousands of tiny spiders on the back of your neck and hands, feeling the little spider legs piercing like little needles, dancing and frolicking on the back of your neck and the backs of your hands.

3. Let it go.

LSD, Peyote, Mescaline and Other Psychedelics

Because people who are into psychedelics are feeling creatively and intellectually repressed, you must establish a personal and present need to be creative. Look at the part of your life that is staid, uneventful and uninspiring. Tripping will be the right prescription to fix your sense of being trapped within the norm and the mundane by bringing you color, light and inspiring revelations.

Formula for a Psychedelic High

1. Begin by thinking that your brain has been replaced by a large gob of pink cotton candy. Think of the fluff, think of the pinkness of it, the sweetness of it and see how the air hits the cotton candy and how it becomes tiny sugar icicles . . .

   Now, attempt to *think* and see *through* the fluff, the pink and the drippy warmed sugar . . . your brain no longer exists, *think* and see *through* that pink, pink, fluffy, sugary hairy filaments, whipped up, sugary cottony mass . . . your brain no longer exists, it is now a large gob of pink cotton candy. . . . *think* and see *through* the fluff, the pink and the drippy warmed sugar . . . your brain is gone and that feels so good . . . continue to *think* and find a way to see *through* all that pink, pink, fluffy, whipped up, sugary-sweet cottony mass . . .

2. Now look at the inside of your hand. Notice closely and carefully all the wrinkles and various colors that you see there. Explore the pink, blue and green

of the veins, the yellow-, brown- and red-stained pigments of your skin, the purple where the stronger indentations are. Marvel at the intricacies and details of something as seemingly simple as your hand.

3. Now lift your head from your hand and notice the infinite details of a particular item around you. See the textures, the various colors, the quality of surface, and marvel at its incredible capacity and its earth-shattering purpose. Example: A toaster. See the toaster's silver and black tarnish and veneer. See how well it shines in some spots and is dull in others. Look at the inside and notice the crevices and intricate wirework and revel in the fact that those wires turn cold to hot, gray to red in just a few seconds. As you're staring at the toaster, marvel that this amazing contraption can actually change something white to brown, and sometimes even black in a matter of moments. "How does it know how to do that?!"

4. Let it go. Start the scene, and as you do the scene continue to pinpoint specific things around you to examine and explore in extreme detail and fascination. This includes the other actor's face as you are speaking to him or her.

Substance Abuser Ritual

Along with the feeling of being high, substance abusers get off on the ritual of imbibing. It's the foreplay of the orgasm. And just as foreplay is an integral part of sex, the ritual of using is key to an addiction. Let's look at some sample substance abuser rituals.

- **Cocaine:** Calling the dealer. Pouring it onto a shiny surface. Tasting it. Cutting it with a credit card or razor blade into fine lines. Snorting it with a particular device—a dollar bill, the right knuckle, a spoon.
- **Heroin:** Measuring the heroin. Loading a spoon. Pouring the precise amount of water into the spoon. Cooking the heroin with your favorite lighter. Putting a piece of cotton in the heroin. Filling the syringe. Tying off with a belt. Finding a good vein. Slapping and pumping the vein. Injecting.
- **Alcohol:** First identify your alcohol of choice—beer, wine, vodka, gin, whiskey. Most alcoholics stick with one type of alcohol. Going to that special place—a bar, the den, the hall closet or somewhere you keep or hide your alcohol of choice. Ordering a drink in a specific way or checking to see how much is left. Analyzing how many future drinks are possible. Making the drink or

asking for the drink the way you *always* make or have your drink made. The drink's accessories should be precise. For instance, you make your drink with exactly three ice cubes, two olives, a splash of water, one large cocktail onion, a quarter wedge of lime, sugar-free orange juice or a pink umbrella. And the glass should be filled to a specific level. Drinking.

• **Marijuana:** Opening the plastic bag. Burying your nose inside the bag and smelling and breathing in the woody, spicy smell with anticipation. Taking it out of the bag. Rolling it around your fingers. Selecting your favorite pipe or bong or rolling papers. Rolling the joint or loading the marijuana into the bong. Putting your mouth to the stem. Lighting up with your favorite lighter. Inhaling.

• **Pills:** Going to your favorite secure hiding place. Taking the lid off the pill container and counting how many you have left. Figuring out how many more times you have left in this bottle to get high. Putting in your mouth and swallowing.

Drugs and alcohol allow the user to feel pain-free and powerful, at least while the drug is at its peak potency. When the good feelings start to go away, the user chases the high in order to feel good again. An actor who plays a substance abuser should keep this in mind—when the bad feelings emerge you fix it by snorting, injecting, drinking, ingesting or smoking some more. This need, along with the ritual, should become part of your DOINGS throughout the scene/story.

Creating an Addictive Personality

Beyond the emotional need to use and the love of the ritual, addicts find a deep sense of safety and security in the actual handling of the substance they are addicted to. This is because they know, absolutely, that the substance they are handling gives them power and strength when they need it the most. People are unreliable, events are unpredictable, but the one thing an addict can count on, again and again, is their substance of choice, which gives them the sense of well-being they so desperately need.

Formula for Creating an Addictive Personality

1. Take the alcohol bottle (pill container, bag with the powder, binge food, whatever your character is addicted to) and press it against your face as you close your eyes.
2. Now feel a sense of *peace, power, warmth, well-being and love* emanating from the container and pouring into your heart and soul.
3. Take the addictive substance SUBSTITUTE (for example: tea or water substituting for alcohol) and pour it out of the container and into your mouth, letting the liquid settle on your tongue for a while as you feel a sense of *peace, power, warmth, well-being and love*. Then swallow.
   - If it's food, chew slowly and feel a sense of *peace, power, warmth, well-being and love* as you taste and savor your character's binge food. Then swallow.
   - If it's pills (substitutes like candy, vitamins, mints, etc., will work), shake the pill into your mouth and let it sit there, feeling a sense of *peace, power, warmth, well-being and love*. Then swallow.
   - If it's cocaine (use a substitute like powdered milk, etc.), snort it up and feel a sense of *peace, power, warmth, well-being and love* as the substance SUBSTITUTE drains down your throat.
   - If it's marijuana (use tobacco or herbal cigarette filling), take a hit and feel a sense of *peace, power, warmth, well-being and love* from the smoke that's filling your mouth and lungs.

Like an addict, you'll find after doing this exercise that you'll want to ingest the substance whenever you're triggered by anxiety, angst, turmoil, confrontation or any uncomfortable situation. You will organically feel the need to go to your addiction as a way to cope, responding to specific emotional triggers that come from the scripted material. This is the way it happens with real addictive personalities, not the way so many actors portray an addict by randomly ingesting their substance as a scene progresses.

Feeling the Influence of Anesthesia

Going into or just coming out of anesthesia gives you a feeling of discombobulation—your vision is distorted and your mind feels hazy, you have the sense of being off-balance, with no equilibrium. In many ways it is not unlike being in a drug fog—it's just a different kind of drug fog. To truly feel this sensory experience, follow these steps.

Formula for Feeling the Influence of Anesthesia

1. Replace your brain with a big lump of gray cotton in your head.

2. Picture the cotton. It is dense and lead gray.

3. Attempt to *see and think through* the heavy, cottony, gnarled gray threads. You have no brain, just a big hunk of dense, dark gray cotton that extends to every inch of your skull. Very little light filters through the lead-gray hairy fibers. Continue to try to see and think through the gray, fluffy, fibrous mass.

4. Create a feeling of nausea by imagining the semidigested food you last ate churning and spinning in gruesome chunks in your gut. Feel the nausea rise in your stomach and up your throat, and taste the sour, fetid flavor of this molten mass of semiliquefied food, letting the taste further your nausea.

5. Let it go.

CHAPTER 14

Creating Sexual Chemistry

> An essential part
> of the performance.

Watching two actors who are supposed to love each other but have no natural heat between them can be a tedious and unsatisfying experience. An audience gets what you feed them. If there's no chemistry between you and the other actor, the audience won't feel any more need to get involved with your story than you do with your co-star. On the other hand, if there's a palpable connection between you and your co-star, then they'll root for your relationship to prosper and survive, making it interactive and exciting. The chemistry factor can often determine the success or failure of a movie, play or television show.

Creating chemistry should never be left to chance. There are ways to make it happen by looking at the reasons why chemistry occurs in life and then learning how to duplicate it in your performance.

Chemistry comes from a deep connection between two people. Most people assume chemistry comes from a simplistic sexual connection, but sex without an emotional connection is not very satisfying to experience, nor is it fulfilling to view. In order to create chemistry, you must have both an emotional and sexual affinity. It's important to recognize that chemistry should go far deeper than just simple sexual attraction to become truly captivating.

The emotional connection, the part that makes people fall in love or bond as friends, doesn't come from two people who like the color red and both like to ski. At its highest intensity it comes from a bond that emanates from a *commonality of pain.* What this means is that both people have experienced similar emotionally painful experiences that touched them and that they reacted to in similar primal ways. If you look at your own personal history with lovers and friends, you'll find that your traumas or reactions to the traumas have been comparable. For example:

- Both of you have experienced the death of a loved one at an early age in life.
- Both of you have experienced physical and/or emotional abuse at the hands of a parent or sibling.
- Both of you have experienced abandonment from a family member.
- Both of you have become addicts as a result of your disturbing past.
- Both of you have experienced cheating ex-mates.
- Both of you have experienced painful parental divorces.
- Both of you have experienced life-threatening disease, personally or with people who are close to you.

- Both of you have the same insecurities based in similar childhood experiences—not being good-looking enough, smart enough, strong enough, etc.
- Both of you have some kind of physical handicap.
- Both of you have a distant, alcoholic (or any-aholic) father or mother.
- Both of you have a doting, overprotective mother or father.
- Both of you use the same M.O. as a way to survive life's adversities.

Once you find a common emotional pain, you have a bond, a touchstone to the other actor's delicate, fragile inner self. You are now privy to the part of their soul that they struggle to hide and protect. This connection—your ability to understand, protect and relate to the other actor from a similar pain source—will draw the two of you closer together than you can imagine. In fact, these are the tenets of love. You can achieve chemistry with authenticity because you identify with and have a profound empathy for the other person. You really get each other, and that's extremely rare.

Formula for Creating an Emotional Connection

Simply think about the trauma or insecurity that most defines you and see the pain, sadness and rage in the other actor's eyes that comes from having experienced the same thing. This can be done anywhere you see the other actor—makeup chair, readings, waiting for the cameras to roll—because you are surreptitiously looking at him or her.

Emotional chemistry is heightened and infused with a much more intriguing complexity when combined with sexual chemistry. Adding a sexual connection to the equation is essential in producing chemistry between people. Usually, there's an inherent sexuality that permeates all loving relationships. This is obviously true in lover relationships, but is just as real between friends and even within the family. Freud, the father of psychology, maintains that there is an innate sexuality between a mother and a son, a father and a daughter and between siblings. Sexual feelings are repressed and usually remain in the subconscious, but they nevertheless exist. As an actor you have to bring this information from the subconscious to the conscious mind and use whatever it takes to recreate someone who is a living, breathing, flesh-and-blood human being. Without the primal connection created by sexuality, you're overlooking a very basic human need. One that is not to be judged, but used to complete your character and your character's important relationships.

In creating sexuality, you must use the other actor, not a SUBSTITUTION.

Sexuality requires physical intimacy, and SUBSTITUTION is used only to generate emotional history.

Formula for Creating a Sexual Connection

Begin by sexually fantasizing about the other actor. Imagine your most dangerously intriguing fantasies as you include the other actor in the sexual scenario. The reason you don't just use generic sex in your fantasy work is because sexuality that includes danger and the forbidden is inherently more erotic. This transcends being straight or gay because it becomes a part of the forbidden and therefore creates a more heightened carnality.

You can do this alone or (secretly) in front of the other actor. It doesn't hurt to fantasize more than once, so do it alone *and* in front of the other actor. After you accomplish this, the other actor will absolutely respond and not know why they all of a sudden feel this new bond. They will not know that you're thinking of them sexually, they'll just feel this unexplainable sense of closeness—otherwise known as chemistry.

I coached one Academy Award–winning actress on a movie where she met her co-star love interest and had an immediate dislike for him (and him for her). Using the following "formula for creating emotional and sexual chemistry" was so effective that not only did they develop a real-life crush on each other, but the tabloids also published that they were involved in a torrid affair—which, by the way, they were not.

Formula for Creating Emotional and Sexual Chemistry

1. Identify the trauma or insecurity that most defines you.
2. Then, look into the other actor's eyes and see the same pain, sadness and rage that you have. Relate it to having experienced the same trauma and insecurity as you. Say in your head to the other actor, "You really understand me because you know what it feels like to (fill in your personal trauma and insecurity)." Be specific. Let that give you a sense of deep connection that the other actor truly and profoundly understands you like no one else.
3. Then sexually fantasize about the other actor, using your kinkiest fantasy in your sexual scenario.
4. Let it go.

You can use this exercise to produce chemistry that is necessary in your acting relationships, such as:

- Friendships
- Between extended family members (cousins, in-laws, aunts, uncles, et al)

- Workplace relationships
- Lover relationships
- Marriage partnerships

It's not just within your acting that this exercise works. Try it yourself with anyone you might come across: the cashier at your local mini-mart, or that hottie you spy at a party, or a potential employer at a job interview—you'll find an immediate chemistry with that person and they will feel the same way. It only takes a few seconds to do, and you'll see an instant change come over the other person. The fun part is that it's so subtle that they'll feel connected to you by an indefinable something, and they won't know why.

Creating Chemistry in the Audition

You can do this exercise in an audition situation, as well. Despite what actors often think, casting directors, producers and directors are human beings and will respond as such. If they like you, feel a chemistry with you, they'll want to have you around, and that essentially means getting cast (of course, you must add to this equation a good reading).

Formula for Creating Chemistry in the Audition

1. See in the casting director's (producer's, director's, et al) eyes the same pain, sadness and rage that comes from a trauma similar to that of your own. Understand and relate.
2. Then, sexually fantasize about the person in front of you (your most twisted and compelling fantasies).
3. Let it go.

All of this should take less than thirty seconds. Do the exercise with the person you're reading with before you start the reading. The exercise helps build the necessary chemistry and intimacy that is such an important component in building the role. (This is additional to the other work you do in your script analysis—not in place of.)

CHAPTER 15

Playing a Serial Killer

No matter how cruel someone is,
there's always a reason.

When a person becomes a serial killer, it is usually a response to heinous physical, emotional and/or sexual abuse they endured as a child. A child is powerless to respond to the abuse because of size, authority control and reliance on the abuser for money, home and sustenance. However, when the child becomes an adult, he then has the power to avenge the abuser. There is no greater power that a human being can have than to have the power over whether someone lives or dies. A serial killer's victims almost always symbolize their original abuser. When a killer murders his victim, he feels he is finally winning his power back from the person who took it away. Because the person being killed is not the actual perpetrator of the abuse, the acquired power is momentary. And because the relief is fleeting, the serial killer, like a drug addict, chases this high by killing again. His (or her) killing becomes essential in maintaining his sense of control and power. Thus, a series of murders are committed, and a serial killer is produced.

Case in point is the infamous serial killer Ed Kemper. Growing up, Ed was tormented by his mother. She accused him of molesting his sister and of wanting to rape the coeds on a college campus. She verbally abused him and locked him in a suffocating, windowless, dark and damp cellar filled with vermin so that he wouldn't harm anyone. All this for crimes he didn't commit. Then, when Ed was old enough to fend for himself, guess what he did? He raped and killed. Who? Yup, those very coeds his mother had unfairly imprisoned and chastised him over. His first victim?

His mother. Ed beat her to death with a claw hammer, cut off her head and carefully extracted her larynx—the part of the body that gave his mother the capacity to shower Ed with her brutal accusations and hateful admonishments. And then Ed had sexual intercourse with the detached head. He was punishing *her* sexually, the equivalent of being punished for sexual crimes that he, to this point, had never committed.

You have to be aware of the manner in which your character kills, because it is always fraught with symbolism—symbolism that makes sense and matches the childhood abuse that was inflicted upon the killer.

More often than not, sexuality plays a key role in a mass murderer's M.O. Why? Because both killing and sex involve power. For a killer, murder is an aphrodisiac. For most murderers, even if there is no actual sex, the act of killing is sexually stimulating. So arousing, in fact, that it often reaches the point of orgasm.

When playing a serial killer, the act of killing can be compared to a seduction and should be performed that way.

Another aspect of being a serial killer is that they don't just kill upon contact with their victim. Like a cat with a mouse, there's the joy of the hunt—playing with his food—before the murder is committed. This gives the killer additional power in watching the victim squirm and beg.

A serial killer will say and do things that push the buttons of the victim until the victim retaliates with behavior similar to the original abuser. This enables the killer to justify his murder. In the killer's mind, the victim actually deserves to die.

There's a stunted emotional growth and a childlike quality to a serial killer.

Their traumas are often so severe that their development is arrested and they remain emotionally very immature. Mature adults rationalize their history so that they can emotionally survive life's dilemmas. A serial killer doesn't understand this and, like a child, acts out, immaturely striking back without thought to the act or its repercussions.

How does that relate to you, someone who is a rational adult?

*All acting is taking a fraction of who you are and turning it
into a whole, so you can become and
live the character on the page.*

Everyone has homicidal urges at one time or another in their life, but
few actually act upon them. You have to look at your life and the times
you've felt the homicidal urge. Who caused it? In the fantasy land of acting, you get to have the upper hand for a change by taking someone from
your life that you feel has abused you horribly, preferably someone from
your childhood, but it could be an abuser from your more present life,
and killing them in your performance. The symbolic SUBSTITUTION for
your victims may stem from childhood issues, such as dealing with someone who:

- Abandoned you when you were a child
- Sexually molested or raped you
- Beat you up emotionally and/or physically
- Didn't protect you from someone who abused you—
  emotionally, sexually or physically
- Humiliated you in vast proportions

Or from your adult issues, such as dealing with a person who:

- Stole a mate away
- Maliciously sued you
- Hurt someone you loved in a hideous manner
- Viciously abused you
- Was your mate, but had sexual intercourse with someone near
  and dear to you
- Had you fired or caused you to lose your job
- Lied about you with disastrous results

All these deeds deserve to be punished. And as an actor playing a
murderer, it's payback time!

Formula for Organically Realizing the Mind-set of a Serial Killer

1. Identify your most potent abuser, the one you'll use as a SUBSTITUTION for your victims.

2. Then figure out the best, most pleasurable way to take your revenge. In other words, what manner of killing, in your fantasy, would be equivalent to what was done to you?

3. Then, viscerally fantasize about doing exactly that to your SUBSTITUTION.

4. Feel the joy of getting your power back, both emotionally and sexually. Let it elate you. Let it empower you.

5. Look at the actor who is playing the victim, knowing that everything you've just experienced in your mind will soon be physicalized.

6. Let it go.

Symbolically killing this person within the confines of acting should give you great joy in your newfound power over someone who has, in the past, cruelly had it over you.

Reminder: Don't ever judge your characters. Even serial killers feel their behavior is justified. Making your victims into SUBSTITUTIONS for the major abuser in your life makes your homicidal act appropriate and valid. What would seem to the healthy adult as sick, evil and immoral now seems to make more justifiable sense.

CHAPTER 16

Creating Organic Fear

Fear Is the Most Difficult Feeling for an Actor to Re-create

This is because most of the telltale physical responses that indicate fear are involuntary to your system, such as:

- Pupils contracting
- Heart beating fast
- Adrenaline pumping into your system
- Skin blanching
- Body and mind exhibiting unusual levels of courage and strength.

In order to make these physical reactions really happen in your body, you have to investigate what actually causes fear to happen. Fear is our body's way of protecting ourselves when we suspect that we might be or truly are in danger. Fear emanates from the need to stay alive—it's part of our innate survival instinct. Because fear motivates the parts of your body that control action—blood and adrenaline flowing faster and in greater amounts through your system—it creates faster movement, a quicker thought process, and physical prowess that we wouldn't ordinarily have.

It's a common misconception that fear comes from a rush of information. It's actually *one* aspect of our lives that we think about when we're afraid that makes us want and need to survive. For example, if someone has a gun to your head, you might think about the fact that you are the only person around who can take care of an ailing parent. You have to survive to keep that parent from being left alone to fend for him- or herself.

> **When creating organic fear, you must find that personal issue that, if you were to face a life-and-death situation, you would regret not living to see, do or resolve.**

To establish your specific personal issue in creating fear, make a list of all the regret possibilities. The list should include any and all issues that, if you were to die today, you'd never be able to accomplish, resolve or take care of.

List at least ten to fifteen ideas. Don't stop at five. The issues that emerge after number five are often the most affecting because they stem from your subconscious—the material that is deepest, darkest and that you don't necessarily want to admit to yourself. Logically, the issues we hide even from ourselves are always going to be more deeply felt.

The following is an example of a "Fear List" (which you'd handwrite on lined paper):

Fear List

(Think, "If I die today . . .")

1. I'll never have a child.
2. (Or, if you do have a child) I'll never be able to watch my child grow up and they'll never know me as their mother (or father).
3. I'll never find true love.
4. I'll never know what it feels like to be truly loved.
5. I'll never be married.
6. I'll never know if my mother (father) ever really loved me.
7. I'll never make my father (mother, child, sibling, mate) proud of me.
8. My mate (parent, sibling, friend, etc.) will believe I died a loser.
9. I won't be there to take care of my financially bereft (or ailing) mother (father, sibling, mate, child, etc.) who was always there for me.

10. I'll never resolve or have closure in my relationship with my father (mother, child, sibling, mate, ex-mate, best friend, etc.).

11. I'll never hear the words "I love you" from my father (mother, sibling, child, mate, etc.).

12. I'll never be able to say, "I love you" and "I'll miss you" to my mother (father, sibling, mate, ex-mate, friend, child, etc.).

13. I'll never hear the words "I'm sorry" from my father (mother, mate, ex-mate, sibling, friend, uncle, etc.) for their abuse (molestation, abandonment, cheating, etc.).

14. I'll never prove to my child (father, mother, mate, etc.) I could be successful.

15. I'll never know my real mother (father—if adopted or abandoned).

Before you can do the fear formula for performance, you have to first determine which regret issue from your fear list would affect you the most. You must pinpoint precisely the regret issue from your fear list before your actual performance. This will enable you, during your performance, to realize organic fear within a minute of using the fear formula.

Finding Which Regret Issue from Your Fear List Will Be the Most Effective

Once you're done with your list, read each one aloud (alone, you'll feel more available, and less judged). There will be one particular "regret" on your fear list that will pull at you more emotionally than the others. If two or three seem to "speak" to you equally, then try the following exercise with each one and see which creates the most tangible fear response.

After you've picked the one (or two or three) from your fear list that inspires the largest emotional reaction in you, close your eyes and picture what it would feel like to accomplish or fix the regret in the best possible way. Enjoy picturing your success. Then open your eyes and imagine your achievement or resolution taken from you in an abrupt and tragic manner. Then say over and over again in your head, "I have to survive to keep this from happening," "I have to survive to keep this from happening. . . ."

You repeat a survival mantra because it's the need to survive that actually creates fear, not the fearful situation itself.

Applying the fear list.

Using regret issue #1: *If I die today* . . . "I'll never have a child" (which, by the way, is frequently a highly effective regret issue, because procreation is such a strong, primal need):

1. *If you're a woman:* Picture a baby that looks just as you did when you were an infant and imagine "baby-you" floating in your womb.
    If you're a man: Picture holding a baby that looks just as you did when you were an infant and see it in your mind's eye placed gently in your arms. (The reason you see the baby as yourself as a child is because a parent sees his offspring as a little version of themselves, a second chance, if you will, at fixing the woes and devastations that happened in the parent's childhood. That's why pride and letdowns are so intensified with regard to your own child, because basically it's just "little you" having to deal, yet again, with life's trials and tribulations.)

2. Look into your baby's eyes and see your baby's unconditional love, the kind of love you've never received before, and feel it wash all over you. Then look down at your baby and silently speak to your child, vowing to protect and love and keep all the bad things that have happened to you from happening to your baby. Be specific in remembering your personal traumatic events and your personal insecurities that you're going to shield your baby from. This should take only a few moments. Now, see the baby look at you with unconditional love, thanking you for protecting him (or her) from all the bad things that happened to you and allowing him (or her) to stay safe, hopeful and innocent. Feel the love wash over you again.

3. Feel the baby pulled from your womb (or arms). Forever. Feel the profound emptiness—an emptiness that will never go away if you die. Then quickly open your eyes and realize that the last image is going to happen if you die today. Then say in your head, like a mantra, "I have to survive to keep this from happening," "I have to survive to keep this from happening," "I have to survive to keep this from happening. . . ."

4. Let it go and begin the scene. The *fear* should stay with you, driving you to survive.

Let's look at another example so that you really get the idea. We'll use #7 from the sample list: *If I die today* . . . "I'll never make my father proud of me."

1. Get comfortable. Relax. Close your eyes and picture a close-up of your father's face beaming with pride at your future accomplishments—the kind of look you've never seen from him, but have always hoped you would see one day. Take a few seconds to let the feeling of your father's pride wash over you, the feeling that, "I've finally gotten what I've always wanted from him."
2. Abruptly change the image to your father looking at your tombstone, shaking his head in disappointment, thinking what a loser and screwup you were and how much you let him down. Watch him cry because you were such a failure and a mistake. Let that feeling make you sick.
3. Quickly open your eyes and realize that the last image is going to happen if you die today, and say in your head, like a mantra, "I have to survive to keep this from happening," "I have to survive to keep this from happening," "I have to survive to keep this from happening. . . ."
4. Let it go and begin the scene. The *fear* should stay with you, driving you to survive.

After you've figured out your most effective regret issue from your fear list, you can go ahead and use the formula for creating fear.

Formula for Creating Organic Fear

1. Take the regret issue that you've previously chosen from your fear list and see the upside of what you want to accomplish, resolve or take care of happening in the most wonderful and vivid way—exactly the way you'd always wanted and imagined it would be. Thoroughly enjoy it.
2. Then imagine the worst that can happen if you were to die today without having a chance to fulfill your need. Picture it in all of its horrible details. Let the image fill you with anxiety.
3. Then, with great angst, acknowledge that the worst image is definitely going

> to happen if you die today, and internally do the survival mantra, "I have to
> survive to keep this from happening," "I have to survive to keep this from
> happening," "I have to survive to keep this from happening. . . ."
> **4.** Let it go and let the *fear* happen organically.

This whole process should take only a minute, which will allow you to be in fear mode quickly when the director says, "Action!" or when the curtain goes up.

Remember: Always do the fear list as part of the homework you do *before* you arrive on set or stage, so you'll know in advance which regret issue will be the most effective—it takes time to make the list and figure out which one will work best for you. In this way, when it's time to shoot or make your entrance on stage, it will take less than a minute to take the choice you've already made from your list and do the fear exercise.

It's also important to note that just because the choices you make to create fear work for you today, it doesn't mean that they're going to work forever. Priorities change, needs change and circumstances change as your life progresses, and so will the issue that will be most crucial to motivate a need to survive. For every new script you analyze in which a need for fear comes into play, do an entirely new list and rework it as if you're doing it for the first time.

Place-Motivated Fear

If the fear is more place motivated—such as in a haunted house, or in a scene in which some unknown entity is chasing you—there's another technique available to you.

Formula for Place-Motivated Fear

1. Figure out which vermin or creatures give you the creeps: spiders, rats, roaches, snakes, worms, maggots, pit bulls, possums, etc.
2. In the space in which you're acting, imagine that every dark corner, space, light fixture and drawer is grotesquely swarming with whatever vermin you've selected. Now think, "If I can't escape, I will be covered by them—in my hair, filling my mouth, up my nose, up my sleeves and pant legs."
3. Let it viscerally get to you by imagining the creatures of choice, in masses—biting, sliming and crawling all over you.
4. Let it go.

CHAPTER 17

Creating Organic Feelings
of Death and Dying

Experience dying from the P.O.V. of the dying.

Many actors see dying and death as a final giving up on life. The truth is that when someone is dying, that person grasps onto life like never before. Even the breath that a dying person takes is an attempt to desperately take in more air. Physiologically, when we are dying, our organs shut down, and the intensive struggle to get breath—which brings life-building oxygen—becomes impossible. It's sort of like trying to put gas in a broken engine—no matter how much fuel you attempt to get in, the engine still won't get the motor running and, for all intents and purposes, the car dies.

Because breath brings oxygen, which feeds the body and keeps it alive, physicalizing the obstruction of breathing is where you want to begin when you are playing someone who is dying. After you truly feel that you are aching with the need for life-giving oxygen, then you would do the formula for creating organic fear.

The reason you use the formula for creating organic fear when you're playing someone who is dying is because dying and fear are inextricably connected. In the same way that we struggle for physical life (via the need to breathe), we also struggle to keep our emotional lives. In other words, when we die, we don't want to give in to death because we don't want to lose our emotional connections, so we voraciously fight to stay alive. There's usually one climactic emotional reason that will make you feel like you have to stay alive. Therefore, just like the fear list, you make up a dying list of your regret issues that you'd never be able to accomplish, resolve or take care of if your death were about to happen. In the same way you dealt with the fear list, you would explore and discover the particular regret issue from your dying list in *advance* of performance.

Once you've figured out the best, most effective regret issue from your fear list, then you can duplicate the terrifying feeling of someone who is imminently dying by doing the following exercise.

Formula for Dying, from the P.O.V of the Person Dying:

1. Create labored breathing by imagining a large rock on your chest and throat and attempting to breathe around the pressure of the excessive weight. Grapple to gain breath around the weight on your chest, throat and esophagus. It will sound gravelly and make you cough. Then struggle to gain back the air that the coughing let escape.
2. Fight to breathe as you would fight for life.
3. Once you really feel that you're desperately and agonizingly trying to get some air in your lungs to survive, do the previously described formula for creating organic fear. (Taking the regret issue that you've previously chosen from your fear list, and see the upside of what you want to accomplish, resolve or take care of—happening in the most wonderful and vivid way—exactly the way you'd always wanted and imagined it would be. Thoroughly enjoy it.

   Then imagine the worst that can happen if you were to die immediately and never get a chance to fulfill your need. Picture it in all its horrible details. Let the image fill you with anxiety.

   Then, with great angst, acknowledge the worst image is definitely going to happen if you die today, and internally do the survival mantra, "I have to survive to keep this from happening," "I have to survive to keep this from happening," "I have to survive to keep this from happening. . . .")
4. Continue the fight for breath and life, because so much depends on it.
5. Let it go.

Why does it work? Since you are fighting to live, instead of surrendering to death, it makes your work active and eventful and eventually cathartic. Fighting to live makes the dying feel real because this is what we do—our inherent survival instinct doesn't allow us to give in and give up. This formula infuses the dying process with passion and the human will to live. If you give up and let death take you, the audience will give up as well. Your specific needs, which will be revealed by your fight for life, will engage your audience. They will identify and root for you to overcome death. And when you don't, your audience will be moved.

Experiencing Death
When a Loved One Is Dying

Whenever someone we love is dying, our natural instinct is to deny their impending death and to try to keep them alive. We usually have unfinished business that needs closure or that requires more time with this person. This is why you'd use the SCENE OBJECTIVE *"to keep you alive"* when you are playing a character who is experiencing the death of a loved one. This drives you to fight for their life, thereby furthering the goal that needs to be achieved (SCENE OBJECTIVE). If you were to just accept the loved one's death, there would be nothing to do and nowhere to go.

Next, identify a SUBSTITUTION. Ask yourself, "Who is it that I need to keep alive?" If someone that you are close to is very sick or dying, or has recently passed away, then it's easy. Use that person. However, if you are fortunate enough not to be dealing with sickness, dying or death in your present life, then ask yourself the question, "The death of which person in my life would devastate me if he or she were to die today because important issues would remain painfully unresolved?"

Choosing a relationship-fraught SUBSTITUTION adds a higher charge to your hypothetical situation. If someone that you feel is safe and loving dies, it will leave you feeling sad, but you won't have the extra inner turmoil that comes from unresolved issues. And if that person dies, it will be unresolved forever. This intensifies your passion to win your SCENE OBJECTIVE of *"to keep you alive,"* because if you fail, you'll be left with permanent emotional scars.

Once you select your SUBSTITUTION, you must identify precisely what it is you will lose if that particular loved one dies. As with the fear/dying list, what you lose, regret and do not resolve must be significant and specific to your own life and relevant to your issues with your SUBSTITUTION choice. This gives you a very personal and emotionally charged reason to fight to keep that person alive. Generalities are hard for our brains and hearts to latch onto. It's always specific intimate information that makes us think and feel. The truth is that when someone you love is dying, there's usually a momentous reason why we feel that person must stay alive.

As with the fear list, identify the specific issue that needs to be ac-

complished, resolved or taken care of before your choice of SUBSTITU-
TION dies. Make a list. In your handwritten list, state at least ten regret
issues that are relevant to your SUBSTITUTION.

Sample Loved One Is Dying List

(Think, "If *you* die today . . .")

1. I'll never know what you could have become or achieved.
2. You'll never know what I could have become or achieved.
3. I'll never know if you were ever proud of me.
4. I'll never know if you loved me.
5. I'll never resolve and understand why you abandoned me.
6. I'll never resolve and understand why you abused me.
7. I'll never know if you forgave me for what I did to you.
8. You'll never see me happy and in love.
9. You'll never meet your grandchild (if you're using a parent as SUBSTITUTION).
10. You'll go to your grave thinking I'm a loser.
11. You won't be there to love and take care of me.
12. I'll be all alone.
13. I'll never hear you say the words "I love you."
14. You'll never know how much I love you.
15. I'll never know if you're sorry for what you did to me.
16. I'll never know if you forgive me for not being able to protect and save you (if you're using your child as a SUBSTITUTION).

As with the lists in the previous exercises, evaluate which regret is the
strongest by reading each one aloud and feeling which one emotionally
pulls at you the most. If more than one feels viable, try all of your final
contenders and evaluate which one affects you the most.

Always identify in advance which SUBSTITUTION as well as which issue from your loved one's dying list you'll be using to exemplify your
need to keep your SUBSTITUTION alive.

Formula for Organically Feeling a Loved One's Impending Death

1. Think of your SUBSTITUTION as dying, then use the issue from your list that will never be resolved, accomplished or taken care of if the person were to die right now. Now *close your eyes* and picture the accomplishment or resolution as you would most like to see it come to pass if that person were to stay alive. (For example, if "I need you to say I love you before you die" is your regret issue, see and hear the dying loved one say "I love you" with great emotion in your mind's eye, precisely the way you'd always wanted it to happen.)
2. Open your eyes and see your SUBSTITUTION die before you can get what you want (as per the example: death before the loved one can say "I love you") and feel the desperation and disappointment of never hearing those words or having resolution with your selected regret issue.
3. Attempt to keep your SUBSTITUTION alive with sounds and behavior as you imagine the worst event if death were to happen and recite this mantra over and over in your head: "I have to keep you alive to keep that from happening, I have to keep you alive to keep that from happening. . . ."
4. Let it go.

You'll be surprised by the emotions that surge out of you. They will not necessarily be what you expect. How we really respond to a loved one when they are dying is always different than how we imagine it will happen. And the only way to have real, spontaneous and present feelings is to put yourself in a similar predicament by using the formula.

Experiencing the Dying of a Loved One That Is Highly Unexpected and Happens Quickly

You are driving, hit black ice, spin out of control, hit a telephone pole, your best friend who is in the passenger seat gets thrown through the windshield, you get pinned to the steering wheel and must watch her die. You witness your child being shot in a drive-by shooting. While you are working at the local convenience store, you see your friend and coworker get stabbed. Your home is invaded and you're forced to watch your wife be raped and stabbed. These are examples of unexpected, out-of-the-blue circumstances of dying. Because your brain doesn't have time to react and your emotions don't have time to percolate, these particular life-and-death situations provoke different internal, instinctual reactions. Here is a formula that triggers the feelings that come from unexpected traumatic deaths.

Formula to Experience the Dying of a Loved One That Comes Unexpectedly and Quickly

1. See your SUBSTITUTION in an open coffin.
2. Look at the face, lifeless, for the last time.
3. Memorize the face, because this is the last time you'll ever see your SUBSTITUTION, and say in your mind, "Good-bye. I love you and I'll miss you."
4. Taking the specific issue you're using from your "loved one is dying list," know now that you'll never accomplish, resolve and take care of it . . . and feel the finality of the loss.
5. Then see the coffin lid slowly close over your loved one's face, enveloping your SUBSTITUTION with ultimate darkness. Forever.
6. See the coffin dropping slowly into the six-foot dirt hole.
7. Watch dirt fill the hole, surrounding the coffin with cold, dark, suffocating, heavy and hopeless finality.
8. Then, feel the need to keep the coffin image from happening by keeping your SUBSTITUTION alive. In your head, say over and over to your SUBSTITUTION, "You've got to survive to keep that from happening, you've got to survive to keep that from happening. . . ."
9. Let it go.
10. Then launch into the scene.

Experiencing the Actual Death of a Loved One

If you are at a funeral or some venue where a loved one is long past saving, you still must make active choices that further your story. Death may have stopped your character's loved one, but it shouldn't stop your character. There's always something to be learned from the loss, as well as revelations and change that occurs from the pain. With this in mind . . .

Formula for Feeling the Actual Death of a Loved One

1. Close your eyes and picture your SUBSTITUTION in an open coffin.
2. See the lifeless face for the last time.
3. Memorize their face, because this is the last time you'll ever see him or her. Say in your mind, "Good-bye. I'll miss you. I love you." And know this is it, forever.
4. Watch the coffin lid slowly close over the face. Imagine the coffin filling with darkness.
5. See the coffin dropping slowly into the six-foot dirt hole.
6. Watch the dirt fill the hole, enveloping the coffin with cold, dark, suffocating, heavy and hopeless finality.
7. Take the issue that you've chosen from your "loved one is dying list" that, because of your SUBSTITUTION's death, will never be accomplished, resolved or taken care of, and mull over what you could and should have done differently in your life that would have kept it from happening.
8. Resolve to fix that issue in the future with an appropriate person in your present life who is still alive.
9. Let it go.

This way of looking at death allows for the tragedy of death to promote growth, change and hope in your character's future, which gives your audience hope that there is a conceivable chance for growth and change within their own lives. Looking at death—one of life's inevitabilities—and the horrible pain that accompanies it as a way to inspire growth, and change enables your audience to grow and learn from it, too.

CHAPTER 18

Experiencing Feeling Pregnant (from the Male and Female P.O.V.)

Pregnancy—There Is No SUBSTITUTION

When you are pregnant, or someone is carrying your child, there is no SUBSTITUTION that can correlate to the baby in you or the mother of your child. Some actors believe that thinking about a pet or a niece or nephew will elicit a similar feeling of love. But unfortunately, as much as you love Fluffy your dog, or Amy your godchild, or even Adam, your beloved sister's son, how you feel about your own flesh-and-blood child is inherently different.

The best way to describe how we feel about our children is to say that we see them as little versions of ourselves. That's why when someone compliments your child by saying things like, "Your child is gorgeous," or "Your child is so smart," you respond with, "Thank you!" as if the compliment was meant for you. That's because your child is "little-you," giving you a second chance to cure the insecurities that have arisen from your bad experiences. That's why a parent sees red when they observe anyone dealing with their child in a way that is similar to an abuser from their own history. They're not seeing the actual person in front of them, but rather the symbolic version of their own abuser, motivating them to change it *this time* because they couldn't change it the *first time*. This is where the strong innate urge to protect and nurture your child comes from—it's the same urge that comes from one's own need to survive. And thus this formula was, to excuse the expression, born.

Formula for Feeling Pregnant (from the Male and Female P.O.V.)

1. Sit. Get comfortable. Close your eyes.

2. If you are a female, take your hand and rest it on your stomach where your womb is. If you are a man, put your hand on the stomach of the woman playing your pregnant partner.

3. Think about a picture that was taken of you when you were an infant and imagine you, as that infant, floating in your (or her) womb.

4. Zero in on the eyes of baby-you and see the innocence, purity and hopefulness (the kind of hope where anything is possible). The innocence, purity and hope that can only happen before any of your painful experiences have taken place.

5. Then, in your head, talk to baby-you, and tell him or her that you vow to keep any of those painful events and bad self-images that you've personally experienced from happening to him or her. And vow to protect baby-you from experiencing the awful moments that you were forced to endure, because you know how bad it felt and know all too well the aftermath of those terrible events. How insecure, self-sabotaging and self-loathing you became as a result. How you made stupid decisions for a mate, how you allowed people to take advantage and abuse you, how you made harmful life choices, all because of those horrible experiences. You continue to speak, in your mind, to baby-you and assure him or her profusely that you are bound and determined to keep your baby, your child, from ever having to suffer what you had to suffer. Be extremely specific about the events and feelings that you don't want baby-you to go through. (Examples: "I will never abandon you like my father did to me when I was seven, only coming to see me when it was convenient for him. I will always be there for you." Or, "I won't let anyone make you feel ugly, stupid and worthless like my mother did to me." Or, "I won't ever hit or abuse you like my brother did to me. I'll make sure no one ever hurts you the way I was hurt.") Talk to baby-you for about a minute.

6. Now, look at baby-you smiling that gummy, toothless, innocent grin, looking back at you with pure unconditional love, thanking you for your love and protection. Let the unconditional love wash over you, the kind of love that you've never experienced before . . . a love without conditions.

7. Now protectively and nurturingly rub the stomach area and say in your head, "I won't ever let you feel the pain that I felt growing up, you will always feel cherished and loved, taken care of, I'll always be there for you because I'm your mommy (or your daddy) and I love you."

8. Feel the eyes of baby-you look back at you again with unconditional love, thanking you and feeling safe in your love and protection. Feelings you've given your child that were not given to you, not so purely and completely as you are giving them to baby-you. Feel your child's love wash over you, making you feel special and cherished. Let it feel really good.

9. Let it go.

Procreation is such an inherently human drive that, even if you're someone who has no desire to have children, this exercise will trigger feelings that you didn't know you had.

CHAPTER 19

Experiencing Parenthood

Creating an Organic Connection
Between a Parent and a Child

A connection needs to be made between you and the child actor when you are playing their parent. No matter how good an actor you are, it's easy to tell when an actor is pretending to be a parent. When I worked with Anna Friel on the movie *The War Bride* (directed by a brilliant director who also happens to share the split credential as my husband), she had to play a mother of an infant. At twenty-three, Anna wasn't a mother, nor did she have any concept of being one. Yet she had to deal with a screaming, three-month-old infant. The baby scene was about to be shot, so I told her to do the following exercise as she held the unruly baby in her arms. The baby was hollering and screeching (in decibels that only a baby can reach) and pulling away from Anna, desperately trying to get back to his real mother. She began to do the exercise, and within moments, the baby had quieted down and began to lovingly snuggle into Anna, his pudgy little hand reaching for her baby finger and grabbing on. This was the behavior of a baby who feels he is with someone who loves him like a parent. A baby can't be directed nor can a baby take acting classes (well, he can, but I don't know how much good it would do), but doing this easy exercise made the parent/child connection real and organic for both the actress and the child.

Formula for Organically Feeling Like a Parent

1. Look directly into the eyes of the baby, child or teenager that is playing your child and see the same exact pain, insecurities, anger, paranoia, traumas and emotional issues that you possess. These might include:

- Issues of abandonment
- Self-loathing
- Self-consciousness and/or hatred of some physical trait
- Fear of rejection
- Trust issues
- History of abuse or being the victim of violence
- Inordinate insecurity and fearfulness
- People-pleasing
- Suicidal tendencies

2. As you continue to look into the child's eyes, think about the specific events that caused these problems and visualize the child in front of you experiencing the same traumas in exactly the same way you did. By doing this you are creating a kindred spirit—someone you will feel you need to protect and nurture, because for all intents and purposes, this is little-you.

3. Let it go.

By utilizing this formula, you are essentially turning a virtual stranger into the child version of yourself. This exercise works because that is precisely how we see our own children.

CHAPTER 20

Playing a Paraplegic
or Quadriplegic

Organically Replicating Extreme Physical Handicaps

There's always a traumatic event that has occurred that has created this handicapped condition. It's important to not only supply the reality of the physical condition to your characterization, but to add the constant reminder of the emotional trauma that was involved in *causing* the crippled state. The following formula will combine both these elements into a truthful and organic duplication of someone who's lost the use of their limbs.

Formula for Organically Feeling Like a Paraplegic or Quadriplegic

I. Sit down. Take the afflicted areas (paraplegic—the lower part of your body; quadriplegic—everything below the neck) and relax all of the muscles in those areas until they no longer feel like muscles but like warm gelatin melting into the ground. There's no form or substance, just a mass of warm gelatin melting into the ground. Sit still and feel this until you feel like you truly can't move.

2. Then, place your hands on top of your legs and take yourself to a hopeless emotional place, where you feel like a failure and a loser. Using *real events, fears and emotions* from your life that make you feel depressed and despondent,

press those feelings and images into your legs. Or, if you're playing a quadriplegic, press them into your torso and then your legs.

3. Let it go.

Your OVERALL OBJECTIVE in the script will include finding other
ways to physically and emotionally survive despite your character's
predicament. Also, use the handicap as an emotional and physical OB-
STACLE in your script analysis. Being a paraplegic or quadriplegic is a
powerful OBSTACLE to overcome in surviving any OBJECTIVE, and will
produce a dynamic result.

CHAPTER 21

Creating Emotional Realities for Scars and Bruises

Organically Realizing Physical Traumas

In drama, a character's bruise or scar is usually a result of abuse—self-inflicted or otherwise—or a consequence of some form of a traumatic event. To make the scar or bruise real to you . . .

Formula for Organically Feeling Your Character's Scars and Bruises

1. Find an event from your life that emotionally duplicates the event in the script that caused the bruise or scar. For example:

   - If the character has a scar from a parent's abuse, think of the strongest, most profound time when you felt physically and emotionally destroyed, decimated by an authority figure (it doesn't have to be a parent, if there is an emotional scar that has been more severely caused by a teacher, older sibling, uncle, grandparent, employer, etc.).
   - If your character's bruises are caused by a mate punching them in the face, recall an event where you loved someone so much and they rewarded you with blame for their failures and decimated you with words of discouragement, making you feel dejected and heartbroken. Or use an actual violent event committed against you by someone you cared about.

- If the bruises and lacerations are the result of a terrible car accident or a violent crime, recall an event where you felt emotionally helpless and all alone, or use an actual event of violence.

2. Press two fingers onto the area where the bruise or scar is supposed to be.
3. As you press down, picture the event you've chosen to emotionally duplicate the story's event, remembering the space, words and deeds and refeeling the painful emotions as if they were happening today. Be very specific and detailed as you viscerally relive the horrible event, infusing the pictures and emotions into the appropriate area with the pressure of your two fingers.
4. Remove your fingers and let it go.

When referring to the bruise or scar or touching it, it will feel tender and the wound will feel real.

CHAPTER 22

Organically Realizing the Character's Occupation, Profession or Career

Career Defines You

Too often actors play the obvious characteristics of their character's profession without regard to the *how* and *why* that character has chosen his or her career. Our careers are how we spend most of our time. It's what defines us. And there's always a reason why someone picks his or her chosen profession. Whether the occupation is something that the character aspires to be, or is a profession that the character has accomplished to a great degree of success, there is always a purpose and incentive for picking that particular career. More often than not, it is to resolve and accomplish something that is essential to their emotional survival.

In your analysis of your character, you must not only understand *what* your character does, but also *why*. I've analyzed a few common occupations to give you an idea of how to think about why someone chooses the career path that they do, which will provide you with a more comprehensive understanding of your character.

- **Police Officer.**
  A person often chooses police work as a career because that person has been deeply affected by crime, in one form or another. They have family members who are cops or they have witnessed a tragic crime or the results of a tragedy (like murder, molestation, victimization at the hands of a con-man, arson and rape) that involved them or a loved one. A child who is victim or

a witness to a crime feels helpless, and rightfully so, because there's not much that a young person can do. As an adult, they are capable of making choices and choosing a career that can empower themselves or the victims that they couldn't save as a child. Becoming a police officer enables the young victim/witness to affect change in a troubled area of their past.

In this way, we can consider that playing a character who is a police officer is a means to rectify something that happened in your childhood. The cases that your character is involved with are symbolic of the crimes that you dealt with or witnessed as a child. As a cop, you are finally in the position and have the power to make a difference. Your pained past will fuel the interrogation or investigation because the need to solve the scripted crime is part of your and your character's healing. The antagonist in the script then becomes the symbolic perpetrator of the original, childhood crime experience and an effective SUBSTITUTION. This creates an arena that allows possible closure to a childhood trauma that will ultimately lead to a more profound resolution. Thus, with every criminal you arrest and prosecute in performance, you are doing something that is much deeper than just doing a job—you are healing past wounds.

• **Thief/Crime Career.**

A good many people who have chosen a life of crime grew up in financial poverty. They grew up noticing that the few who manage to escape their poor circumstances easily and with panache are those that have chosen life within the underworld. In a place like the projects, it's the criminals that are living large, wearing fancy duds and with ready cash. Enviable, sure, but more important, it's those with money that have position, dignity and power.

This kind of character's backstory might be that the father was a working stiff, providing for his family, living a hand-to-mouth existence, suffering an abusive boss, all to ensure that food was on the table and a roof was over his family's head. As a child, this future underworld character would have grown up to hate the fact that those with money hold the power, whereas the people he loved, who deserved better, were made to kowtow. By becoming a thief (or any underworld character), they would not only provide more money than the family is used to, but would also create a sense of empowerment and superiority in being successful at mocking authority and the law.

When playing someone of this ilk, it's about getting the power back from who you feel symbolizes the person (SUBSTITU-TION) who made you and/or your loved ones feel diminished and insignificant. A lower station in life was foisted upon you through the social system—whether by issues of race, money, gender or familial roots—and it was absolutely inequitable and unfair. Therefore you wouldn't view the crime activity your character is engaged in as wrongdoing, but rather, righting the wrongs of your personal circumstances, which justifies any illegal actions as righteously motivated.

- **Psychiatrist/Psychologist.**

A person usually chooses psychiatry or psychology as a profession due to some unresolved childhood emotional trauma. Being a psychiatrist or psychologist allows that person, as an adult, to attempt to resolve the problem. There are many different fields that a therapist can focus on. A specialist in sex crimes might have been a victim of a sexual assault or molestation when they were a child, or come from a family where this was an issue. A couples' therapist might come from a broken home or have parents who came from one. A child psychiatrist might have trouble with the responsibility of adulthood or relating to adults.

When playing a therapist, realize that the patient is that part of your character that needs fixing in their area of expertise. Essentially, the patient symbolizes you. (For this reason, it can be very effective to use yourself as a SUBSTITUTION for the patient.) Playing a therapist with this understanding and focus creates a more critical need to heal the patient's mental illness, because you're doing it to heal yourself. This humanizes your psychiatrist role. This is important, because too often actors play doctors, lawyers, teachers or any authority figure as one-dimensionally officious—acting out authoritative behavior without concerning themselves that there is actually an individual human being behind the official trappings.

Once you've figured out the character's focus in his or her practice, you must relate that to a specific emotional issue of your own. See the patient in front of you as your chance to rectify the dire emotional issue that has been plaguing you.

- **Doctor.**

    It takes years of premed studies, then several more years of medical school and another couple of years of residency to launch a career in medicine. It is not a career path you choose or follow on a whim. Becoming a doctor is a life mission to heal.

    Think of a childhood or current event in which you were or are powerless to heal someone you loved and that person died, became handicapped, or suffered a downward quality-of-life change. Becoming a doctor gives you a second chance to cure the loved one that, in life, you were helpless to make well.

- **Hooker/Stripper.**

    Although prostitutes and strippers work in professions that are ostensibly sexually oriented, being a hooker or stripper actually has very little to do with sex. It is, conversely, an act of retribution and power that stems from a little girl or young woman who has been raped or molested while growing up. A prostitute's johns or a stripper's audience is a symbol for the man who raped or molested her. The sexual power that a hooker/stripper has over a john or her audience is an attempt to reclaim the power that was taken away from her as a young girl or woman. She uses the same vehicle that was used to take away her power—sex—to turn her helplessness into empowerment. (The same dynamic applies to a male prostitute/stripper.)

    If you've been raped or molested, you can use the person responsible for the assault as the SUBSTITUTION for your character's clients. Fortunately, not everyone is a victim of a sexual crime. However, rape takes many forms. If you feel you have been violated emotionally, you can use that person as your SUBSTITUTION in your power-plays enacted with your john or lap-dance partner.

- **Lawyer**

    Good lawyers personalize their cases, making them about an issue that he or she needs to personally rectify. Yes, there are those cases that a lawyer might be less interested in and might simply go through the legal motions to win, but detached commitment is not what we want to see on the stage or screen. With nothing personally at stake, the fight will be removed and dispassionate for you and the audience. A great lawyer personalizes the crime or damage that has been done in the case at hand as if it has happened to him (or her) or to someone they love, like a family member, because they will fight harder and more ardently to win the case if it becomes a personal vendetta. Drama isn't re-creating a slice of life, drama is dramatizing life, taking life to its extreme. So infusing your own heightened personalizations with the scripted material is a necessity.

In order to do this you have to take some current altercation, crime or mystery that presents itself in your life today (you can also use an unresolved problem that comes from your past history) that is affecting you or someone dear to you. In your role as a lawyer, you must attempt to solve, affix blame or get payback, depending on what the best resolution would be to the personal crime with which you've endowed the crime in the script. Or, if it seems fitting, all three. As inner work, personalize the bad guys (meaning those detrimental to you—they don't have to actually be bad people) in the script with the bad guys that make sense to your personalized legal scenario. Personalize the good guys (meaning important to you—they don't actually have to be good people)—the ones you want to protect or who have been victimized in the script—with the appropriate good guys from your personal legal scenario. There are often many players involved in legal battles. Personalizing all the players in the script who are of importance to the law case provides detailed realism as well as a more impassioned drive to win.

- **Armed Forces/Military.**

A person who is determined to join the military is someone seeking order, stringent rules and regulations and a chain of command. Perhaps that person's childhood was out of control and lacked an effective authority figure. Children require guidance through rules and boundaries. It helps them understand how to deal with life as an adult. If a child doesn't get enough of this, he or she will grow up seeking it. What better way to get the feeling of *order* that comes from following many stringent rules and regulations than by being a member of the military?

- **From an Enlisted Man/Private P.O.V.:**

To play an enlisted man, you have to look at your feelings about a particular parent, teacher, aunt, uncle or some other authority figure who wasn't there to guide you as you grew up. Someone who made you feel that you simply were not worth the effort. In this way, the officer who is in charge of your character's unit, platoon, etc., will serve as a SUBSTITUTION for the offending childhood authority figure. Your relationship with your presiding officer becomes more like the parent you felt you never had but needed. This personalizes the relationship beyond the plot, making you need to affect and be more affected by the officer in charge. This also makes the relationship that transpires throughout the script more remarkable, deeper and more emotionally urgent than a simple and undeveloped interplay between an officer and a private.

• From an Officer P.O.V.:

An officer in the military is in a position of life-and-death power. An officer's orders can determine whether someone lives or dies. Being an officer in the military is one of the few legal occupations with such a huge power base. Someone who requires such a power-infused job is usually someone who was made to feel powerless growing up. This could have happened because the child was emotionally or physically beaten up by a parent, neighborhood kids, babysitter, etc., or horribly ridiculed by the same. A child is powerless to do anything about it, but an adult has choices—ways to turn around the power positions.

Being an officer in the military gives that person the power of life and death over a group of people who, given the rules of the military, must obey every order.

When playing an officer, think of a person or a group of people (a group that makes sense together, like your siblings, the members of a club you belong to, classmates, coworkers, the popular group, etc.) that you feel has abused you in some way and for whom some form of retribution would be especially sweet. Endow that person or group as SUBSTITUTION(s) for those who are playing your subordinates. In this way, harshly giving orders and humiliating the man or men who are below you in your chain of command is righteous and satisfying. This takes away the cruelty factor, and we as an audience will support you because your motivation isn't to be malicious, but to get your power back from the person or persons who symbolically took it away from you.

• **Actor.**

The essence of what drives a person to become an actor is the need for attention and to be loved unconditionally by vast numbers of people. That need causes an actor to have a tendency to overdramatize anything that happens in their lives. To be an actor you must always have your emotions on the surface, available for the roles that you play. Covering or being introspective isn't conducive to a great performance—an actor has to be ready to bring up whatever charged emotion is called for. Because of this, actors enjoy their emotions—the more painful, the better. They view it as fodder for performance, whether it's onstage or not. And like it or not, there's very little disparity between an actor's onstage and offstage behavior.

This is why, when playing the role of an actor, you have permission to be a drama queen or king. The fun of playing an actor is that nothing is too much. You can do anything in the name of getting attention and love, because anyone and everyone who is in an actor's general vicinity becomes an instant audience for their award-winning performance of life. The trap of playing an actor is to do a caricature, a cartoon version. You must keep in mind that the OVERALL OBJECTIVE and passion that drives the inner work to get the SCENE OBJECTIVE must be real—ultra-dramatically real. An actor, on-screen and off, always knows how to find the light, cheats to the audience (real or imagined) and is always trying to win the Oscar.

In terms of the inner work, well, you *are* an actor—identify the issues and events that made you personally want to become an actor in the first place and let that drive you to want to win your OVERALL and SCENE OBJECTIVE with dramatic intention and without restraint.

• **Wall Street Stockbrokers/Financial Expert/CEO, et al**

People attracted to these high-powered jobs are people willing to do anything to win. To even get these particular positions of power, you have to be uncompromisingly driven. And you have to have a deep, deep love of money and understand, profoundly, the power of what money can buy.

To play this type of character, you need to find what would motivate *you* to become aggressive and ruthless and at the same time would make you feel righteous in doing so. Find a person or a group that in some way destroyed you or a loved one's life. Make the person or group from your personal life the SUBSTI- TUTION(S) for the people you are wreaking havoc with in the script. Then the person or group will *deserve* your merciless power plays and acts of vengeance.

But no matter what your character does career-wise . . .

Acting gives you the chance to realize a fantasy, something that you'll never be able to do in life. Acting is an opportunity to influence and change events that you are powerless to change in real life.

PART III

The Practical Application of the 12 Tools

Part III will show you how to apply the twelve tools to a single piece of material. I have chosen a script from Act III from Anton Chekhov's play *Uncle Vanya* as an example. Think of this scene as a comprehensive model of how to apply the technique to any script.

Theatrical material can be broken down into two categories:

- Stories with *power* as the driving force.
- Stories with *love* as the primary motivation.

Of course, no script is this black and white. All love stories have power elements and all power stories will contain issues of love. You must just look at what the principal driving force of the script is.

Ask yourself, "Is it power or is it love that is motivating the goals of my character?"

The scene from *Uncle Vanya*, Act III, is an example of material where love propels the action, although that doesn't negate that there will be subtle underpinnings of power issues. Life experience has forced us to consider that there are always inherent power struggles in matters of the heart.

Script Analysis for *Uncle Vanya* Using the 12 Tools

As with every script you will ever work with, you must first read the entire script. This is so you'll have the story's facts and details, which you'll need to inform the choices you'll make for the twelve acting tools. I know how easy it is to either read those oh-so-available *Cliff's Notes* or quickly skim the material. But a more careful reading will inspire a deeper, more textured and distinct characterization.

An Overview of *Uncle Vanya*

Briefly, *Uncle Vanya* tells the story of Professor Alexander Serebriakov and his beautiful young wife, Yelena, who leave St. Petersburg, Russia, in the mid-1800s to settle on Alexander's late-wife's country estate. For years, Sonya, the professor's daughter from his first marriage, and her uncle, Vanya, have lived and labored on the estate, accepting small wages and sending the bulk of their earnings to St. Petersburg to support Alexander and his studies.

Alexander and Yelena's arrival sends the estate into chaos, disrupting the daily routines of country life and sparking passions. Triangles of tension develop as the characters struggle with their frustrated desires and disillusionment. Vanya and his friend Astrov, the local doctor, vie for Yelena's attention, while Sonya and Yelena find themselves irresistibly attracted to Astrov.

The relevant facts surrounding a scene from Act III of *Uncle Vanya*.

The following are the key points that will be necessary for understanding how this scene fits into the arc of the play's story. This includes the immediate actions before and after this particular scene, along with the denouement of the story, which will help you understand where each character needs to go and what they need to win for there to be a resolution to their journey:

- Uncle Vanya is Professor Alexander Serebriakov's brother-in-law from his first marriage. Since Alexander's wife died, he has taken care of the family estate and Alexander's daughter.
- Astrov is a conscientious doctor, whose bachelorhood and other personal difficulties have made this once-idealistic man cynical. He uses excess amounts of alcohol to numb his pain.
- Sonya, Alexander's daughter, is about the same age as his second wife, Yelena, and has been in love with Astrov for a long time. Astrov, however, has no interest in Sonya—it's Yelena he's after.
- Uncle Vanya and Astrov are both in love with the sexually charismatic Yelena.
- Yelena, who is clearly not in love with Alexander, pits Vanya and Astrov against one another to vie for her attention.
- ***Prior to this scene:*** Yelena promises Sonya to help get Astrov to love Sonya. Pretending to be Sonya's friend, Yelena persuades her to confide in her and trust her. Her mission, she tells Sonya, is to selflessly aide Sonya in creating a relationship with Astrov. It would seem, however, that Yelena has a hidden agenda that is more selfishly motivated than what she's communicated to Sonya.
- ***In the following scene:*** Uncle Vanya catches Yelena and Astrov having a romantic interlude.
- ***After the following scene:*** If that's not enough, Vanya is even more enraged when Alexander attempts to sell the estate of his former wife, and he tries to kill him.
- ***In the end:*** Alexander survives Vanya's lame attempt at murder. The entire household is torn asunder by Yelena's manipulations, and Alexander and Yelena move out of the estate.

And now, the scene to be analyzed . . .

UNCLE VANYA
Anton Chekhov
(A scene from Act III)

ASTROV
[*Enters with drawing*]
Hello, I understand you wanted to see
some of my artistry?

YELENA
Yesterday, you assured me you would show
me your drawings. Are you available now?

ASTROV
I'd love to!

[*He spreads the drawing on a nearby table and fixes it with stick-
pins. She helps him.*]

Where were you born?

YELENA
In Petersburg.

ASTROV
And where did you go to school?

YELENA
At the conservatory.

ASTROV
I doubt very much this will intrigue you
in any way.

YELENA
Why not? You're right in assuming I don't
know much about the country, but I'm well read.

ASTROV
Look here. It's a map of this area as it was
fifty years ago. The green color indicates the
forest. Half of the area was surfaced with
forest. Where you see the red over the green—
deer, wild goats and all sorts of wildlife were
prevalent. Look at the third part and you'll see my
rendition of how it is today. There's green, but it's
sporadic. There is no wildlife.
[*Pause*]

ASTROV

You might say it's progress and I'd agree if the
destroyed forests were making way for
factories or schools. But, no, there is a lot of
unusable muddied land filled with disease
and people who are destitute.

[*He looks at her askance . . .*]

It seems to me that you have little interest
in any of this.

YELENA

No, it's simply that I don't comprehend much
of it.

ASTROV

It doesn't take much to comprehend it, I just
don't think you're all that interested.

YELENA

Please excuse my lack of concentration as my
mind is someplace else. To be honest I wanted
to ask you something but I don't know how to
begin.
[*Pause*]
It's a question about someone you know.
Like friends, let's talk, being totally open with
each other and then forget we ever had this
conversation. What do you say?

ASTROV

All-right.

YELENA

It's about Sonya, my stepdaughter. What do
you think of her, do you like her?

ASTROV

I can admire her spirit.

YELENA

But do you like her as a woman?

ASTROV
[*Pause*]
No.

YELENA
[*Kissing his hand*]
You don't love her, I can see that from your
eyes. You know, she's suffering. Try to
understand that you must stop coming here.
[*Pause*]
Ouch! I hate this, I feel like I've been carrying
the weight of the world on my shoulders. Anyway,
it's done, thank God, so now we can forget we
ever had this conversation and move on. You're
a smart man, I'm sure you realize why you must . . .
[*Pause*]
I feel all the blood rushing to my head.

ASTROV
If you had told me about her feelings a month or
two ago I might have thought about it . . . but if
she is sick at heart because of me then I guess
there's no other recourse . . .
[*Pause*]
But tell me, why is it *you* had to ask me?

[*He looks at her a moment.*]

Ohhhh, I get it!

YELENA
What are you talking about?

ASTROV
You know. Sure, Sonya may be in love, but
why is it you're asking the questions? Why do
you look so surprised? You know why I come
every day, you're very well aware of the effect
you have on me, you lovely "bird of prey."

YELENA
Bird of prey! What are you talking about?!

ASTROV
You are a gorgeous, frisky rascal . . . and I am
your victim. Well, you win, you can have me.

[*He opens his arms and bows his head like a martyr on the cross.*]

I give in, I'm here and ready to be consumed!

YELENA
Have you gone mad?!

ASTROV
Oh, you are so coy.

YELENA
I'm not as cunning or as cruel as you're making
me out to be. Honestly, I'm not.

[*She tries to leave. Astrov rushes to block her way.*]

ASTROV
I'll leave and I won't return. Just tell me . . .

[*He takes her hand and glances about to see if anyone is looking.*]

Where should we meet? Hurry, someone may
catch us—please tell me where.
            [*Whispering lustfully*]
Your hair smells wonderful. One little kiss,
please let me kiss you.

YELENA
I beg of you . . .

ASTROV
[*Stops her from talking*]
No need to beg, I'm yours. You are so beautiful.
And your lovely hands, I need to kiss your hands.

[*He kisses her hands.*]

YELENA
Stop it, please stop . . . go . . .

[*She pulls her hand away.*]

ASTROV
You know it's inescapable, we are meant
to be together.

[*He kisses her and at that very moment Uncle Vanya shows up carrying a dozen roses and stops just inside the door. Neither Astrov nor Yelena see him.*]

YELENA
[*Not seeing Vanya*]
Don't. We shouldn't be doing this . . .

[*She lays her head on Astrov's chest.*]

ASTROV
At two o'clock meet me at the plantation.
Promise me you'll come.

[*Yelena sees Vanya looking at them.*]

YELENA
Let go of me!

[*She forcefully pulls away from Astrov. Then she goes to the window.*]

[*Muttering to herself*]
This is just awful.

[*Vanya carefully puts the roses on a nearby chair. Yelena continues to look out the window trying to figure out what she's going to say or do next as Astrov looks painfully guilty and attempts to cover up.*]

Before We Begin Analyzing . . .

The following choices made in using each of the tools are suggestions. Because acting is an art form, everything is subjective. There are no absolutes. As you read and work with the twelve tools, use your imagination, your history, your needs and incorporate your point of view. And always, always (one more time), always write in pencil.

Write directly on your script.

It is critical that you write directly on your script, putting the tools precisely by the words or activities that the tool relates to. This way, as you memorize the script and glance down to prompt yourself, you'll see the attached thoughts and choices right away. As a result, you will be memorizing the words and thoughts together, creating associations and relating the analysis accurately to the story.

Memorize your lines only after you've done your work.

If you memorize your lines before you've done your work, the dialogue becomes a bunch of meaningless words strung together. When the meaning and intentions of the words are unclear, you can't help but memorize one way of saying it. It becomes a line reading and line readings will sound the same way every time you speak the dialogue. This kind of memorized interpretation is cemented in your mind, and like cement, it is extremely difficult to undo. Obviously, this spoils any chance of spontaneity and truly living the role. Whereas, if you apply the twelve acting tools first and then memorize your lines, the words will have associated information that means something personal to you, allowing organic impulses to emerge.

Tool #1: OVERALL OBJECTIVE

The character's life goal that is pursued throughout the entire script.

Yelena's OVERALL OBJECTIVE.

After having studied the script and gathering pertinent and specific information about Yelena, you must explore why such a beautiful and young woman would marry such a crotchety old man. Perhaps for security? Alexander is old and not in very good health. Yelena stands to inherit money and freedom sooner than later. Maybe she has father issues and Alexander gives her the feeling of the father she never had.

You must also ask, "Why does Yelena move from the city, a city where she was born and raised, to a place she considers to be tedious and lackluster?" In the script, she often talks about being bored, yet when the others give her suggestions for activities, she has no interest. However, the country is a new arena for her to wreak her own personal brand of havoc. Creating chaos and turmoil makes her feel alive. Taking risks and pushing the envelope makes the adrenaline flow, makes the blood pump faster and creates an emotional roller coaster for her and those around her. Now, *that* is exciting! And it's also Yelena's way of validating her existence. How?

She cruelly leads Uncle Vanya on with no intention whatsoever of making good on her "promises." She makes Sonya act on her feelings for Dr. Astrov, knowing full well that it is a fool's journey and Sonya is going to get hurt. Meanwhile, she competes with the naive Sonya for both Alexander's and Astrov's affections by making Sonya think she's her friend—creating even more chaos. Yelena is the catalyst for the climax of the story, which unhinges everyone's once-safe relationships and leaves her husband virtually unscathed by all of her games and subterfuge. Why does Yelena do it?

We must assume that she is not an inherently evil person. So she must be motivated by extreme insecurities. In Russia in the mid-1800s, women didn't have the opportunities to have careers to define themselves. They were defined by *if* they were married and *who* they were married to. A smart woman had few outlets for her intelligence. For Yelena, domesticity was simply not enough. Moreover, Yelena doesn't have a sense of purpose. She is not a mother, is in a loveless marriage, has no jobs or passions and no charity to pour herself into. As a result, she makes a lot of noise to feel like she is doing something. Like a bratty child acting out, getting attention—any attention, negative or positive— becomes the goal. Often, children who act out feel like they will disappear if they don't do something shocking or drastic (this is especially true for children with abandonment issues). Likewise, Yelena wreaks emotional destruction to feel a sense of life. She makes people fall in love with her and look up to her. This makes her feel empowered and gives her a sense of purpose and a reason to be alive. So . . .

Yelena's OVERALL OBJECTIVE.

- *"To get everyone to love me, body and soul."*

Astrov's OVERALL OBJECTIVE

Astrov is a doctor in a rural community. He became a doctor in an idealistic pursuit to heal. But, after years of treating rich hypochondriacs, he has grown cynical and lonely and has resorted to alcohol to soothe these wounds. Astrov began his practice as a way to conquer diseases that were rampant in his rural community, yet he soon learned that he was helpless and it was hopeless. In short, the big changes he was going to make for mankind never came to pass.

Before Yelena's arrival, he would come to Vanya's home once a month. (Yes, he was the kind of extinct doctor who made house visits and was gladly innocent of the horrors of HMOs.) This all changed with Yelena's arrival. With her presence in the house, Astrov uses Alexander's frequent and mostly imaginary complaints of pain and disease as an excuse for daily visits.

Before Yelena, Astrov had all but given up hope that he would find love. His hopelessness caused him to act surly, overly critical and to drink enormous amounts of vodka. Since his efforts in medicine were without reward, he tried immersing himself in an effort to save the ecology. Unfortunately, he is also failing in curing the land of its modern ills.

Yelena changes his perspective. Because of his strong feelings for her (mostly manipulated by the lovely and calculating lady herself), Astrov feels romantic, hopeful and almost giddy. It also doesn't hurt his ego that Sonya reveals her long-term crush on him. In the end, he's so crushed by Yelena's machinations that he proclaims to Vanya and Sonya (the remaining characters in the household) that he will not return for at least a year. The bottom line is that love has a huge effect on his life. We see how the lack of it causes him to be hopeless and cynical and a drunk, while the input of love causes him to feel hopeful and industrious. So . . .

Astrov's OVERALL OBJECTIVE.

- *"I want to be loved."*

> **As you look over the elements of your character's life circumstances and goals, always be attentive to how they can be emotionally translated into those of your own.**

Tool #2: SCENE OBJECTIVE.

The goal that your character would like to achieve over the course of an individual scene. It must support the goal of the OVERALL OBJECTIVE.

Yelena's SCENE OBJECTIVE.

Facts of the scene that affect Yelena:

1. Yelena doesn't have much interest in Astrov's drawings or in his enthusiasm for forestry.
2. What seems to appeal to Yelena as a prime topic of conversation is anything about and for Yelena. Even when she talks about Sonya to Astrov, it's a way to make him say he doesn't want Sonya, but instead yearns for her.

3. Yelena may say "no" to Astrov's advances, but her behavior goads him on, giving him the kind of mixed signals that have plagued men for centuries: "There's 'no-no' in your words, but 'yes-yes' in your eyes."

4. Yelena is married to someone she doesn't love.

5. Yelena knows that Vanya is in love with her (as well she should know—after all, she made it happen).

In supporting Yelena's OVERALL OBJECTIVE *"to get everyone to love me, body and soul,"* it would make sense that Yelena's SCENE OBJECTIVE would be *"to get you (Astrov) to fall in love with me."* While this might also be Astrov's SCENE OBJECTIVE, because he is truly in love with her, Yelena would go after Astrov's heart to have power over him, which would make her feel alive and validated. Making Astrov fall in love with her will make Yelena his reason for being as well as someone he's willing to destroy his life for. This enables her to become a person of great consequence. We know she doesn't love him, because when she has the option to leave her husband at the end of the story, she chooses to stay with her much richer husband and move on in her life's journey to another locale and make more unsuspecting men fall for her. In order for Yelena to give herself a feeling of significance, which validates her existence, it would be logical that . . .

Yelena's SCENE OBJECTIVE.

- *"To get you to fall in love with me."*

Astrov's SCENE OBJECTIVE.

Facts of the scene that affect Astrov:

1. Astrov showing off his drawings and erudite concerns about ecology as a way to impress Yelena.

2. He blurts out, in a moment of weakness, that he only comes to the house to see her. His obvious romantic and sexual intentions for her create awkward I-like-you-too-much behavior.

3. Astrov wants a love relationship, one that he's never had before.

4. He's lonely and desperate because he feels that Yelena may be his last chance to find love.

5. Yelena is married and Astrov's good friend is in love with her, too, which makes getting her to love him complicated and problematic.

You could look at all the sexuality in the scene and say that Astrov's SCENE OBJECTIVE could be *"to get you to have sex with me,"* but that would undermine his life's intentions as stated in his OVERALL OBJECTIVE of *"I want to be loved."* If sex were all he desired, he could easily bed Sonya, who has behaved like a lovesick schoolgirl for a long time. Additionally, Astrov mentions throughout the script how much he doesn't want to be alone anymore, but he just can't find the right woman. That is, until . . . Yelena. Being married, Yelena also has the draw of being forbidden fruit, which always makes someone or something more desirable. Thus . . .

Astrov's SCENE OBJECTIVE.

- *"To get you to fall in love with me."*

The SCENE OBJECTIVE must always support the OVERALL OBJECTIVE and be worded in a way to get a response.

Tool #3: OBSTACLES

The physical, emotional and mental hurdles and conflicts that prevent the SCENE OBJECTIVE from being accomplished, thereby making the quest more exciting and fulfilling.

Yelena's OBSTACLES.

Some of the OBSTACLES getting in the way of Yelena's SCENE OBJECTIVE, *"to get you to fall in love with me,"* are:

1. Possible rejection.
2. Yelena is married.
3. Sonya, Yelena's stepdaughter, is in love with Astrov.

4. Vanya, owner of the house, her husband's brother-in-law and Astrov's good friend, is in love with Yelena.

5. Yelena has zero interest in ecology, which Astrov loves.

6. She comes from the city. Astrov comes from the country. She has very little in common with Astrov. And she has no interest in what someone from the country has to offer, anyway.

7. Yelena has an extremely competitive nature. When it comes to competition, she likes the stakes to be high—in this case, competing with Sonya for Astrov.

8. Her need to play games with people's minds.

9. She might get caught. (By Alexander, her husband; Sonya, her stepdaughter and professed new best friend; Vanya, Astrov's friend, owner of the house, her husband's brother-in-law and a man who is dangerously enamored of her; or any combination thereof.)

10. She does get caught.

These are just a few of Yelena's general OBSTACLES.

Now we must read the scene again and pinpoint some of the more specific OBSTACLES from Yelena's P.O.V.

UNCLE VANYA
Anton Chekhov
(A scene from Act III)

ASTROV
[*Enters with drawing*]
Hello, I understand you wanted to see
some of my artistry?

[OBSTACLE: A possible negative reaction to his drawing and an unconvincing cover.]

YELENA
Yesterday, you assured me you would show
me your drawings. Are you available now?

ASTROV
I'd love to!

[*He spreads the drawing on a nearby table and fixes it with stick-pins. She helps him.*]

[OBSTACLE: A misinterpretation of Yelena's accidental touching while helping him spread out the drawing as her being easy, which, for most men, is a turn-off.]

ASTROV
Where were you born?

YELENA
In Petersburg.

[OBSTACLE: Social disparity. Yelena is from the city. He is from the country.]

ASTROV
And where did you go to school?

YELENA
At the conservatory.

[OBSTACLE: Educational disparity. She's far better educated than him.]

ASTROV
I doubt very much this will intrigue you
in any way.

[OBSTACLE: Astrov is suspicious of Yelena's interest in his drawing].

YELENA
Why not? You're right in assuming I don't
know much about the country, but I'm well read.

[OBSTACLE: Without being patronizing, convincing a relatively savvy man that she is truly intrigued when she could not care less.]

ASTROV
Look here. It's a map of this area as it was
fifty years ago. The green color indicates the
forest. Half of the area was surfaced with
forest. Where you see the red over the green—
deer, wild goats and all sorts of wildlife were
prevalent. Look at the third part and you'll see my
rendition of how it is today. There's green, but it's
sporadic. There is no wildlife.
                    [*Pause*]

[OBSTACLE: Being totally bored.]

ASTROV
You might say it's progress and I'd agree if the
destroyed forests were making way for
factories or schools. But, no, there is a lot of
unusable muddied land filled with disease
and people who are destitute.

[OBSTACLE: Total indifference to Astrov's passion.]

[*He looks at her askance . . .*]

It seems to me that you have little interest
in any of this.

[OBSTACLE: Having Astrov discover that she really doesn't
care.]

YELENA
No, it's simply that I don't comprehend much
of it.

ASTROV
It doesn't take much to comprehend it, I just
don't think you're all that interested.

[OBSTACLE: Astrov *is* suspicious.]

YELENA
Please excuse my lack of concentration as my
mind is someplace else. To be honest I wanted
to ask you something but I don't know how to begin.
[*Pause*]
It's a question about someone you know.
Like friends, let's talk, being totally open with
each other and then forget we ever had this
conversation. What do you say?

ASTROV
All-right.

YELENA
It's about Sonya, my stepdaughter. What do
you think of her, do you like her?

[OBSTACLE: A very risky question—Astrov might say he's in
love with Sonya and then Yelena will never win her SCENE
OBJECTIVE.]

ASTROV

I can admire her spirit.

YELENA

But do you like her as a woman?

ASTROV
[*Pause*]

No.

YELENA
[*Kissing his hand*]

[OBSTACLE: A bold and sexual move, which could be misinter-
preted by him as her being too loose.]

You don't love her, I can see that from your
eyes. You know, she's suffering. Try to
understand that you must stop coming here.
[*Pause*]
Ouch! I hate this, I feel like I've been carrying
the weight of the world on my shoulders. Anyway,
it's done, thank God, so now we can forget we
ever had this conversation and move on. You're
a smart man, I'm sure you realize why you must . . .
[*Pause*]
I feel all the blood rushing to my head.

[OBSTACLE: Astrov's cynical nature. What if he doesn't trust
Yelena?]

ASTROV

If you had told me about her feelings a month or
two ago I might have thought about it . . . but if
she is sick at heart because of me then I guess
there's no other recourse . . .
[*Pause*]
But tell me, why is it *you* had to ask me?

[*He looks at her a moment.*]

Ohhhh, I get it!

YELENA

What are you talking about?

ASTROV
You know. Sure, Sonya may be in love, but
why is it you're asking the questions? Why do
you look so surprised? You know why I come
every day, you're very well aware of the effect
you have on me, you lovely "bird of prey."

[OBSTACLE: Astrov sees through Yelena's innocent act.]

YELENA
Bird of prey! What are you talking about?!

ASTROV
You are a gorgeous, frisky rascal . . . and I am
your victim. Well, you win, you can have me.

[*He opens his arms and bows his head like a martyr on the cross.*]

I give in, I'm here and ready to be consumed!

YELENA
Have you gone mad?!

ASTROV
Oh, you are so coy.

YELENA
I'm not as cunning or as cruel as you're making
me out to be. Honestly, I'm not.

[*She tries to leave . . .*

[OBSTACLE: An audacious move. What if Astrov doesn't try to
stop her? All of her manipulations will be for naught.]

Astrov rushes to block her way.]

ASTROV
I'll leave and I won't return. Just tell me . . .

[*He takes her hand and glances about to see if anyone is looking.*]

Where should we meet? Hurry, someone may
catch us—please tell me where.
            [*Whispering lustfully*]
Your hair smells wonderful. One little kiss,
please let me kiss you.

[OBSTACLE: Out-of-control sexual feelings. NOTE: Sex is always
a natural OBSTACLE. A woman loses power once she goes all

the way. A man loses power if he can't get a woman to go there.
And sexual feelings are naturally very hard to control.]

YELENA
I beg of you . . .

ASTROV
[*Stops her from talking*]
No need to beg, I'm yours. You are so beautiful.
And your lovely hands, I need to kiss your hands.

[*He kisses her hands.*]

YELENA
Stop it, please stop . . . go . . .

[*She pulls her hand away.*]

ASTROV
You know it's inescapable, we are meant
to be together.

[*He kisses her and at that very moment Uncle Vanya shows up car-rying a dozen roses and stops just inside the door. Neither Astrov nor Yelena see him.*]

YELENA
[*Not seeing Vanya*]
Don't. We shouldn't be doing this . . .

[*She lays her head on Astrov's chest*]

[OBSTACLE: The huge possibility of getting caught.]

ASTROV
At two o'clock meet me at the plantation.
Promise me you'll come.

[*Yelena sees Vanya looking at them.*]

[OBSTACLE: Getting caught.]

YELENA
Let go of me!

[OBSTACLE: Not knowing the length of time Vanya's been there—how much he has seen and heard.]

[*She forcefully pulls away from Astrov. Then she goes to the window.*]
[*Muttering to herself*]

YELENA
[cont.]
This is just awful.

[Vanya carefully puts the roses on a nearby chair. Yelena continues
to look out the window trying to figure out what she's going to say
or do next as Astrov looks painfully guilty and attempts to cover up.]

[OBSTACLE: Extricating herself from an obvious indiscretion.]

Astrov's OBSTACLES.

Some of the OBSTACLES getting in the way of Astrov's SCENE OBJEC-
TIVE, *"to get you to fall in love with me,"* are:

1. Possible rejection.
2. Astrov is in love with Yelena. (As we all know, being in love has
   inherent OBSTACLES.)
3. Yelena is married.
4. Astrov has never had a long-term relationship and is naive.
5. Sonya is in love with Astrov and could pose a problem.
6. Astrov's best friend, Vanya, also wants Yelena.
7. His drinking problem.
8. Desperation. (Desperation always creates strange and unwanted behavior.)
9. Social and educational disparity.
10. Astrov's cynical nature.
11. A guilty conscience.

Specific OBSTACLES from Astrov's P.O.V.

UNCLE VANYA

Anton Chekhov
(A scene from Act III)

ASTROV
[Enters with drawing]
Hello, I understand you wanted to see
some of my artistry?

[OBSTACLE: Yelena's possible dislike or rejection of the drawing and the topic.]

YELENA
Yesterday, you assured me you would show
me your drawings. Are you available now?

ASTROV
I'd love to!

[OBSTACLE: Too eager. This reads as obvious desperation.]

[*He spreads the drawing on a nearby table and fixes it with stick-pins. She helps him.*]

[OBSTACLE: Lack of savvy. What if Astrov misinterprets Yelena's frequent touching as romantic when it truly might be accidental?]

Where were you born?

YELENA
In Petersburg.

[OBSTACLE: Social disparity.]

ASTROV
And where did you go to school?

YELENA
At the conservatory.

[OBSTACLE: Educational disparity. Yelena is better educated and more socially adept, making Astrov feel somewhat emasculated.]

ASTROV
I doubt very much this will intrigue you
in any way.

[OBSTACLE: Astrov's insecurity.]

YELENA
Why not? You're right in assuming I don't
know much about the country, but I'm well read.

ASTROV

Look here. It's a map of this area as it was
fifty years ago. The green color indicates the
forest. Half of the area was surfaced with
forest. Where you see the red over the green—
deer, wild goats and all sorts of wildlife were
prevalent. Look at the third part and you'll see my
rendition of how it is today. There's green, but it's
sporadic. There is no wildlife.
                    [Pause]
You might say it's progress and I'd agree if the
destroyed forests were making way for
factories or schools. But, no, there is a lot of
unusable muddied land filled with disease
and people who are destitute.

[He looks at her askance . . .]

[OBSTACLE: Yelena's obvious lack of interest.]

ASTROV

It seems to me that you have little interest
in any of this.

YELENA

No, it's simply that I don't comprehend much
of it.

ASTROV

It doesn't take much to comprehend it, I just
don't think you're all that interested.

YELENA

Please excuse my lack of concentration as my
mind is someplace else. To be honest I wanted
to ask you something but I don't know how to
begin.
                    [Pause]
It's a question about someone you know.
Like friends, let's talk, being totally open with
each other and then forget we ever had this
conversation. What do you say?

[OBSTACLE: A leading, unnerving and possibly embarrassing
question.]

ASTROV

All-right.

YELENA
It's about Sonya, my stepdaughter. What do
you think of her, do you like her?

[OBSTACLE: A loaded question—this could be a trick.]

ASTROV
I can admire her spirit.

YELENA
But do you like her as a woman?

ASTROV
[Pause]
No.

[OBSTACLE: The possibility of giving the answer Yelena doesn't
want to hear.]

YELENA
[Kissing his hand]
You don't love her, I can see that from your
eyes. You know, she's suffering. Try to
understand that you must stop coming here.
[Pause]
Ouch! I hate this, I feel like I've been carrying
the weight of the world on my shoulders. Anyway,
it's done, thank God, so now we can forget we
ever had this conversation and move on. You're
a smart man, I'm sure you realize why you must . . .
[Pause]
I feel all the blood rushing to my head.

[OBSTACLE: Her mixed message.]

ASTROV
If you had told me about her feelings a month or
two ago I might have thought about it . . . but if
she is sick at heart because of me then I guess
there's no other recourse . . .
[Pause]
But tell me, why is it *you* had to ask me?

[He looks at her a moment.]

Ohhhh, I get it!

YELENA
What are you talking about?

ASTROV
You know. Sure, Sonya may be in love, but
why is it you're asking the questions? Why do
you look so surprised? You know why I come
every day, you're very well aware of the effect
you have on me, you lovely "bird of prey."

[OBSTACLES: Time constraints. Astrov has to hurry. There's a
houseful of people who can interrupt and this could possibly
be the only time he'll ever have alone with Yelena.]

YELENA
Bird of prey! What are you talking about?!

ASTROV
You are a gorgeous, frisky rascal . . . and I am
your victim. Well, you win, you can have me.

[*He opens his arms and bows his head like a martyr on the cross.*]

I give in, I'm here and ready to be consumed!

[OBSTACLE: Bold and risky behavior. Yelena may think Astrov is
too weird to love.]

YELENA
Have you gone mad?!

ASTROV
Oh, you are so coy.

YELENA
I'm not as cunning or as cruel as you're making
me out to be. Honestly, I'm not.

[*She tries to leave.*]

[OBSTACLE: Yelena leaving.]

[*Astrov rushes to block her way.*]

ASTROV
I'll leave and I won't return. Just tell me . . .

[*He takes her hand and glances about to see if anyone is looking.*]

[OBSTACLE: Possible unwanted witnesses—Alexander, Sonya
and/or Vanya.]

ASTROV
[*cont.*]
Where should we meet? Hurry, someone may
catch us—please tell me where.
                    [*Whispering lustfully*]
Your hair smells wonderful. One little kiss,
please let me kiss you.

YELENA
I beg of you . . .

ASTROV
[*Stops her from talking*]
No need to beg, I'm yours. You are so beautiful.
And your lovely hands, I need to kiss your hands.

[*He kisses her hands.*]

[OBSTACLE: Possible rebuff.]

YELENA
Stop it, please stop . . . go . . .

[*She pulls her hand away.*]

[OBSTACLE: Actual rebuff.]

ASTROV
You know it's inescapable, we are meant
to be together.

[*He kisses her and at that very moment Uncle Vanya shows up carrying a dozen roses and stops just inside the door. Neither Astrov
nor Yelena see him.*]

YELENA
[*Not seeing Vanya*]
Don't. We shouldn't be doing this . . .

[*She lays her head on Astrov's chest.*]

[OBSTACLE: Another baffling mixed message.]

ASTROV
At two o'clock meet me at the plantation.
Promise me you'll come.

[*Yelena sees Vanya looking at them.*]

YELENA
Let go of me!

[OBSTACLE: Getting caught.]

[*She forcefully pulls away from Astrov. Then she goes to the window.*]

[*Muttering to herself*]
This is just awful.

[*Vanya carefully puts the roses on a nearby chair. Yelena continues to look out the window trying to figure out what she's going to say or do next as Astrov looks painfully guilty and attempts to cover up.*]

[OBSTACLE: Extricating himself from an obvious indiscretion.]

Never, ever give up on going after your SCENE OBJECTIVE, even if the OBSTACLES seem impossible to overcome.

Tool #4: SUBSTITUTION

Endowing the other actor/character with someone from your own life that inspires a personal need to accomplish your character's SCENE OBJECTIVE.

Keep in mind that when making a SUBSTITUTION choice, it must create a personal desire to win, because the SUBSTITUTION contains the appropriate history and inherent OBSTACLES that relate to your character's predicament. Pick someone necessary and difficult, because if you can get your SCENE OBJECTIVE too easily from your SUBSTITUTION choice, the journey will be uneventful.

Do not judge or moralize in picking a SUBSTITUTION.

Acting is an arena where you can be evil, immoral and manipulative, because it's not real. It is your fantasy life having a field day. Don't censor yourself. This art form is just about the only place where you can legitimately do what you'd never dare do in your real life. So enjoy it.

The following suggestions are merely a few in an infinite field of possibilities. SUBSTITUTION choices are as varied and numerous as your life experiences. Come up with a few choices that are logical, then think outside the box and come up with some that make less sense. Try them all and let the best SUBSTITUTION win.

Yelena's Astrov SUBSTITUTION

Ask yourself the question, "From whom in my life do I want my SCENE OBJECTIVE, *'to get you to fall in love with me,'* who also inspires the need to play games, take risks and has inherently charged OBSTACLES?"

SUBSTITUTION suggestions.

- **Your ex-mate:** There's a reason why this person is no longer in your life. Lying, cheating, constant condescension and abuse are all good reasons to play games as payback for all the games that were originally played on you. The risk is that through all of your manipulations you can very well fall in love with him again, making it a dangerous walk to walk. Think of the people who could walk in on you: your present mate, a disapproving parent or friend, his friend or family member who never liked you, etc.

- **Your friend's mate:** Perhaps you have a friend who has in some way been cruel to you. We've all had a friend (past or present) like this. It may be your masochism, but this person nevertheless deserves some sort of game that gives you some power reversal. Going after your friend's mate and getting him to fall in love with you would do just that. The risk is loss of her friendship and perhaps the loss of other friends who might learn about your behavior and would no longer trust you. The uninvited guests who might walk in could be the friend, your other friends who would be appalled or your present mate.

- **Your boss, teacher, director, producer (people in positions of authority):** People in positions of authority often abuse it. If this has happened to you, all bets are on. This person deserves some righteous game-playing and manipulations of the heart. Possible choices for the dangerous interrupter could be your mate, their mate, another student or employee, etc.

- **Extended family member (cousin, uncle, stepfather, brother-in-law et al):** This is not an immediate family member and isn't as reprehensible as, say, a blood father or brother, but it's still considered amoral and a social no-no. Yet, if this extended family member has in some way hurt you (or the family member that this person is attached to has caused you emotional pain), then all of your calculating manipulations will feel absolutely justified. The intruders could be another family member, the family member that this person is attached to, your present mate, etc.

- **Your male friend:** You know the friend I'm talking about. The one you've always been attracted to, but were afraid to pursue for fear that the friendship would be lost. There are intrinsic power issues in this particular kind of friendship because the friend usually knows and often feels the same attraction. Whether this friend fails to act out of fear or because withholding gives them power, it doesn't matter—you feel as though they have too much power over you. Those who could walk in and cause heart failure could be another friend who knows both of you, your mate, his mate, etc.

Astrov's Yelena SUBSTITUTION

Ask yourself the question, "From whom in my life do I want to win my SCENE OBJECTIVE, *'to get you to fall in love with me,'* in which the relationship feels forbidden, guilty and there's a sense of unrequited love?"

SUBSTITUTION suggestions.

- **Your ex-mate:** Whatever issue caused this person to be an ex is always present. It's unlikely that this person has changed much, and the ugliness of the past is bound to rear its ugly head. We all know this, yet most of us ignore probability for the tiny possibility that they've seen the error of their ways and have changed. The more wrong this relationship seems to be, the more we want it. This makes the ex feel forbidden, which makes you feel stupid for wanting them so badly, which makes you feel guilty and the love unrequited (ah, human nature rearing its ugly head). Those who can enter causing you distress might be your present mate, family members or friends who never liked this person in your life, etc.

- **Your student, your employee or stepchild:** When you are in a position of authority, it is considered inappropriate, sometimes even illegal, to take advantage of the person over whom you have power. You can be reviled and ostracized by the people you care about, because they simply don't understand the depth of your love for your student, employee or stepchild, and that it transcends convention. This doesn't negate your feelings of guilt or the fact that it is love that is enormously forbidden. Those who can interrupt . . . well, just about anyone would be a problem in these circumstances.

- **A man to whom you're attracted:** If you're straight and you find yourself attracted or even obsessed with a man, it will bring up organic feelings of the forbidden, guilt and, because of societal stigma, it will be unrequited. Bottom line, it would be damn scary to pursue the SCENE OBJECTIVE from this SUBSTITUTION, making it a powerful choice. Problem interceders—anyone.

- **A woman who's financially, socially, intellectually or age-wise "out of your league":** If a woman makes more money, is more educated or is from a substantially higher socioeconomic background, it can be extremely intimidating and emasculating. You might wonder if you're silently and secretly being viewed as a buffoon by your friends and family. However, you'll do anything and everything to get this person to fall in love with you— no matter how extreme the disparity—because, on another level, it will boost your ego. Those who can enter without invitation who might be problematic: any friend or family member who feels you're reaching too high, your present mate, her friends or family that look down on you, etc.

- **Your friend's mate, your stepmother, sister-in-law (anyone attached to someone you love):** This would fall under the category of "you're not supposed to go there." Your guilt is obvious . . . forbidden, clear, probably unrequited . . . but that doesn't stop you from pursuing—because love might conquer all, as it's supposed to. That is, if she loves you back, which she might not, and then all is lost because you've lost her *and* the loved one whom she's attached to. Those who enter at your risk: the loved one that she is attached to, other family members, your present mate, a friend who would disapprove, your preacher or rabbi who would call you immoral, etc.

Personalizing OBSTACLES Considering Your SUBSTITUTION Choice

Once you've selected and tried a few people from your life as possible SUBSTITUTION choices and have found a SUBSTITUTION that works, you must go back through the script and personalize your character's OBSTACLES as they relate to this person. The personalization of OB-STACLES will be innately determined from the SUBSTITUTION you end up using in the scene. This means that if you change your SUBSTI-TUTION, you must accordingly change your personalizations.

When personalizing your OBSTACLES, make vivid and in-depth choices—be specific and detailed when infusing personal information into your OBSTACLES. This will create an intensified struggle to accomplish your SCENE OBJECTIVE, because it makes you hyperaware of precisely what will happen if you don't win.

Personalizing Yelena's OBSTACLES.

1. Possible rejection.
Personalization: As a human being, it's more than likely that you've experienced rejection, and lots of it. Think about the choice you've made for a SUBSTITUTION for Astrov and remember viscerally the event(s) that involved rejection from that particular person. Or, using an event in a similar venue, remember the rejection moment with all your senses and be afraid it's going to happen again, this time with your SUBSTI-TUTION for Astrov. For example: Your SUBSTITUTION for Astrov is your current employer, so be aware of exactly what could happen to you if you're rejected (being fired, loss of fellow employee friendship and trust, losing your car, apartment, becoming homeless because you no longer have money, etc.). Or take a past rejection event from a prior employment venue

and replay the whole nasty incident in your mind. Allow your natural paranoia to surge forward in the form of intensified fear that it could very well happen again today. Create precise pictures in your mind that match up to your rejection scenario and accompanying fears.

2. Yelena is married.

   Personalization: If you are married or attached to someone, then you simply personalize the natural OBSTACLES that exist in your relationship when and if you were to stray. This includes: possible loss of your mate, a loss of trust from your mate, possible loss of financial stability, loss of children, the extreme difficulty of finding a new mate. Realize these possibilities as if they have actually happened in vivid detail and color. If you are not connected at this time, then look at the OBSTACLES that exist if you were to lose a friend, family member, job, or social standing because you were "caught in the act" with your SUBSTITUTION for Astrov.

3. Sonya, Yelena's stepdaughter, is in love with Astrov.

   Personalization: Figure out exactly what could befall you if you were caught in a sexual tryst with your SUBSTITUTION for Astrov by your SUBSTITUTION for Sonya. Make the loss specific to your SUBSTITUTION for Sonya. Is it loss of a mate? A loss of a friend? A loss of financial security? A loss of a home? Or a loss of a job and all the disturbing ramifications that would go along with it?

4. Vanya, owner of the house, her husband's brother-in-law and Astrov's good friend, is in love with Yelena.

   Personalization: How you fear Vanya would react to being scorned would vary depending on your SUBSTITUTION choice for Vanya. For instance:

- Violence (directed at you and/or your SUBSTITUTION for Astrov).
- Payback in some form, which would cause you to be kicked out of the house, family or job.
- Bad-mouthing you to your mate, family member, employer or producer/director, which would cause great damage to your family or career.
- Severing all ties with you, and making your friends and/or family members do it, too.

Pick the appropriate reaction that would make the most sense to your SUBSTITUTION for Vanya and picture the response in all of its gory detail.

5. Yelena has zero interest in ecology, which Astrov loves.

Personalization: This is more complex, because not only do you have to pick a topic of passionate interest to your SUBSTITUTION for Astrov, but also a topic that you could care less about. Your SUBSTITUTION might love to talk your ear off about football, but if you like football, it doesn't initiate the right dynamic. Typical examples of topics that elicit passion in the speaker and are a great sleeping aid for the listener might be: the virtues of vegetarianism, religion, sports, politics, mechanics, cars or current events. You have to pick a particular topic to your SUBSTITUTION for Astrov that absolutely inspires him and completely numbs you.

6. She comes from the city. Astrov comes from the country. She has very little in common with Astrov.

Personalization: Considering your SUBSTITUTION for Astrov, look at the differences that exist. Are you from a big city while he is from the suburbs? Do you come from money, whereas he grew up poor? Are you educated and he is not? Are you funny while he is intense and serious? Are you outgoing while he's a loner? Are you outspoken and opinionated, and he's quiet and without conviction? Are you apolitical while he's political? Are you right-brained (artistic) while he's left-brained (analytical)? Are you an atheist while he is religious? Remember and picture how the differences have played out in creating difficulty in your relationship.

7. Yelena has an extremely competitive nature. When it comes to competition, she likes the stakes to be high: in this case, competing with Sonya for Astrov.

Personalization: Everyone has felt a strong competitive drive in some aspect of their lives. In fact, it's usually the case that the more successful the person, the more competitive the spirit. Have you noticed that the saying "It's not whether you win or lose, it's how you play the game" is almost always quoted by the winner? Recall any event or circumstance that has motivated the desire to win at all costs. Also, look at your SUBSTITUTION for Sonya to determine why it's especially important to not let *her* win. Examples of this dynamic include:

- A sister. Sibling rivalry and all that this includes. If you're using your sister as your SUBSTITUTION for Sonya, use whatever she has done better than you and tends to gloat about. In this case, if you win the prize of Astrov, it enables you to do the gloating.
- A good friend. If you're using a good friend as your SUBSTITUTION for Sonya, find something that your good friend has always done better than you (better grades, better boyfriends, better jobs, more money, etc.) and think how wonderful it would be to beat her out on this occasion. Getting the man that your friend has expressed interest in could be quite the coup.

With this OBSTACLE you have to personalize both *why* you need to compete with your SUBSTITUTION for Sonya and *what* are the specific repercussions you'd suffer if she were to become aware of your scheme.

8. Her need to play games with people's minds.

Personalization: Look at the specific mind games that were played on you by your SUBSTITUTION for Astrov, and know that turnabout is fair play.

9. She might get caught (by Alexander, Sonya or Vanya).

Personalization: You have to identify what could specifically go wrong in your own personal life as a result of being caught by your SUBSTITUTION for Vanya, Sonya and Alexander. When a plan goes terribly wrong, we never think in vague thoughts like, "Uh-oh, this is really bad. . . ." The natural human response is to picture precisely the worst that you can imagine happening. In this case, the picture is determined by your SUBSTITUTION for Vanya, Sonya and Alexander, and it will give you explicit images of the consequences.

10. She does get caught (by Vanya).

Personalization: When personalizing the OBSTACLE of "getting caught," you should consider two points:

    a. The damage that would come as a result if you were caught in mid-seduction by your SUBSTITUTION for Vanya, like:
- Loss of a job
- Loss of a friend
- Estrangement of family
- Loss of a mate

- Loss of integrity
- Loss of custody

b. The long-term consequences versus the immediate damage, like:
- Not being able to get another job.
- Other friends will leave you because they don't trust you.
- Your family will lose respect for you, forever.
- Loss of a mate may make you financially and/or emotionally insecure.
- Your reputation is muddied, perhaps for the rest of your life.
- You'll never get to see your children grow up.

Personalizing Astrov's OBSTACLES.

1. Possible rejection.

Personalization: Think about the choice you've made for a SUBSTITUTION for Yelena and remember viscerally the event(s) that involved rejection from that particular person. Or, using an event in a similar venue, remember the rejection moment with all your senses and be afraid it's going to happen again, this time with your SUBSTITUTION for Yelena. For example:

- If you're using a good friend as a SUBSTITUTION for Yelena, remember an event from your past when a different friend whom you wanted more from expressed that she *didn't see you in that way*, which, of course, made you feel like a total loser. Feel the fear that this could happen again with the present friend and SUBSTITUTION for Yelena when you express deeper feelings within the scene.
- If you're using your cousin as a SUBSTITUTION for Yelena, they, as a family member, might know you too well. This person knows embarrassing secrets about you and, as a result, might reject you. Identify the personal humiliations. For instance, you had a grotesque skin disease when you were growing up, you were a bed wetter until you were five, you

were the school nerd, you were held back a year in school, your lifelong difficulty with making and keeping friends, etc.

Remember the rejection experience as a reminder that it could happen again, in the present moment of the scene.

2. Astrov is in love with Yelena.

Personalization: If you're over the age of twelve, you've experienced the pain of being in love. Use it. Remember your own personal trials that were part of that rickety, harrowing theme-park ride called "being in love."

3. Yelena is married.

Personalization: Yelena, for all intents and purposes, is unattainable. If the person you are using for a SUBSTITUTION is attached to someone else, then personalize the OBSTACLES in these circumstances, like: Is her husband/boyfriend your friend? Do you feel guilty, immoral? Is this the first time you've gone after a married person? The thirtieth time? And so on.

- Say your SUBSTITUTION for Yelena is a longtime friend. She becomes unattainable, because changing a friendship to a sexual relationship (or even suggesting it) almost always destroys the friendship. Making the "move" is riddled with OBSTACLES.
- If your SUBSTITUTION for Yelena is work-related, the OBSTACLE is losing your job or respect from your peers. How does that bode for a future in your career?

Figure out exactly what makes your SUBSTITUTION for Yelena beyond your reach and the exact repercussions of seeking and exploring this forbidden relationship.

4. Astrov has never had a long-term relationship and is naive.

Personalization: Even if you're involved with someone or it's easy for you to score, there's always someone in your life that makes you perspire and feel awkward, shy and inarticulate. These feelings are identical to what a naive and inexperienced person feels. Your SUBSTITUTION choice should make you feel this way. You should pinpoint the various behaviors that happen specifically to you when faced with that very hot person. Do you get tongue-tied, blurt out idiotic or shocking statements, have inordinately sweaty palms, sigh a lot, want to vomit, actually vomit, mumble or pick at the skin of your fingers or lips? Whatever it is that you personally tend to do when confronted with your stressful love object, be aware of it. Then, when the behavior starts to emerge, let it be an ever-present OBSTACLE that you have to attempt to overcome by overcompensating.

5. **Sonya is in love with Astrov and could pose a problem.**

    Personalization: There's usually someone lurking in the shadows of everyone's life who is either obsessed with you—an ex who isn't as done with you as you are with them, or a friend, parent or sibling who is so possessive that he/she doesn't want you to be with anybody else. Whoever this is in your life would be your SUBSTITUTION for Sonya. This OBSTACLE is potent because these kinds of people are often crazy, unbalanced or, at best, irrational. You just might have to deal with emotionally violent outbursts if that person finds out that your feelings for your SUBSTITUTION for Yelena supercedes any sentiment you have for them.

6. **Astrov's best friend, Vanya, also wants Yelena.**

    Personalization: Who you are using as a SUBSTITUTION for Vanya determines exactly what your loss factor would be if your feelings and seduction of your SUBSTITUTION for Yelena were to be revealed. Would it be the loss of a friend, family member, or mate, and specifically what would be lost if the friendship was severed? Loss of a job, confidante, social standing, financial support? Identify exactly what would be gone and how difficult it would be to endure without it. This would make the OBSTACLE tangible, because you would know precisely what would happen if you were exposed, and this would make the need to keep it from happening all the more necessary.

7. **His drinking problem.**

    Personalization: Addictions of any sort are innate OBSTACLES. Overeating, sexual excess, alcohol, drugs, tobacco, computer obsession—any addiction has an inescapable control over you. As much as you think, "Heck, I could stop tomorrow if I wanted," it just isn't so. Take your vice—you know the one you feel you *must* do or have when the stress meter is registering on high, and endow your need to drink with it. You won't want your SUBSTITUTION for Yelena to know that you have this weakness, and you'll feel a push/pull when finally giving in to imbibing within the scene.

8. Desperation.

    Personalization: Desperation is a natural OBSTACLE. It's never attractive and causes undesirable behavior. Your personalized desperation can emanate from many different places.

- If you haven't been with someone in a long time, then too much rides on this relationship to be successful.
- If you are married, or have a longtime attachment to someone, the desperation comes from the possibility that you won't attain your SUBSTITUTION for Yelena. You'll be found out and lose your mate, and be left with absolutely no one.
- Your brand of desperation can come from a pattern and history of painful past relationships that you fear will happen again with your SUBSTITUTION for Yelena.
- Desperation can come from nagging friends or relatives who insist that you'll die alone if you don't hurry up and find someone.
- Your desperation can stem from the dire need to procreate and have children. Until science finds a new way, having a woman in your life is key.
- If you're using a work situation, your desperation can come from the fact that you haven't worked for a long time and this person can give you your dream job or catapult you to the top.

    Identify what personal events or fears color your desperation.

9. Social and educational disparity.

    Personalization: Establish, specifically, what makes you feel intimidated and inferior and just plain not good enough with regard to your SUBSTITUTION for Yelena. Is this person famous, better-looking, more educated, from a large metropolis while you're from the sticks, makes more money than you, is older and more experienced, or is your superior at work? Whatever emasculating issue(s) really exists is a powerful OBSTACLE to overcome in getting her to fall in love with you.

10. **Astrov's cynical nature.**

    Personalization: Look at your own life experiences, the ones that have decimated your personal idealism and caused you to assume the worst, to not trust, and to be dubious of people's motives. Even if you're generally a Pollyannish type of person, there is some area of your life in which you've been stepped on enough to feel cynical about it. Pinpoint where it exists and use it as your OBSTACLE to overcoming a skeptical attitude in achieving your SCENE OBJECTIVE.

11. **A guilty conscience.**

    Personalization: Guilt is your conscience coming forward, giving you a reason to right the wrongs you've committed. Of course, this implies that you know your behavior is on the shady side, which further implies guilt's organic OBSTACLES. In exactly what way do you feel guilty in regard to fully pursuing your SUBSTITUTION for Yelena? Are you married and being unfaithful? Is your SUBSTITUTION for Yelena your friend's wife or girlfriend, which makes what you're doing really, really *un*friendly? Are you sure of your intentions? I mean, if this turns out to be merely a sexual liaison, you're not being completely honest with her or yourself. Are you the kind of friend who can unscrupulously go after the same person that your best friend is clearly in love with? And if your SUBSTITUTION is married, are you prepared to deal with the moral consequences of being with a woman who's seen by God and the state as attached to someone else? Pick the circumstance that motivates the greatest amount of guilt and you'll see how tricky it is to overcome.

SUBSTITUTION infuses all the other acting tools with personal history and need.

Tool #5: INNER OBJECTS

These are the visuals attached to the people, places, things or events from your own life that you think about when you or the other character(s) are talking about the script's people, places, things or events.

INNER OBJECTS are pictures, not words. Picturing these personal images of people, places, things and events creates *real* associations for the words that you speak and listen to. The inner work you've done thus far will help you define your INNER OBJECT choices. Also, make sure your INNER OBJECTS have inherent OBSTACLES (this is true for all the acting tools). If your INNER OBJECT choices aren't infused with history and a highly charged conflict, then the images you've created will not naturally come forward when it comes time for you to perform.

Here are some possible INNER OBJECT choices for *Uncle Vanya*. Again, as with all the tools we've discussed so far, these are merely suggestions to help inspire a deeper understanding of the technique and guide you to come up with your own ideas. The INNER OBJECTS that most affect you will be unique to who you are as a person. Always make choices based on *your* life experiences.

For the purposes of the book and so that you can fully understand how INNER OBJECTS operate, the *Uncle Vanya* dialogue that need IN-NER OBJECTS will be *underlined,* and my list of possible choices for the INNER OBJECTS will be *handwritten* in pencil. While you will see a list here, in practice, you will handwrite only *one* choice directly under the word that needs an INNER OBJECT. If you change your INNER OBJECT during the rehearsal process, erase and replace the original choice with the new choice. Once again, this must be written directly beneath the scripted word that needs an INNER OBJECT (the same way it was illustrated in Part I, Tool #5, in *The Importance of Being Earnest*).

INNER OBJECTS from Yelena's P.O.V.

UNCLE VANYA
Anton Chekhov
(A scene from Act III)

ASTROV
[*Enters with <u>drawing</u>*]
Hello, I understand you wanted to see
some of my <u>artistry</u>?

"... <u>drawing</u>," "... <u>artistry</u>" =
Think about your SUBSTITUTION for Astrov. What subject is he obsessed with?
What topic does he go on and on about that utterly bores you?

• The mayoral campaign in Juneau, Alaska

• The Free the Ferrets Act

• Ecology

• The Washington Redskins

• Stock futures

YELENA
Yesterday, you assured me you would show
me your <u>drawings</u>. Are you available now?

"... <u>drawings</u>." =
Same INNER OBJECT as above.

ASTROV
I'd love to!

[*He spreads the drawing on a nearby table and fixes it with stick-
pins. She helps him.*]

Where were you born?

YELENA
In <u>Petersburg</u>.

"... <u>Petersburg</u>." =
You have to choose an INNER OBJECT visual of a place that your SUBSTITU-
TION for Astrov might be intimidated by. This doesn't have to be a city,
state or country where you actually grew up. It could be where you reside
today, or a section of the city you live in that is socially or economically
superior to where your SUBSTITUTION for Astrov lives. You have to also be
aware of how your SUBSTITUTION for Astrov will be distressed when he makes
the comparison to his life.

- Beverly Hills (he lives in "The Valley")
- Manhattan (he's from the Bronx)
- Suburbs (he's from the ghetto)
- A large house (he lives in a one-room apartment with a hot plate)
- No roommates (he has several)

ASTROV
And where did you go to <u>school</u>?

YELENA
At the <u>conservatory</u>.

"... <u>school</u>" "... <u>conservatory</u>." =
Your INNER OBJECT picture must be something that will make your SUBSTI-
TUTION for Astrov appear less educated, intelligent or savvy. It's an additional OBSTACLE for you to overcome, because at the same time you want to
impress Astrov, you certainly don't want to emasculate him. For in this answer
resides both "good news and bad" . . .

- Ivy League university (he went to City College, or didn't get a B.A.)
- School for the gifted (he went to public school)
- Street smarts from the school of hard knocks (he comes from a naïve subur-
  ban upbringing)
- Same school as SUBSTITUTION for Astrov but getting better grades or in
  accelerated classes
- Big shot at a big conglomerate (he's got a small position in a small com-
  pany)

ASTROV
**I doubt very much this will intrigue you
in any way.**

YELENA
**Why not? You're right in assuming I don't
know much about <u>the country</u>, but I'm well read.**

"... <u>the country</u> ..."=
The same INNER OBJECT visuals you used for "drawings" and "artistry."

ASTROV
Look here. It's a <u>map of this area</u> as it was
<u>fifty years ago</u>. The green color indicates the
<u>forest</u>. Half of the area was surfaced with
<u>forest</u>. Where you see the red over the green—
<u>deer, wild goats and all sorts of wildlife</u> were
prevalent. Look at the third part and you'll see my
rendition of how it is today. There's green, but it's
sporadic. There is <u>no wildlife</u>.
[*Pause*]
You might say it's progress and I'd agree if the
<u>destroyed forests</u> were making way for <u>factories or
schools</u>. But, no, there is a lot of <u>unusable muddied land
filled with disease</u> and <u>people who are destitute</u>.

Now you have to fill in the details of the topic you've chosen that motivates your
SUBSTITUTION for Astrov's passion and your need to take a nap. Let's use
"U.S. politicians" as the subject that you find dull. As you hear the script's words,
you'll perceive the meaning as follows:

- "... <u>map of this area</u> ..." =
  A diagram of the history of high-powered U.S. politicians, including what
  their accomplishments and disgraces were.
- "... <u>fifty years ago</u> ..." =
  Two hundred years ago, America's beginnings.
- "... <u>forest</u> ..." & "... <u>deer, wild goats and all sorts of wildlife</u> ..." =
  Freedom of speech, freedom of religion, et al.
- "... <u>no wildlife</u> ..." =
  No truth or integrity in politics and politicians.
- "... <u>destroyed forests</u> ..." =
  Destructive political scandals.
- <u>factories or schools</u> ..." =
  Helping poor people.
- "... <u>unusable muddied land filled with disease</u> ..." =
  Ghettos and poor areas.
- "... <u>people who are destitute</u>." =
  ... poor people, drugs addicts, AIDS victims.

[*He looks at her askance ...*]

ASTROV
It seems to me that you have little interest
in any of this.

YELENA

No, it's simply that I don't comprehend much
of it.

ASTROV

It doesn't take much to comprehend it, I just
don't think you're all that interested.

YELENA

Please excuse my lack of concentration as my
mind is someplace else. To be honest I wanted
to <u>ask you something</u> but don't know how to begin.
   [*Pause*]
It's <u>a question about someone you know</u>. Like
friends, let's talk, being totally open with each
other and then forget we ever had this conversation.
What do you say?

"... <u>ask you something</u> ..." and "<u>a question about someone you know</u>" =
Although Sonya's name isn't stated in the text, she must be an INNER OBJECT
here because she is the subject of Yelena's mysterious question. Obviously, your
INNER OBJECT visual for Sonya is the SUBSTITUTION you're using for
Sonya.

ASTROV

All-right.

YELENA

It's about <u>Sonya, my stepdaughter</u>. What do
you think of her, do you like her?

"... <u>Sonya, my stepdaughter</u>." =
Same INNER OBJECT for "Sonya."

ASTROV

I can admire her spirit.

YELENA

But do you like her as <u>a woman</u>?

"... <u>a woman</u>" =

Sex

ASTROV
[*Pause*]

No.

YELENA
[*Kissing his hand*]
You don't love her, I can see that from your
eyes. You know, she's suffering. Try to
understand that you must stop coming <u>here</u>.

YELENA

Your SUBSTITUTION for Astrov will determine what your INNER OBJECT will be. According to the circumstances you have created, where are you? ". . . <u>here</u>."=

- My home
- My office
- My school
- My family's home
- My boyfriend's home

> Ouch! I hate this, I feel like I've been carrying
> the weight of the world on my shoulders. Anyway,
> it's done, thank God, so now we can forget we
> ever had this conversation and move on. You're
> a smart man, I'm sure you realize why you must . . .
> > [*Pause*]
> I feel all the <u>blood rushing to my head</u>.

". . . <u>blood rushing to my head</u>." =

- Sexually turned on (picture favorite sex with Astrov)
- Dizzy and feeling faint (and if I faint, I can legitimately fall into his arms . . .)

ASTROV
> If you had told me about her feelings a month
> or two ago I might have thought about it . . . but
> if she is sick at heart because of me then I guess
> there's no other recourse . . . But tell me, why is
> it that *you* had to ask me?

[*He looks at her a moment.*]

> Ohhhh, I get it!

YELENA
> What are you talking about?

ASTROV
> You know. Sure, Sonya may be in love, but
> why is it you're asking the questions? Why do
> you look so surprised? You know why I come
> every day, you're very well aware of the effect
> you have on me, you lovely <u>"bird of prey."</u>

YELENA
> <u>Bird of prey!</u> What are you talking about?!

"... <u>bird of prey</u>." =
Again, Astrov is being ambiguous. Let the paranoid possibilities run wild.

* Two-faced
* Untrustworthy
* Liar
* Vulture-like.
* Slut
* Weasel-like

ASTROV
You are a gorgeous, frisky rascal . . . and I am
your victim. Well, you win, you can have me.

[He opens his arms and bows his head like a martyr on the cross.]

I give in, I'm here and ready to be consumed!

YELENA
Have you gone mad?!

ASTROV
Oh, you are so <u>coy</u>.

"... <u>coy</u>." =

* Liar
* Sneaky
* Slutty
* Two-faced
* A game-player

YELENA
I'm not as cunning or as cruel as you're making
me out to be. Honestly I'm not.

[She tries to leave. Astrov rushes to block her way.]

ASTROV
I'll leave and I won't return. Just tell me . . .

[He takes her hand and glances about to see if anyone is looking.]

Where should we meet? Hurry, someone may
catch us—please tell me where.
          [Whispering lustfully]
Your <u>hair smells wonderful</u>. One little kiss,
please <u>let me kiss you</u>.

"*. . . hair smells wonderful.*" =

• My perfume

• My natural scent

• My shampoo

"*. . . let me kiss you.*" =
The INNER OBJECT here is a vivid and specific "sexual" fantasy that would motivate a heightened sexuality in you—a fantasy visual that is so titillating that part of the OBSTACLE is not being able to stay in control of your sexual urges. Therefore there is the possibility of going further than you ever intended to go.

YELENA

I beg of you . . .

ASTROV
[*Stops her from talking*]
No need to beg, I'm yours. You are so beautiful.
And your lovely <u>hands</u>, I need to <u>kiss your hands</u>.

[*He kisses her hands.*]

"*. . . <u>hands</u> . . .*" and "*. . . <u>kiss your hands</u>.*" (and the INNER OBJECT attached to the act of kissing the hands) =
The pictured fantasy has to get more illicit, the hands symbolizing the part of your body that is most sensitive. When he talks about your hands, and kisses your hands, you are fantasizing that he's actually doing it to the part of your body that is most easily stimulated.

• Nibbling my neck

• Licking the inside of my knees

• Sucking my fingers or toes

• Nibbling my ears

• Kissing my inner thighs

YELENA
Stop it, please stop . . . go . . .

[*She pulls her hand away.*]

ASTROV
You know it's inescapable, we are meant to be
together.

[*He kisses her and at that very moment Uncle Vanya shows up carrying a dozen roses and stops just inside the door. Neither Astrov or Yelena see him.*]

YELENA
[*Not seeing Vanya*]
Don't. We shouldn't be doing this . . .

"We shouldn't be doing this . . ." =
The INNER OBJECT here is the visual image that expresses the danger of your
personal circumstances if you get caught . . .

- Divorce
- Loss of job
- Death or maiming
- No future job
- Expulsion
- Loss of family
- Loss of children
- Loss of friends
- Alone forever

[*She lays her head on Astrov's chest.*]

ASTROV
At two o'clock meet me at the plantation.
Promise me you'll come.

". . . the plantation." =
Use an INNER OBJECT visual of a place that will make sense for you and your
SUBSTITUTION for Astrov to have a private meeting.

- His home
- A local park
- A friend's home
- His or my office
- A specific hotel or motel room
- An empty classroom

[*Yelena sees Vanya looking at them.*]

YELENA
Let go of me!

[*She forcefully pulls away from Astrov. Then she goes to the
window.*]

[*Muttering to herself*]
This is just awful.

[Vanya carefully puts the roses on a nearby chair. Yelena continues to look out the window trying to figure out what she's going to say or do next as Astrov looks painfully guilty and attempts to cover up.]

INNER OBJECTS from Astrov's P.O.V.

ANTON CHEKHOV
Uncle Vanya
(A scene from Act III)

ASTROV
[Enters with <u>drawing</u>]
Hello, I understand you wanted to see
some of my <u>artistry</u>?

" . . . <u>drawing</u>," " . . . <u>artistry</u>" =
Choose an INNER OBJECT picture that displays what you are personally passionate about, because these are drawings to help illustrate Astrov's long-term passion for ecology.
• The Detroit Redwings
• Democratic politics
• Governmental programming for the mentally handicapped
• Born-again Christianity
• PETA

YELENA
Yesterday, you assured me you would show
me your <u>drawings</u>. Are you available now?
" . . . <u>drawings</u>." =
Same as above.

ASTROV
I'd love to!

[He spreads the drawing on a nearby table and fixes it with stick-pins. She helps him.]

Where were you born?

YELENA
In <u>Petersburg</u>.

" . . . <u>Petersburg.</u>" =
The INNER OBJECT picture here is a place that intimidates you in some way. It doesn't have to be a place where your SUBSTITUTION for Yelena was born. It can be where she lives now, or a "state of mind" place that makes you feel less than confident.

• New York City (versus my coming from Hicksville)
• Her high-powered career (versus my serving fries at Mickey D's)
• Upper class (versus my lower-middle-class upbringing)
• Her wealth (versus my poverty)
• Her fame/famous family (versus my average anonymous self/family)

ASTROV
And where did you go to <u>school</u>?

YELENA
At the <u>conservatory</u>.

" . . . <u>school</u>" and " . . . <u>conservatory.</u>" =
Here choose an INNER OBJECT visual that makes you feel less educated, intelligent or socially equal.

• Harvard (versus my vocational school)
• Personally trained by a famous acting teacher (versus my being trained by Aunt Lucy, whose big claim to fame is being an extra on <u>The Poseidon Adventure</u>)
• Graduated magna cum laude (versus my barely passing)
• Coming from a famous family that knows the joys of nepotism (versus my not being able to even get a cup of sugar from the trailer parked next door)
• A school for gifted (versus my trying to get into the same school and their refusing to take me)

ASTROV
I doubt very much this will intrigue you
in any way.

YELENA
Why not? You're right in assuming I don't
know much about <u>the country</u>, but I'm well read.

" . . . <u>the country</u> . . ."=
The same INNER OBJECT images you used for the "drawings."

ASTROV

Look here. It's a <u>map of this area as it was</u>
<u>fifty years ago</u>. The green color indicates the
<u>forest.</u> Half of the area was <u>surfaced with</u>
<u>forest.</u> Where you see the red over the green—
<u>deer, wild goats and all sorts of wildlife</u> were
<u>prevalent.</u> Look at the third part and you'll see
my rendition of how it is today. There's green,
but it's sporadic. There is <u>no wildlife</u>.
                    [*Pause*]
You might say it's progress and I'd agree if the
<u>destroyed forests</u> were <u>making way for factories or</u>
<u>schools</u>. But, no, there is <u>a lot of unusable muddied</u>
<u>land filled with disease and people who are destitute</u>.

You have to match the images described in the text to images that correlate to the topic you have chosen. Example: using the issue of the mishandling of the mentally handicapped.

- "... <u>map of this area as it was fifty years ago</u> ..." "... <u>forest</u>." "... <u>surfaced</u> with <u>forest</u> ..." =
A diagram of social programming the way it was forty years ago when social programming was fully funded by the government and the mentally handicapped were being taken care of.

- "... <u>deer, wild goats and all sorts of wildlife were prevalent</u> ..." =
Varied government social programs were prevalent.

- "... <u>no wildlife</u>" ... "<u>destroyed forests</u>" ... "<u>making way for factories or</u> schools" ... "<u>a lot of unusable muddied land filled with disease and people</u> ho are destitute."=
No government-subsidized social programs. Larger corporations run the world. Social programs destroyed. Mentally handicapped are left homeless and destitute.

[You can take any topic that you are obsessed with, as
you will have many facts and figures at your fingertips to
which you can correlate the words in the script with
pictures from your personal issue.]

[*He looks at her askance* . . .]

ASTROV

It seems to me that you have little interest
in any of this.

YELENA
No, it's simply that I don't comprehend much
of it.

ASTROV
It doesn't take much to comprehend it, I just
don't think you're all that interested.

YELENA
Please excuse my lack of concentration as my
mind is someplace else. To be honest I wanted
to ask you something but don't know how to begin.
[*Pause*]
It's a question about someone you know. Like
friends, let's talk, being totally open with each
other and then forget we ever had this conversation.
What do you say?

"*. . . ask you something . . .*" "*. . . question about someone you know.*" =
Thinking of your SUBSTITUTION for Yelena, what could be a possible question that would make sense to something she would ask, as well as something that would be personally disquieting to you? As part of the INNER
OBJECT visual, you have to deal with the great possibility that she might know
something about you that is revealing, humiliating or disparaging (don't forget
the human paranoia factor). Your "skeleton in the closet" might very well be the
topic to her question that's taking oh-so-long to ask you. The INNER OBJECT
pictures would be of you engaged in the activity you don't want exposed through
answering her question.
Yelena's "*question*" possibilities =

- "(Are you) an alcoholic?"
- "(Do you like to) torture small animals?"
- "(Are you) a homosexual?"
- "(Are you) sexually perverted (specify your perversion of choice)?"
- "(Have you ever) been in prison?"
- "(Do you have a history of) beating up on women?"

ASTROV
All-right.

YELENA
It's about Sonya, my stepdaughter. What do
you think of her, do you like her?

"*. . . Sonya, my stepdaughter.*" =
Your SUBSTITUTION for Sonya.

ASTROV
I can admire her spirit.

YELENA
But do you like her as <u>a woman</u>?

"... <u>a woman</u>" =

Sex

ASTROV
[*Pause*]
No.

YELENA
[*Kissing his hand*]
You don't love her, I can see that from your
eyes. You know, she's suffering. Try to
understand that you must stop coming <u>here</u>.

"... <u>here</u>." =
This INNER OBJECT picture would be the place that you've been inordinately
visiting to see your SUBSTITUTION for Yelena and contains some kind of risk
if you had to stop showing up.

• Your SUBSTITUTION for Yelena's home (which means you'll never see her
again)

• Your SUBSTITUTION for Yelena's relative's home

• Your SUBSTITUTION for Yelena's workplace (and if you work in the same
place, that means you have to quit and be jobless)

• The school we both attend (which means you have to drop out of school)

• My friend's (SUBSTITUTION for Vanya) home (which means you lose
your friend)

YELENA
Ouch! I hate this, I feel like I've been carrying
the weight of the world on my shoulders. Anyway,
it's done, thank God, so now we can forget we
ever had this conversation and move on. You're
a smart man, I'm sure you realize why you must ...
[*Pause*]
<u>I feel all the blood rushing to my head.</u>

"<u>I feel all the blood rushing to my head</u>." =
This could have many meanings. The INNER OBJECT images here are the different possibilities of what she means by that, both wishful and fearful.

• Sexually turned on

• Uncomfortable

• Needs to vomit

ASTROV

If you had told me about her feelings a month
or two ago I might have thought about it . . . but
if she is sick at heart because of me then I guess
there's no other recourse . . . But tell me, why is
it that *you* had to ask me?

[*He looks at her a moment.*]

Ohhhh, I get it!

YELENA

What are you talking about?

ASTROV

You know. Sure, Sonya may be in love, but
why is it you're asking the questions? Why do
you look so surprised? You know why I come
every day, you're very well aware of the effect
you have on me, you lovely "<u>bird of prey</u>."

". . . <u>bird of prey</u>." =
• Elegant eagle
• Fox
• Slut
• Nymphomaniac
• Naked woman

YELENA

Bird of prey! What are you talking about?!

ASTROV

You are a <u>gorgeous, frisky rascal</u> . . . and I am
your victim. Well, you win, you can have me.

". . . <u>gorgeous, frisky rascal</u> . . ." =
Same as above

[*He opens his arms and bows his head like a martyr on the cross.*]

I give in, I'm here and ready to be <u>consumed</u>!

". . . <u>consumed</u>" =
• Kissing
• Foreplay
• Oral sex

- Full-out sex
- Deviant sex that is geared toward your predilection
- A nonsexual expression of love (i.e., Yelena's loving words, hugging, kiss on the cheek, etc.)

                         YELENA
            Have you gone mad?!

                         ASTROV
            Oh, you are so coy.

                         YELENA
            I'm not as cunning or as cruel as you're making
            me out to be. Honestly I'm not.

[*She tries to leave. Astrov rushes to block her way.*]

                         ASTROV
            I'll leave and I won't return. Just tell me . . .

[*He takes her hand and glances about to see if anyone is looking.*]

            Where should we meet? Hurry, someone may
            catch us—please tell me where.
                    [*Whispering lustfully*]
            Your hair smells wonderful. One little kiss,
            please let me kiss you.

"*. . . hair smells wonderful.*" =
- Strawberry smell
- Her natural body smell
- Favorite perfume
- Sexy musk smell
- Favorite food smell

                         YELENA
            I beg of you . . .

                         ASTROV
                    [*Stops her from talking*]
            No need to beg, I'm yours. You are so beautiful.
            And your lovely hands, I need to kiss your hands.

"*. . . your lovely hands, I need to kiss your hands.*" =
Picture your favorite sexual activity using your favorite female body part as your INNER OBJECT when looking at Yelena's hands. This way you truly will need to "kiss" her hands.

[*He kisses her hands.*]

YELENA
Stop it, please stop . . . go . . .

[*She pulls her hand away.*]

ASTROV
Tell me, where do you want to meet tomorrow?
You know it's inescapable, we are meant to be
together.

[*He kisses her and at that very moment Uncle Vanya shows up carrying a dozen roses and stops just inside the door. Neither Astrov
or Yelena see him.*]

YELENA
[*Not seeing Vanya*]
Don't. We shouldn't be doing this . . .

[*She lays her head on Astrov's chest.*]

ASTROV
At two o'clock meet me at <u>the plantation</u>.
Promise me you'll come.

"*. . . the plantation.*" =
Picture a place that would make sense for you to meet considering your SUBSTI-
TUTION for Yelena.
- My home
- A local beach
- My parents' home
- A particular hotel or motel room
- Under the football field's bleachers at our school

[*Yelena sees Vanya looking at them.*]

YELENA
Let go of me!

[*She forcefully pulls away from Astrov. Then she goes to the window.*]

[*Muttering to herself*]
This is just awful.

[*Vanya carefully puts the roses on a nearby chair. Yelena continues
to look out the window trying to figure out what she's going to say
or do next as Astrov looks painfully guilty and attempts to cover up.*]

INNER OBJECTS provide more detail, texturing and truth
to the inner story you've established.

Tool #6: BEATS and ACTIONS

Consider each BEAT and ACTION pair as a mini-OBJECTIVE.

A BEAT is a thought change. A BEAT can be one line or a whole page. There is an ACTION attached to each BEAT. An ACTION is the specific tack or tactics you take to achieve your SCENE'S OBJECTIVE. (Don't confuse ACTIONS with DOINGS.)

Although it's been explained quite thoroughly in PART I, BEATS and ACTIONS are such an important and integral part of the technique that it bears repeating. BEATS and ACTIONS bring various facets to the forward motion of getting your SCENE OBJECTIVE. They inform precise ways to achieve the goal stated in the SCENE OBJECTIVE. That's why the BEATS and ACTIONS are phrased the same way you word your SCENE OBJECTIVE: to get a reaction. This is so you are not talking at the person, but eliciting a response.

Never stop going after your BEAT and ACTION when you stop talking and the other person speaks. Continue to pursue the BEAT and ACTION. Look to see if you are getting the desired reaction. Be open to the other actor's response to your BEAT and ACTION, and in turn, let that motivate an emotional reACTION in you. Then, based on what it is that you feel (your reACTION), let that reACTION inspire a reason to go on to the next ACTION.

You will find the BEATS bracketed and the ACTION for each BEAT handwritten (in pencil) out to the *right* side (DOINGS are written on the left) of the bracketed area in the analyzed scene that follows. This is exactly how you should write on any and every script when establishing your BEATS and ACTIONS. Once again: There are many choices you can make in determining your BEATS and ACTIONS. The following are only suggestions. It's up to you to find the most effective ACTION for each BEAT that will most befit the who-am-I of the character, as well as your own personality.

BEATS and ACTIONS from Yelena's P.O.V.

Keep in mind Yelena's SCENE OBJECTIVE of *"to get you to fall in love with me"* in order to substantiate her shallow existence. It is often the case that when you empower another person they are more likely to fall in love with you. You become indispensable to his or her personal validation. This is how gurus, cult masters, mentors and leaders of any type inspire fanatically dedicated followers. Most of us are fairly self-involved, our favorite topic being me, myself and I. So, when someone makes it all about us and what makes us feel brilliant and special, it's like an addict with a drug—we want more and more, because it feels so damn good. Empowering the object of your desire is an extremely effective way to make someone fall—hard—in your direction.

Yelena's BEATS and ACTIONS suggestions.

UNCLE VANYA
Anton Chekhov
(A scene from Act III)

ASTROV
(*Enters with drawing*)
[Hello, I understand you wanted to see
some of my artistry?

YELENA

*Make you feel
important*

Yesterday, you assured me you would show
me your drawings. Are you available now?

ASTROV
I'd love to!

(*He spreads the drawing on a nearby table and fixes it with stick-
pins. She helps him.*)]

[Where were you born?

*To diminish my higher
position in life for your benefit*

YELENA
In Petersburg.

ASTROV
And where did you go to school?

YELENA
At the conservatory.]

ASTROV
[I doubt very much this will intrigue you
in any way.

*Make you believe
I'm intrigued*

YELENA
Why not? You're right in assuming I don't know much
about the country, but I'm well read.]

ASTROV
[Look here. It's a map of this area as it was
fifty years ago. The green color indicates the
forest. Half of the area was surfaced with   *Make you feel*
forest. Where you see the red over the green—   *like a genius*
deer, wild goats and all sorts of wildlife were
prevalent. Look at the third part and you'll   *Make you*
see my rendition of how it is today. There's   *believe I am*
green, but it's sporadic. There is no wildlife].   *fascinated*
(*Pause*)
[You might say it's progress and I'd agree if *make you*
the destroyed forests were making way for   *Make you*
factories or schools. But, no, there is a lot of   *believe I*
unusable muddied land filled with disease   *sympathize*
and people who are destitute.]

[(*He looks at her askance . . .*)

It seems to me that you have little interest
in any of this.

*Make you feel
smarter than me*

YELENA
No, it's simply that I don't comprehend much
of it.

ASTROV
It doesn't take much to comprehend it, I just
don't think you're all that interested.]

YELENA
[Please excuse my lack of concentration   *Make you feel how*
as my mind is someplace else. To be   *grateful I am that you*
honest I wanted to ask you something   *deign to speak to me*
but don't know how to begin.]
(*Pause*)
[It's a question about someone you know.
Like friends, let's talk, being totally open with *Empower you*
each other and then forget we ever had this   *by sharing a*
conversation. What do you say?   *secret*

ASTROV

All-right.]

YELENA

[It's about Sonya, my stepdaughter. What do
you think of her, do you like her?

ASTROV

I can admire her spirit.

Make you say you're not
attracted to

YELENA   *(SUBSTITUTION*

But do you like her as a woman?   *for) Sonya*

ASTROV
(*Pause*)

No.]

YELENA
(*Kissing his hand*)   *Make you feel rewarded*
[You don't love her, I can see that from your   *for giving the*
eyes. You know, she's suffering.]   *right answer*
[Try to understand that you must stop
coming here.   *Make you believe what a*
(*Pause*)   *sacrifice this is for me*
Ouch! I hate this, I feel like I've been carrying
the weight of the world on my shoulders. Anyway,
it's done, thank God, so now we can forget we
ever had this conversation and move on. You're
a smart man, I'm sure you realize why you must . . .]
(*Pause*)
[I feel all the blood rushing to
my head.   *Make you rush over and hold*
me to keep me from fainting

ASTROV

If you had told me about her feelings a month
or two ago I might have thought about it . . . but
if she is sick at heart because of me then I guess
there's no other recourse . . .]
(*Pause*)
[But tell me, why is
it that *you* had to ask me?

(*He looks at her a moment.*)

Ohhhh, I get it!

YELENA   *Impress you with*

What are you talking about?   *my innocence*

ASTROV
You know. Sure, Sonya may be in love, but
why is it you're asking the questions? Why do
you look so surprised? You know why I come
every day, you're very well aware of the effect
you have on me, you lovely "bird of prey."

YELENA
Bird of prey! What are you talking about?!

ASTROV
You are a gorgeous, frisky rascal . . . and I am
your victim. Well, you win, you can have me.]

[(*He opens his arms and bows his head like a martyr on the cross.*)

I give in, I'm here and ready to be consumed!

Make you chase after me

YELENA
Have you gone mad?!

ASTROV
Oh, you are so coy.

YELENA
I'm not as cunning or as cruel as you're making
me out to be. Honestly I'm not.]

[(*She tries to leave. Astrov rushes to block her way.*)]

*Make you stop me
from leaving*

ASTROV
[I'll leave and I won't return. Just tell me . . .

Make you seduce me

(*He takes her hand and glances about to see if anyone is looking.*)

Where should we meet? Hurry, someone may
catch us—please tell me where?
            (*Whispering lustfully*)
Your hair smells wonderful. One little kiss,
please let me kiss you.]

YELENA
[I beg of you . . .

ASTROV   *Make you beg me to
(Stops her from talking)   be with you*
No need to beg, I'm yours. You are so beautiful.
And your lovely hands, I need to kiss your hands.

(*He kisses her hands.*)
                    YELENA
          Stop it, please stop . . . go . . .

(*She pulls her hand away.*)]

                    ASTROV
[You know it's inescapable, we are meant to be
together.

(*He kisses her and at that very moment Uncle Vanya shows up carrying a dozen roses and stops just inside the door. Neither Astrov
or Yelena see him.*)

                                        Get you to continue to
                                        seduce me (no matter how
                    YELENA   *much I tell you to stop)*
               (*Not seeing Vanya*)
          Don't. We shouldn't be doing this . . .

(*She lays her head on Astrov's chest.*)

                    ASTROV
          At two o'clock meet me at the plantation.
          Promise me you'll come.]

[(*Yelena sees Vanya looking at them.*)
                              Get Vanya to believe you (Astrov) are
                    YELENA   *forcing me to be "with" you and*
          Let go of me!   *that I'm an innocent victim*
                               and make you (Astrov)
                               back me up in my lie

(*She forcefully pulls away from Astrov. Then she goes to the window.*)

               (*Muttering to herself*)
          This is just awful.

(*Vanya carefully puts the roses on a nearby chair. Yelena continues
to look out the window trying to figure out what she's going to say
or do next as Astrov looks painfully guilty and attempts to cover up.*)]

BEATS and ACTIONS from Astrov's P.O.V.

Consider Astrov's SCENE OBJECTIVE of *"to make you fall in love
with me."*

Astrov's BEATS and ACTIONS suggestions.

UNCLE VANYA

Anton Chekhov
(A scene from Act III)

ASTROV
(*Enters with drawing*)
[Hello, I understand you wanted to see
some of my artistry?   *To intrigue you*

YELENA
Yesterday, you assured me you would show
me your drawings. Are you available now?]

ASTROV
[I'd love to!   *Get you excited*

(*He spreads the drawing on a nearby table and fixes it with stick-
pins. She helps him.*)]

[Where were you born?

YELENA
In Petersburg.   *Get you to open up to me*

ASTROV
And where did you go to school?

YELENA
At the conservatory.]

ASTROV
[I doubt very much this will intrigue you
in any way.   *Make you beg me*
                                              to continue

YELENA
Why not? You're right in assuming I don't know much
about the country, but I'm well read.]

ASTROV
[Look here. It's a map of this area as it was
fifty years ago. The green color indicates the   *Get you to*
forest. Half of the area was surfaced with forest. *anticipate*
Where you see the red over the green—deer,
wild goats and all sorts of wildlife were
prevalent. Look at the third part and you'll   *Rile you up*
see how it is today. There's green, but it's sporadic.
There is no wildlife.]

ASTROV
(*Pause*)
[You might say it's progress
and I'd agree if the destroyed forests were making
way for factories or schools. But, no, there is a   *Get you*
lot of unusable muddied land filled with disease   *to agree*
and people who are destitute.]   *with me*

[(*He looks at her askance.*)

It seems to me that you have little interest
in any of this.
                                        Challenge your honesty

YELENA
No, it's simply that I don't comprehend much
of it.

ASTROV
It doesn't take much to comprehend it, I just
don't think you're all that interested.]

YELENA
[Please excuse my lack of concentration as my
mind is someplace else. To be honest I wanted
to ask you something but don't know how to begin.
                                        Get you to ask me
                (*Pause*)   *the question quickly*
It's a question about someone you know. Like
friends, let's talk, being totally open with each
other and then forget we ever had this conversation.
What do you say?

ASTROV
All-right.]

YELENA
[It's about Sonya, my stepdaughter. What do
you think of her, do you like her?
                                        Make you happy
                                    with my vague answer

ASTROV
I can admire her spirit.]

YELENA
[But do you like her as a woman?

ASTROV
(*Pause*)   *Make you aware I*
No.]   *am available to you*

YELENA
(*Kissing his hand*)   *Make you keep*
[You don't love her, I can see that from your   *kissing me*
eyes. You know, she's suffering. Try to
understand that you must stop coming here.]
(*Pause*)
[Ouch! I hate this, I feel like I've been carrying
the weight of the world on my shoulders. Anyway,
it's done, thank God, so now we can forget we
ever had this conversation and move on. You're
a smart man, I'm sure you realize why you must . . .
(*Pause*)   *Get you to help me*
I feel all the blood rushing to my head.   *understand why I*
                                                have to go

ASTROV
If you had told me about her feelings a month
or two ago I might have thought about it . . . but
if she is sick at heart because of me then I guess
there's no other recourse . . .]
(*Pause*)
[But tell me, why is
it that *you* had to ask me?

(*He looks at her a moment.*)

Oh, I get it!   *Make you admit you*
                                            like me

YELENA
What are you talking about?

ASTROV
You know. Sure, Sonya may be in love, but
why is it you're asking the questions? Why do
you look so surprised? You know why I come
every day, you're very well aware of the effect
you have on me, you lovely "bird of prey."]

YELENA
[Bird of prey! What are you talking about?!
                    Make you run into my arms
ASTROV   *and have your way with me*
You are a gorgeous, frisky rascal . . . and I am
your victim. Well, you win, you can have me.

(*He opens his arms and bows his head like a martyr on the cross.*)

ASTROV
[*cont.*]

I give in, I'm here and ready to be consumed!]

YELENA
[Have you gone mad?!

ASTROV   *Make you play the*
Oh, you are so coy.   *game with me*

YELENA
I'm not as cunning or as cruel as you're making
me out to be. Honestly, I'm not.]

[(*She tries to leave. Astrov rushes to block her way.*)]   *Stop you*
from leaving

ASTROV
[I'll leave and I won't return. Just tell me . . .

(*He takes her hand and glances about to see if anyone is looking.*)
Make you commit to a time and a
and place (so you can't back out)
Where should we meet, hurry someone may
catch us—please tell me where.]

(*Whispering lustfully*)
[Your hair smells wonderful. One little kiss,
please let me kiss you.
Get you turned on
YELENA   *sexually*
I beg of you . . .

ASTROV
(*Stops her from talking*)
No need to beg, I'm yours. You are so beautiful.
And your lovely hands, I need to kiss your hands.

(*He kisses her hands.*)

YELENA
Stop it, please stop . . . go . . .]

(*She pulls her hand away.*)

ASTROV
[You know it's inescapable, we are meant to be
together.   *Make you admit*
you love me

(He kisses her and at that very moment Uncle Vanya shows up carrying a dozen roses and stops just inside the door. Neither Astrov or Yelena see him.)

YELENA
(Not seeing Vanya)

Don't. We shouldn't be doing this . . .

(She lays her head on Astrov's chest.)]

ASTROV

[At two o'clock meet me at the plantation. *Make you promise*
Promise me you'll come.]   *to meet me*

(Yelena sees Vanya looking at them.)

YELENA

[Let go of me!   *Make you want to stay*
                                                   in my arms
(She forcefully pulls away from Astrov.) [*Then she goes to the window.)*

YELENA
(Muttering to herself)   *Make Vanya believe in our*

                                            innocence (and be
                                                  your hero)

This is just awful.

(Vanya carefully puts the roses on a nearby chair. Yelena continues to look out the window trying to figure out what she's going to say or do next as Astrov looks painfully guilty and attempts to cover up.)]

ACTIONS *and* BEATS *give you the colors and specificity of how your character wins the scene.*

Tool #7: MOMENT BEFORE

This is the event that takes place before the scene begins.

The MOMENT BEFORE gives you a dire reason for you to want to win your SCENE OBJECTIVE. It tells you *where* you're coming from and *why* you need your SCENE OBJECTIVE so badly, right now. Remember, you use events that include *present* unresolved issues that are based on real or what-if my-worst-fear-were-to-come-true situations.

Remember: The MOMENT BEFORE is a visceral reliving of the event just before you launch into the scene, and should take no more

than thirty to sixty seconds. As always, write in pencil, putting your MO-
MENT BEFORE choice on the top of the first page of the scene.

Yelena's MOMENT BEFORE

In the scene from Act III of *Uncle Vanya*, the scripted MOMENT BE-
FORE is Yelena ruminating about her utter boredom with life as she
speaks to Vanya and Sonya. She explains that she is without purpose or
direction. Vanya and Sonya make some helpful suggestions. They offer
solutions like running the home, teaching children, caring for the sick
and less fortunate. These are worthy endeavors for anyone, but Yelena
declares that these activities are for heroines in a novel. She, of flesh and
blood, will leave charity work to those that are charitable. She thinks all
those activities would be dull and uninteresting, so what would be the
point? Vanya exits, leaving Sonya and Yelena alone. Yelena insists that
she is Sonya's really good friend, and new friendship always requires a
tell-all session. Sonya, in the spirit of friendship and floodgates gone
wild, confesses that she loves Astrov. She goes on to say how hopeless
she feels and that she fears that her affections will never be returned.
Sonya's new best friend, Yelena, offers to help her find out exactly how
Astrov feels about her. Sonya is so tortured by her unrequited love that
she agrees. Yelena tells Sonya that she will use the ruse of telling Astrov
that she has an interest in his drawings and seeks an immediate audience
with him. After Sonya goes to fetch Astrov, Yelena muses about what
she's about to do, admitting to herself that she feels a tad guilty because
she, too, has an attraction to him. While she waits for Astrov to show up,
she forgets her guilt as she develops a hearty appetite for the doctor.

Considering the script's MOMENT BEFORE, you have to emotionally
correlate them to real events from your own life that make the SCENE
OBJECTIVE more honest and important to you. Yelena's SCENE OBJEC-
TIVE is *"to get you to fall in love with me."* Yelena is bored stiff and
Sonya's unrequited love is an intriguing game for Yelena to play. Wouldn't
it be exciting to set up a competition between her and the unknowing
Sonya, with Astrov being the prize? What better way to win the competi-
tion and prove self-worth than to make Astrov *"fall in love with me."*

Bottom line.

Yelena feels like a loser and a nobody because she does nothing with her life. Being able to win the affections of Dr. Astrov over Sonya will validate her importance, essentially making her a winner, a somebody. Therefore, getting Astrov (who becomes quite the catch by virtue of Sonya's obsession with him) to fall in love with her becomes more than just the petty manipulations of an idle woman. It becomes crucial for helping her feel like she has a purpose in her life, an importance of being. With this in mind . . .

MOMENT BEFORE suggestions for Yelena.

- MOMENT BEFORE: Could be any event that makes you feel like a loser. An event that makes you feel that you need to be immediately validated. This could be a real or what-if event, like failing a class, being dumped by a friend or mate, having to claim bankruptcy, being fired from a job.

  Let's use being fired from your job as an example. Say you were just fired from a job (or what-if you fear being fired from a job, and you visualized it actually happened) and your SUBSTITUTION for Sonya is prospering in the workplace. Although, as luck would have it, your SUBSTITUTION for Sonya is having major troubles with her love life. Replay the real firing event in your head (or how you imagine you'd be fired if you're using a what-if event) and then launch into the scene, knowing that getting your SUBSTITUTION for Astrov so easily to fall in love with you will make you the better person and the winner. What will happen is that you will feel like a loser in the workplace but damn it, you're going to win in the social arena!

- MOMENT BEFORE: Think about a specific event in which you had some form of a competition with your SUBSTITUTION for Sonya and she won (for example, she got better grades, a better job, a better home, a better man, a better review, better financial opportunities, won an athletic event, etc). This will make you want to win today's competition with enormous enthusiasm. Relive this event (where you were the loser and your

SUBSTITUTION for Sonya was the winner) in your mind as if it just happened, and then launch into the scene.

- MOMENT BEFORE: Think about your SUBSTITUTION for Sonya, a person with whom you have an inherently competitive relationship and who is rarely a good sport about it, gloating and bragging at your expense. Your SUBSTITUTION for Sonya has been regaling you with her constant woes about some man she loves (a conversation that seems to take place more frequently between *girl*friends). Whether you like this guy or not doesn't matter. Going after him and getting him would make you the victor in your own mind, because she'd never have to know about it. As your MOMENT BEFORE, relive the event where your SUBSTITUTION for Sonya was particularly broken up about something that happened with the object of her obsession and launch into the scene with the mission—maybe she can't get him, but *I* can.

- MOMENT BEFORE: You feel that your SUBSTITUTION for Sonya has betrayed you, diminished you or showed a blatant lack of respect (and she has a boyfriend/husband.) Using the event that exemplifies this, relive it in your mind as if it's currently happening and launch into the scene using her boyfriend/husband as your SUBSTITUTION for Astrov. You making her boyfriend/husband fall in love with you then becomes a form of righteous payback.

- MOMENT BEFORE: You feel that your SUBSTITUTION for Astrov has betrayed you, diminished you or shown a blatant lack of respect. Getting this culprit to *fall in love* with you would give you the power back in this relationship. Using an event you felt was the most egregious as your MOMENT BEFORE will make you need to help this rogue feel what you felt, and hurt like you hurt. Use his present girlfriend as your SUBSTITUTION for Sonja.

Astrov's MOMENT BEFORE

In Astrov's case, there is no scripted MOMENT BEFORE. For all we know, he's floating around the house someplace thinking thoughts only

Astrov would be privy to. Although we don't have an actual scene that takes place directly before that includes Astrov, we can surmise from previous scenes that he is probably consumed with thoughts about Yelena. After all, he does come to the home daily, and before her arrival he hardly ever showed up. He also goes on and on about how lonely he is and how hopeless he feels about fixing his bachelor status. He is also readily available when she summons him.

MOMENT BEFORE suggestions for Astrov.

- MOMENT BEFORE: Fantasizing the particular kind of fantasies that you entertain about your SUBSTITUTION for Yelena. For instance, the fantasy sequences in your head could include your SUBSTITUTION for Yelena smothering you with kisses and telling you she loves you more than life itself. Thus when you find out she wants to see you, you can entertain the idea that maybe your fantasy is about to come true.

- MOMENT BEFORE: Fantasize sexually about the actress who is playing Yelena, then launch into the scene. This will make you aroused and physically needy of Yelena's love.

- MOMENT BEFORE: Fantasize about your SUBSTITUTION for Yelena giving you a job or promotion (if you are using career issues instead of romantic issues as your underlying inner work). Imagine actually having the job or promotion and all the perks that come with it (say it's an acting job—imagine being on set, having your makeup put on, meeting stars and giving out autographs, etc.). Then launch into the scene by attempting to woo her into giving it to you. The imagery will make it more conceivable and force you to do more to get it, because you're so close you can taste it.

- MOMENT BEFORE: Relive an event in the relationship you're presently in that has gone terribly awry. Replay this horrid event in your mind and launch into the scene. This will make you need your SUBSTITUTION for Yelena to fall in love with you, because she seems so much better in comparison to your mate.

- MOMENT BEFORE: An event that typifies your loneliness. It could be imagining your place of residence, staring at four walls, feeling all alone and empty. Or you could use a what-if event like seeing yourself old and dying and there's no one there to mourn your passing. Live it for a few moments and then launch into the scene. This will make you work harder to get Yelena to fall in love with you so you can avoid these horrible pictures from either continuing or ever taking place.

MOMENT BEFORE gives you the urgency to accomplish your SCENE OBJECTIVE immediately. A strong MOMENT BEFORE choice catapults you into real time and real need.

Tool #8: PLACE and FOURTH WALL

Endowing the PLACE/FOURTH WALL that you're acting in with a PLACE/FOURTH WALL from your own life.

Applying information from the inner story you have created from your OVERALL OBJECTIVE, SCENE OBJECTIVE, OBSTACLES, SUBSTITUTION, INNER OBJECTS and MOMENT BEFORE, ask yourself the question: "What PLACE from my life would best inform and add conflict to the choices I've already made?" Once you make the choice of what PLACE you're using, endow the FOURTH WALL with what would be there when you look in that direction. *Uncle Vanya* may take place in the nineteenth century, but your PLACE/FOURTH WALL will not, because this is not *your* reality. It's difficult to feel private in entirely make-believe surroundings. On the other hand, if you infuse the set with an appropriate PLACE/FOURTH WALL from your own life, the audience will believe you are from this bygone century, because you'll look so at home in your nineteenth-century surroundings.

Keep in mind that when making your PLACE and FOURTH WALL choice for both Astrov and Yelena, there is the reality of your SUBSTITUTION for Uncle Vanya lurking around the outskirts of your PLACE. This person can easily enter the PLACE and interfere with accomplishing your SCENE OBJECTIVE.

Write, in pencil, your choice for PLACE/FOURTH WALL at the top of the scene's script page.

PLACE/FOURTH WALL from Yelena's P.O.V.

Choose a PLACE/FOURTH WALL that would be highly charged and that lines up with the circumstances you have created with the other tools. The PLACE/FOURTH WALL also has to instill a danger in accomplishing your SCENE OBJECTIVE of *"to get you to fall in love with me."*

PLACE/FOURTH WALL suggestions (depending on your SUBSTITUTION choices for Astrov and Vanya).

- **Your living room or bedroom:** Where your mate (or parent, sister, brother, friend, anyone who hates your SUBSTITUTION for Astrov) can show up and, as a result of what they see, sever all ties with you.
- **Your boss's office:** (When the boss is your SUBSTITUTION for Astrov.) His wife (or his secretary, a fellow employee, his boss) could enter any minute, causing you to lose your job, promotion possibilities, respect from coworkers, etc.
- **A classroom at your school:** (When a student is your SUBSTITUTION for Astrov.) It would be devastating both morally and maybe even legally to be caught by the dean or principal (or fellow teacher or another student).
- **Your friend's bedroom:** (When using a friend's boyfriend/husband as your SUBSTITUTION for Astrov.) There's a huge potential for your friend to unexpectedly arrive home early and catch you in the act.
- **Your boyfriend's apartment:** (When using a boyfriend's good friend or relative as your SUBSTITUTION for Astrov.) This is perilous by virtue of the fact that your boyfriend can uninvitingly walk in at any time—it doesn't usually require an invite to walk into your own home.

PLACE from Astrov's P.O.V.

Choose a PLACE that you would feel the probable disruptive presence of a person who would be hazardous to your achieving your goal of *"to get you to fall in love with me."*

PLACE suggestions (depending on your SUBSTITUTION choices for Yelena and Vanya).

- **Your friend's living room or bedroom:** Where your friend can come in from another part of the house and discover you trying to seduce his woman.
- **Your or her office:** Where your boss (or fellow employee, mate to Yelena, etc.) can catch you in the act of seduction, creating the possibility of losing your job or your life.
- **A classroom at the school you attend:** Where a teacher (or fellow student, her mate, the principal, dean, etc.) is capable of interrupting your attempt to achieve your SCENE OBJECTIVE and possibly putting a damper on your school career.
- **Your bedroom:** Where her mate (or friend, father, mother, sister, brother—anyone who is adversarial to your getting together with your SUBSTITUTION for Yelena) can barge in at any time.
- **Your living room:** Where your mate (or father, mother, friend, sister, brother, roommate—anyone who would be hostile to you about your SUBSTITUTION for Yelena) can come in and wreak havoc on your life.

In script analysis, PLACE and FOURTH WALL are easy elements to overlook. But don't skip using them. They truly augment and reinforce your character's emotional life and goals.

Tool #9: DOINGS

DOINGS are the handling of props to produce behavior.

The handling of props allows you to behave naturally, as if you were really in the environment your character is inhabiting. And all of the technique's other tools will temper *what* and *how* you handle the props—whether you pick up a book angrily, with lust or as a way to impress. As a result, using props informs the audience about what you are really thinking and feeling.

Remember: What you DO in the scene isn't only prescribed by the DOINGS described in the text of the scene. It's up to you, the actor, to bring in more of the character's life and behavior by introducing more than what is literally called for in the script.

In *Uncle Vanya*, the DOINGS must relate to the fact that the story takes place in a fairly wealthy country home in nineteenth-century Russia. You must also consider that Yelena and Dr. Astrov are well-educated and socially savvy.

The following are suggestions for possible DOINGS. They should be handwritten (as always, in pencil) and located to the left of the dialogue, where the DOING will most likely take place. These suggestions are here to whet your imagination. As you read, try to come up with some DOINGS of your own.

Possible doings from Yelena's P.O.V.

UNCLE VANYA
Anton Chekhov
(A scene from Act III)

Eating a ripe peach
(There is a non-
threatening
sexuality in
eating something that's drippy and pulpy.
When it drips on a chin, Astrov will
likely "help" wipe it off with his finger—
making him feel safe
in starting
a seduction.)

ASTROV
[*Enters with drawing*]
Hello, I understand you wanted to see some of my artistry?

YELENA
Yesterday, you assured me you would show me your drawings. Are you available now?

ASTROV
I'd love to!

[*He spreads the drawing on a nearby table and fixes it with stick-pins. She helps him.*]

Where were you born?

Help him spread the drawing
(In this way you have a legitimate
excuse to "accidentally" touch.)

YELENA
In Petersburg.

ASTROV
And where did you go to school?

YELENA
At the conservatory.

ASTROV
I doubt very much this will intrigue you
in any way.

YELENA
Why not? You're right in assuming I don't
know much about the country, but I'm well read.

Examine the drawing
closely as he points out each item.   ASTROV
(This is   Look here. It's a map of this area as it was
a way   fifty years ago. The green color indicates the
to appear   forest. Half of the area was surfaced with
engrossed   forest. Where you see the red over the green—
and to be   deer, wild goats and all sorts of wildlife were
physically   prevalent. Look at the third part and you'll
close.)   see my rendition of how it is today. There's green,
                  but it's sporadic. There is no wildlife.
                            [*Pause*]
                  You might say it's progress and I'd agree
                  if the destroyed forests were making
                  way for factories or schools. But, no, there is a
                  lot of unusable muddied land filled with disease
                  and people who are destitute.

[*He looks at her askance . . .*]

It seems to me that you have little interest
in any of this.

YELENA
No, it's simply that I don't comprehend much
of it.

ASTROV
It doesn't take much to comprehend it, I just
don't think you're all that interested.

Pick up a photograph   YELENA
of Sonya   Please excuse my lack of concentration as my
from a   mind is someplace else. To be honest I wanted
nearby table to ask you something but I don't know how to
or chest,   begin.
stare at it with concern.   [*Pause*]
Touch the   It's a question about someone you know.
photo with   Like friends, let's talk, being totally open with
love and   each other and then forget we ever had this
pathos.
                            ASTROV
                  All-right.

YELENA

It's about Sonya, my stepdaughter. What do
you think of her, do you like her?

ASTROV

I can admire her spirit.

YELENA

But do you like her as a woman?

ASTROV
[Pause]

No.

YELENA

Kissing his hand   [*Kissing his hand*]
at the same   You don't love her, I can see that from your
time you are eyes. You know, she's suffering. Try to
telling him   understand that you must stop coming here.
to go away is a mixed   [*Pause*]
message.   Ouch! I hate this, I feel like I've been carrying
Your lack of the weight of the world on my shoulders. Anyway,
predictability it's done, thank God, so now we can forget we
is appealing. ever had this conversation and move on. You're
                  a smart man, I'm sure you realize why you must . . .
                           [*Pause*]
                  I feel all the blood rushing to my head.
Loosening up your collar or unbuttoning
your blouse in order to get some air
(and it also reveals more skin
and is provocative).   ASTROV
                  If you had told me about her feelings a month or
                  two ago I might have thought about it . . .
                  but if she is sick at heart because of me then I guess
                  there's no other recourse . . .
                           [*Pause*]
                  But tell me, why is it *you* had to ask me?

[*He looks at her a moment.*]

Ohhhh, I get it!

YELENA

Pulling out   What are you talking about?
a fan that is tucked snugly in your
bodice, and frantically fanning yourself.

ASTROV
You know. Sure, Sonya may be in love, but
why is it you're asking the questions? Why do
you look so surprised? You know why I come
every day, you're very well aware of the effect
you have on me, you lovely "bird of prey."

YELENA
Bird of prey! What are you talking about?!

ASTROV
You are a gorgeous, frisky rascal . . . and I am
your victim. Well, you win, you can have me.

[*He opens his arms and bows his head like a martyr on the cross.*]

I give in, I'm here and ready to be consumed!

YELENA
Have you gone mad?!

ASTROV
Oh, you are so coy.

YELENA
I'm not as cunning or as cruel as you're making
me out to be. Honestly, I'm not.

[*She tries to leave. Astrov rushes to block her way.*]

*"Accidentally" run into a piece of furniture
on the way out (fall if you must—buy as
much time as possible so Astrov has time
to stop you. Also, things that are on the
furniture are bound to fall. Astrov's attempt
to help you up or help you pick up what fell will
give him legitimate close proximity and an
opportunity to take it further).*

ASTROV
I'll leave and I won't return. Just tell me . . .

[*He takes her hand and glances about to see if anyone is looking.*]

Where should we meet? Hurry, someone may
catch us—please tell me where.
          [*Whispering lustfully*]
Your hair smells wonderful. One little kiss,
please let me kiss you.

YELENA

I beg of you . . .

*unbutton another button
(because you're so flustered).*

ASTROV
[*Stops her from talking*]
No need to beg, I'm yours. You are so beautiful.
And your lovely hands, I need to kiss your hands.

[*He kisses her hands.*]

YELENA
Stop it, please stop . . . go . . .

[*She pulls her hand away.*]
*(. . . in a way that makes him want
to take it back)*

ASTROV
You know it's inescapable, we are meant to be
together.

[*He kisses her and at that very moment Uncle Vanya shows up carrying a dozen roses and stops just inside the door. Neither Astrov
nor Yelena see him.*]

YELENA
[*Not seeing Vanya*]
Don't. We shouldn't be doing this . . .

[*She lays her head on Astrov's chest.*]

ASTROV
At two o'clock meet me at the plantation.
Promise me you'll come.

[*Yelena sees Vanya looking at them.*]

YELENA
Let go of me!

*Angrily buttoning up your blouse (as if to imply that Astrov
is the one who unbuttoned it in the first place).*
[*She forcefully pulls away from Astrov. Then she goes to the window.*]

[*Muttering to herself*]
This is just awful.

*Playing with the window cord or latch
(so it looks like you have a real reason
to be there).*

[*Vanya carefully puts the roses on a nearby chair. Yelena continues
to look out the window trying to figure out what she's going to say
or do next as Astrov looks painfully guilty and attempts to cover up.*]

Possible DOINGS from Astrov's P.O.V.

UNCLE VANYA

Anton Chekhov
(A scene from Act III)

*A briefcase held protectively
under your arm.*

ASTROV
[*Enters with drawing*]
Hello, I understand you wanted to see
some of my artistry?

YELENA
Yesterday, you assured me you would show
me your drawings. Are you available now?

ASTROV
I'd love to!

[*He spreads the drawing on a nearby table and fixes it with stick-
pins. She helps him.*]

Where were you born?

*Manipulate spreading
the drawing in a way that enables
you to legitimately touch her.*

YELENA
In Petersburg.

ASTROV
And where did you go to school?

YELENA
At the conservatory.

ASTROV
I doubt very much this will intrigue you
in any way.

YELENA
Why not? You're right in assuming I don't
know much about the country, but I'm well read.

Point at the different items
displayed in the drawing in a   ASTROV
way that   Look here. It's a map of this area as it was
forces her to   fifty years ago. The green color indicates the
have to   forest. Half of the area was surfaced with
move in   forest. Where you see the red over the green—
close to you. deer, wild goats and all sorts of wildlife were
               prevalent. Look at the third part and you'll see
               my rendition of how it is today. There's green,
               but it's sporadic. There is no wildlife.
                    [*Pause*]
               You might say it's progress and I'd agree if
               the destroyed forests were making way for
               factories or schools. But, no, there is a
               lot of unusable muddied land filled with disease
               and people who are destitute.

[*He looks at her askance . . .*]

               It seems to me that you have little interest in any of
               this.

                   YELENA
               No, it's simply that I don't comprehend much
               of it.

Pour some vodka from a   ASTROV
nearby table It doesn't take much to comprehend it, I just
and down it don't think you're all that interested.
(as if to say, "You've upset me").

                   YELENA
               Please excuse my lack of concentration as my
Play with   mind is someplace else. To be honest I wanted
a box   to ask you something but I don't know how to
or any item begin.
that's displayed on top of a table   [*Pause*]
or chest   It's a question about someone you know.
(so Yelena   Like friends, let's talk, being totally open with
won't see   each other and then forget we ever had this
your fear   conversation. What do you say?
of the question).
                   ASTROV
               All-right.

                   YELENA
               It's about Sonya, my stepdaughter. What do
               you think of her, do you like her?

                   ASTROV
               I can admire her spirit.

YELENA
But do you like her as a woman?

ASTROV
[*Pause*]
No.

YELENA
[*Kissing his hand*]
You don't love her, I can see that from your
eyes. You know, she's suffering. Try to
understand that you must stop coming here.

Packing up the drawing   [*Pause*]
and putting Ouch! I hate this, I feel like I've been carrying
it back in the weight of the world on my shoulders. Anyway,
your it's done, thank God, so now we can forget we
briefcase ever had this conversation and move on. You're
(call her a smart man, I'm sure you realize why you must . . .
bluff, make it look like you're   [*Pause*]
leaving). I feel all the blood rushing to my head.

ASTROV
If you had told me about her feelings a month or
two ago I might have thought about it . . . but if
Abruptly she is sick at heart because of me then I guess
stop there's no other recourse . . .
packing your   [*Pause*]
drawing to But tell me, why is it *you* had to ask me?
make a
point.

[*He looks at her a moment.*]

Ohhhh, I get it!

YELENA
What are you talking about?

Take a comb out of
your pocket and groom   ASTROV
yourself. You know. Sure, Sonya may be in love, but
why is it you're asking the questions? Why do
you look so surprised? You know why I come
every day, you're very well aware of the effect
you have on me, you lovely "bird of prey."

YELENA
Bird of prey! What are you talking about?!

ASTROV
You are a gorgeous, frisky rascal . . . and I am
your victim. Well, you win, you can have me.

ASTROV
[cont.]
[He opens his arms and bows his head like a martyr on the cross.]

Pick a grape, a piece of candy, or I give in, I'm here and ready to be consumed! *or a nut out of a bowl on a nearby table and pop it into your mouth—to illustrate "consumed."*

YELENA
Have you gone mad?!

ASTROV
Oh, you are so coy.

YELENA
I'm not as cunning or as cruel as you're making me out to be. Honestly, I'm not.

[She tries to leave. Astrov rushes to block her way.]

ASTROV
I'll leave and I won't return. Just tell me . . .

[He takes her hand and glances about to see if anyone is looking.]

Where should we meet? Hurry, someone may catch us—please tell me where.

Play with her hair—lift it, smell it, twirl it, play with it.   [Whispering lustfully]
Your hair smells wonderful. One little kiss, please let me kiss you.

YELENA
I beg of you . . .

ASTROV
[Stops her from talking]
No need to beg, I'm yours. You are so beautiful. And your lovely hands, I need to kiss your hands.

[He kisses her hands.]

YELENA
Stop it, please stop . . . go . . .

[She pulls her hand away.]

Pull her hand back to you (just because it's not written in the stage directions, doesn't mean you can't do it).   ASTROV
You know it's inescapable, we are meant to be together.

[*He kisses her and at that very moment Uncle Vanya shows up carrying a dozen roses and stops just inside the door. Neither Astrov nor Yelena see him.*]

YELENA
[*Not seeing Vanya*]
Don't. We shouldn't be doing this . . .

[*She lays her head on Astrov's chest.*]

Kiss her head, play with her
hair, pull her in close.

ASTROV
At two o'clock meet me at the plantation.
Promise me you'll come.

[*Yelena sees Vanya looking at them.*]

YELENA
Let go of me!

[*She forcefully pulls away from Astrov. Then she goes to the window.*]

Maniacally eat
what's in the   [*Muttering to herself*]
bowl, trying This is just awful.
to appear innocent.

[*Vanya carefully puts the roses on a nearby chair. Yelena continues to look out the window trying to figure out what she's going to say or do next as Astrov looks painfully guilty and attempts to cover up.*]

People are complex by nature, and it's the actor's job to duplicate that complexity. There's a layered effect to your characterization when you're using DOINGS. Because words can lie, behavior always tells the truth.

Tool #10: INNER MONOLOGUE

INNER MONOLOGUE is the dialogue going on inside your head that you don't speak out loud.

Our minds are one continuous scroll of thoughts when we're speaking, listening and even when we're alone. INNER MONOLOGUE is a way to replicate this innate mind-processing system.

Remember: INNER MONOLOGUE is defined paranoia. It's all those thoughts you can't say out loud because it will make you seem insecure, vulgar, crazy, stupid or prejudiced. The INNER MONOLOGUE should be written the way your mind really thinks. This means that the INNER MONOLOGUE should be stated not as introspective musings, but as a way to communicate with the other people in the scene. When crafting your INNER MONOLOGUE always use "you" instead of "he" or "she." Acting is all about creating relationships—it is never a self-indulgent, it's-all-about-me exercise.

The INNER MONOLOGUE you write is just a guideline. It is not additional dialogue to memorize. What you write is a base that provides the initial spark and direction for your thoughts to naturally flow. Whether you're rehearsing or performing, the INNER MONOLOGUE will vary slightly each time you run the scene.

Your guide for your INNER MONOLOGUE should be handwritten in pencil between the dialogue (exactly where you would use the INNER MONOLOGUE when you are acting the script). Put the INNER MONOLOGUE between quotes and under the dialogue so that you can distinguish it from the other choices you've already made.

INNER MONOLOGUE from Yelena's P.O.V.

Once again, Yelena's OBJECTIVE is *"to get you to fall in love with me,"* to give her a purpose and a reason for being. Therefore her INNER MONOLOGUE must be colored by her need to feel enhanced by his falling in love with her so as to ultimately validate her existence. The INNER MONOLOGUE will also include her weaknesses, vulnerabilities, crudeness, modus operandi and neuroses.

The following are suggestions that are geared toward the character of Yelena in the script. When writing your own INNER MONOLOGUE, it is up to you to make it personal with the thoughts, ideas, needs and people that are distinct to your own life.

INNER MONOLOGUE starts before the scripted dialogue.

UNCLE VANYA

Anton Chekhov
(A scene from Act III)

"I hope I like his drawing, it's so hard for me to pretend when I don't like something. I'm not a good liar . . . uh-oh, here he comes . . . I'm gonna strike that pose that displays both 'come-hither' and 'pure innocence.' It's a surefire winner . . ."

ASTROV
[*Enters with drawing*]
Hello, I understand you wanted to see
some of my artistry?

"Oh yeah, I'm just chafing at the bit to see your crude and amateurish attempts . . ."

YELENA
Yesterday, you assured me you would show
me your drawings. Are you available now?

"Of course you're available. You don't do anything all day except drool whenever I walk by . . ."

ASTROV
I'd love to!

"That was easy. It's gonna be fun watching you sweat as I accidentally on purpose expose my cleavage to you as I bend down to help spread your drawing on the table . . ."

[*He spreads the drawing on a nearby table and fixes it with stickpins. She helps him.*]

"Whoops, I dropped one of the stickpins. So I'm just going to have to bend down to pick it up, making sure I bend in such a way so as to make sure my firm buttocks are in your full view . . ."

ASTROV
Where were you born?

"What a weird thing to ask. Usually the sight of my butt and breasts doesn't inspire talk of my birthplace. Except, if you really think about it, one can't be born unless you have sex, so it does make sense, kind of . . ."

YELENA
In Petersburg.
"You're looking at me strangely. Why? Does the fact that I'm from a cosmopolitan, sophisticated, cultured city and you're a hick from the sticks have something to do with it? . . ."

ASTROV
And where did you go to school?
"Not a good line of questioning. I'm going to tell you and it's just going to make you feel bad. I mean, it's real hard to beat out having gone to the conservatory. But I'm not a liar (at least not about my credentials) so . . ."

YELENA
At the conservatory.
"There's that disgruntled face. I knew you wouldn't like the answer. My suggestion, my dear Astrov, is to stop asking leading questions. You'll be a lot happier for it . . ."

ASTROV
I doubt very much this will intrigue you in any way.
"You got that right. I don't know about the country, nor do I care about the country . . . but I'm really good at making men feel virile and smart . . ."

YELENA
Why not? You're right in assuming I don't know much about the country, but I'm well read.
"Nobody does better 'sincere' than me. You believe me, don't you? That I care about what you care about and I'm excited about learning at your scholarly feet, oh wise and boring one . . ."

ASTROV
Look here. It's a map of this area as it was fifty years ago. The green color indicates the forest. Half of the area was surfaced with forest. Where you see the red over the green— deer, wild goats and all sorts of wildlife were prevalent.
"Green, red, deer, goats, forests . . . who cares?"

Look at the third part and you'll see my rendition of how it is today. There's green, but it's sporadic. There is no wildlife.
"Speaking of wildlife, I'm hungry . . ."

You might say it's progress and I'd agree if the destroyed forests were making way for factories or schools.
"Whatever. I'll just keep nodding my head, and make him believe I'm really listening . . ."

ASTROV
[*cont.*]
But, no, there is a lot of unusable muddied land filled
with disease and people who are destitute.

"I hate disease and poor people . . ."

[*He looks at her askance . . .*]

"I hope there won't be a pop quiz later, because I haven't been listening . . ."

It seems to me that you have little interest
in any of this.

"Ya think?!"

YELENA
No, it's simply that I don't comprehend much of it.

"You know, I'm highly educated, so I hope the ignorant defense is convincing to you."

ASTROV
It doesn't take much to comprehend it, I just
don't think you're all that interested.

*"Yikes, you caught me. I've got to find another way to keep you bonding with me.
Perhaps I've underestimated you. You've got spunk. I find that sexy . . ."*

YELENA
Please excuse my lack of concentration as my
mind is someplace else. To be honest I wanted
to ask you something but I don't know how to
begin.

*"I'm going to string you along for a while. That always makes men nervous. You
don't have a clue what I'm going to ask. It could be anything. Boy, do you look
nervous. Gee, this is fun . . ."*

[*Pause*]
It's a question about someone you know.

"I'm really going to milk this. Hmm . . . Let me make it sound ominous. . . ."

Like friends, let's talk, being totally open with
each other and then forget we ever had this
conversation. What do you say?

*"I am so brilliant, look at you squirm. You look like a worm on the end of a fish-
ing hook. Either that or you're suspicious and I'm reading you all wrong. I love a
good challenge. This is better than chess . . ."*

ASTROV
All-right.

*"This could easily backfire. It's a risky question to ask you. What if you do love
Sonya? Then I would be the fool . . ."*

YELENA
It's about Sonya, my stepdaughter. What do
you think of her, do you like her?

"You're taking a long time to answer. This is not a good sign . . ."

ASTROV

I can admire her spirit.

"What the hell does that mean?! Are you messing with my mind? You're better at this than I thought. God, you're cute . . ."

YELENA

But do you like her as a woman?

"Now you can't wriggle out of answering this question, there's no obtuse way you can answer my genius choice of words . . ."

ASTROV
[*Pause*]

No.

"Yes! I knew it! Sonya's the loser. LOSER!! And now that that homely skank is out of the way, there's nothing keeping you from falling head over heels in love with me . . ."

YELENA
[*Kissing his hand*]

"We've come to the point of the game, my love, called "mixed message." I'm gonna get you all turned on by kissing your hand in that special Yelena way (I should have it patented) . . ."

You don't love her, I can see that from your
eyes. You know, she's suffering. Try to
understand that you must stop coming here.

". . . and then tell you to go away. What am I really trying to say to you? Can you figure it out? Every man loves a mystery woman, and they don't get any more mysterious than me!"

Ouch! I hate this, I feel like I've been carrying
the weight of the world on my shoulders.

"It's so hard being the kind of person that cares about others so much. Don't you think? I'm so compassionate . . ."

Anyway, it's done, thank God, so now we
can forget we ever had this conversation and move on.
You're a smart man, I'm sure you realize why you
must . . .

"Here comes the never-fails money-move . . . ooooh, I feel so faint, I might fall and you must hold me up, you big-hunk-of-man you . . ."
[*Pause*]
I feel all the blood rushing to my head.

"Come to me you moron, can't you see I'm about to faint?! Why aren't you moving—it can't get any simpler than this. This is your cue to have a legitimate reason to touch and hold me . . ."

ASTROV

If you had told me about her feelings a month or
"Hold me, come to me . . ."

two ago I might have thought about it . . . but if
she is sick at heart because of me then I guess

"Hold me, kiss me . . ."
there's no other recourse . . .
                    ASTROV
                    [*Pause*]
But tell me, why is it *you* had to ask me?
"Uh-oh, good question, you're really good at this game and that really turns me
on. How should I answer? I want to inspire you with my clever response. What
should I say? Nothing's coming to my mind . . . hurry up brain, do your stuff . . ."

[*He looks at her a moment.*]

Ohhhh, I get it!
". . . I'm just gonna play innocent. That should work . . ."

                    YELENA
What are you talking about?
"Are you buying my innocent act? You're not looking too sold on it . . . uh-oh,
better come up with another tactic . . ."

                    ASTROV
You know. Sure, Sonya may be in love, but
why is it you're asking the questions? Why do
you look so surprised? You know why I come
every day, you're very well aware of the effect
you have on me, you lovely "bird of prey."
"Bird of prey? Whoa, good word usage to describe what I'm doing. Good for you.
Bad for me. New ploy: indignant and offended . . ."

                    YELENA
Bird of prey! What are you talking about?!
"I can't look at you. If you see my face, you'll know I'm full of it . . ."

                    ASTROV
You are a gorgeous, frisky rascal . . . and I am
your victim. Well, you win, you can have me.
"You're going for it. Good move! You're so sexy when you're winning . . ."

[*He opens his arms and bows his head like a martyr on the cross.*]

"What's with the Jesus bit?! Talk about mixed messages. Is this about sex or religion?"

I give in, I'm here and ready to be consumed!
"You want me to come to *you*?! *You're* supposed to be all over *me*!"

                    YELENA
Have you gone mad?!
"No one's ever outsmarted me before. I'm really at a loss . . . and that gets me so
hot . . ."

ASTROV
Oh, you are so coy.

"You're relentless. How do I counter?!"

YELENA
I'm not as cunning or as cruel as you're making
me out to be. Honestly, I'm not.

"Believe me. Please believe me . . . you're such a good player and I'm feeling the heat, in more ways than one . . . I better get out of here before it ceases to be a game and we're rolling all over the floor making mad, passionate love. All I've been used to is old-man sex, and I bet you can last longer than three seconds . . . oh, boy, I gotta get out of here!"

[*She tries to leave. Astrov rushes to block her way.*]

ASTROV
I'll leave and I won't return. Just tell me . . .

[*He takes her hand and glances about to see if anyone is looking.*]

"You grabbing me is so strong, so arousing. I want you. I'm married. I can't. Yeah, I'm married to an old, old man, there are wrinkles in places you don't even want to know about . . . look at your clear skin—sure you've got broken blood vessels from way too much vodka, but who cares? I want you, badly! What if we get caught? Oh, that thought gets me even hotter. I'm doomed . . ."

Where should we meet? Hurry, someone may
catch us—please tell me where.
[*Whispering lustfully*]
Your hair smells wonderful. One little kiss,
please let me kiss you.

"Help me to be strong. I don't know how much longer I can pull away . . ."

YELENA
I beg of you . . .

"I'm not kidding. Help me get out of here before I get to that place when I can't say no any longer . . ."

ASTROV
[*Stops her from talking*]
No need to beg, I'm yours. You are so beautiful.
And your lovely hands, I need to kiss your hands.

"No, not the hands. I'm so sensitive there . . ."
[*He kisses her hands.*]

"It feels so good, too good, stop, please stop, I'm losing control . . ."

YELENA
Stop it, please stop . . . go . . .

"I gotta be strong, I can't lose control. Then I'll lose everything . . . what if someone shows up?!"

[*She pulls her hand away.*]

"I've got to get it together, I'm totally out of control! . . . oh, I want you . . . I won't rest 'til I have you. Oh, my God . . . you've got to stop! . . ."

ASTROV
You know it's inescapable, we are meant
to be together.

". . . Oh, what the hell. Come here. Take me . . ."

[*He kisses her and at that very moment Uncle Vanya shows up carrying a dozen roses and stops just inside the door. Neither Astrov nor Yelena see him.*]

YELENA
[*Not seeing Vanya*]
Don't. We shouldn't be doing this . . .

"Don't stop! This feels way too good! Hold me, touch me, engulf me . . ."

[*She lays her head on Astrov's chest.*]

ASTROV
At two o'clock meet me at the plantation.
Promise me you'll come.

"What's wrong with now?! Oh, I want you so much. Take me . . . wait a second, I feel eyes on me . . ."

[*Yelena sees Vanya looking at them.*]

"Oh no, this looks really bad. I've got to get away from you . . . It's not my fault, Vanya, Astrov forced me! . . ."

YELENA
Let go of me!

[*She forcefully pulls away from Astrov. Then she goes to the window.*]

"Should I lie? Should I cry rape? My husband is going to find out and divorce me and I'll have no money. Should I say I was drunk? Or, better yet, Astrov hypnotized me and made me do his bidding? I'll be left with nothing . . ."

[*Muttering to herself*]

                        YELENA
                        [*cont.*]
            This is just awful.

". . . *Temporary insanity? Or sleepwalking? Maybe I should come on to Vanya. He's always wanted me. Oh no, what if Vanya kills Astrov?! Or worse, what if he tries to kill me?!!!! . . .*"

[*Vanya carefully puts the roses on a nearby chair. Yelena continues to look out the window trying to figure out what she's going to say or do next as Astrov looks painfully guilty and attempts to cover up.*]

". . . *Amnesia? That's good. I could say I bumped my head or something. But if he doesn't believe me, I'll be homeless and without a clothing allowance! Maybe I can convince Vanya he didn't see what he thought he saw. My head was resting on Astrov's chest because he was checking for head lice . . . I mean, he is a doctor, he could've been doing something doctory . . . ahhh jeez, the world's gonna see me as a slut and a whore . . .*"

Continue the INNER MONOLOGUE until the director yells, "Cut!" or the curtain comes down, or until after you finish your exit.

INNER MONOLOGUE from Astrov's P.O.V.

Astrov's SCENE OBJECTIVE is *"to get you to fall in love with me."* Astrov's SCENE OBJECTIVE is steeped in obsession and sexuality. Create your INNER MONOLOGUE for Astrov with this in mind. Again, the following thoughts are merely suggestions based on what the character in the script might have as an INNER MONOLOGUE. You, however, must personalize your INNER MONOLOGUE to what makes sense to your SUBSTITUTIONS for Yelena, Sonya and Vanya, your personalized OBSTACLES and INNER OBJECTS. How you manifest your specific INNER MONOLOGUE will fluctuate depending upon how you individually deal with life—thoughts that emanate from your own unique history and background.

UNCLE VANYA

Anton Chekhov
(A scene from Act III)

"*I hope you like my drawings, and please don't think they're stupid and crude. I mean, you're more sophisticated than me, and my drawings may make me look like a rube . . .*"

ASTROV
[*Enters with drawing*]
Hello, I understand you wanted to see
some of my artistry?

"Maybe 'artistry' is too strong a word. Sounds like I'm full of myself. Maybe you're patronizing me when you said you wanted to see my drawing yesterday. Maybe you have no interest at all and I'm looking way too desperate."

YELENA
Yesterday, you assured me you would show
me your drawings. Are you available now?

"Oh, yeah, I always just stand around with my drawing in my hand. Of course I'm available. I think that they're pretty damn good. Maybe you'll be so impressed that you'll like me, maybe even fall in love with me, marry me and have my babies . . ."

ASTROV
I'd love to!

"Whoa, whoa, whoa, way too eager . . . and too desperate, eager and desperate. Now that's an appealing combo. How can she resist. Just call me 'el blurto'! . . ."

[*He spreads the drawing on a nearby table and fixes it with stick-pins. She helps him.*]

"You're hovering over me and accidentally touching me. Do you want me sexually, or are you just being helpful and the touches are truly incidental? Well, I better figure it out soon because the conversation has stopped and I'm looking really dumb. I better say something, but I don't know what to say. What to say? What to say? . . ."

Where were you born?

"Well, that was really stupid. I'm a stupid, stupid man. 'Where were you born?'! Could I have asked anything more boring? Note to self: next time, bring my brain . . ."

YELENA
In Petersburg.

"You come from the city. You're cosmopolitan and sophisticated and let's not forget married . . . and I'm not. Why would you want to be with me?! As far as you're concerned, I'm just a country bumpkin. Although I am a doctor. Perhaps I can outdo you with my educational background . . ."

ASTROV
And where did you go to school?

Oh yeah! There's no way you're going beat me, no way in hell . . ."

YELENA
At the conservatory.

"Ohhhkay, maybe not. Why couldn't it be any place but the heralded conservatory?! Boy oh boy, a shot of vodka would feel real good right about now . . ."

ASTROV
I doubt very much this will intrigue you in any way.

"How can anything that interests me interest you?! Why should it? You're young and hot and I'm drunk and sweaty. Why did I start this conversation?! I must be more interesting than your wrinkled, crotchety, impotent (and I should know, I'm his doctor) husband. What am I doing?! You're married and my best friend is in love with you. God help me, I'm a louse . . . a very horny louse . . . but a louse nonetheless . . ."

YELENA
Why not? You're right in assuming I don't know much about the country, but I'm well read.

"Are you patronizing me? Huh? Huh?! Ah, what does it matter, as long as you're here and I'm here, who knows? Maybe you'll like what I have to say. I mean, it is exciting to me. So here goes . . ."

ASTROV
Look here. It's a map of this area as it was fifty years ago. The green color indicates the forest. Half of the area was surfaced with forest. Where you see the red over the green— deer, wild goats and all sorts of wildlife were prevalent.

"This is good stuff. I love talking about it. It's controversial yet benevolent. Makes me look real smart . . ."

Look at the third part and you'll see my rendition of how it is today. There's green, but it's sporadic. There is no wildlife.

"This is the best part, you're gonna love this . . ."

You might say it's progress and I'd agree if the destroyed forests were making way for factories or schools. But, no, there is a lot of unusable muddied land filled with disease and people who are destitute.

"You look so bored. Why did I go on and on? You must think I'm a babbling loser. You hate me. I hate me . . ."

[He looks at her askance . . .]

It seems to me that you have little interest in any of this.

"How could you have any interest in this? Why did I think you would? What am I, nuts?! Ooooh, I love the way your breasts jiggle when you walk . . ."

YELENA
No, it's simply that I don't comprehend much of it.

"Yeah right. It's not like I'm explaining rocket science here . . ."

ASTROV

It doesn't take much to comprehend it, I just
don't think you're all that interested.

*"That's telling ya. No fool I. Now you're going to think I'm strong, not a wuss,
because I stood up to you. On the other hand, what if you take it badly and leave?!
Oh no, I wish I could take it back. Don't go, please don't go . . ."*

YELENA

Please excuse my lack of concentration as my
mind is someplace else. To be honest I wanted
to ask you something but I don't know how to
begin.

*"This question could be really, really bad . . . Maybe you're going to ask me, 'Why
do you keep coming to visit so often when nobody is ill? Doesn't anyone else
require your services?' Why am I here all the time? 'Cuz you got me wrapped
around your nasty little finger, you. . . . Okay, Astrov, that was a little harsh,
wait and see what she's gonna ask, don't assume anything . . ."*

[*Pause*]

It's a question about someone you know.
Like friends, let's talk, being totally open with
each other, and then forget we ever had this
conversation. What do you say?

"You want to forget we had this conversation? This can't be good . . ."

ASTROV

All-right.

"Please don't prolong the agony. I'm dying here. Ask me already . . ."

YELENA

It's about Sonya, my stepdaughter. What do
you think of her, do you like her?

*"Is this a trap? What if I don't answer in the right way? Then you'll hate me.
Should I lie? Tell you I like Sonya and make you jealous? . . . That could backfire
big time. Or should I tell the truth and let you know I'm available? More than
available, desperate, in fact. Oh, that's real attractive. Every woman loves the
stank sweat of a desperate man. Yeah, right. Think, Astrov, think . . . okay, here
goes—I'll try to respond in a way that's real vague . . ."*

ASTROV

I can admire her spirit.

*"That's good. Nice, but noncommittal. Please accept this and change the subject to
something else, like how handsome and sexy you find me . . ."*

YELENA

But do you like her as a woman?

*"What do you want me to say? Give me a hint. Why can't you make this easy on
me? My life is hard enough. What if I make the wrong choice? I suck at tests. Oh
boy, could I use a shot or two of vodka . . . Okay, answer now, vodka later . . . I'll
tell you the truth and hope it flies . . ."*

ASTROV
[*Pause*]
No.
"Do you like my answer? Do ya, huh, do ya?"

YELENA
[*Kissing his hand*]
You don't love her, I can see that from your
eyes. You know, she's suffering. Try to
understand that you must stop coming here.
"Nothing like the ol' mixed message. You kiss my hand yet you tell me to leave.
What do you want and how should I respond?!"

Ouch! I hate this, I feel like I've been carrying
the weight of the world on my shoulders. Anyway,
it's done, thank God, so now we can forget we
ever had this conversation and move on. You're
a smart man, I'm sure you realize why you must . . .
"This can't be good. You see me as a weight on your shoulders, not as a virile
man . . ."
[*Pause*]
I feel all the blood rushing to my head.
"Yet you seem to want me to hold you . . . but what if I'm wrong and you push me
away?! Woman, you are so hard to read and I am so aroused . . ."

ASTROV
If you had told me about her feelings a month or
two ago I might have thought about it . . . but if
she is sick at heart because of me then I guess
there's no other recourse . . .

"I'm babbling and babbling. I sound like a stupid moron, but wait a minute . . .
you didn't have to ask me this question . . . maybe you _do_ like me . . ."

But tell me, why is it you had to ask me?
"Come on. Admit it. You like me. You want me just as much as I want you,
right?! . . ."

[*He looks at her a moment.*]

"You're not answering. That means you're too afraid to answer. I hope this means
you want me as much as I want you. I'm going for it . . ."

Ohhhh, I get it!
"Just say it. You have the hots for me! Oh yes you do . . ."

YELENA
What are you talking about?
"Don't pretend you don't know. You know what I'm talking about. You want me,
you want me bad . . ."

ASTROV

You know. Sure, Sonya may be in love, but
why is it you're asking the questions? Why do
you look so surprised? You know why I come
every day, you're very well aware of the effect
you have on me, you lovely "bird of prey."

"I'd like to feel my lips against yours, hungrily tasting you, you wanting me like the tigress that you are . . ."

YELENA

Bird of prey! What are you talking about?!

". . . I want you squirming against me, begging me for more and more, grrrrr . . ."

ASTROV

You are a gorgeous, frisky rascal . . . and I am
your victim. Well, you win, you can have me.

[*He opens his arms and bows his head like a martyr on the cross.*]

". . . Come to me. Hold me. Touch me. Eat me up . . ."

I give in, I'm here and ready to be consumed!

". . . What's taking you so long? I'm starting to look insane just standing here, arms akimbo, looking like Jesus on the cross. And how the hell do I get out of this position?! . . ."

YELENA

Have you gone mad?!

". . . Uh-oh, you do think I'm nuts. Or maybe you're just playing 'hard to get' . . ."

ASTROV

Oh, you are so coy.

"That gets me even hotter. Oooooh, I want you soooo much . . ."

YELENA

I'm not as cunning or as cruel as you're making
me out to be. Honestly, I'm not.

[*She tries to leave. Astrov rushes to block her way.*]

"You can't leave. If you do, I'll never get another chance. I've gotta stop you or else I'll never get another chance to make you mine . . . and besides, I'm so horny . . ."

ASTROV

I'll leave and I won't return. Just tell me . . .

"I'll promise you anything you want . . ."

[*He takes her hand and glances about to see if anyone is looking.*]

ASTROV
[*cont.*]
"... Uh-oh, what if someone walks in and interrupts? I hate when that happens. Hurry up. We don't have much time. Tell me. Where do you want go to get down and dirty? ..."

Where should we meet? Hurry, someone may
catch us—please tell me where.
"Is that perfume or you? Oh, baby, I want to eat you up. ..."

[*Whispering lustfully*]
Your hair smells wonderful. One little kiss,
please let me kiss you.
"Your body, your hair, your luscious lips are really getting to me! Press your full lips against mine, kiss me like you've never kissed anyone before ... please, please, please, please ..."

YELENA
I beg of you ...
"Oh yeah! You're begging now, huh? You want me, huh? ..."

ASTROV
[*Stops her from talking*]
No need to beg, I'm yours. You are so beautiful.
And your lovely hands, I need to kiss your hands.
"I could get away with saying hands. That's safe to say, but what I'd really like to wrap my lips around is ..."

[*He kisses her hands.*]
"Oh yeah, don't stop now ..."

YELENA
Stop it, please stop ... go ...

[*She pulls her hand away.*]

"No, no, no, don't do that! Don't pull away! You're a Leo and I'm a Scorpio—astrologically we're supposed to be together!"

ASTROV
You know it's inescapable, we are meant
to be together.
"What if I'm wrong about you wanting me?! And what if you tell Alexander and Vanya that I've been coming on to you?! What to do? What to do? ... Oh, those luscious lips. I want to devour them, suck them, lick them ... Oh, what the hell? I'm going in!"

[*He kisses her and at that very moment Uncle Vanya shows up carrying a dozen roses and stops just inside the door. Neither Astrov nor Yelena see him.*]

                              YELENA
                        [*Not seeing Vanya*]
                  Don't. We shouldn't be doing this . . .

"Come to me. Be with me. Come on. You want to. You know you do . . ."

          [*She lays her head on Astrov's chest.*]

"Ahh, a little taste of heaven . . ."

                              ASTROV
                  At two o'clock meet me at the plantation.
                  Promise me you'll come.

"I'm so close. I can see it in your eyes. You can't wait for two o'clock. You love me
and I love you. And Astrov, you stud, you are gonna get lucky . . ."

          [*Yelena sees Vanya looking at them.*]

". . . Wait. What are you looking at? Oh no, it's Vanya. He's got rage issues and
is gonna kill me and then what will I do?! . . ."

                              YELENA
                        Let go of me!
"How am I gonna explain this?! This looks really, really bad . . ."

          [*She forcefully pulls away from Astrov. Then she goes to the
          window.*]

"Why are you making me look like the bad guy, like I forced you or
something?! . . ."

                        [*Muttering to herself*]
                  This is just awful.

"I gotta claim innocence, but I look guilty as hell. What should I say or do that
will fix it for both of us?! Vanya, what have you seen? What have you heard?
When in hell did you come in and how'd I miss it?! It's gotta be that last shot of
vodka because otherwise I'm usually very observant . . ."

          [*Vanya carefully puts the roses on a nearby chair. Yelena continues
          to look out the window trying to figure out what she's going to say
          or do next as Astrov looks painfully guilty and attempts to cover up.*]

"I could say I was so drunk that I didn't know what I was doing. He's witnessed
some of my infamous blackouts. Or I could say it was a parlor game we were
playing. Or she came to me with some aches and pains and I was just examining
her. Being the family doctor that could fly. Except what I was doing didn't look
very medicinal . . . I gotta come up with something believable so that I can be
Yelena's hero and still have a chance to get her to love me . . . there's gotta be a way.
Here's one that just might work. I could say, 'I was warming her up for you . . .'"

INNER MONOLOGUE keeps something going on behind your eyes, further establishing a scripted character into a flesh-and-blood human being.

Tool #11: PREVIOUS CIRCUMSTANCES

This is a character's history that makes them the kind of person they are today.

With PREVIOUS CIRCUMSTANCES you must first discover your character's history as it relates to the script. Then you connect the script's PREVIOUS CIRCUMSTANCES to parallel emotional experiences from your own life, so that you can identify with your character with such insight and depth that you ultimately "become" the character.

PREVIOUS CIRCUMSTANCES for Yelena

The script's PREVIOUS CIRCUMSTANCES.

In mid-nineteenth-century Russia, being married to a wealthy and well-regarded man was the best a woman could aspire to. Despite her beauty, upper-class education and manners, Yelena didn't marry at the age most young women did. For some reason, she waited. As a result, with the feared label of spinster nipping at her heels, she married Alexander, a man who is at least twice her age, is a retired professor, a hypochondriac, acerbic, stubborn and asexual. And to Yelena's dismay, her husband chooses to move back to the country, a place she considers to be backward and remote.

Alexander has the means to be quite comfortable, but he is not uber-rich. So, Yelena's motivation for marrying him would not be to amass huge sums of money. Nor is she with Alexander for his looks. If Alexander was ever handsome, it has withered away with age. Then why would she marry this particular man? We must assume that Yelena is drawn to him because he is well-respected. Why is respect something that Yelena craves? Given her behavior over the time that has elapsed in the script, we can say Yelena is willful, self-centered, obstinate, mischievous, spirited, unrestrained, fiery—a she-devil. What brought this behavior on? Obviously something she did or had done to her has colored her fortunate beginnings, making her somehow disreputable and no longer worthy of getting a good husband. So she married the best she could. Someone who may be old and ugly but was a highly regarded professor, someone from whom she could earn vicarious respectability through association.

Here are some of the PREVIOUS CIRCUMSTANCES you must personalize.

> 1. **Script's PREVIOUS CIRCUMSTANCE: Yelena's history of self-destructive behavior.**
> **Personalized PRIOR CIRCUMSTANCES suggestions:** In one's zest to live life to the fullest, one often jumps in head-first without considering the ramifications. Looking back at some of those specific events when you have personally experienced a backlash as a result of an attempt to create excitement in your life, see becoming Yelena as a continuation of your misadventures. What Yelena does in the time frame that takes place in *Uncle Vanya* is not new behavior. She has been getting herself and those foolish enough to be around her in hot water for a long time. The PREVIOUS CIRCUMSTANCES you've paralleled to the scripted character could be:
>
> - A history of numerous sexual liaisons
> - A history of stealing
> - A history of irresponsible partying
> - A history of drug and/or alcohol abuse
> - A history of pathological lying
> - Getting pregnant and having abortion(s)
> - Getting caught having an affair or having numerous affairs with married men.
>
> Now, consider what happened as a result of your undisciplined behavior. This may have meant getting a bad reputation, jail, pregnancy, a lack of trust from those around you, loss of a mate, loss of friendships, loss of a job, others seeing you in a bad light so they don't even give you a chance to be a friend, a mate or a job opportunity.
>
> 2. **Script's PREVIOUS CIRCUMSTANCE: The time period's expectations of a woman's need to be married.**

Personalized PRIOR CIRCUMSTANCES suggestions:
You have to duplicate the kind of high pressure to get married
that would force the need to enter a loveless marriage, as well
as the need for "extra-curricular" activities (wink-wink). The
following are some possibilities for creating a similar PREVI-
OUS CIRCUMSTANCES from your own life:

- Social demands haven't changed that much since the mid-
  nineteenth-century. There's still huge social status associated with having a boyfriend, fiancé or husband. Friends
  and family make too big a deal over the proposal, the en-
  gagement ring, the bridal shower and the marriage ceremony. If you are a woman who is unattached, never been
  married, or don't have any prospects of getting attached, it's
  likely you're looked down upon as someone to pity and put
  in the category of don't-invite or as a must-set-up-with-nice-
  doctor-or-lawyer emergency case. This set of PREVIOUS CIR-
  CUMSTANCES will give you the need to change your single
  status ASAP.
- You are married, but had originally gotten married out of
  pressurized PREVIOUS CIRCUMSTANCES like pregnancy,
  no one else around, who you really wanted wasn't available,
  planned by the family, expected because you had been going
  together for so long or all your girlfriends are married so you
  said yes to the first guy who asked you. If so, use these PRE-
  VIOUS CIRCUMSTANCES from your life as the impetus to
  risk everything to go after your SUBSTITUTION for Astrov.
- Perhaps your present relationship sprung from love, but
  now you've grown apart, you're different from one another
  and bored. If so, use the past events that illustrate this as the
  PREVIOUS CIRCUMSTANCES that would make you feel it
  necessary to get your SUBSTITUTION for Astrov to fall in
  love with you so you can *mix it up.* . . .
- Maybe the PREVIOUS CIRCUMSTANCES in your life don't
  include the importance of long-term or marital relationships, but in your case you do have the need to prove your
  worth in a long-term relationship with a job. Personal useful
  PREVIOUS CIRCUMSTANCES in this venue could be: a history of problems holding onto a job, always being skipped over
  when it comes time for raises or promotions, a background

of many interviews (auditions) with the tally sheet for jobs booked at zero. This would make you want to risk your marriage with Alexander (who would be a SUBSTITUTION for a boss, producer or some work-related authority who isn't presently satisfying) for Astrov (who would be a SUBSTITUTION for someone that could give you a job or the kind of career that you dream of).

3. **Script's PREVIOUS CIRCUMSTANCE: Yelena's past of being shocking, outrageous, scandalous, shameful and socially out of control as a way to feel alive.**

   Personalized PRIOR CIRCUMSTANCE suggestions: What is it that you have historically done that might risk your security, but feel compelled to do anyway so as to keep your life from being dull and monotonous? This could be PREVIOUS CIRCUMSTANCES of your own such as:

- Having extramarital affairs
- Gossiping in massive doses
- A problem with kleptomania (thievery can produce adrenaline)
- Constantly blurting out shock-speak
- Being prone to inordinate amounts of swearing
- Being loud and obnoxious in inappropriate places
- Brazen joking (and you may even be funny, but too much of a good thing . . .)
- Dressing indecently or simply for shock value

4. **Script's PREVIOUS CIRCUMSTANCE: Yelena's background of manipulation and game-playing in relationships.**

   Personalized PRIOR CIRCUMSTANCE suggestions: Relationships aren't solely motivated by love. We've all had PREVIOUS CIRCUMSTANCES in which we sought out a relationship for other purposes that were reasonable to us but unclear to those looking in from the outside. Reasons such as:

- Security
- Money
- Getting a job
- Social position

- Power
- Because someone you compete with wants him
- Good looks
- Loneliness

Look at some of the friendships and relationships you have instigated because of factors other than undying love as your PREVIOUS CIRCUMSTANCES in order to make the part of you that is manipulative come from a real place when becoming Yelena.

5. **Script's PREVIOUS CIRCUMSTANCE: Yelena's inordinate need to make men love her.** Where alcohol is Astrov's addiction, *"love"*—and bushels of it—is Yelena's drug of choice. Yelena has Alexander, who loves her, Vanya, who is clearly smitten, Sonya, who is caught under her spell as a friend and confidante, and Astrov, who's constant presence in the house since her arrival can only mean one thing—he loves her, too. This didn't occur by accident—Yelena needs people to fall for her, and she's obsessed with the drive to make that happen.

   Personalized PRIOR CIRCUMSTANCE suggestions: What are your PREVIOUS CIRCUMSTANCES that make you personally *need* people to fall in love with you? Could it be:

- Events of abandonment
- Emotionally nondemonstrative parents
- Being the "reject" kid when you were growing up
- A previous mate relationship where you were the one *more* in love and got severely hurt because of it
- You always thought you were ugly and need constant attention to prove otherwise
- You were horribly abused as a child

Remember events and PREVIOUS CIRCUMSTANCES in which you were especially needy for love. Let this motivate your behavior as Yelena.

PREVIOUS CIRCUMSTANCES for Astrov

The script's PREVIOUS CIRCUMSTANCES.

Astrov comes from Russia at a time when changing your career or social position was nearly impossible. He is a country doctor who is always going to practice and live in the country. In the nineteenth century, it was the practice to make house calls, which were often miles apart, and the constant traveling made a doctor's social life difficult. In this era, age was also an issue. Having been a confirmed bachelor for a long time doesn't bode well for a future of matrimony. All the good girls his age are spoken for, and the other women—spinsters—are unmarried for a reason. He is alone with no prospects for change. But he still wants a wife and family, and this desire is growing. Unfortunately, despite this desire, Astrov thinks his chances for a happy domestic life are slim. This makes him cynical. Because of his ever-growing pessimism, Astrov has transferred his primal need to love and protect a family to a focus on loving and protecting the environment.

We can presuppose that Astrov has probably had commitment issues at the key marrying junctures in his life. It's also important to note that he has the opportunity to have a wife and child with the clearly available Sonya, but chooses instead to fall in love with the unattainable Yelena.

The other characters in the play talk about how much he drinks, and he indeed appears to have a drinking problem, something that clearly isn't new to him. Alcoholism is usually learned or genetically motivated from primal sources. Here it may also be a way for him to manage his desires and his reality.

Here are some of the PREVIOUS CIRCUMSTANCES that you must personalize.

1. **Script's PREVIOUS CIRCUMSTANCE: Astrov chose medicine as his career path.**
   Personalized PRIOR CIRCUMSTANCE suggestions: Whatever career we choose, we do so for a reason. Our careers are what defines us. You must find events from your past that would drive you to want to become a doctor. Perhaps:

- A parent or mentor is in the field of medicine, and you want to please and emulate someone whom you love and respect.
- You have had a loved one (a parent, sibling, friend, etc.) die from an illness and at the time felt helpless to do anything about it. Becoming a doctor would satisfy you by offering you the power to do something about it if it were to happen again today.
- A parent who had a blue-collar job and wants you to have more out of life than just a daily grind. Becoming a doctor would give that parent a sense of pride in you because you have risen above the family "blue-collar" legacy.

2. **Script's PREVIOUS CIRCUMSTANCE: Stuck in a lower social strata—geographically, educationally and socially.** This will affect Astrov's ability to go after Yelena, who bests him in all these areas.
   Personalized PRIOR CIRCUMSTANCE suggestions:

- You came from or still live in a small, backwoods town. Think about past experiences that remind you of your feelings of social inferiority (such as times you were humiliated for your way of speaking, dressing or your lack of savvy).
- You came from or still live in a part of the city that would be considered poor, the ghetto or ethnically segregated. Remember events when being poor or ethnic caused you emotional pain, or perhaps even caused you to get into physical battles.
- Your family came from or you and your family still live in a city or town in which your family was castigated because they were the sole residents representing an unpopular racial or religious group (the only black family in an all-white neighborhood, the only Muslim family in a Jewish part of town, etc.) and all of the degradation that came with it.
- You are a member of a castigated minority group (African American, Hispanic, Asian, Arabic, Jewish, etc.). Use the history of bigotry you've experienced.
- You grew up with poverty, remembering the events of your past that affect you today (going to bed hungry, being made fun of at school because of your shabby clothes, etc.).

- You were not formally educated, or you were a bad student. Think of the specific PREVIOUS CIRCUMSTANCES that caused you shame, such as having been constantly tutored, mocked by fellow students and teachers, consistently given bad grades that your parents berated you over, etc.

3. **Script's PREVIOUS CIRCUMSTANCE: Past opportunities to meet women are limited, creating a currently desperate and lonely Astrov.**
   Personalized PRIOR CIRCUMSTANCES suggestions: You have to find emotionally similar PREVIOUS CIRCUMSTANCES from your life that make you feel that you have limited opportunities.

- You have a history of feeling unattractive in some way (too fat, too skinny, blemished skin, bad hair, racial differences, too short, too tall, plain or homely, etc.).
- You have had a long relationship or marriage that has broken up and you're out of practice, feeling unprepared and awkward.
- You have a history of women who just wanted to be friends, excluding any other form of relationship.
- You have been in a long-term relationship that has been so abusive that you're feeling insecure that all future mates are going to treat you the same way.
- You are homosexual, and being around a woman in that way makes you feel uncomfortable.
- You haven't had a relationship in a very long time and don't have a lot of hope that that's going to change.

4. **Script's PREVIOUS CIRCUMSTANCES: Mid-1800s in Russia—age issues revolving around finding a mate have produced Astrov's present hopelessness.**
   Personalized PRIOR CIRCUMSTANCE suggestions:

- Even today, it is a common perception that the older you get the fewer options you have. The field of choices for a mate, career and social circumstances narrow. Taking any age-riddled events that have caused you to feel hopeless in making changes in your life, elaborate in detail on what changes you'd like to make and how difficult it would be to do so given your current age. For example: You've been working as an electrical engineer, which took some training and time. In order to make a change to be an actor, you'd have to start from the bottom, and you're always fearful that the younger actors will take precedence over you in the casting process. Use PREVIOUS CIRCUMSTANCES from your own life—actual experiences that make this true.

• What if actual age is not your problem? Hopelessness doesn't have to necessarily stem from age. Your personal PREVIOUS CIRCUMSTANCES may include the experience that, no matter how hard you've tried, you've failed at most of your attempts to succeed. It could be consistently bad grades in school, friendships that always seem to turn on you, girls who time after time ridicule you and won't give you the time of day, being fired from job after job. Use personal PREVIOUS CIRCUMSTANCE events from your life that seem to thwart you at every turn.

5. **Script's PREVIOUS CIRCUMSTANCE: Astrov's history of commitment problems.**

    Personalized PRIOR CIRCUMSTANCES suggestions: Personalize how commitment has been a problem for you by looking at important events and experiences that may have caused you to have a sense of leeriness and fear when it comes to making the "Big C" (otherwise known as *commitment*).

• Perhaps you have been brought up in a family that went through a messy divorce and you don't want to repeat in your life what you witnessed growing up, and therefore commitment scares you.

• You watched your parents stay together, but not get along. You don't want to commit to someone and feel smothered in a bad relationship the same way your parents were—so you avoid commitment.

• You personally have had a history of bad relationships and don't want to repeat history with yet another painful, devastating commitment.

• You watched your parents, who are loving and amazing, give up their dreams and aspirations to support a family, and you

don't want that to happen to you. Because of this, you subconsciously feel that commitment will always equal drudg-
ery and an elimination of your dreams.

6. **Script's PREVIOUS CIRCUMSTANCE: Astrov's background
and the reason for his obsession with environmental
issues.**
   Personalized PRIOR CIRCUMSTANCE suggestions:

• Astrov's love and concern for the country is not new to him.
  A devotion like his increases over time—largely because
  he doesn't have anywhere else to put all those feelings of
  passion. People are not arbitrarily caught up in an issue unless they feel motivated by personal PREVIOUS CIRCUM-
  STANCES. You have to look at yourself and consider what
  are you obsessed with rectifying and why. A person who is
  caught up in changing drunken driving laws is usually someone who's had some past tragedy caused by a drunken
  driver. A person who is troubled by the way the mentally
  handicapped are dealt with usually has a family member
  who is disabled and has witnessed their abuse firsthand.
  Whatever issue you have chosen as an INNER OBJECT for
  the theme contained in Astrov's "drawings," think about
  your own personal history (PREVIOUS CIRCUMSTANCES)
  that would cause you to be concerned about your issue as
  Astrov is of his.

7. **Script's PREVIOUS CIRCUMSTANCE: Astrov's alcoholism.**
   Personalized PRIOR CIRCUMSTANCES suggestions:
   First you have to identify the "drug" that is an addiction for
   you. What is the thing you do to endure life's torments?
   Overeating? Drugs—prescription or street? Sex? Sleeping?
   Isolation? Pathological lying? Computer obsession? Then elab-
   orate how and why you have a problem in this area by looking
   at your own PREVIOUS CIRCUMSTANCES.

• If you're a Valium addict, remember the event that triggered the first time you ever took it, and what specifically
  happened later to create an escalating problem. Was it

trauma, or was it just rising insecurity coming from daily events that became increasingly harder to deal with? How did you know about Valium in the first place? Was your mother, a role model, someone predisposed to taking it? Or did a friend or lover have a problem with it and it seemed to work for him or her? Did it begin as a peer group activity and end with you being the only one who continued after the phase was over for everyone else? Understanding and knowing your PREVIOUS CIRCUMSTANCES in this area will determine how your personal addiction was learned and/or genetically induced.

PREVIOUS CIRCUMSTANCES put the final layer on becoming a living, breathing, three-dimensional human being. You are Astrov. Or you are Yelena. At this point there should be no distinction between you and the character. All that's left to do is to . . .

Tool #12: LET IT GO

Trust the work that you've done.

Trust that you've created a strong foundation for spontaneity to emerge. Trust the choices you've made. Trust . . . and LET IT GO.

Practical Application:
Three-or-More-Person Scenes

What to Do When There Are More Than Two Characters

In a three-or-more-person scene, each character works with one SCENE OBJECTIVE and then selects a hot person in the scene to focus on. A hot person is the person your character wants to win their SCENE OBJECTIVE from. This doesn't always mean that this is the person your character is talking to or even necessarily knows. This is the person your character wants to most *affect*. All the other people in the scene are *witting* or *unwitting* allies in gaining your SCENE OBJECTIVE.

Let's look at another scene from *Uncle Vanya* so that you can have a more comprehensive view of how the hot person, unwitting/witting ally system works.

The following scene takes place after the disastrous seduction scene between Astrov and Yelena. Vanya is extremely distressed—he, too, loves Yelena and can't believe that his good friend Astrov could and in fact, did, come on to her. So he decides that making a big show of "attempting" suicide is his best revenge. Being a typical Russian with a flair for the dramatic, Vanya figures that if he uses Astrov's morphine as his tool of self-destruction, he'd be making the statement that it's all Astrov's fault. He has no intention of really killing himself. He's making a point—a theatrical point, but a point nonetheless. If he uses Astrov's medicine, which is meant to kill pain, as a way to kill himself (and therefore his personal pain) he's making a grand gesture that would make Dostoevsky proud. Astrov learns of this and, completely believing that Vanya means to do away with himself because of what Astrov has done, tries to get Vanya to give back the morphine. Sonya enters mid-conversation.

UNCLE VANYA
Anton Chekhov
(A scene from Act III)

ASTROV

You took a little bottle of morphine out of my medicine bag.
[*Pause*]
Listen to me! If you're hell-bent on killing yourself, go outside and shoot yourself. Surrender the morphine or everyone will assume I gave it to you and will accuse me of doing you in. As your friend, I really don't want to have to perform an autopsy on you. Do you think I'd like that?!

[*Sonya enters.*]

VANYA

Leave me alone.

ASTROV
[*To Sonya*]
Sonya, your uncle has stolen some morphine from out of my medicine bag and won't give it back to me. Tell him he's being stupid. I don't have time for all this foolishness, I really have to be going.

SONYA

Uncle Vanya, did you take the morphine from Astrov?

ASTROV

He took it. I'm sure of it.

SONYA

Admit it, Uncle! Why do you want to frighten us?
[*Gently*] Give it up, Uncle Vanya. My life is far worse than yours, but I'm not feeling sorry for myself. I will keep going in spite of my pain and will continue to do so until the day I naturally die. You must endure as well, Uncle.
[*Pause*]
Give it to us! You are a nice person and you mean well, so I know you will return the morphine. You have to try to overcome your sadness, you've just got to . . .

[*Vanya opens a drawer on the table and takes out the bottle of morphine and hands it to Astrov.*]

VANYA
Then take it. [*To Sonya*] Now, let's get to work
immediately, because if I don't have something
to occupy my mind I will not be able to survive.

SONYA
Yes, let's work. As soon as father and Yelena go,
we will get back to work.

[*She attempts to clean the mess of papers on the table, but is too upset to do much good.*]

Everything is such a mess.

ASTROV
I've really got to get going.

[*He packs the morphine in a safe place in his medicine bag, collects himself and exits.*]

Three-Person Scene from Astrov's P.O.V.

If Vanya kills himself with Astrov's morphine, then Astrov will have a guilty conscience for the rest of his life, because it is his fault that Vanya is so upset. Astrov seducing Yelena—in Vanya's home, no less—was a callous act. Astrov had to know that Vanya was obsessed with Yelena. Vanya never made a secret of it. And a good friend just doesn't do that to a good friend. Astrov rightfully feels guilty, and since guilt is a very unpleasant feeling to hold on to, it would make sense that his SCENE OBJECTIVE would be "*to get you to absolve me of my guilt.*" Vanya is the hot person that he wants his SCENE OBJECTIVE from, because Vanya is the only person who could really absolve Astrov. By getting Vanya to return the morphine, with Sonya's help, he's absolved his guilt by saving Vanya's life—with witnesses to prove his virtue. By making Sonya a witness as well as a willing participant in retrieving the morphine (and keeping Vanya alive), she becomes his witting ally.

- **Astrov's SCENE OBJECTIVE:** "*to get you to absolve me of my guilt*"

- **Hot person:** (that you want your SCENE OBJECTIVE from):
  Vanya
- **Witting ally:** Sonya

Three-Person Scene from Vanya's P.O.V.

Vanya feels terribly betrayed by his friend, Astrov. It's only natural for Vanya to feel vindictive, to make Astrov feel the agony he feels would be righteous payback. Thus, Vanya's SCENE OBJECTIVE would be *"to make you feel guilty,"* with Astrov being the hot person he wants his SCENE OBJECTIVE from. Vanya chooses the dark and dramatic to make his point. He also needs an audience for his fabulous death scene as well as a witness who will see his side and turn against Astrov. This is where Sonya comes in. However, Sonya doesn't support Vanya's flamboyant and theatrical show of pain, thereby making her an unwitting ally.

- **Vanya's SCENE OBJECTIVE:** *"to make you feel guilty"*
- **Hot person:** Astrov
- **Unwitting ally:** Sonya

Three-Person Scene from Sonya's P.O.V.

Sonya wants Astrov, badly, and has for a long, long time. She's a woman with a mission: get Astrov to love her at any cost. She believes if she supports Astrov, no matter what he asks of her, she just might earn his love. Clearly Sonya's SCENE OBJECTIVE is *"to get you to love me,"* with Astrov being her very hot person. Vanya, who currently hates his good buddy Astrov, is hardly going to willingly aid Sonya in her pursuit, thereby making Vanya the unwitting ally. Unwitting, as well, because the more Vanya protests and the more Sonya stands by Astrov (not Vanya), the better she looks to Astrov. Vanya doesn't fare well in this dynamic.

- **Sonya's SCENE OBJECTIVE:** *"to get you* (Astrov) *to love me"*
- **Hot person:** Astrov
- **Unwitting ally:** Vanya

Using the hot person, witting/unwitting ally system allows you to focus on one SCENE OBJECTIVE. This keeps you from the confusion of trying to recall many SCENE OBJECTIVES for many people and more accurately represents what we really do when we are in the midst of more than two people.

Epilogue

························

A Word About Auditioning

There's so much myth and mystique about the auditioning process. There are tricks that actors feel they need to pull off, rules that are supposed to be followed. The bottom line and key to auditioning, however, is good acting. That's it. It's as simple as that. This is what the casting director, producers and director are looking for.

Do your script analysis as detailed in Part I. When you're in the auditioning room, let go of all the work, trust that it will be retained and focus on your SCENE OBJECTIVE, so that you have a forward motion and through-line. Let the words and behavior flow naturally, spontaneously.

Don't just pick up the cues. The behavior is more important than the words—it will, in fact, drive the words. If you pick up the cues too quickly, you're not allowing for the natural thought process it takes to sort out what you've just heard. Spoken interchange goes like this: First you listen. Then you take it in and respond internally. Then you figure out how you want to respond to what was said (or done). And then, and only then, do you speak. If you're in such a hurry to get to the words, behavior can't happen.

Take your time.

I can't tell you how many instances a student booked a role from an audition because the director or producer felt that he or she was the only one who brought physical behavior to the audition. That's the reason they got cast. Unless you're playing someone who can't move due to illness or incapacity, don't just sit in the casting chair. Own the room by working the room. This doesn't mean that you should in any way hurt, destroy or even move the casting paraphernalia or furniture, but by all means be comfortable in the space.

Don't try to prove what a good actor you are.

Just do the work—with blinders on, endow the person reading with you with your SUBSTITUTION and go after your SCENE OBJECTIVE. Let all the script analysis inner work that you've done naturally and effortlessly emerge. It will help you live and become the character with a goal, which is what they want to see.

Don't strive for perfection.

People are flawed—sometimes they fail, and the character you're playing is no different. If you give that perfect reading, you've just taken the humanity out of it, which makes you uncastable. What they want to cast is that diamond in the rough, the imperfection that comes from someone who *is* the role, not the best acting of it. They want to see the character come alive off the page—this means you have to *be* the character, not act it out. The tools are there for your use as a way to enable you to *live* the character, not to show them how much work you've done. Be aware, the acting tools are there for you as a means to an end, not the end itself.

Allow who you are as a person to come forward within the interview portion and the reading itself. That's what makes you special and distinct. They're more likely to remember you if you're not a cookie-cutter version of the character they're casting. Believe me, it seems like a simple concept, but having been a producer of four films and having worked as a casting assistant, I know that few actors actually let their mannered, quirky and individual selves come through.

It's okay to be nervous.

They expect it. And if you try to squelch your nerves, you'll only make yourself more panicked. A good trick is to talk yourself *into* the nerves. In the same way that if you try *not* to cry, all you can do is cry. If you try *not* to laugh, all you can do is laugh. On the other hand, if you try *to* cry or laugh, you cannot. Give yourself permission to be nervous. You have a legitimate reason, because auditions can be scary. Let the work you've done on your role become your anchor. Accepting your nerves removes the crippling part of your nerves and leaves the part of the nerves that actually is good and helpful.

Don't be taken in by niceties.

If you continue to come in second, or you don't get called back at all, don't get taken in by casting's "nice" comments. It's not their job to be your mother and tell you the truth. They will often kindly and gently try to extract you from their office with words like, "That was 'good,'" or "Interesting choices" or "Nice work." Using my translation book of casting-director-speak, these can be roughly translated to "Get the hell out of here and never darken my office again!" And hearing again and again from casting that "you just weren't right for the role" really means you weren't good enough. Which means you have to go back to the drawing board and work harder on your craft.

Do the Work

There is no magic to becoming a successful working actor. That's why renowned actors come in all shapes and sizes. You don't have to be the most beautiful, the most intelligent, nor even the most talented to make it. Like any other prestigious profession, having a flourishing career takes:

- Focus
- Tenacity
- Drive
- Love of what you do
- The freedom to explore and discover
- Taking risks
- Openness to continue learning (never become so jaded that you think you know it all—be aware, you are never done learning)

- Belief in yourself
- Concentrated practicing of
  the craft

• Hard work

Acting is an art form and art is infinite—there's always something more to learn, another risk to explore, another facet to discover. Edison said the equation for success is 99 percent perspiration and 1 percent inspiration—that is, only one percent is actual talent, the rest is hard work. Taking what you've learned, don't cut corners and get lazy. The more work you do, following the steps, the more satisfying the result will be for you.

Acknowledgments

....

I'd like to thank Mollie Doyle for keeping me grammatically focused and artistically motivated. Brian DeFiore for making me stay the course and knowing how to make a great deal. William Shinker, Lauren Marino and Hilary Terrell for their conviction in the book and their publishing savvy. Halle Berry for being a friend, ally, kindred spirit and unwavering support system. Many of my revelations are because of her soulful intuitiveness that was explored through our friendship and in the work we've done together. The Gottfrieds, and my family: Nan, Linda, Heidi, Hagen, Joe, Erika, Helene and Bernard—for providing me with that ever-important neurotic base one needs to be an actor. My Chubbuck in-laws: John, Syble, Gary, June, John Robert and Travis for being a second family to me. The thousands of students I've taught over the years, thank you for your dedication to the craft—we've learned and grown together, particularly those who have inspired stories for this book. Bob Wallerstein, who is the best legal advisor, ever, and a really cool guy. Claire, my daughter, who, as I've loved and lived with her, has enabled me to truly understand the machinations of being human (and how to use it in acting) from its most primal form. My studly husband, Lyndon, whose steadfast belief in my abilities has enabled me to truly believe in myself. This book never would have been written without his inspiration, his knowledge, his insights . . . and most important, because it was his idea to write the book in the first place.